*The Life and Times of*
SIR THOMAS ELYOT
ENGLISHMAN

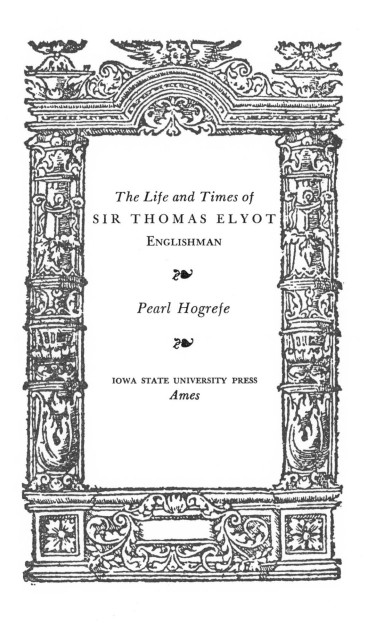

*The Life and Times of*
SIR THOMAS ELYOT
ENGLISHMAN

~

*Pearl Hogrefe*

~

IOWA STATE UNIVERSITY PRESS
*Ames*

PEARL HOGREFE is Professor of English, Iowa State University. Among her other writings are articles for the professional journals of her field, and the books *The Process of Creative Writing* and *The Sir Thomas More Circle*.

/

*The title page reproduces a picture-frame design often used by Thomas Berthelet, who became the king's printer about 1530 and who published every known edition of every work of Sir Thomas Elyot that appeared in the author's lifetime. This design was used on the first edition of* The Castle of Health *(ca. 1536–1539) (Cf. Plate V), the 1537 edition and some other editions of the* Governour, *and on many other books printed by Berthelet. Apparently the design was made in 1534, but it was used with that date on many books printed later.*

Composed and printed by
The Iowa State University Press

First edition, 1967

Library of Congress Catalog Card Number: 67–10601

# Preface

HE AIM of this work is to give a complete account (or as complete as the remaining material permits) of the life and writings of Sir Thomas Elyot, to indicate his relationship to major events of the period, and to emphasize the English elements in his life and in his writings.

The plan is chronological, beginning with early records about Elyot's father, and wills, mostly unpublished ones, drawn by members of the families with whom the Elyots were connected. The wills give us additional facts about the families; thus they reveal formative influences of Elyot's childhood. The legal training he received is clarified with information about the Inns of Chancery and of Court. His classical education is discussed in relation to conditions at the universities and to the opportunities for study in London, when Linacre, Grocyn, and William Lily had returned from study abroad, and More and Erasmus were learning Greek. Elyot's work for the government, as clerk of the assize, clerk of the king's Council, sheriff, and member of commissions of the peace is not merely listed but explained. In subsequent chapters, the events of his life, the ideas in his letters and books, small biographical details that seem to have been overlooked before, and political events of the time have been carefully studied in relation to each other; and since some of his books are related to immediate happenings, careful conclusions have been drawn from the interrelation of these sources.

The material available for the study is limited, especially the personal material. We have no family letters, no letters of friendship from others to Elyot, no private papers, and except for his name on commissions, few public documents that mention him. Among the letters Elyot wrote to others we have one to the Duke of Norfolk, one to Sir John Hacket, and several to Thomas Cromwell. Few as they are, some of them give invaluable details about Elyot's thinking. We do have the wills, both of Thomas Elyot and his father, giving information about their possessions and their personalities, and the other wills mentioned above. Most of these have been examined before for family relationships but have not been studied in depth; and some (for example, the will of Dame Susan Kingston, Thomas Elyot's stepsister) seem not to have been used at all.

The nonpersonal material has a broad scope. Since the biography aims at completeness, it is necessary to use, with appropriate credit, the contributions of others to our knowledge of Elyot. It is also necessary to build on information about the character and motives of such public figures as Wolsey, More, Cromwell, and Henry VIII, and to use, whenever they are pertinent, events recorded in the *Letters and Papers* and in the *Statutes of Parliament*. It is even more necessary to know the literary work of others in the period in order to evaluate Elyot's contribution through his books. For example, one who examines Elyot's 1538 *Dictionary* without realizing the lack of classical Latin or English dictionaries in the period underestimates his work. And one who evaluates *The Defense of Good Women* without knowing what More, Erasmus, Vives, and Herde had said earlier about the capabilities of women overestimates the work of Elyot. It is imperative to know and use the whole educational, religious, and political

background of the period instead of interpreting a fact
about Elyot in a void or in a modern context. The whole
meaning of his life, so far as we can understand it, must be
clarified through its relation to a period of conflict.

The Selected Bibliography at the close of the volume
includes only the sources that seem most valuable. The
pioneer work of H. H. S. Croft, in his edition *The Boke
Named the Gouernour* (London, 1883) must always be respected for what he accomplished without some of the materials now available. Stanford E. Lehmberg, in *Sir
Thomas Elyot: Tudor Humanist* (Austin, Texas, 1960)
made a real contribution with facts from documents,
though this writer must disagree with some of his conclusions. John M. Major, in *Sir Thomas Elyot and Renaissance Humanism* (Lincoln, Nebraska, 1964) presents a detailed study of influences; thus his aim is different from
mine. Though the volume came into my hands when my
own manuscript was ready for submission to a publisher,
the work has been stimulating and had led to additions,
especially in Chapter VII.

In this study of Elyot's life I have used, especially in
Chapter I, a technique which is common in modern
historical and biographical studies: some account of probable *mental* events. The assumption back of Chapter I,
for example, is that a man going to make an official report
to Henry VIII on his embassy and preparing to remon-
strate with him would probably be recalling events in the
life of the king and the queen, as well as significant events
in his own life and his hopes for the future. The *materials* of thought so presented are fully documented as
absorbing interests of the time and the man.

In sixteenth-century material, spelling is a problem.
I have used the modern form for proper names whenever
a reasonable number of authorities support me. *Fettiplace,*
for example, is consistently used by all the Victoria County
Histories that I have examined. *Perkins,* not *Parkyns*

alone, is used in the *STC* and the *DNB*. *Grocyn* is preferred over *Grocin* by many, perhaps by most, modern authorities, though not by P. S. Allen; doubtfully I have chosen *Grocyn*, hoping to achieve consistency except in some quotations where another form appears. Four spellings are given by Thieme and Becker, an outstanding authority, for the artist named in Chapter I, Matsys. I have chosen one that is frequent but not invariable in English and American authorities. The spelling *Syon*, not *Sion House*, is confirmed by present usage in England. For titles named in the discussion I have usually used modern spelling since several early editions with different spellings may be referred to, but when a specific edition is named in the notes, I have followed the original spelling.

In the debatable area of quotations from early sixteenth-century material I have retained original spelling for short quotations. However I have changed the printer's *u*'s to *v*'s where there is no doubt about the meaning and have expanded obvious contractions, such as signs for *and* and *that*, and for double consonants. Though even a change in punctuation is a form of editing, it has seemed better in some quotations to make changes in an effort to clarify meaning. Several letters of Elyot, especially longer ones where he is explaining his religious opinions, make extremely difficult reading in the original spelling. The writer was emotional, perhaps agitated by his own fears, and there is a large chance that he was intent on concealing his real views. For these letters I have used modern spelling, adding in brackets information about doubtful words. All these letters have been reprinted at some time in the original spelling; and references to these versions are given in the notes. After all, spelling was often not determined by the author but by his printer. It is interesting to speculate on what would have happened to Shakespeare's plays if editors had always reprinted them in the exact spelling of the First Folio.

My warm thanks are extended to Giles Dawson and to Dorothy Mason of the Folger Shakespeare Library, for reading chapters in their early form, as well as for other helps, and to Professor Kathrine Koller, the University of Rochester, for reading an entire first draft. All three gave encouragement and valuable suggestions. Professor Albert L. Walker, Chairman of the Department of English and Speech, Iowa State University, also read some of the early chapters and gave unusually helpful comments on organization. Professor Norris Yates, a colleague at Iowa State University, read the chapters on the *Governour* and gave stimulating suggestions on them. Professor William S. Heckscher, formerly of the University of Utrecht but now at Duke University, was a friendly consultant while we were fellow readers at the Folger Shakespeare Library. Other fellow readers at the same library form a great company of anonymous helpers, since I profited from the discussion of ideas at lunch or at tea or from their answers to my questions. They are part of the nameless and unnameable influences extending far into the past. Professor William Nelson, Columbia University, who read an earlier version of the work, saved me from many small blunders and stimulated me to new thinking about larger areas of the work. None of these individuals should be held responsible for my own shortcomings or errors.

Letters from many people, in answer to my inquiries, constitute another area of indebtedness: letters from the late W. A. Jackson and his assistants, Harvard University; from Madeline Stanton, Librarian of the Historical Collections, Yale Medical Library; the Art Division, New York Public Library; the Keeper of Prints and Drawings, Royal Library, Windsor Castle; the Asst. Comptroller, Lord Chamberlain's Office, St. James's Palace; T. S. Wragg, Librarian, Chatsworth, Bakewell; E. J. Freeman, Wellcome Medical Library, London; David Piper, Asst. Keeper, National Portrait Gallery, London; L. W. Hanson, Keeper of

Printed Books, Bodleian, Oxford; H. M. Nixon, Deputy
Keeper, Department of Printed Books, British Museum,
London. To all, my appreciation and thanks.

To Louis B. Wright, Director of the Folger Shakespeare Library, and to the entire staff of that friendly,
efficient place, I am indebted beyond repayment. In addition to other services and courtesies, a Folger fellowship,
extending over several months, made it possible to get the
book under way. Another grant, from the Alumni Achievement Fund, Iowa State University, provided money for
necessary travel in the United States, photostats, and other
materials. Both these grants gave encouragement as well
as financial aid. I am grateful to other libraries also: to
the Henry E. Huntington Library for welcome and help
during the few days I could spend there; to the Newberry Library for answers to questions and for photostats;
to D. Pepys Whitely, Deputy Keeper of the Pepys Collection, Magdalene College, Cambridge; and to many helpful and efficient people during my brief period of work at
the British Museum.

The British Museum has granted permission for the
use of the line drawing of the king by Cornelys Matsys. The
Holbein drawings of Sir Thomas and Lady Margaret Elyot
at Windsor Castle, the undated portrait of Henry VIII by
an unidentified artist (perhaps by van Cleve) at Hampton
Court, and another painting of the king (School of Holbein) at Windsor Castle are all reproduced by gracious
permission of Her Majesty Queen Elizabeth II. I am
grateful for these additions to the book.

# Table of Contents

xi

*The Life and Times of*
SIR THOMAS ELYOT
ENGLISHMAN

# CHAPTER I

*Return From an Embassy.* *1532*

BOUT the first of June, 1532, Sir Thomas Elyot, just returned from his embassy for Henry VIII, was hurrying from London to report to his king. He had been at the court of Charles V, ruler of all the kingdoms of Spain, Holy Roman Emperor, and nephew also of Catherine of Aragon. In this most important ambassadorship Elyot had spent seven or eight months on the Continent. His mission was chiefly to persuade Charles into accepting the English king's separation from Catherine without making trouble. Riding horseback, with a retinue of servants, Elyot started from the Middle Temple on his ten-mile trip, past Greenwich, down to the magnificent country palace of Eltham, Kent.

As Elyot rode through the city that day, he noted the unchanged physical details: St. Paul's, other churches and more churches, priests, friars, papal envoys, the markets, the Steelyard, the narrow streets with filth in the gutters, the sanctuary of St. Martin's with its human derelicts—and everywhere the restless, passionate crowds. He watched London eagerly, even the human dregs and the ugliness as well as the towers and the fresh summer beauty, for his whole life was dominated by a love of England. Impatiently he had tried to arrange an earlier return from his only trip to foreign lands—through the Duke of Norfolk and also through his wife, who apparently had appealed to the king about bringing him home.

As Elyot and his attendants moved eastward through the city, perhaps the London crowds seemed more passionate than he remembered them. For some time they had been giving noisy expression to their love for Catherine of Aragon when she appeared, so that Henry did not dare to establish a residence for her near the great city or to send her to the Tower as a prisoner. Some Londoners supported Catherine and the emperor with an additional motive: a loss of trade with the imperial domains would bring financial disaster. Whenever Anne Boleyn appeared, the crowds greeted her with cold silence or with outbursts of disapproval. About the time Elyot started on his embassy, 7,000 or 8,000 Londoners (some women and others dressed as women) had tried to kill her. They learned that she was having supper, without the protection of the king, at a country place on the river. But she was warned in time to escape.[1]

Though London looked almost unchanged in physical details, Elyot must have been conscious of grave threats to the religious and political order that day as he rode toward Eltham Palace. Henry VIII and Cromwell had begun their attack on the religious orders that were obstinate in opposing the king's separation from Catherine: the Carthusians, the Franciscan Observants, and the Bridgettines at Syon House. On Easter Sunday, March 21, 1532, while the clergy in Convocation were debating the question of submission to the temporal power, William Peto, provincial of the Observants at Greenwich, had preached against the king's plans (even though members of the court were present) and had indicted his evil counselors. On the following Sunday, when Peto was absent, a defender of the king had preached, expressing a wish that Peto were there to answer him. As if on cue, Father Henry Elston, the warden, rose in the rood loft and refuted his statements. On April 15, Peto and Elston were imprisoned by order of the king.[2]

On May 15, the clergy in Convocation had yielded to the king. They agreed to submit to him all existing church laws for his approval or veto and to make no new laws without his consent.

On May 16, Sir Thomas More had resigned his office as lord chancellor. He pleaded poor health, and the king accepted with a gracious surface. But as More's action was precisely timed to follow the Submission of the Clergy, probably neither Henry VIII nor anyone else with the ability to think was left in doubt about the basic reason for the resignation. When Elyot returned from his embassy, London and all the capitals of Western Europe were buzzing with the news.

With these winds of change blowing across England, Elyot's mind must have been a whirling kaleidoscope of memories, hopes, and fears. Though we cannot know what came into a man's mind at a specific moment, it would be strange indeed if he did not think of his embassy, his king, his queen, and also of his own past and future as he rode along to make his official report.

Memories of strange cities, perhaps—Tournai, Ratisbon, Brussels—alien sounds and the chatter of foreign tongues, a modified Mass from which he had hastily departed at Nuremberg, where his own chaplain was not permitted to conduct service for him; memories of people: Guevara, De Puebla, Charles V.

Older memories of his father's years of service under Henry VII and Henry VIII, of his own work for six and a half years as clerk of the king's Council without the usual pay, of the sums beyond the royal allowance that he had been forced to spend on his embassy.

Memories of his king and queen: Catherine of Aragon

at her coronation, in a litter of gold cloth between white palfreys, with her shining hair and her embroidered dress of white satin, the costume of a virgin bride; memories or reports of the trial before Campeggio at Blackfriars, when Catherine had suddenly knelt before the king, imploring him, for the love that had existed between them in the past, to say whether she had been a virgin when she married him—and the king's confused silence; Henry in his Council, affable but eager to leave Wolsey in charge and be off to his hunting.

Memories blending with hopes and fears: hopes that what he meant to say to the king might help change the future of England and that he might be called to Council with other diplomats; hopes that his own conflicting loyalties to his church, to Catherine, and to his sovereign lord might be resolved; fears about the swift-moving political and religious changes.


Elyot had learned officially, of course, that the king was in residence at Eltham, the finest of his country palaces. Excited street gossip told him that Anne Boleyn was not with the king, that sixteen of the royal watermen had attended her to her father's residence at Durham House.[3] There would be no sharp black eyes and no alert ears to spy on his talk with the king. That was good, since he had a purpose in mind besides his report on his embassy.

As they drew nearer to Eltham, where a period of royal residence had become unusual,[4] activity was stirring along the roads leading into the palace. A countrywoman was bringing beans and chickens as a welcome to her king. Servants were exercising the king's horses. Escorts attended a swarthy foreigner who might have necklaces or tiaras for the king's approval. Couriers, riding hard from Dover, brought news from foreign capitals.

When Elyot reached the palace, he dismounted and was ushered in alone for his audience. Attendants hurried to summon the king, perhaps from his new bowling alley or his examination of some newly acquired diamond or ruby. In the first five months of 1532, Henry had spent 8,000 crowns for such adornments. On June 5, he paid 600 crowns more, and on June 12, another 1,000 crowns for jewels.[5] Anne Boleyn might have managed, it seems, without acquiring those Catherine gave up, at the king's command, in the early autumn of 1532.[6] But the king left his pleasures and came quickly to hear the report of his ambassador.

The Henry VIII and the Sir Thomas Elyot who confronted each other that day were strangely different in character and personality. Elyot did not see the athletic St. George who had rescued Catherine from the dragons of neglect and poverty in 1509, married her, and continued for an unbelievable time to present himself in all tournaments as her "Knight of the Loyal Heart." He did not see the paragon of wisdom and virtue whom William Blount described at the accession, when he summoned Erasmus back to an earthly Paradise. Perhaps that paragon had never existed in the flesh, not quite. He did not see the beefy, bullnecked figure with the truculent stance, familiar to us from the alleged Holbeins, or the sinister boarlike face in the likeness by Cornelys Matsys. Instead, Elyot saw a king more like the Hampton Court picture, with an effect of lightness, pleasure, and youth. His great body was thicker than it had once been; his face was shrewd, sensual, and self-willed, but still beautiful.[7] He was like the Henry whom Lodovici Falier described in 1531: "His face is angelic rather than handsome; his head imperial and bald; and he wears a beard, contrary to the English custom." Falier added praise of his physical

feats, his intellectual attainments, his affability, gracious-
ness, and his lessening but still active generosity; he noted
that the king usually attended two Masses daily, with an
additional high Mass on Sunday.[8]

Such a man was the Henry VIII whom Elyot hoped to
influence. Since the king at this time had taken no irre-
trievable steps away from the church at Rome but only
those he might use as threats or clubs, and since he had not
declared Anne Boleyn his queen, Elyot may have had a
slight basis for hope.

Elyot and the king were about the same age—perhaps
their only likeness. Elyot craved chiefly scholarship and
service to the state. He was reticent but with an unusual
capacity for friendship, and so self-controlled that he never,
in his life or his writings, approved an illicit passion. His
straight hair made his long, thin face, without beard or
mustache, seem even longer. His mouth was firm; his eyes
were candid and farseeing. His slender figure, plain dress,
and serious expression were a strange contrast to the king's
thick body, extravagant costume, jewels, and calculating,
sensual face.[9]

Henry was anxious, as usual, for reports about Charles
V. Some years earlier the English lion had become conscious of his strength: with the execution of the Duke of
Buckingham in 1521 he had learned "how easy it was to
kill so great a man."[10] While Wolsey managed everything
and left him to his pleasures, he had scarcely needed that
knowledge. But in the last few years, his desires had grown.
He had been working hand in glove with Thomas Cromwell for more than a year and a half; he had been learning
what he might have to do if he gratified those desires. But
since his actions would be partly dependent on foreign
powers, he was eager for news.

Unfortunately we do not have the complete details

about the talk between Elyot and the king. But judging from the king's instructions to him, dated October 7, 1531, Elyot must have answered questions like these:

"Did you fish out the mind of the emperor toward us? Does he despair of our old friendship toward him and fear our communication with France?

"Does he seek out ways and means to our detriment?

"Does he realize that the Pope wrongs us by wishing to call us to Rome, either ourself in person or by proctor, to make answer to our pretended marriage, which is contrary to human and divine law and to the law of nature? Does he know that all unprejudiced lawyers, including those of France, tell us this? With the Turk threatening all Christendom, does he realize that a trip to Rome would put us in jeopardy?

"Does he remember his promise to us, not to meddle in our great cause except that he do so with justice?

"Has the Pope wrongfully reported him to us, and if so, is the emperor, like a man of honor, willing to cease from doing us wrong?"[11]

We have only some general ideas about the answers to such questions. On June 3, after his audience with the king, Elyot visited Chapuys, the emperor's ambassador in London. On June 5, Chapuys wrote the emperor about their talk. From this letter we know that the king asked about all the details of the embassy, even those he had already had in formal reports. We learn also that Elyot took it upon himself to speak frankly to his king and to urge upon him a course of action that would be beneficial to Catherine, to the emperor, and to Henry himself. We learn further that Elyot concluded his audience in the belief that his remonstrances had had a desirable effect. Such an effect, Chapuys suggested, would not be permanent. Others had remonstrated, but a smile or a tear from Anne Boleyn always brought the king back to agreement with her.

Elyot also told Chapuys that he was writing down the substance of his talk with the king, and, as the emperor wished, was ending it to Fernando De Puebla, in the cipher Puebla had given him for the purpose.[12] Puebla, the son of that former ambassador to England who had struggled to help Catherine while she was the widow of Prince Arthur, was at this time a chaplain to Charles V.

Elyot's talk with his king and with Chapuys and his report to Puebla appear in a new perspective when we find that prominent men in England who were sympathetic with Catherine had been avoiding contacts with Chapuys. As early as April, 1531, Sir Thomas More had begged Chapuys, for the honor of God, not to visit him. Though he had given ample proof of his loyalty, he said, a visit might not only endanger him but also deprive him of his freedom to speak frankly about affairs connected with the emperor and Queen Catherine—affairs he valued as he valued his life, his country, and his king.[13] On January 11, 1532, Bishop John Fisher was receiving the emperor's messages through a third person, Chapuys reported, because he would not risk speaking with him directly. Again, on January 22, Chapuys wrote, Fisher thanked the emperor and offered his services, but asked that messages be sent to him only in cipher.[14]

But in early June, 1532, Elyot not only visited Chapuys and sent the emperor's chaplain a report of his audience but he even remonstrated with his king. Henry was not a patient man at best, and his passion for Anne Boleyn, unrequited physically for five and a half or six years, had done little to increase a quality that was normally in short supply.[15] But Elyot was not arrested or imprisoned; he was allowed to leave the king with the illusion that his words had had a desirable effect.

Perhaps Henry, who still had doubts and fears in 1532 about his future course of action, as well as unassuaged passion, did respond for a few moments as if his own early conscience were speaking. Perhaps he dismissed the protests without rancor because Elyot held no important office in church or state and thus was no roadblock to his desires. Perhaps he regarded Elyot with sardonic amusement.

What sort of man was Thomas Elyot? What were his motives? Did he have affection for his king, as Reginald Pole apparently had in December, 1530, when he thought that he had found a way to reconcile his views with those of his sovereign? While Pole waited at York Place for the audience he had requested, Henry entered suddenly from a secret gallery. For a moment Pole was unable to speak. Then he began pouring out a passionate remonstrance—the exact opposite of what he had planned to say. The king seized his dagger as if to kill Pole, stopped, and then rushed from the room, slamming the door behind him and leaving Pole in tears. He spent the next hour, it is said, in an agony of self-appraisal. Pole's biographers suggest that his concern for the king's honor and his affection overcame him.[16] Elyot may also have had a real affection for the younger Henry VIII.

If Elyot had heard some account of Pole's talk with the king, did he hope to succeed where Pole had failed? Or did he have the kind of integrity that impelled him to try, with little hope of success? Was he bold? Was he naïve? Did he believe with simple sincerity that kings, if only told the truth often enough, would apply the ethical theories on government that he had emphasized in the *Governour?*

Like many other educated, intelligent men of the 1530's who felt the need of a strong government, was he eager to serve a temporal ruler with loyalty but also to worship in a church uniting all Western Europe, as his grandfather and his father had done? Was his life a struggle between these loyalties?

If answers to these questions can be found, they will rise from a study of the whole life and all the writings of

Thomas Elyot. If the answers have validity, they must be
based on a realization of the complexity in men's motives
—not from a single-minded search for evidence that he
supported the temporal power and not from an equally
single-minded search for evidence that he supported, so
far as circumstances allowed him, the Catholic doctrines of
the "old religion."

# CHAPTER II

## *Early Background and Family*

HE EXACT DATE and the place of Thomas Elyot's birth are unknown. But since he was born in the latter part of the fifteenth century, before the keeping of parish registers was established by law, there is nothing unusual about the fact. Either the date or the place of birth is uncertain for many prominent men of the period; for example, Archbishop Warham, Cardinal Wolsey, and Thomas Cromwell. Thomas Elyot was born about 1489 or 1490, probably at some place in Wiltshire, but we can only infer the facts from chance references and property records.

Both Thomas Elyot and Sir Richard Elyot, his father, referred many times to places in Wiltshire, especially to those in or near Salisbury. Thomas Elyot's youthful memories, recorded in the 1542 edition of his Latin-English dictionary, are centered in Ivychurch, when it was still an Augustinian monastery as well as a village two or three miles from Salisbury. Explaining *gigas*, he says that he and his father had once seen at that monastery the excavated bones of a fourteen-foot giant with teeth the size of walnuts. Explaining *Britania*, he says that men digging for a foundation at the same monastery had found an old book, with leaves of thick vellum, which seemed to be an early history of Britain. When a single defaced leaf of the book

came into his hands later, he took it to Richard Pace, then
secretary to the king, to see if he could read it.[1]  Thomas
Elyot had another connection with Ivychurch through his
marriage with Margaret Barrow; when the father, Sir
Maurice, made his will in 1521 he identified his daughter
as Margaret Elyot and described himself as a resident of
that place.[2]

Richard Elyot emphasized Salisbury and other places
in Wiltshire in his will as if they were a large center of his
interests, though he still used the terms Old and New
Sarum.  In his bequests to friars he included Salisbury and
also Fisherton, which later became a part of the larger
city.  Though he left small sums for churches in London,
Oxfordshire, and Berkshire, he was more concerned with
Wiltshire.  He left money for repairs at three parish
churches in Salisbury and for repairs in the cathedral, and
he asked to be buried there in the place prepared for him
and his wife unless circumstances caused his executor to
choose another place.  He willed his cousin, Alice Winbourn, the use for her life of a house in that city.  He had
some connection with Wanborough, a manor in north
Wiltshire, but there he was probably acting only as the
king's agent while the heir was a minor.[3]  His will mentioned property in Winterslow, northeast of Salisbury,
and in Chalk, presumably the Hundred of Chalk in south
Wiltshire.  As he wished the profits from the Chalk property
to provide prayers for his soul, the souls of his relatives,
and all Christian souls, he made a tripartite indenture for
this purpose, leaving one part in the hands of his heir, one
in Salisbury Cathedral, and the other with the mayor and
council of the city.  In bequeathing the uses of his property
to his only son as chief heir and arranging for new trustees
whenever the need should arise, he provided that eight out
of twelve should be of Salisbury, either men who had been
mayors or who were named among the twenty-four likely
to be mayors in the future.[4]  Many of the legal commissions

on which he served also suggest connections with Salisbury. What were the influences of the West Country background on Thomas Elyot?

His father's prosperity, so important to his own future, apparently began in the Wiltshire area. Though the term West Country may refer to all southwest England, including Devon and Cornwall, an economic historian has said that the heart of the West Country "was 'the low flat country, full of rivers and towns and infinitely populous,' comprising part of the three counties of Somerset, Wiltshire, and Gloucestershire, and stretching from Cirencester in the north to Sherborne in the south, and from Devizes in the east to Bristol in the west."[5] In this area, people in the market towns carried on the woolen trade and produced the finest broadcloth in England which was sold mainly to the Low Countries.[6] In this general area Richard Elyot not only held the lands which he mentioned in his will but also owned many hundreds of sheep. He willed one wether for every year of service to every manservant (excepting his clerks) who was with him at the time of his death; and to one servant, Edward Harrison, in addition to a cow and other personal gifts, twenty wethers. He gave his daughter Margery one hundred of his best wethers, with other livestock, whenever she began a household of her own. According to an indenture that he and his second wife had made between them, perhaps at the time of their marriage, he left to her children by Richard Fettiplace 340 ewes. Probably for his only son Thomas, his chief heir, he provided many more sheep than all these others together.

The residents in the heart of the West Country, including Richard Elyot, had many advantages helping them to prosper in the woolen trade. They held unusually fine grazing lands, especially those in the chalk districts. They had available the waters of the River Avon, which clothiers considered especially effective for fulling, dressing, and dyeing the finest cloth.[7] They also had two great commercial outlets for the sale of their products, London and Bristol. Comparatively good roads led to London, where they probably marketed, through the staple of Calais, the fine broadcloth sold to the Low Countries. Bristol was accessible for the sale of any other cloth they might have. With a population of 11,000 to 13,000 it had become the third city and the second seaport of the kingdom. The Severn furnished "a deep river system fanning out into Wales and the Midlands," bringing the produce which helped to give Bristol an early, bold development in seafaring. As early as 1467 the Merchant Venturers were organized there as a separate company with a master and wardens, and before 1474 William Canning had developed a large cloth trade in the Baltic area.[8] In 1521, when Wolsey approached the great companies about a venture to Cathay and to the Spice Islands, London merchants met the plan with passive resistance, saying that there was no rutter, or marine guide, for those areas and there were no English-born mariners to take charge. But Bristol men readily promised two ships for the venture: they were already familiar with the Newfoundland trade.[9]

It is clear that Richard Elyot's prosperity, which began in the West Country though later it was not limited to that area, would enable him to provide his son with advantages and leave him a solid inheritance.

Since Thomas Elyot probably spent his childhood in the West Country, there may have been general influences from the area. Perhaps the region then resembled the Wiltshire described a century later by John Aubrey, even if Aubrey's accounts are tinged with fancy and nostalgia. There were no alehouses except along the great roads, he says; people went to the friaries to drink; travelers were entertained three days at the religious houses if they had need of such accommodations; and country gentlemen did not meet at tippling houses but in the fields, with hawks, hounds, and bugles. A traveler met the wearers of many different kinds of religious habits, and heard often the "tingle-tangle" of convent bells.[10] Aubrey also describes Ivychurch, with which Elyot had associations, saying that Sidney often came there with his sister and wrote part of his *Arcadia* there. He adds that Ivychurch is situated on a hill overlooking all the country to the west, to the north over Sarum, and across the plains into beautiful Clarendon Park.[11] Earlier it was a monastery, he says, with the cloisters still remaining. In an occasional work where Elyot is moved by personal feelings to become less bookish and classical than usual, such as in *Pasquil the Plain*, he uses an earthy vocabulary including the diseases of animals; in a philosophical discourse, *Of the Knowledge Which Maketh a Wise Man*, he adds quite unexpectedly realistic details about horses, dogs, and hunting, and his Plato speaks of fat sheep as if he might once have lived in Wiltshire. It is possible that such details in both works are influences from the West Country childhood.

It is doubtful whether the primitive background of Wiltshire, though it lingered long after Elyot's time, had any effect on him. Antiquarians tell us of cucking stools used to punish women whose tongues were habitually unruly, dograppers who whipped dogs out of churches long after other places had given up their services, and mummers who blended the earliest traditions with later history. Like the other humanists of the period, Elyot probably regarded such folk traditions with indifference or scorn. Charms and superstitions to cure illness also flourished in Wiltshire and developed even more rapidly after the religious houses were dissolved.[12] One may wonder whether Elyot's *Castle of Health* had any connection with an early distaste for these futile treatments, but there is no evidence.

Thomas Elyot's ancestry and family connections were important in his life, but, except for the dominant and many-sided influence of his father, his paternal relatives were probably unimportant. Richard Elyot's people seem to have been residents of Somersetshire, and no doubt they were honest and thrifty. In his will, he names his grandfather, Michell Elyot; his father, Simon Elyot; two sisters, Alice Gilpurn and Johanne Crouch; their sons, John Gilpurn and Richard Crouch; his father's sister, Katherine Lydford, her daughter Alice, and two sons of Alice, John Huet of Taunton and John Soper. He mentions also a John Michell or Elyot, of Coker (he uses both names), the son of Philip, who was the son of his grandfather, Michell Elyot. On his mother's side, his great-grandfather, he says, was Brice Bassett; his uncle, John Brice of Bassett; John had a daughter Johanne and a son James. His mother had a sister Katherine, with a daughter Isabel; Isabel's son was Thomas Somer. He leaves gifts to three cousins: Agnes, daughter of John Brice; Margaret, formerly the wife of John Hawkins; and Alice Winbourn of Sarum. The Ballards of Kent, including a daughter who was a nun at Barking, must have been relatives; for he gives them small sums provided they do not trouble his executor. He has forgotten, it seems, only one detail: the Ballard daughter receives a blank line instead of a Christian name. But for every other relative, he knows the full name and the exact relationship.

Here is God's plenty, so far as the names of relatives are concerned. But only a few of them can be traced through the usual channels of wills, the records of visitations by heralds, county histories, and state papers. A Margery Ballard, later pensioned as a nun of Barking, is probably the one Richard Elyot mentioned in his will.[13] A John Michell, named along with Richard Elyot in 1493–1494 on a large commission to inquire into concealed or forfeited lands in several counties including Somerset, may possibly be the relative mentioned in the will.[14] Since the others elude the searcher, one can only conclude that Richard Elyot knew well his background, paternal and maternal, but that his ancestors were undis-

tinguished. Probably they had little influence on Thomas
Elyot.

The two marriages of Richard Elyot were certainly
influences on the life of his son Thomas. But before we
can reach conclusions about why they were important, it
is necessary to examine such facts as we have about them.
Richard Elyot married as his first wife Alice, the
widow of Sir Thomas Daubridgecourt; she became the
mother of Elyot's children. She was the daughter of Sir
Thomas Delamere and his wife, Elizabeth, who was a
Findern. As Daubridgecourt died in 1485, Alice and
Richard Elyot may have been married about 1486, since
a second marriage often followed hard upon the death of
a first husband. During her first marriage, Alice had given
birth to several children: a suit in chancery that she and
Richard Elyot brought later states that Thomas Daubridgecourt had as issue two sons and three daughters.[15] Since
Alice was young enough to bear children to her second
husband, it is likely that children by her first husband
became for a time part of the Elyot household and that
some of them were there when Thomas Elyot was born.
It seems strange that Richard Elyot made no mention in
his will of any Daubridgecourts, though he made many
provisions for the Fettiplace children connected with his
second marriage. Thomas Elyot, too, left us no comments
on the Daubridgecourts, though he may have purchased
the wardship of Erasmus Pym in 1528 partly because the
mother of Erasmus was a Daubridgecourt. Without more
facts we do not know whether relationships with the children of his mother's first marriage were a happiness, a
source of irritation, a cause of his reticence, or whether
they had no influence.

Richard Elyot and his wife Alice had three children
not merely the Thomas and Margery known to previous
biographers. The third (and she may have been the
oldest) was a daughter, Eleanor. Her father identifies her

clearly in his will as "my doughter Elynour, mynchyn of Shaftisbury." He names another Eleanor but distinguishes her clearly by describing her as the daughter of Richard Fettiplace and calling her his daughter-in-law, a term used in the early sixteenth century to mean stepdaughter. He provides funds for the marriage of Eleanor Fettiplace or her entry into a convent when she decides about her future. He mentions his own daughter Eleanor twice, the first time willing her two spoons, a little mazer, and twenty shillings in money. Further on in the will, when he is arranging the proceeds from immovable property, he provides for her an annual income of fourteen shillings and fourpence as long as she may live.

The evidence from her father's will is supported by a list of Shaftesbury nuns, in 1504, on the election of a new abbess. Eleanor Elyot is named as one of twenty-two *tacitae professae*, apparently probationers.[16] If she was the oldest of the three Elyot children and born about 1487, she would have been perhaps seventeen at this time. In the early sixteenth century a girl entered a religious house for one of three main reasons: she was from a large family with limited finances and forced into it to save a dowry, she had a strong desire for a religious life, or she had some handicap that made marriage impossible. For Eleanor Elyot we may eliminate the first reason, since she was one of three children, and by the early 1500's her father had property from other sources besides the West Country beginings. Perhaps she had both the strong desire for a religious life and some handicap that forbade marriage. She seems to have died early. Thomas Elyot described Margery as his only, entirely beloved sister in the preface to *The Education or Bringing Up of Children*, some years later, and Eleanor's name does not appear on later lists of nuns at Shaftesbury.

With no brothers and the two sisters, Thomas Elyot may possibly have had a rather lonely childhood unless he was on good terms with some of the Daubridgecourt children. So far as we know, his sister Margery (who married a Puttenham and became the mother of Richard and George, associated with *The Art of English Poesy*) had no special influence on him. His sister Eleanor may have developed in him a gentleness for her frailty or strengthened his religious feeling, depending on her main reason for becoming a nun. At least he had gentleness and religious feeling, as he had reticence. But again we lack the facts for firm conclusions about these personal influences.

After the death of Alice Elyot about 1510, when her son Thomas was perhaps twenty-one, Richard Elyot married Elizabeth Bessils Fettiplace, widow of Richard Fettiplace, East Shefford, Berkshire. The Bessils connection is made clear because the wife's father, William Bessils, is named as one of the two supervisors of the Fettiplace will. As the will was probated in 1511, the marriage took place perhaps late that year or in 1512.

By this second marriage Richard Elyot acquired five stepsons and seven stepdaughters, though he never used the prefix *step* in describing any of these relationships. Richard Fettiplace and Elizabeth, his wife, had had five sons and seven daughters, not merely the four sons and three daughters a previous biographer has mentioned. Few men, it can safely be said, have ever become stepfathers to twelve children. In his will Richard Elyot mentions five men, speaking of each as his son but adding the name Fettiplace: John Fettiplace the elder, Edward, Antony, Thomas, and John Fettiplace the younger. Other wills of the Fettiplace family carefully distinguish the two Johns, the elder and the younger, leaving no doubt about their separate identities. The seven daughters named in various records are these: Susan, who married John Kingston; Dorothy, wife of John Codrington, perhaps of Gloucester; Jane, wife of a John More, of Haddon, Oxford; Anne, wife of Edward Purefoy, of Shalston, Buckingham; Mary, wife of James

Yate; Elizabeth, a nun at Amesbury; and Eleanor, a nun at Syon House.[17] The will of Dame Susan Kingston, which seems not to have been examined before, clearly identifies Mary Yate as a sister, and names several children in her large family, including a nephew, John Yate of the Middle Temple, who is one of her two executors, with Edward Purefoy. The John More whom she mentions was probably the husband of her sister Jane. She also names Elizabeth and Eleanor Fettiplace as her sisters, providing annual sums for them if they have need in illness or other unusual circumstances. At this time, after the Dissolution, they were on the pension lists of their religious houses.[18] Thus the will of Dame Susan either confirms or gives new evidence about the large Fettiplace family.

By this second marriage of his father, Thomas Elyot also acquired some connections with stepuncles, probably four of them: Anthony, William, John, and Sir Thomas Fettiplace. Two of these, William and Sir Thomas, are important enough to furnish illustrations for the next chapter; but all of them, it has been said, had achieved a higher status than Richard Fettiplace.

It is not necessary to think that Thomas Elyot was suddenly immersed in an enormous household as a result of the Fettiplace connection. First, it is probable that some of these twelve children were already married and in households of their own. Second, since Richard Elyot's second marriage could hardly have taken place before 1511, Thomas Elyot was already spending much time in London and was assisting his father as clerk of the assize for the Western Circuit. There are also reasons for supposing that he was in London even earlier and that London had become the center of his life. We know very little about his personal feelings for any of the Fettiplace connections. Only once, in 1534, he did express concern and admiration for three of his Fettiplace sisters—the two who had become nuns and Dame Susan Kingston—at a time of danger to Syon House.

Though ideas about the personal relationships of Thomas Elyot resulting from his father's marriages must remain tentative and conjectural, we are able to draw definite conclusions about material advantages. Each time he married, Richard Elyot chose a widow with property. Though the will of Sir Thomas Daubridgecourt is not available, a man was not asked to assume knighthood until he had a clear income of forty pounds from his lands. A widow had her dower rights, and, if the children were minors, might for a time have the control of all the property. The chancery document about the Daubridgecourt property, cited earlier in the chapter, stated that Richard Elyot and Alice, his wife, were at that time the executors. Thus property no doubt came to the Elyots. As for the second marriage, Richard Fettiplace described himself as esquire, but named substantial holdings, and controlled enough scattered lands so that his will was probated in the archbishop's court of Canterbury. He left to his wife all that he had not given to churches or the poor, and he made her the sole executor, asking her to use the property for herself and the children at her discretion. Hence Thomas Elyot must eventually have received a substantial amount of property from his father because of these marriages.

The ties that developed between Elyots and Finderns must have given Thomas Elyot an added sense of security as well as more property. When Sir William Findern made his will about 1517, he named Richard Elyot, Justice of the Common Pleas, as one of his executors, calling him "my cosyn." He willed his cousin Elyot's son Thomas all the "stuff" that might happen to be in his chamber in London, possibly at the Middle Temple, at the time of his death. Richard Elyot and William Findern also made indentures confirming an agreement that if either were left without an heir, certain possessions should go to the chief heir of the other. In 1523, young Thomas Findern, grandson and heir of Sir William, died suddenly without issue.

Thomas Elyot laid claim to the specified lands, including the manor of Carlton, probably Little Carlton, sometimes called Loppams, or Barbedors. After much delay, expense, and litigation he won this Findern property.[19]

Both marriages of Richard Elyot, connecting his family with the Delameres, Daubridgecourts, and the Finderns, and with the Bessils and Fettiplace families, gave Thomas Elyot firm roots and social status among the landed gentry of the West Country and adjoining areas. Some eighty years ago, H. H. S. Croft did pioneer work in establishing these relationships, and a recent biographer has added many details.[20] New information has been added here from a close scrutiny of wills and from the will of Dame Susan Kingston. In the next chapter, the ideas and attitudes of these people will be analyzed to evaluate their possible influence on Thomas Elyot.

Though this chapter has dealt mainly with Wiltshire and West Country background, it would be unrealistic to begin thinking of the Elyots as confined to the heart or even to the whole of the West Country. The Delamere and the Daubridgecourt families had holdings in Berkshire and other counties. The Fettiplace families had widely scattered holdings, including those in Berkshire. Sir William Findern lived in Cambridge and had possessions in many places. Richard Elyot was establishing himself in London as an expert in the English common law while his son Thomas was still a child, and was acquiring property in London and its environs. Later he willed his son the use of his manor of Long Combe, Oxford. In 1546, when Thomas Elyot died, he owned a manor in Dorset, one in Southampton, and four in Cambridge. But in the beginning, the prosperity of the Elyots was apparently based on the woolen trade in the heart of the West Country and on the marriages of Richard Elyot.

# CHAPTER III

## West Country Landed Gentry: Their Ideas and Attitudes

s no human being can slough off his environment, the members of the Delamere, Bessils, Findern, and Fettiplace families—most of them landed gentry in the West Country—must have exerted an influence on the life and the thinking of Thomas Elyot. His father, Richard Elyot, prosperous and highly successful in practicing the common law, probably influenced him more than any other member of this group was able to do. Hence it seems worthwhile to inquire into the background of these people and to draw conclusions from their wills. These documents give us the best insight, and for some of them the only available insight, into their manner of life, their attitudes, and their loyalties.

These men were not an adventurous lot. They were not ambassadors, and they did not set off to strange lands on voyages of discovery. In avoiding the unknown at sea, they were like other Englishmen about 1485 to 1550. Looking back from the twentieth century, one might assume an adventurous spirit, since Richard Elyot was about forty-two and his son Thomas about three years old when Columbus first sighted land. But admitting notable exceptions of the Bristol seamen and some others, it is not in the records.  One Englishman, the well-known John Rastell, brother-in-law of Sir Thomas More, tried exploring, but his abortive venture stranded him in Ireland. When he wrote that strange play *The Nature of the Four Elements* urging other Englishmen to discovery, he was a voice crying in the wilderness. The early Tudor kings did little to foster voyages. Henry VII aided and encouraged the Cabots, but he was a thrifty conservative, interested in trade. The adventurous element in Henry VIII was not directed to geography.

They were not an intellectual group, these families connected with Thomas Elyot, but neither were they the uncouth illiterates, interested only in hawking and hunting, whom Pace and Erasmus loved to attack. Of course they were conditioned by their own Age. Richard Elyot was perhaps twenty-six years old when Caxton set up his printing press in Westminster; and his education, including his law training, must have proceeded without benefit of printed books. Even by 1500, when Thomas Elyot was ten or eleven years old, only a half-dozen printers were working in England; by 1550, four years after his death, there were perhaps twenty of them in the whole country.[1] In the early part of the century nearly all Latin and Greek books were published on the Continent. One wonders what books, in addition to the usual textbooks, Thomas Elyot had as a child in his father's house. His tutor may have lent him a few volumes, and perhaps his father brought him an occasional book from London.

It is not surprising, then, that the wills of these men seldom mention books. Sir William Findern directed that the books as well as the chalices and ornaments in the chapel at Carlton should remain there forever. Richard Elyot bequeathed his English books to his daughter Margery, and his Latin and French books to his son Thomas. Those he left to his son may have been law books,

but he did not name even one. He willed to his daughter
a prayer book described as his "faire great primer with
silver clasps," and to his son his "faire great sawter written," a collection of Psalms in manuscript. He gave his
son also "my prymer that I wrote myself and my little
prymer that I occupie daily." None of the Fettiplace men
or the other writers of wills that have been examined mention any books.[2]

They took great care about amassing property and
then willing it to others—these men who formed the background of Thomas Elyot's youth. Out of the details in
many wills, a few examples will serve. Richard Elyot left
personal gifts to many people: a gilt spoon with his in-
itials to the abbess of Shaftesbury and another to the abbess
of Barking; a fur-trimmed gown to James Brice; a gilt
spoon and a black cloth gown to each of a half dozen clerks;
the canopy of his bed in London and the hanging in his
chamber to his daughter Margery, except that his son was
to have the border of the hanging. To his son, John Fettiplace the elder, he left the bedding at East Shefford, the
hangings of the chambers and halls, cushions, boards,
forms, chairs, sheets, napery, brass pots and pans, cauldrons,
broaches, spits, chaffers, pewter vessels, and other instruments of the brewhouse—perhaps all the furnishings that
had belonged to his father, Richard Fettiplace, of East
Shefford. To other friends and relatives he willed black
gowns, cloth coats, other fur-trimmed gowns, a riding
gown, white petticoats, shoes, hose, smocks, a white bonnet, a kerchief, gilt salts, standing cups, ale pots with covers,
other drinking cups, and mazers. He must have owned a
considerable amount of movable property, for his period;
and his careful assigning of gifts suggests a pride in his
possessions and a concern for his friends and relatives.

Thomas Elyot's stepuncle, Sir Thomas Fettiplace, indicated by details in his will that his possessions, both movable and immovable, were finer than those of other men in this group. For example, he left his daughter Katherine his silver basin and silver pitcher with the griffin's head, two pots of silver of "the highest sort," three white embossed goblets with covers, and the standing gilt cup that the queen had given her. Among his gifts to his nephew, John Fettiplace the elder, he included his gown of russet velvet furred with martin and his doublet of crimson satin. In his house he named a great room called the chapel chamber, a gatehouse chamber, a white chamber next the gatehouse, the king's chamber, and the queen's chamber. Probably his status was such that he had at one time entertained Henry VIII and Catherine of Aragon, when the queen had given his daughter the standing gilt cup.

Of course these men conveyed with meticulous care the rights to the uses of farms, tenements, and manors. The will of Sir Richard Elyot is an excellent example, with its detailed provisions about the right to certain properties in default of heirs to his body or in default of heirs to the body of his son Thomas. The will of Dame Susan Kingston also cites a maze of court decisions and statutes in regard to her property.

These men of property had also a feeling of obligation to others outside the family circle. They made gifts to servants who may have been indispensable in acquiring and caring for the possessions. Besides Richard Elyot's gifts to clerks and menservants, he willed sums of money to maidservants, sometimes designating the amounts as marriage portions. Sir William Findern made provision for all his servants, but the details are better adapted to the discussion of religious orthodoxy later in this chapter. Dorothy Barrow, the mother-in-law of Thomas Elyot, left to one servant, William Saunders, a hundred sheep, half wethers and half ewes, one of her best carts, and three horses with all their furnishings. As she had been a widow for some ten years when she died, perhaps the man had been a competent steward. Dame Susan Kingston left to her old servants, Thomas and Helen Hopkinson, a gift of twenty-five pounds. Since she was a widow many years and a vowess living at Syon House, and since she must have traveled her area looking after property for herself and others, a husband and wife pair of servants, as these seem to have been, were perhaps her best escort and protection.

They made gifts to the poor, to churches, to friars and parish priests, or to the fellows of All Souls' College or Lincoln College. Sir Thomas Fettiplace, in 1524, left twenty pounds for poor scholars at Oxford—for one a coat, for another a gown, for another a small sum of money, according to need and at the discretion of his executors. Thomas Elyot left money for the aged and bedridden, for poor maidens (to help them toward their marriages) and directed that all his books be sold and the money given to poor scholars who were also good students. He did not ask prayers in return for these gifts. Of the other donors, some asked prayers and some did not.

Sometimes the gifts might be called philanthropy. Sir William Findern left the profits of his manor of Lacey's near Duxford in Cambridge, to Claire College for the next fifty years. William Fettiplace, stepuncle of Thomas Elyot, by indentures made in 1526, established at Childrey, Berkshire, an almshouse, a perpetual chantry, and a free school. His priest and teacher was to receive eight pounds a year, a good salary then, and he must be skilled in grammar. He was to teach his pupils religion, in both Latin and English, so that the boys might learn to assist the priest in services; but if any persons were disposed to learn grammar, he was to teach them diligently and even to seek the "sage counsel of learned men." Queen's College, Lincoln College, and the rector of Childrey were to keep a qualified man in the position. The indentures also provided a house for the school. The teacherpriest was to accept "such children and persons as shall come" for instruction, and to take no money from any resident of Childrey.[3] The plan of William Fettiplace was not without precedent, for free schools were being established in other places outside London. In 1508 a merchant tailor and mayor of London established a school under the care of the Merchant Taylors at his birthplace, Wolverhampton, Staffordshire. In 1515 a draper and mayor of London established one at Walthamstow, Essex.[4]

Dame Susan Kingston, Thomas Elyot's stepsister, whose will was proved in 1541, directed that four marks sterling be taken annually from the profits of her holdings and applied to the support of a priest to teach poor children at Shalston, Buckinghamshire. Her executors were to carry out the plan. Doubtless she chose Shalston because her sister Anne lived there; and since she was buried there, one might suppose that she made it her home after Syon House was dissolved in 1539.

The families connected with Thomas Elyot also assumed that their wives and daughters were able to manage the property they left to their heirs. In 1492 Sir Thomas Delamere named his wife as his principal executor with two men as her helpers. Though the will of Thomas Daubridgecourt is not available, his wife, who later married Richard Elyot, stated in a chancery plea that her husband had named her as his executor, directing that she use certain parts of the property for the support of the sons and the marriages of the daughters.[5] In 1511, as we have seen, Richard Fettiplace named his wife as his sole executor, leaving her all the property not assigned to the church and to charity, to be used for herself and children at her discretion. With her he named as supervisors his brother William and her father, William Bessils. In 1515, William Bessils gave his wife half his property, both movable and immovable, allowing her to choose her half;

he named John Fettiplace the elder as his executor. In 1521, Sir Maurice Barrow, Thomas Elyot's father-in-law, named his brother, John, and his wife Dorothy as his executors. About 1521–1522, Sir Richard Elyot named his daughter as the one supervisor and his son Thomas as the executor of his will. In 1524 John Fettiplace the elder, after making some bequests, left the residue, both movable and immovable, to his wife Dorothy; he named her as one executor, his uncle William Fettiplace as the other, and his grandmother as the overseer of his will. When Sir Thomas Elyot died in 1546, without children, he left his considerable property to his wife Margaret and named her as his sole executor.

But the outstanding woman of business in these families was Dame Susan Kingston, who did not retire to a nunnery but made the best of two worlds after her widowhood by living as a vowess (one who had taken a vow of chastity) at Syon House, where she paid board for herself and her servants. When her husband, John Kingston, died about 1514, he made gifts to religion and arranged for funeral expenses; then he left to her the order and disposition of his will and gave her all his possessions, both movable and immovable. Like many others connected with the Fettiplaces, he left much property, including six manors and other lands in six different counties. From the records of his father's death and his inheritance, he must have been about twenty-five when he died,[6] and the chances are that Susan was younger than he was. As a result of his death, she probably began early to accept the responsibilities for her own property. In 1524 she took charge of some business for her uncle, Sir Thomas Fettiplace. He specified in his will that £400 and much plate were to go to his daughter Katherine if his unborn child were a son and would thus receive his lands. He put the money and the plate into the keeping of his niece, Dame Susan, at Syon House; she was to make indentures for this property with his executors. About 1526, when Dame

Alice Bessils made her will and wished to leave some property for Edmund Fettiplace, she appointed Dame Susan,
Dorothy Fettiplace (who was Edmund's mother), and
James Yate, to keep the property until Edmund was
twenty-four years old. She also named the same Susan as
her executor. In 1529 William Fettiplace named among
seven executors his sister, Dame Marie Englefield, and his
niece, Susan Kingston. Perhaps Susan had the leisure as
well as the ability to manage business affairs. At least she
bears the palm for the number of these appointments.

The families connected with Thomas Elyot were orthodox and conventional so far as religion is concerned,
with no indication of anticlerical feeling. In this period
some men were anticlerical because they were irreligious.
Others, like Erasmus, seemed anticlerical because they had
analyzed the essentials of religion as love of God and man
expressed in worthy action; they attacked mere formality,
superstition, ignorance, and evil living concealed under
the robes of friars, monks, and priests. But so far as we
know, no prominent man associated with these families
(except Thomas Elyot himself) attacked evil in his church;
and Elyot seldom admitted that churchmen had human
frailties.

When we judge these men and women by the provisions they made for their funerals and for subsequent
events, we find them orthodox and conventional. They
left funds for torches, tapers, and black gowns to be worn
by relatives or by poor men who would pray for the souls
of the dead. They made gifts to parish churches, to priests,
and to friars, sometimes to orders of friars in many different places. They left money for every priest who came
to the burial to say dirige and Mass. They arranged for
the burial, the month's mind, and the year's mind. They
bequeathed their souls to the Holy Trinity, to Saint Mary
the Virgin, or to all the saints of heaven.

Several people made individual arrangements about prayers for their souls. Maurice Barrow directed his house priest to serve six years in Ivychurch before the image of Our Lady of Pity, where his body was to lie, and to pray as he felt disposed for his soul, his wife's soul and her welfare while she lived, his children's souls, and all Christian souls. Dorothy Barrow left her own chaplain the generous sum of £6, 13s., and 6d. a year to sing for her soul and all Christian souls, at the place where she should be buried. Sir William Findern directed that his household should be maintained for a full year after his death, and that every servant, man or woman, should have meat, drink, and wages as usual, but that each might be released as he found other employment. In return, each servant was to be at Mass daily, either in the chapel at Carlton or at high Mass in the parish church, from three until five o'clock in the afternoon; to hear evensong and to pray for the souls of Sir William, his wife, his son William, and all his family. During the other hours of the day, the servants were to work in the gardens and pastures or to be at prayers; they were not to live in idleness. William Fettiplace in addition to his other provisions for prayers, left a sum of money for two prisons in London, Ludgate and Newgate; and for two prisons in Southwark, Marshalsea and King's Bench. The money was to be divided equally among the prisoners, to pray for his soul, his wife's soul, and all Christian souls.

An interest in Lincoln College furnishes some evidence of orthodoxy, since it was founded to oppose heretics and later was refounded on the same principle.[7] Sir Richard Elyot, Sir William Findern, and William Fettiplace remembered the college in their wills, though several men connected with the group also indicated an interest in other colleges.

Many of these people had some connection with Syon House, one of the wealthiest and strictest of the religious houses. Sir Thomas Delamere, his wife Elizabeth, and

Dame Alice Bessils all gave directions under certain conditions for burial there. Since Dame Susan Kingston had
chosen to live there as a young widow and a "vowess," paying board for her servants and herself, perhaps she would
have chosen burial there but the house was dissolved in
1539 and she died in 1540. An Ursala Fettiplace, also pensioned from Syon House, was probably a relative. Eleanor
Fettiplace became a nun there, and her sister Dorothy, as
the widow of John Codrington, seems to have entered the
same house. At least a Dorothy Codrington was being
paid a pension later as a former nun there; and John Yate
sometimes collected her pension along with Fettiplace
pensions.

The daughters of some of these families became nuns
elsewhere. As we have seen, Eleanor Elyot entered the
Abbey of Shaftesbury, Elizabeth Fettiplace became a nun
at Amesbury, and the Margery Ballard who drew a pension as a former nun of Barking Abbey was probably a
relative of the Elyots.[8] The religious houses these girls
entered were usually the wealthiest, the most aristocratic,
and the strictest in England. In wealth, Syon House was
first, Shaftesbury second, and Barking third. The abbess
of Barking had precedence over all other abbesses, and
earlier, at least, she was held responsible for the same contribution to military service as abbots and bishops.[9] In
spite of any regulations, families tended to pay fees when
their daughters entered these great houses; and perhaps
most of the girls connected with the Elyots really sought a
religious life, instead of entering to save the family payment of a dowry. Either the girls or the parents or both,
then, were orthodox in their acceptance of the religious life.


To these West Country landed gentry and other families connected with them, manor life apparently seemed

the normal method of living. Though there is no evidence
that Thomas Elyot lived on a manor in his childhood, he
must have been quite familiar with manors from his connection with the Finderns and the Fettiplaces. He inherited manors: Long Combe, Oxford, from his father, and
Little Carlton from Sir William Findern. Others, including Dame Susan Kingston and William Fettiplace, had
possession of numerous manors. After the death of Thomas
Elyot's father, the manor of Long Combe, Oxford, became
his chief country home; after he was knighted, in 1530, the
manor of Carlton, Cambridge, became his chief residence.

The English manor was the descendant of a dying
feudalism. (It was also the ancestor of the Southern planta-
tion in the United States.) It was an independent, self-
sustaining community, comparatively speaking; but in a
day of poor roads and slow, uncomfortable travel, it was
the center of an isolated life. Legally speaking, it was a
place where the lord of the manor was bound to hold court
at intervals and his freehold tenants were bound to attend,
or if absent without good reasons, to pay their fines. To
this court the tenants also brought their own grievances.
and those who had broken manor laws had fines or penalties assessed against them. With other technicalities of the
manor we are not concerned here—they have been
thoroughly discussed in other sources—but only with the
way of life provided for the lord and lady of the manor.

Certainly the legal duties of a manor lord, in addition
to the supervision of animals, crops, and people, made a
considerable burden—especially when the same lord was
likely to be on commissions of the peace, of assize, or of
gaol delivery and to spend days and weeks helping to ad-
minister the local government of England. Hence the
manor lord with much property had a steward who could
travel about and supervise different holdings. The steward
was usually a man of some education, perhaps a younger
son of the manor lord himself or of some other good

family, and he was chosen by the lord to look after his interests. In addition, a reeve, chosen by the tenants or at least approved by them, usually looked after the work of an individual manor. The reeve might be unable to read or write, keeping his accounts by some highly individual system of tallies, and he was often a serf. But he was shrewd, and he probably knew better than his lord both the duties and the people of his manor. One fourteenth-century reeve, according to H. S. Bennett, traveled from Oxfordshire to Southampton, bought five new millstones for his lord at a cost of more than fifteen pounds, took them to Henley by water, and hired carts there to take them on to his lord's manor.[10] Reeves like this one could do much to make life bearable for a manor lord who had government duties in London or must travel miles on horseback to deliver gaols or hold assizes.

Besides the steward and the reeve, the manor personnel included freehold tenants, subject to military duty for the lord, and copyhold tenants whose ancient land rights were written into the records of the manor. The latter owed occasional fines or heriots to the lord but were free men who might usually convey land rights to their heirs. There were serfs, holding small cottages and performing agricultural or other duties. The lord of the manor needed a miller, a blacksmith, a carpenter, and perhaps a pound-keeper; some of these might also serve his tenants. He must have shepherds, cattleherders, a tiddler to look after the young cattle, and perhaps others for specific kinds of work. The lord had his personal servants, including one or more who rode horseback to carry messages, and enough servants in the household to manage activities for his family and guests. Sometimes he had a family chaplain who might also be a schoolmaster, a secretary, or even an agent for the land. While the details varied from manor to manor, each person, according to his abilities and to his degree, made some contribution to the common welfare.

The physical plant of a manor included the lord's house, either a church and a churchyard or a chapel as part of the house, perhaps a rectory, barns, a mill, a smithy, a bakehouse, a brewhouse, a slaughterhouse, oxstalls, pigsties, a sheepfold, a dovecote, other outbuildings, land reserved for the manor lord, the better houses of the free tenants, the cottages of others (sometimes two rooms with one of them shared by the stock), the common fields, and the wastes, with trees or shrubbery and undergrowth.

The house of the manor lord tended to be a set of low, rambling buildings around a countyard or two, with the entrance through a gatehouse. Here a manor family lived as comfortably, perhaps, as the same family might do in London. The great hall of the house, if typical, had an entrance at one end from a passageway which was cut off by screens, with a minstrels gallery above it. At the other end of this hall was a raised dais, with a table of boards on trestles; here sat the master, the mistress, and special guests. Two tables at right angles to the main one were used by the other people. At the high table there might be either a settle with a back or several elaborate chairs with high backs. For the lower tables there were benches without backs and some stools. None of the seats had upholstering, but at least for the high table plenty of loose cushions were provided. The hall was decorated with hangings, either with cheaper painted cloths or tapestries, according to the wealth and the taste of the manor lord. By the late fifteenth century, fireplaces no longer were in the center of the room but at the wall, so that smoke found an easier exit. In Thomas Elyot's time the windows were probably glass, since the Pastons a generation earlier were having problems with glass because it was new; but his father probably spent his boyhood in more primitive conditions. Lighting came from candles, either in wooden candlesticks or in wooden or metal candelabra hung from the ceiling. Small chests at the foot of beds usually served instead of cupboards or chests of drawers. Huge beds had canopy frames and handsome canopies, such as the one Sir Richard mentioned in his will; and there were coverlets and feather-beds, with plenty of truckle beds to be shoved under the big ones. Perhaps the families in these manor houses found their greatest physical comfort in their beds, where they could be warm all through—at least a modern American is likely to think so.

When a manor had a resident chaplain, the whole household attended matins and Mass before breakfast, and evensong before dinner, as a part of the daily routine. A family who lived near a parish church probably attended services there. Sir Maurice Barrow and his widow, Dorothy, each provided an income for a chaplain who was to pray for souls. Sir Richard Elyot did not mention a chaplain. If he lived in Salisbury, perhaps he always had a parish church within easy reach, as he had St. Dunstan's or the Temple Church in London. Though Thomas Elyot took his own chaplain with him on his embassy, he did not mention a chaplain in his will, though he did name the curate of Combe as a witness to the early part of that document.

When the family was living on the manor (instead of being in London) the lady of the manor needed administrative skill to keep her household clothed and fed. Since much or all of the household linen was made at home and all was kept in repair at home, she had to direct mending, spinning, weaving. She must make at home all wearing apparel except hose, girdles, and hats. She must order ahead any fur, silk, or velvet that might be needed for the finer garments. She would have to order early, perhaps from London or Bristol, such supplies as wine, pepper, other spices, oranges, dates, sugar, and treacle. She could buy salt fish in quantities, direct the killing of sheep, or even plan a beef supply for the winter. Much meat and game came from the manor itself and fresh fish from the manor pond; the meal was ground at home, and bread, butter, and beer or ale were made on the premises. The lady of the manor had much to supervise for adequate food supplies.

In earlier, less settled times, a Paston wife sometimes found herself fighting her husband's battles, both figuratively and literally, while he was in London; but so far as we know, the Fettiplace and Elyot women fought only the normal battles of the household. If the wife of Thomas Elyot, who had once been a student in More's household school, spent much of her married life on a manor, this may be one reason why she did not follow the example of Margaret More Roper and publish translations of Latin and Greek classics.

In winter or in rainy weather with muddy roads, a manor wife must sometimes have craved social life with equals other than those in her immediate family, even though she did not expect the entertainment available to a modern woman. At least one Paston wife, a little earlier, looked forward eagerly to a party for the queen in Norwich, and wrote begging her husband in London to send her some ornament for her neck, so that she need not go unadorned and ashamed.

For Thomas Elyot, the manors owned by men connected with his family may have seemed a living example of degrees in government. Certainly the manor lord, the steward, the reeve, free tenants, copyhold tenants, and servants for every kind of duty might cause him to consider such degrees as normal living. If one cannot say with certainty that manor life was the cause, one might conjecture that it intensified natural tendencies. At least he was the aristocrat of the early sixteenth-century humanists in England, expressing his theory consistently from the *Governour*, 1531, to *The Image of Governance*, 1541. He argued for classes in the state as if they were the will of providence, but he was careful to add that leaders must have wisdom and virtue. He asserted that men of virtue, education, and ability made better governors if they were of noble birth. The other humanists of the period were more concerned with the right of the humble man, when he had virtue and ability, to rise to a new status in the aristocracy of learning.

With this background and these family connections, Thomas Elyot cannot be considered as one who made his way upward in life from ignorance and poverty. Even if he had no university education and even if he learned his Greek as More and Erasmus did, he cannot by any reasonable stretch of the imagination be considered a self-made man. The men who belong to his boyhood and youth were the foundation of Tudor society. They amassed, conserved, and passed on its real wealth in their flocks, herds, and the uses of their lands. Through their work on commissions of the peace, for the assizes, and for gaol delivery, they carried on a substantial part of Tudor government. They were the extension of the king's power and the power of his Council—an extension which served at the same time their own interests in bringing peace and preserving property. They needed a stable government and a strong king. They were also the secular support of the religious houses and of an orthodox church. They were thrifty and ambitious but public-spirited and sincerely religious. These qualities of the West Country gentry, which Thomas Elyot had by inheritance and association, were important in his life—perhaps even more important than his aristocratic tendencies.

# CHAPTER IV

## *Unknown Years. 1503–1510*

HOUGH Thomas Elyot's father, Richard Elyot, may have sprung from undistinguished ancestry, he developed gradually a legal eminence greater than that achieved by any Findern, Bessils, or Fettiplace. The record of his activities begins in 1493 with a commission directing him and others to inquire into concealed or forfeited lands, including those acquired by Edward IV or Richard III, in a half dozen western counties. Then he was on commissions to deliver the gaol of Old Sarum (Salisbury) and to investigate the escape of prisoners there and in the entire county of Wiltshire. He helped to conduct inquisitions *post mortem* and to demise a group of manors that came into the king's hands about 1500 because the heir was a minor. From 1494 to 1507 he was on the Commission of the Peace for Wiltshire, and from 1501 to 1508 on the same commission for Essex.[1]

His special appointments, beginning in 1503, were even more important. In that year he became a serjeant-at-law, and as a result of the honor, he was asked to be a reader at his Inn of Court, the Middle Temple. Two other men from his own inn, Lewis Pollard and Guy Palmes, and seven men from other inns became serjeants at the same time. One of them was John More, of Lincoln's Inn, the father of Thomas More, the future chancellor of

England.[2] All serjeants-to-be received notice of the honor by letters patent from the king, and each must have practiced law for at least sixteen years. A serjeant ranked as the equal of a knight; he did not doff his white silk coif, or cap, in the presence of the king, even when the two were in personal conversation. Unless some unusual circumstance led the king to issue a letter depriving him of his status, he held his position for life.[3]

In keeping with the exalted position, the ceremonies held for men when they became serjeants-at-law were both elaborate and expensive. About 1468–1471, Fortescue estimated that the honor cost each man no less than £266, 13s., and 4d.; and the expense in 1503 probably did not differ greatly from that sum.[4] The ceremonies for 1503 happen to be described in considerable detail in the Middle Temple minutes. On Friday, the first day of the festivities, the members of that inn assembled in their hall, sent older members to bring the serjeants-to-be, and when they had arrived, made speeches praising them, and "delivered to them 20 marks of silver enclosed in a new glove." They in turn thanked the society, not only for the money but for the learning and the good rules "which had restrained them in their youth from their dislike of study." Then after all had drunk together, the others accompanied the future serjeants to the barge which was to convey them to the Inn at Lambeth, and there they left them.

On Saturday the newly chosen serjeants asked the members of their own inn to dine with them.

On Sunday all the justices assembled before ten o'clock in the Chapel of the Inn at Lambeth. The new serjeants, kneeling, made declarations on certain writs which had been delivered to them earlier. Afterward the Chief Justice praised them "and showed to them more good examples of their predecessors." Then he placed the coifs on their heads, tied them under their chins, and clothed them one by one with hoods of scarlet (which they had provided at their own cost), placing the hoods on their shoulders like those of doctors. And "so they were created Serjeants-at-law in the presence of the public, before the whole Inn, the folk standing around." Then the justices and the serjeants entered the inn, and all dined together. On Monday the serjeants came to Westminster Hall, and before them marched "all men of their livery and well ranked." Two who had been made serjeants at some earlier time led the senior one of the new serjeants to the bar before the Chancellor of England, the Treasurer of England, and the justices, who were all present. This senior made his declaration, a former serjeant made a defense, "and the Prothonotary read the writ." Each new serjeant in his turn went through the same ceremony. Then they went to their inn—probably meaning the one at Lambeth—and the king with his whole household had breakfast with them, so that a thousand people sat down together.[5] Presumably the new serjeants paid the bills for this and for the earlier feasts.

As one might suppose, this account from the Middle Temple records stresses the legal part of the ceremonies, but Fortescue emphasizes the gold rings which must be given to every prince, duke, archibishop, chief justice, earl, knight, and every important official of England who attended the ceremony, and also the great "livery of cloth" which every new serjeant gave to his servants and to his friends and acquaintances who attended and served him at these celebrations.[6] A man who became a serjeant-at-law, then, must have acquired enough property so that he could pay his share of the costs, but such a man also expected enough extra profit in the future to compensate him many times over.

After his appointment as a serjeant-at-law in 1503, Richard Elyot continued to receive other honors. In 1507, he and Lewis Pollard were designated as king's serjeants.[7] Though any serjeant may have been called a king's serjeant in certain eras, it was not true of this period. Holdsworth says: "Of the more distinguished serjeants, the crown retained certain to be king's serjeants." They performed some special legal duties, received a fixed salary from the crown, and were summoned by a special writ to attend Parliament.[8] When Henry VIII came to the throne in 1509 he confirmed the appointment of Richard Elyot and Lewis Pollard as king's serjeants; and the two, along with the king's attorney, were listed to receive yards of scarlet and red cloth for robes at the coronation.[9] Again, in 1513, Richard Elyot received another outstanding honor when he was named as a justice of the Court of Common Pleas.[10]

What effect would the legal eminence of Richard Elyot have, in the early sixteenth century, on the life of his son? What sort of education would he wish his son to have? Probably, either with or without his growing eminence, he would wish his son to have a sound training in the English common law, because conditions in the period made a knowledge of the law important. Every property owner needed such knowledge to protect his holdings and to acquire more property, for property, especially immovable property, was important in giving a man citizenship and rank. As a result, men were hungry for land—and then more land—to establish themselves and to provide their sons with the means for carrying on the family name. As feudal tenures had broken down also, shrewd interpreters were needed for the laws of property.

Richard Elyot could hardly have been sympathetic with an education in the classics for his son. Such sympathy from him would be a minor miracle. Nor would be consider desirable the education that the universities about 1500 were actually giving. He probably realized also that the universities, in the late fifteenth and early sixteenth centuries, even if they were improving, offered little control for young boys.[11] From experience, as a man of the

Middle Temple, he knew that the centers for law training in London enforced strict discipline based on residence. In London, too, Thomas Elyot could be under his father's eye part of the time; and there he could study the English common law.

Definite parallels between Richard Elyot and John More, the father of Thomas More, the future chancellor, lend strong support to these ideas. Young Thomas More was sent to Oxford by Cardinal Morton, not by his father; and after two years his father recalled him, fearing that he might turn away from the common law. The son came home and entered New Inn; later he went on to Lincoln's Inn, where his grandfather and his father had studied law. The More and the Elyot fathers were of the same generation, neither had a university education himself, both came from rather humble ancestry, both were trained at Inns of Court, both were shrewd lawyers and were made serjeants-at-law. Eventually each was made a justice, John More of the King's Bench and Elyot of the Court of Common Pleas. Probably both thought that a university education in this period was for clerks, not for men of affairs. They may have been confirmed in this opinion by the fact that the universities, using Latin, taught only civil and canon law; but the law schools in London, using English and law French, were the only places where one might study the English common law.

Another question, perhaps equally important, concerns the kind of education that young Thomas Elyot himself wished to have. If one may judge his desires from his future activities, he wished to learn Greek, to improve his skill in classical Latin, and to read widely in the classics. About 1500 to 1518, he could achieve that aim far better in London than at either of the universities.

The universities were in a period of stagnation followed by one of transition. The testimony of Erasmus and of Bishop John Fisher, who worked together at Cambridge about 1511 to 1514, shows the condition there. Writing in 1516, Erasmus said that earlier little had been taught but the *Parva logicalia,* the old 'dictates' from Aristotle, and questions from Duns Scotus. Now some were starting to learn Greek and to read authors who had formerly been unknown.[12] Though Erasmus had himself taught a little Greek there informally, that language was not officially established until the appointment of Richard Croke in 1518. Modern curricula as approved by the classicists began only when Bishop Fisher opened St. John's College in 1516; and the college needed several years to reach its full development.[13]

Conditions at Oxford were little better than they were at Cambridge. In the late fifteenth century some visitors to Oxford knew Greek. Cornelio Vitelli reached there in 1490, gave a public lecture in Latin the next year, paid for a room at Exeter College for several terms up to the summer of 1492, and then disappeared from the records. Grocyn, who had apparently learned some Greek in England before 1488, went to Italy that year for study, returned to Oxford about 1491, and paid room rent there until 1493. Perhaps he was at the university part of the time after this date; he was given a living in London about 1496.[14] Some suppose that he gave public lectures on Greek without a formal appointment for teaching it, but exact evidence is lacking. It is possible that More's interest in Greek and some knowledge of it began in Oxford with Grocyn, since More went to the university in 1492; but his own comment in a letter of 1504 tends to imply that he was beginning the study of it in London with Grocyn.

Granting that some Greek may have been taught informally at Oxford by Vitelli or by Grocyn about 1490 to 1493 or 1494, opposition to liberal studies was strong many years later. We learn this fact from More's well-known letter to that university in 1518. Speaking for the king and other leaders in church and state, not merely for himself,

More soundly reproved the "Trojans," who were attacking Greek and Latin literature, all the liberal arts, and all polite learning. He warned that "learning will perish if the university continues to suffer from the contentions of lazy idiots, and the liberal arts are allowed to be made sport of with impunity."[15] Modern curricula as approved by the humanists made a beginning at Oxford when Bishop Fox established Corpus Christi College about 1517; and that college needed time for its development. Greek did not become a part of the curriculum until John Clement, More's protégé, was appointed in 1518 as a reader.[16]

While the universities were in this period of transition, from about 1500 to 1518, London was the great center in England for a man who wished to study the classics. Thomas Linacre, William Grocyn, and William Lily were in or near London, after study in Italy and other Mediterranean countries, with knowledge, enthusiasm, and perhaps books they had bought abroad. If classics, the books would be newly translated direct from the Greek, not through the Arabic, and they would be sources for the vocabulary of classical Latin which these men prized.

Thomas Linacre had gone to Italy about 1485 or 1486 with William Selling of Canterbury, who had started him in Greek. He continued to study it with Politian at the court of Lorenzo de Medici in Florence; he went on to Rome and Ferrara, where he probably read both Galen and Hippocrates; and about 1496 he took a degree in medicine at Padua. For several years he lived in the house of Aldus Manutius in Venice, helping him edit a Greek edition of Aristotle. About 1499 he returned to England. Because of his learning he was appointed tutor to Prince Arthur, though he may never have served in that position, and later he directed the education of the Princess Mary.

After spending some time at Magdalen College and New College and learning a little Greek in England, perhaps from visitors who spoke the language, William Grocyn

studied in Italy about 1488 to 1489 or 1490, with Politian
and Chalcondyles. Apparently from about 1496, he held
the living of St. Lawrence Jewry, the parish church of Sir
John More, and lectured at St. Paul's in 1501; hence he
must have been in London many years, up to his death in
1519.

William Lily went on a Mediterranean pilgrimage
which included Jerusalem and stopped for some time in
Rhodes, when it was made safe for western Christians by a
garrison of the Knights of St. John. He studied in Italy
under Sulpitius and Pomponius Laetus. He mastered the
Greek and Latin languages and also acquired a vast fund of
information about classical antiquity. After his return to
England he was teaching in or near London, making the
reputation that led Colet to choose him about 1510 or 1511
as his headmaster for St. Paul's school.[17]

These were the men who made London an excellent
place to study the classics in the first decade or two of the
century. They, first Grocyn and then Linacre, were helping
More with his studies. Though More had been a young
student at Oxford when Grocyn was there, his letter to
John Holt about 1501 does not suggest that he had started
Greek at Oxford:

> You ask how I am doing in my studies. Wonderfully, of
> course; things could not be better. I have shelved my
> Latin books to take up the study of Greek; however, while
> dropping the one, I have not as yet, completely caught up
> with the other. . . .
>    Grocin, my instructor, recently made a very successful
> start on his lectures at St. Paul's. . . .

In a letter of 1504 to Colet, More deplored his friend's
absence from London and then added:

> Meanwhile, I shall pass my time with Grocin, Linacre,
> and our dear friend Lily, the first as you know the sole

guide of my life (in your absence), the second my master
in learning, the third the dearest partner of my en-
deavors.[18]

About this time More and Lily were friendly rivals in the
translating of Greek epigrams, though at first Lily probably possessed a superior knowledge of Greek.

During these same years Erasmus was teaching himself Greek, having first tried a private teacher who proved
to be unsatisfactory. He used the system of double translation, from Greek to Latin and then back again; and
when he returned to England in 1506, both he and More
had probably achieved a sound knowledge of Greek.[19]
About 1511 to 1516, Bishop Fisher, working under the influence of Erasmus, tried to learn Greek; he developed
enough skill to discover printer's omissions in Erasmus'
translation of the New Testament.[20] Colet was also doing
his best to learn Greek. In 1516 More wrote to Erasmus:

Colet is working strenuously on his Greek, with the so-
licited help of my boy Clement. I do believe he will per-
severe until he masters the subject, especially if you keep
spurring him on from Louvain; and yet it might be better
to let him follow his own impulse. As you know, he has
the habit of disagreeing with suggestions given him, just
to have an argument, even when those suggestions cor-
respond with his own ideas.[21]

London was a stimulating place about 1500 to 1516
and later, not only because these humanists were teaching
and learning there but because they were guided by a
definite philosophy: education was the way to human
perfectibility for the individual and for society. As a result, they felt an obligation to help others who had the
ability and the desire to learn. Probably a boy who was a
complete stranger but who was "by nature inclined to
knowledge" could have approached Linacre, Grocyn, Lily,
or More, asked for help in learning Greek or Latin, and

received it. Thus London was the place for Thomas Elyot
to gain both the training in law that his father wished him
to have and the informal education in the classics that he
began absorbing.


What did Thomas Elyot tell us himself about his education? He made four brief interesting comments: one in
the preface to his *Dictionary*, 1538; one in the Proheme to
the *Governour;* one in his discussion of law, also in the
*Governour*; and another in the preface to the 1541 edition of *The Castle of Health*. These statements have not
been related to each other and to the life of Elyot.

In the preface to the first edition of his Latin-English
*Dictionary*, Elyot expressed a hope that readers would not
consider him an ignorant knight; though he had had no
formal education after his twelfth year in his father's house,
he had been led by himself into liberal studies and into
both kinds of philosophy.[22] This statement is one that
any biographer must come to terms with: Elyot, so far as
we have other evidence, was scrupulously honest in comments about himself, he never contradicted this estimate
of his education elsewhere, and in this instance he had no
motive for lying. In fact, if he had wished to lie, he would
have pretended to more education. He was no doubt using
the term education as a classicist might use it, meaning the
kind that would prepare him for editing a Latin dictionary,
not his vocational training in law.

In his father's house, Thomas Elyot had had a tutor,
no doubt, according to the custom of the time. Even if his
father lived in Salisbury, no grammar school existed at
Salisbury Cathedral for at least sixty-five years before 1540;
and records reveal no evidence of grammar schools in
Wiltshire or in all the West Country at this time.[23] The
father may have been able to secure for his son a better
than usual tutor chosen from the men attached to the

parish churches or the cathedral staff. Such a tutor would
know classical Latin, perhaps even a little Greek, and
might be skillful enough to whet his young pupil's appetite for learning.

If Elyot was telling the truth, then, he did not have
any university education. Some Thomas Elyot near this
time did receive degrees from Oxford, a B.A. in 1519, and
a B.C.L. in 1524.[24] But there is little reason to believe
that these degrees were given to the future author of the
*Governour.* A number of Thomas Elyots were living in
England at this time. One named Thomas, but one of
the Devon and Cornwall Elyots, was on the commissions
of the peace for those counties about 1494 to 1504; one,
perhaps the same one, was a tax collector at Plymouth in
1488–1489 and again in 1515, and was a prosperous merchant, licensed to export quantities of tin. In 1516 a Sir
Thomas Eliet was listed as a Knight of the Body in the
Royal Household. In the same year a Mr. Elyot, who *may*
have been the future author of the *Governour,* was named
among those for the jousts. He was listed as one of a
number of men for whom the king furnished white satin
costumes with white velvet cut-work and silver of damask.
In 1534 a "Mr. Elyott" (though we do not know his given
name) was asked by the abbot of Rewley at Oxford to teach
his monks; probably this one had a degree or degrees from
Oxford. About 1539 to 1542 a Thomas Elyot is named in
Surrey, one in Staffordshire, and one in London. Between
1493 and 1557 six Thomas Elyots, with enough property
so located that they came under the high jurisdiction, had
wills probated in the Prerogative Court of Canterbury.[25]
Hence it seems unsound to draw conclusions about university degrees when there were many Thomas Elyots in many
different places at this time.

In 1519 the author of the *Governour* was about thirty
years old, and in 1524 about thirty-five—advanced ages in
this period for receiving degrees unless a man wished to

teach at a university. The Thomas Elyot we are dealing
with here indicated no such desire, and for some time before 1519 he was following other paths of preferment. No
evidence seems to suggest that he acquired the knowledge
of civil or Roman law implied in receiving the B.C.L. A
favorable comment on the civil law was a commonplace
among humanists in the period, and men who expressed
the preference may have had no training whatever in law.

The normal age for going to a university in the early
sixteenth century was about fourteen or fifteen. At these
ages boys sometimes went for a few months or a year and
then entered an Inn of Chancery or of Court in London.
(Thomas More, for example, was about fourteen when
Cardinal Morton sent him to Oxford.) Often they left behind them no official evidence of residence at the university
and took no knowledge with them. We learn by chance,
perhaps from letters they wrote, that they had once spent
a brief time at Oxford or Cambridge. But Elyot's firm
statement in the preface to his dictionary seems to disprove
even a brief early attendance, since he was a man of some
integrity and he did not contradict the statement elsewhere. It is not necessary to assume that he was either a
university graduate or a self-made man. An eagerness to
provide him with degrees in an age when they were unessential and when the universities emphasized theology is
like a refusal to believe that Shakespeare wrote his plays because he did not have the blessing of a university.

In the Proheme of the *Governour* Elyot made another
statement about his education. He had gathered his material for the book, he said, from two sources: first, the
most noble Greek and Roman authors; and second, from
"myne owne experience, I being continually trayned in
some dayly affaires of the publike weale of this your moste
noble realme all mooste from my chyldhode." This statement alone may prove little; but related to other details,
it suggests that the best place to secure such practical train-

ing was in London with his father; and he was far from childhood in 1510 when his father entered him at the Middle Temple.

Elyot's third statement about his own education comes in his discussion of law study in the *Governour,* Book I, xiii, xiv. As he concludes chapter xiii, he says that men who put their children to the study of law when the children are fourteen or fifteen years old are doing wrong. He will go on to show good reasons for his opinion, and his opinion is "infourmed partely by myne owne experience." It seems clear that he himself, at too early an age, had been a victim of the practice. In chapter xiv he explains his opinion. Laws are founded on deep reason, he says; the deeper the reason, the more difficult the study. English common law has an additional difficulty because it is expressed in "barbarous" language, in law French. Boys forced too early into the study of law either escape into gambling and other improper pastimes, or they comprehend only a small part of what they study, and as a result, they lose their courage and self-esteem. Children should be permitted to follow their own interests, instead of being forced into the law; but men tend to stop them if they wish to follow artistic pursuits—to carve, embroider, or engrave. Thus their own talents are dulled, and England loses its chance of development in the arts. Perhaps he found the courage to express these ideas partly because he had taken to heart his reading of Erasmus, where he might have found similar theories on permitting a boy to follow his natural bent.

After condemning the early study of law, Elyot proposes his own plans: let children study philosophy or liberal subjects until they are twenty-one; then give them English law expressed either in English, in Latin, or in good French; and train them to use the exordium or pleasant beginning in law pleading, as they already use some of the rules of ancient rhetoric. He is sure that the

earlier study of liberal subjects and of eloquence will not
turn young men against a later study of law.

Elyot's fourth comment on his own education appears
in the preface to his 1541 edition of *The Castle of Health,*
in his defense of himself against detractors who said that a
knight who was not a physician had no business writing a
book on medicine. He does know something about medicine: before he was twenty years old, "a worshipfull phisition, and one of the moste renouined at that tyme in
England, perceyuyng me by nature inclined to knowledge,
rad unto me the workes of Galene of temperamentes, natural faculties, the Introduction of Johannicius, with some
of the Aphorismes of Hippocrates." He follows this with
a list of medical works that he himself had read later.
Several conclusions, in addition to the fact that Elyot had
done a quantity of medical reading before 1510, can be
drawn from his statement. First, his worshipful physician
was certainly Linacre, almost as certainly as if Elyot had
named him. England had few real physicians at this time:
mostly ecclesiastics and a few surgeons; general practice was
carried on mostly by barber surgeons and apothecaries. Of
the few physicians, probably no one in England except
Linacre knew enough Greek and enough medicine to read
Galen to anyone. Galen's treatises "in clear, Attic Greek"
had been lost to Western Europe, though his *Methodus
medendi* was available in a Latin version translated
through Arabic. At this time Linacre, who is recognized as
the first Englishman to read Galen in the original Greek,
was translating his works from Greek into Latin. The six
volumes he published between 1517 and 1524 include *De
temperamentis* . . . and *De facultatibus,* which Elyot
named among those read to him. Linacre was certainly
a worshipful physician; he treated the king, More, Erasmus, and others; he was one of the founders and the
first president of the Royal College of Physicians in London; and he arranged for lectures on medicine at both Ox-

ford and Cambridge.[26] One may wonder why Elyot did not name his physician: he was writing for a nonmedical public, Linacre had been dead for about seventeen years, and Elyot's natural reticence usually caused him to omit personal details.

Let him who doubts that Elyot's worshipful physician was Linacre find another in England who was reading Galen in Greek before 1510.

Since Thomas Elyot was reading medicine in Greek before he was twenty, he must have been spending time in London. If so, why was he there? What else was he doing? No biographer, so far as this writer knows, has raised the question what he was doing from about 1503 to 1510. In the latter date, we know, his father sponsored his admission into the Middle Temple.

It seems sound to suggest that his father brought him to London and placed him in one of the Inns of Chancery, to have him learn early the fundamentals of the English common law. Such an action seems logical for a man of his father's background. The son was old enough to enter one of the lesser inns about this time; for if he was born in 1489, he was fourteen in 1503. This suggestion helps explain much that he told us in detached statements about his own education—especially the one that he was continually trained in affairs of the public weal almost from his childhood and also that his opposition to the early study of law was based partly on his own experience.

Further evidence for the suggestion appears when we examine the system of law education in the early sixteenth century. At this time there were nine or ten Inns of Chancery, called by Fortescue the lesser inns, and also the four well-known Inns of Court, called the greater inns. The lesser inns gave elementary work to prepare students for the greater ones. Though both kinds of inns had residents who were not students, they are not our concern here. According to Holdsworth, Stow, and others, the Inns of

Chancery were connected with certain Inns of Court. New Inn and Strand Inn were related to the Middle Temple; Furnivall's and Thavy's to Lincoln's Inn; Clifford's, Clement's, and Lyon's to the Inner Temple; the Staple and Barnard's to Grey's Inn.[27] A man did not always enter the greater inn to which his lesser one was attached; but if he became a reader at a lesser inn, he read at one connected with his own Inn of Court because there was a bond of responsibility for education. For example, though young Thomas More did his elementary work at New Inn and then entered Lincoln's Inn, where his grandfather and father had studied law, he was later a reader at Furnivall's Inn.

Thomas Elyot's father would have chosen an Inn of Chancery for his son because those places and the Inns of Court were well disciplined. From the beginning both had been *hospitia*, or places of residence for students, basing a strict discipline on residence. Holdsworth says of this period that the education, discipline, and the whole life were collegiate in the best meaning of the term: the hall was the place for breakfast, dinner, and supper, as well as for lectures and arguments. The training, he adds, was moral, religious, educational, and social. Though Holdsworth may be referring primarily to the Inns of Court, they dominated the lesser inns connected with them; and it seems safe to infer that the discipline for younger students was similar. An example of the strict control at the Inns of Court appears in 1517, when the Star Chamber, in a time of unrest, advised the benchers of the inns not to allow their gentlemen students to be out of their houses after six at night or to wear any kind of weapon. It was only toward the close of the sixteenth century that the great number of young men entering the inns was "creating a class of students who lived outside the Inn."[28]

Since the Inns of Chancery took young students,

Thomas Elyot would have been eligible for entrance to any one of them about 1503 to 1505. Fortescue said that their students were "for the most part, young men, learning the originals and something of the elements of the law, who becoming proficient therein, as they mature, are absorbed into the . . . Inns of Court."[29] Stow, after mentioning attorneys, officers, solicitors, and clerks of the court who lived at the Inns of Chancery, added that these inns had young students, "some from the universities, and some immediately from the grammar schools." These, "having performed the exercises of their own houses . . . go on to one of the Inns of Court, where they usually spend seven years or more maturing in the study of the law."[30] Young students in large numbers entered the Inns of Chancery, it seems; for Fortescue estimated that at least a hundred students resided at the smallest of them.

Thomas Elyot's father could have paid the cost of such an education for his only son, judging from his appointment as a serjeant-at-law in 1503 and from the property he mentioned in his will. No figures are available about expenses at the lesser inns but Fortescue assures us that no student could be maintained in an Inn of Court for less than £13, 6s., and 4d., a year; and if he had personal servants, as most of them did, the cost was greater. The so-called Bacon report, in the reign of Henry VIII, tells us that each student paid admission and room fees and also twenty nobles a year for masters commons and a little more than five pounds a year for clerks commons.[31] These were large sums for the period. Probably the scale of living and the cost were both lower at the lesser inns. For example, More, when taking counsel with his family after he gave up the chancellorship, rated New Inn fare below that at Lincoln's Inn but Oxford fare lower than either. Since Richard Elyot had only two daughters, one of them in a convent, and only one son, he could afford an Inn of Chancery for his son.

The best reason for assuming that Thomas Elyot studied at an Inn of Chancery is that he needed a considerable knowledge of the law to be admitted to the Middle Temple. There in 1510 "Elyot, junior, was admitted to the Clerks' commons, and at the instance of his father, Serjeant-at-law, is pardoned Autumn and Lent vacations on consideration that he is a Clerk of Assise in the West Country." At this time the requirements for admission were strict. In 1503 a Master Empson was admitted conditionally but told that he must live at New Inn and be a "fellow commoner" there until he considered himself "capable and sound from his study of the law of England." Then he might obtain "possession of his admission into this inn, as fellow commoner . . . in reality." (The words *hospicio* and *commensalis*, given parenthetically by the translator, add to the evidence that both inns were to receive Empson as a resident student.) In 1505 a Master Twyneo also was to live at New Inn as a fellow commoner until his study of the law had made him "capable and sound in knowledge"; then he might become a fellow commoner of the Middle Temple in reality. In 1511 a certain Hord, junior, admitted at the instance of Christopher Saint German, was permitted to be out of commons at his liking for two weeks at the end of each term "as long as he is employed as deputy of the Clerk of the Warrants." This action was taken "because he was well learned, and others had labored for him at other Inns."[32]

It seems reasonable and almost necessary to suppose, then, that Thomas Elyot studied at some Inn of Chancery, perhaps from 1503, or perhaps from 1504 or 1505, to acquire a foundation in the English common law before he entered the Middle Temple in 1510. The assumption is supported by Elyot's own comments, informed partly by his own experience, about the parents who put their sons to the study of law at fourteen or fifteen years of age.

It seems equally reasonable to assume that in the

same years before 1510 Elyot was perfecting his knowledge
of classical Latin, mastering Greek, and reading widely in
the classics. Other boys who found the law a tough adversary escaped into gambling and various improper pastimes. Thomas Elyot escaped into classical learning.

At this stage a skeptic will remind us that More never
mentioned Thomas Elyot in his letters—and he will be
impeccably correct. One does not need to assume that
More was Elyot's teacher, working with him daily, or that
the two were Damon and Pythias. Since Linacre, Grocyn,
and Lily were also in the London area, plenty of inspired
help was available. Perhaps Linacre, who must have been
Elyot's worshipful physician, was the chief helper of both
Elyot and More, since More was learning his Greek from
1501 on, and in 1504 named Linacre as his teacher.

Perhaps equality in friendship, like that between
More and Erasmus, never developed between More and
Elyot. They differed in age by some twelve years. If they
met in 1503, when the two fathers became serjeants-at-law,
Elyot was perhaps fourteen and More about twenty-six.
At those ages the psychological gap is greater that it would
be at twenty-six and thirty-eight. That gap may never have
closed. If no equal friendship developed, there may still
have been great kindness extended from older to younger.
They differed also in temperament. More, like Erasmus,
had the spirit of Lucian—the ability to make a witty comment with wisdom and imagination; and he was capable of
translating semibawdy epigrams from Greek to Latin.
Elyot was moral and serious almost to the point of solemnity.

Further, why should More mention Elyot in his letters? Those in which he chatted about books and men
were mostly written by 1529, and addressed to men on the
Continent. After that time he was involved in the chancellorship, religious controversy, and efforts to explain himself so that he would not be courting maryrdom. Until

Elyot published the *Governour* in 1531, he was not a literary figure even in England. He was not a future teacher to be placed where he might influence education, a known scholar to be praised, or a theologian to be cited.

The same skeptic will ask how Elyot and More became acquainted, for they did know each other even if they were not intimate. We have already seen some possibilities. First, a boy prone to knowledge could have walked up to any of these men—Linacre, Grocyn, Lily, or More—asked for educational help and received it. Second, the young More and the much younger Elyot may each have been serving his own father at the feasts for the new serjeants-at-law in 1503.

There are other possibilities. A remote one based merely on speculation is that Thomas Elyot's Inn of Chancery may have been Furnivall's Inn, where More was a reader (according to Roper) from about 1501 for more than three years. It is possible, then, that More gave Elyot his first training in the English common law. A solid possibility is the close relationship that must have existed between the More and Elyot fathers from 1503 for as long as they both lived. As soon as they received their new dignities, serjeants-at-law moved from their own Inns of Court to special Serjeants' Inns. These were gentlemen's clubs, not centers for training in law. One cannot say that they moved to the same inn, since there were at least two such inns at this time, one in Fleet Street and one in Chancery Lane; but there must have been some communication between them. Then, since the serjeants-at-law had "the monopoly of practice in the Court of Common Pleas" from the time of Edward IV to the nineteenth century, the two fathers must have known each other well.[33] Firm evidence that Thomas Elyot and Thomas More were associated later appears in property transactions and government commissions about 1515 or 1516; Elyot knew Richard Pace about 1516 to 1521; and Elyot and More were both connected with the king's Council from 1522 or 1523 up to 1530.

The statement that Elyot knew Richard Pace is perhaps worth a fuller explanation at this point, in addition to its brief mention earlier. In the 1542 edition of his dictionary, Elyot told us that workmen, digging for a foundation at the monastery of Ivychurch, found a book with leaves of vellum. None of the men at the monastery could interpret the strange wording. Later a single leaf of the book, torn and water-soaked, came into Elyot's hands. Unable to decipher it, he took it to Richard Pace, who, he adds, was then secretary to the king—a comment that places the happening about 1516 to 1521. Pace was able to make out only one word, *Prytania* for *Brytania*, but he judged it to be an early history of Britain. At this time Pace was in such high favor with the king that Wolsey was jealous of his influence and arranged for him an appointment on the Continent. How did Thomas Elyot know Pace well enough to take him the leaf of vellum? Probably the acquaintance had come about through More and it is one other part of a pattern of relationships, developing before and after 1510, between Elyot and other men who were devoted to Greek and Latin literature.

That a literary relationship existed between Thomas Elyot and Thomas More we learn from Stapleton, a careful, informed scholar who wrote the best early life of More. It would be hard to refute his evidence. He had probably seen Roper's notes, even though the material did not appear in print until later. He had certainly used the expert help of his fellow exiles on the Continent, as he tells us in his preface. They included John Clement, Margaret Gigs Clement (More's foster daughter), John Harris (More's private secretary), Dorothy Colley Harris (Margaret Roper's maid), John Heywood, and William Rastell. After discussing More's intimate friends—Colet, Grocyn, Lily, and William Latimer—Stapleton says: "More had other friends and companions in the pursuit of polite literature." In developing this topic sentence, he discusses Lupset, Elyot, and Croke, and makes this comment on Elyot: "Another was Thomas Eliot, a well-known English writer, whose wife also gave herself to the study of literature in More's school. . . ." It is interesting to note that Stapleton carefully places Elyot with the younger men, Lupset and Croke.[34]

If it seems reasonable, then, to assume that Thomas Elyot was in London studying at an Inn of Chancery for several years before 1510 when his father entered him at the Middle Temple, it seems just as reasonable to assume that he was escaping from the clutches of the English common law into the study of the Greek and Latin classics with the informal help of Linacre and the other experts in London.

If Thomas Elyot spent some years at an Inn of Chancery in London before 1510, it is interesting to speculate about other ideas and events that may have impressed him. When his father was training him in the affairs of the public weal, as he implies in the Proheme of the *Governour*, he must have heard stories about the decline of feudalism, the struggles between kings and powerful nobles, and the final emergence of settled conditions under stronger kings. His father was about ten or eleven years old when Henry VI first lost the throne and about twenty when that feeble king briefly regained it; he had seen the firm handling of the kingdom by Edward IV, especially in his second period, the uncertainty under Richard III, and the return of economic stability under Henry VII. As a thrifty conservative, Richard Elyot was no doubt grateful for middle-class prosperity under firm rule. His son, who also had an ability to accumulate property, must have learned to accept the tradition of supporting a strong king—just as he had already learned from the West Country landed gentry the tradition of orthodoxy in a universal church of Western Europe. Elyot's tribute in the *Governour*, I, xxiv, to Henry VII (for his circumspection, justice, establishment of law and order, and his rebuilding after the destruction of war) indicates that he had learned in some way to value a strong king in England.

As a boy, Thomas Elyot probably heard some discussion about the marriage between Prince Arthur and Catherine of Aragon, without realizing the consequences that would follow in his lifetime. Perhaps he saw the pageantry at the funeral of Henry VII: the chariot, covered with black cloth of gold and drawn by five great horses, bringing the body from Richmond; the cushions of fine gold on top, bearing an image of the dead king in his richest robes, with his crown and ball and scepter; the banners and streamers giving details about his dominions, titles, and ancestry; the servants in black, the nine formal mourners, and the six hundred men carrying torches who came with the body from Richmond. He may have watched as the religious men of London met the body at St. George's field or as the mayor and others joined the cortege at London Bridge. He heard reports, perhaps of dirige, Mass, and a sermon by Bishop Fisher at St. Paul's, of services next day at Westminster Abbey, and finally of burial in the beautiful chapel of Henry VII.

Probably Thomas Elyot saw the magnificent procession of Henry VIII and Catherine of Aragon, coming from the Tower in June, 1509, for their coronation at Westminster. Many streets were hung with tapestry and cloth of arras, and parts of Cheap and Cornhill with cloth of gold. At the end of "Olde Chaunge" the goldsmiths' stall was full of virgins in white, with branches of white wax. Priests and clerks in rich robes, with crosses and censers of silver, scattered incense upon the king and the queen as they passed. The apparel, the jewels, and the other

trappings of the king were magnificent. For this coronation, Richard Elyot, along with others, had received red
and scarlet cloth so that he might appear as a king's serjeant-at-law.

After the coronation, jousts and tournaments were
held, with tapestry houses, castles with fountains, and
beasts running red, white, or claret wine. The Lady Pallas
presented her scholars as challengers for all comers, and the
Knights of the Lady Diana answered the challenge. After
the birth of a prince, in 1511, there were more tournaments. At one time the king entered "under a pavillion of
gold and purple embroidered velvet, powdered with H.
and K. of fine gold, the compass of the pavillion above
embroidered richly and valanced with flat gold, beaten in
wire, with an imperial crown in the top of fine gold. . . ."
These were public or semipublic events, it seems, for on
one occasion, when the king signaled for the ladies and
gentlemen and the ambassadors "to take the letters of their
garmentes, in token of liberalitie," the common people ran
to the king and stripped him and his companions down
to their hose and doublets.[35] Thus the young Thomas
Elyot might have witnessed all of these tournaments if he
had wished to do so. In 1511 the parliament of the Middle
Temple had voted that each of the company should pay
twelvepence as a subsidy for a special stand, to watch the
tournament in honor of the young prince.[36] Perhaps it is
no wonder that a young man who saw such festivals tended
to defend magnificence for kings, at least within the bounds
of reason, when he wrote the *Governour*.

At the coronation, in 1509, he must have caught the
note of optimism in the words and glances of many people.
But he probably had no way of knowing the sentiments
Lord Mountjoy expressed in his letter to Erasmus, when he
called him back to an earthly paradise at the accession of
Henry VIII:

For what may you not promise yourself from a prince with whose extraordinary and almost divine character you are well acquainted . . . ? But when you know what a hero he now shows himself, how wisely he behaves, what a lover he is of justice and goodness, what affection he bears to the learned. . . . Avarice is expelled the country. Liberality scatters wealth with bounteous hand. Our king does not desire gold or gems or precious metals, but virtue, glory, immortality.[37]

The letter was a masterpiece of unconscious irony. It may have been well for Thomas Elyot if he did not know of it in 1509.

# CHAPTER V

## Middle Temple. Clerk of Assize, Western Circuit. 1510–1522

VEN if Thomas Elyot spent several years at some Inn of Chancery, he had need for further study of law after his father entered him at the Middle Temple in 1510. The items mentioned in Chapter IV indicate that men without knowledge of the law were asked to study at a lesser inn before they were allowed to become members of the Middle Temple in reality. Stow tells us also that men who had learned the fundamentals at a lesser inn often spent seven years more of study at some Inn of Court. Thomas More, reputed to be a brilliant student of the common law, entered New Inn in 1494, Lincoln's Inn in 1496, became an utter (outer) barrister and a reader at Furnivall's Inn about 1501, but continued to study law at Lincoln's Inn after his marriage in 1504.[1] So Elyot probably needed further study of the law.

Few items in the Middle Temple records, however, refer definitely to the Thomas Elyot who was to become the author of the *Governour*. His admission as Elyot, junior, in 1510, at the instance of his father, a serjeant-at-law, identifies him beyond doubt;[2] but there is no definite evidence that he ever held an office, acted as reader, or was admitted to the bar. Other men of some prominence are also seldom named in the records. For example, the names of John Rastell and Christopher Saint German appear only once in the extant records, which begin about 1500, when they were fined because they were utter barristers and were absent from a meeting of the parliament. But Thomas Elyot apparently kept a connection with his inn, as men usually did, even to the end of his life. In 1521 his father willed him a joined press he had used, asking him to use it, and when he was through with it, to leave it at the Temple. Sir Richard Elyot's own residence there must have ceased in 1503, since serjeants-at-law moved into their own inns when they achieved the new status.

What was life like for Thomas Elyot at the Middle Temple? Daily life at any Inn of Court was not luxurious, though the cost was high because the societies did not have endowments. The diet at an Inn of Court was probably better than that at an Inn of Chancery; it is said that the daily fare gave the men enough food but it was not adapted to delicate appetites. Drinking cups and dishes were wood or pewter, if many payments to a pewterer are evidence, and there is an occasional mention of green earthenware containers. Sundials marked the time, as they did for most other Englishmen in the period. The plague stalked in boldly, as it entered other places in England. Between 1506 and 1522 there were a number of outbreaks. At one time several servants died; in 1507 when a member suddenly succumbed, the others rushed separately to the country, hoping to find air that was free of pestilence.[3] Thomas Elyot's admission placed him in the clerks commons, of course, not the masters commons. Men remained in the clerks commons about two years, sitting "one more at a mess" than those in masters commons, the term mess seeming to refer to the quantity of food served to a group. Every day, at both dinner and supper, those in the clerks commons served the meat to those in the masters commons.[4]

The members of an Inn of Court were under strict

discipline, as one may learn by glancing at the fines listed for the Middle Temple or any other inns, and this discipline was based on residence. Even if the suggestion from the Court of Star Chamber to the benchers of the inns, in 1517, that the gentlemen students should not be permitted outside their houses after six at night and should not wear arms, was adapted to an emergency, the discipline was still strict. Fortescue tells us that the students in his era attended divine service and read scripture and the chronicles. He adds: "This is indeed a cultivation of virtues and a banishment of all vice. So . . . knights, barons . . . and the nobles of the realm place their sons in these inns . . ." even when they do not especially wish them to learn or to practice law. "Scarcely any turbulence, quarrels or disturbances ever occur there, but delinquents are punished with expulsion . . . a penalty they fear more than criminals elsewhere fear imprisonment and fetters. For a man once expelled from one of these societies is never received into the fellowship of any other. . . ."

In contrast to the ordinary life, Thomas Elyot was involved in special festivities that were elaborate, formal, and ritualistic, because they were a part of the social education. As Fortescue tells us, the lesser and the greater inns are "a kind of academy of all the manners that the nobles learn. There they learn to sing and to exercise themselves in every kind of harmonics. They are also taught . . . to practice dancing and all games proper for nobles, as those brought up in the king's household are accustomed to practice." And the so-called Bacon report, later in the reign of Henry VIII, confirms the evidence for Elyot's period by reporting that the solemn Christmas was kept only that the young men might learn "how to use themselves."[5]

One of the special festivities was the Feast Day of All Saints, when the previous readers were freed from their duties and the new readers for the coming year took office. At this time the judges and the serjeants-at-law who had belonged to the Middle Temple earlier, were invited, we are told, and come in their scarlet robes. The older of the two new readers carries a white staff; the younger, a white rod. They usher in the serjeants and the judges. After music, they usher in the meat, receive it from the young gentlemen who carry it, and place it on the table. After some other ceremonies are over, the elder of the new readers places himself at a certain spot in the hall and calls for the Master of the Revels. "And at the second call, the Auncient, with his white staff, advanceth forward, and begins to lead the measures, followed first by the Baristers, and then the Gentlemen under the Bar, all according to their several antiquities: and when one measure is ended, the Reader . . . calls for another, and so in order." With the last measure of the dance, the reader asks one of the gentlemen at the bar to give the judges a song. He begins with the first line of a Psalm that he considers appropriate, and the rest of the company join in singing with him. Next, with much detailed ceremony, the gentlemen of the bar carry wafers and then bowls of hippocras to the judges, who drink. This part of the ceremony is interspersed with many solemn "congees" or gestures of farewell. The others depart, the new readers usher the judges down the hall to the gate of the court, and the celebration ends.[6]

Readers gave special feasts at some time in their period of service, it seems, for in July, 1513, the parliament of the Middle Temple ruled that if the summer reader sent many bucks for his feast, the company would pay for twelve only, and the reader himself would have to meet the bill for the others.[7] But there is no evidence that these dinners were formal or ritualistic.

The Christmas feasts, which Elyot and other members of these societies attended, were elaborate, lasting a number of days. As we learn from the Paston letters, they were already traditional by the middle of the fifteenth century.[8] And in November, 1510, as well as in other years,

the Middle Temple parliament elected three men to serve
for such occasions.[9] Before Christmas Eve, there was a
grand dinner and a formal bringing in of courses with the
blast of a trumpet and the beating of drums. Carols, revels,
and dancing followed the dinner, with the term *revels*
seeming to imply a stately formality. On Christmas Day,
following divine service, the members gathered for a dinner that began with the bringing in of a boar's head on a
silver platter, as the first course. Other formalities followed.

On St. Stephen's Day, the members of the inn usually enjoyed a drama arranged for by the lord of misrule;
and this is said to have been one of the grandest of all
ceremonies. The records of the Middle Temple are
sprinkled with items about payments to players, minstrels, and singers, sometimes with the notation that the
singers were carollers.[10] One would like more information
about the plays, but it is not reasonable to expect it in a
mere list of bills the parliament voted to pay.

When Elyot was in residence at the Middle Temple
he also had plenty of opportunity for learning the English
common law. For purposes of education and for the government of the society, the masters were divided into three
classes: inner barristers, utter barristers, and benchers. The
inner barristers did not plead or argue any doubtful matter, either because they had not been in the house long
enough or because they did not study or profit in learning.
The utter barristers, who had been in the house five or six
years, were called upon to argue the doubtful points. The
benchers, those utter barristers who had been in the house
fourteen or fifteen years, were asked to be readers for the
whole company in the chief periods of their learning.

The two chief periods for study, called the "learning"
or the grand vacations, were times when the law courts
were not in session, and when more of the seasoned lawyers
presumably could give their assistance. One of these

periods began the first Monday in Lent, and continued for three weeks and three days; the other began the first Monday after Lammas, or the first of August, and continued for the same length of time. In either of these periods, it is said, an elder reads and explains a statute. Then the utter barristers discuss his opinion, either agreeing, disagreeing, or dividing. Finally, if it becomes necessary, the reader confutes them and confirms his own opinion. At night during these same periods, except on Saturdays, Sundays, or festival days, some young learner pleads, or declares some doubtful matter in "homely law French"; then two utter barristers discuss it, taking opposite sides; and finally three benchers express their opinions in English.

In addition to these exercises, every day of the year, except festival days, Saturdays, and Sundays, the students and learners divide into groups of three. One of them puts a question, all argue it in English, and then the one who introduced it shows them the opinion of some authority. After these exercises have ended, the learners argue some question in law French before the utter barristers, who finally give them their opinion in English.[11] Thus Thomas Elyot had a chance to learn law, even if he was pardoned Lent and Lammastide vacations because he was a clerk of the assize with his father on the Western Circuit. The chances are that his father also taught him much property law in a practical way as they traveled the circuit together.

In the early sixteenth century Thomas Elyot and his fellow students of law must have had difficulties that a modern student can scarcely imagine. One problem was the scarcity of printed books. Caxton printed almost nothing about law, and the early publications by Littleton and Fitzherbert were not complete. In 1510, the year Thomas Elyot entered the Middle Temple, Robert Pynson began the first systematic publication of the Year Books, a record of all cases decided according to the common law from the time of Edward I.[12] Without printed books, study was undoubtedly difficult, but the arguing of cases probably sharpened the perceptions of the learners.

Another difficulty Elyot must have met was the lack of any quiet place to study. Dugdale, who was mainly concerned with the time of Henry VIII, said that those who really wished to learn the law were troubled by the walking and talking of those who were not learners, by the clients and servants of clients who kept coming to seek out the attorneys and others who practiced law, so that "the students may as quietly study in the open streets as in their studies." Students had no place where they might talk over their problems except in the Temple Church, and in term time it was no more quiet than the parvis of St. Paul's.[13] Since members kept rooms at their Inns of Court after they were no longer students, using them as offices and places to live when they were in London, clients or their servants would be constantly coming and going. Even in the fifteenth century, as Fortescue has said, the smallest of the lesser inns had at least a hundred students, and the smallest of the greater inns had about two hundred students. As the population of England and the number of law students were both growing, it must have become even more difficult in Elyot's time to find a quiet place for study.

When Thomas Elyot entered the Middle Temple in 1510, he was just beginning that service to the government which he disliked at times, but as a member of the landed gentry could never escape. In 1511, when his name first appears on the lists now in print, he was acting as a clerk of the assize in the West Country. In this office he served, with his father as one of the justices, until the latter's death about 1522, and he continued to be named with other men until 1525. From 1511 for about five years he and Thomas Fitzhugh were associated with Richard Elyot and Lewis Pollard, the latter two being justices. Later, for about three years, Thomas Elyot was named with his father and John Ernley. In June, 1519, a commission had only the names of Richard Elyot and Thomas Pigott, but another the next month added Thomas Elyot. These three were named for the first part of a second year. In July, 1520, the two Elyots were again named but with John Broke. In July, 1521, the two Elyots and Richard Matthew were named, and a blank was left for another name. In February, 1522, the names were "Thomas Elyot, Ric ——, with ——," as if the news of Sir Richard's illness or death had confused the recorder. The next list for the assize on the Western Circuit, in February, 1523, included Thomas Elyot, Sir John Fitzjames, and Robert Norwich; their names were repeated through 1525. In February, 1526, the list had only the names of Fitzjames and Pollard.[14] Such were the variants and the constant, Thomas Elyot, for fifteen years.

When Thomas Elyot's connection with the assize of the West Country finally ended in 1525, Wolsey wished to keep him in London more of the time as clerk of the king's Council. All these years, as he said in later letters to Cromwell, he was acting as a clerk, not as one of the justices. His long service in this position may have resulted in part from his father's desire to keep his son with him, or from the tendency of a busy Wolsey, carrying an enormous burden of responsibilities in the 1520's, to keep a man on a commission until circumstances forced a change.

During these same years, Thomas Elyot and his father were both named also on the Commission of Gaol Delivery for the Western Circuit, their names appearing in 1511, 1512, 1513, 1516, 1519, 1520, and 1522. The name of Thomas Elyot continued to appear on the same commission at intervals through 1526. In 1515 he was named on the Commission of the Peace for Wiltshire; his father, also Sir Maurice Barrow (who became his father-in-law), and Lewis Pollard, who had been with the Elyots on the Western Circuit, were already in this group. He seems to have remained on this commission for years; he is named in 1523, 1526, and 1529, and no lists without his name are available. In July, 1522, Thomas Elyot was named on the Commission of the Peace for Oxfordshire (the group being headed by Cardinal Wolsey); the appointment probably resulted from his inheriting the manor of Long Combe and other Oxford property by his father's death early in the year.[15] About this time or a little later, a more definite connection with Wolsey appeared, when he began serving as clerk of the king's Council.

However, Thomas Elyot's commissions during these years were fewer in number than those of his father. For example, Sir Richard Elyot was also on Commissions of the Peace for Berkshire in 1514; for Cornwall, Devon, Dorset, and Hampshire about 1509 or 1510 to 1514; for the city of Oxford, in 1510 and 1512; for Oxfordshire, from 1509 to 1514; for Somersetshire, from 1509 through 1514; and for Wiltshire, in 1510, 1513, and for many years later. When he was named as Justice of the Common Pleas "during pleasure," on April 5, 1513, and was made a knight about the middle of 1517, one can only conclude that he had earned his honors.[16] There is no record of an exact date when knighthood was conferred upon him; during 1517 he began to appear on official records as Sir Richard Elyot.

When Thomas Elyot was a clerk of the assize, a member of a commission for gaol delivery or for the peace, or when he served as one of the other long arms of the central government, life must have had its difficulties for him.

On the Western Circuit the necessary horseback riding alone might be exhausting. The men in the group were responsible for approximately a sixth of England, since the country was divided into the six circuits established in the reign of Henry II. About 1515 to 1518 they were called the Home, Midland, Norfolk, Northern, Oxford, and Western Circuits. The justices of the assize made the circuit twice a year, it seems, and about a month was required for each trip. The Western Circuit included Hampshire (then called Southampton), Wiltshire, Dorset, Somerset, Devon, and Cornwall.[17]

Though we do not have a detailed account of any trip made by Thomas Elyot on the Western Circuit, there is extant an account of a trip made in 1596 by Thomas Walmesley, Judge of the Common Pleas, and Edward Fenner, Judge of the Queen's Bench, men who were holding the assizes on the same circuit. Their trip began early in July, and they concluded their work about July 24. Starting from Holborn on horseback, they stopped, whenever they could, at the homes of gentlemen along their route; and at such places they had no expenses except tips to servants. On July 5, their accounts indicate, they were at Winchester in Hampshire; July 8, at Salisbury in Wiltshire; July 10, at Blandford Forum in Dorset, and July 12, in Dorchester; July 14, at Chard in Somerset; July 19, at Exeter, in Devon; July 24, at Okington; and July 26, at Launceston, in Cornwall. The details indicate that the men went from Launceston to Bristol.[18] Then they must have taken additional time in returning to London. The amounts spent at each stage of the journey are given; but since the currency had been devalued both by Henry VIII and by the men who managed affairs for Edward VI, these sums have little comparative value.

Even the problems handled by justices of the assize seem prosaic to a nonlegal mind and may not have been thrilling to a young man who found his inspiration in the classical philosophers. The justices had "a limited civil jurisdiction" and were mainly concerned with problems of possession and ownership, including such questions as these: Has A disseised B of his freehold? (That is, has he dispossessed him wrongfully or by force?) Who is the next heir of a person dying in possession of a certain estate? Who was last seised of the right to present to a vacant living? Is a certain piece of land held by lay tenure or by spiritual tenure?[19] Such questions were often extremely difficult; but they may have given Thomas Elyot's father an opportunity to teach his son important principles of the English common law.

Long before Thomas Elyot's fifteen years on the Western Circuit were over, he must have known every man of importance in the region: his food, his wines, his income and its sources, his future aims—even his secret sins! He must have been familiar with every problem likely to come before the judges. He must have recognized as old acquaintances every tree and every flock of sheep along the routes they usually traveled. According to temperament, he might develop a slow-burning boredom or a feeling of coming back home. Perhaps Elyot escaped the boredom, since he was apparently not an adventurer.

Though such knowledge of problems and people might qualify men for effective service, for more than two hundred years Parliament had been passing laws to prevent continuous service and familiar association between justices of the assize and the people among whom they worked. From the reign of Edward III onward, statutes were passed forbidding men to serve as justices of assize or of gaol delivery in their own counties. Later than the time of the Elyots a statute provided a penalty of £100 for breaking this law.[20] But still the law and the practice continued to differ; and sometimes a special license was given men to travel the circuit in their own counties. Not only the Elyots but others had long records for conducting assizes on the Western Circuit. In twenty-two years Thomas Walmesley and Edward Fenner had traveled all the circuits except two and had held every assize in their own areas for five consecutive years. Thus they must have had familiar association with many of the people whose legal problems they handled.

Those who believed in continuity might have advanced the reasons urged for appointments on commissions of the peace: men who lived in an area or owned property there had a vital interest in maintaining law and order, they knew both the men and the problems, and they could command respect better than strangers could do. Thus if they were men of integrity, they were more valuable than srangers. At least the appointment of residents or property owners as justices of the assize continued, and these men went on serving.

The same men seem to have made extra trips when listed on Commissions of Gaol Delivery on the Western Circuit. As the commission for an area directed its members to try the prisoners in all the principal gaols, the work might require days of time compared with the frequent commissions listed for a single town or city, even though this area was sparsely populated. In this work they would be dealing with many criminal cases, but as these were not so difficult as the ones handled regularly by the justices of assize, it was not always necessary to require a member who was a royal judge.

The work that Thomas Elyot did when he served on commissions of the peace was varied and complicated. These commissions had developed along with the decay of feudalism; and quarter sessions, a part of the duties of the members, were ordered as early as 1363. Instead of being a royal bureaucracy, these men formed a system of control by local lords, gentlemen, and esquires who lived in the county part of the time and owned property there. Thus landowners, with an occasional burgess or merchant, were the working members of the group. Usually the list was headed by the lord chancellor, an archbishop, a bishop, or a prince. By 1439, any man appointed must have property with an income of twenty pounds a year; hence Thomas Elyot must have had that amount in his own right about 1515, when his name began appearing on commissions for Wiltshire.[21] Since members of the Council owned property and had local habitations, about half the twenty-nine men on the commission for Surrey in 1518 were also members of the Council—probably a higher number than usual.[22] The number of men in a group varied from time to time, without apparent reasons. Names of men for these commissions were submitted to the king by the lord chancellor, who secured suggestions from local gentry and justices of the assize, but the king confirmed all appointments. Members had competence only for areas to which they were named, they were obliged to serve unless excused for some unusual reason, their names might continue to appear until they died, and they served almost without pay. A statute in the reign of Richard II fixed the amount at four shillings a day for a judge and two shillings for a clerk (apparently the amounts allowed for justices of the assize and their clerks); and in spite of drastic devaluations of the currency, the pay remained the same, though the expense allowance seems to have increased.[23] About 1582 Lambarde said that the men were sometimes forced to spend the entire sum to cover their common diet.

Thomas Elyot or any other man on a commission of the peace found it his duty to work outside formal court sessions as a single justice, as one of two justices, or as one of several justices whenever he happened to be in the county for which he was appointed. That is, a local officer could bring an offender to him at any time or place in his county and expect him and any other justice who happened to be present to deal with the case. When acting alone, a justice had certain powers of criminal jurisdiction, such as handling security for keeping the peace, committing to gaol to stop violence, preventing forcible and illegal entry, and enforcing an almost unbelievable number of statutes about such things as hunting, unlawful games, sanctuaries, or thefts of horses. As for civil jurisdiction, one justice could settle disputes between masters and their servants or apprentices. He had numerous administrative powers about rivers and highways, local taxes, and presenting complaints about hundred or county courts. His trade powers included the assize of fuel and of corn carried by water and some control over the making of malt.[24]

When Elyot or any other member of the commission was acting as one of two justices he had certain additional powers; and when he was acting as one of three, he had some other powers.

An account by a Warwick justice of the peace tells of the activities he carried on in his own hall. The parish constable brought to his house the men and women he arrested as vagrants, poachers, thieves, or brawlers while drunk. The justice had to examine them and decide whether to fine, to punish in some other way, to bind them for appearance at quarter sessions or assizes, or to set them free. He had to deal with some problem every two or three days. Sometimes he felt it necessary to send for another justice so that he might have the right to make a decision. Then he had his notes to write up correctly, since quarrelsome men might call upon him to justify his action before the Court of King's Bench or some other legal body.[25] Such duties of one or more justices outside court sessions must at times have made life a burden.

Members of a commission of the peace were also responsible for the courts of record known as quarter sessions. They were held four times a year, on or near each of these days: Lady Day, March 25; St. Margaret's Day, July 20; Michaelmas, September 29; and St. Nicholas' Day, December 6. Usually they were held in the county town, but occasionally another large town was selected. Since two or three members of a commission could hold quarter sessions, as long as one of them was well trained in law, we have no way of knowing how many times Thomas Elyot attended as a member of the commission. But when he was a sheriff for two counties, in 1528, 1533, and 1544, he had obligations either for himself or his deputy, at eight quarter sessions a year, four in each county. Also, though the obligation to act as a justice of the peace gave the gentleman only a small sum in payment, the work as a sheriff (according to Elyot's statements in his letters to Cromwell) often cost him money from his own pocket. So the landed gentry carried the work of the government and sometimes paid the costs.

Though it is probable that no two places ever held quarter sessions in exactly the same way, the general procedure tended to be somewhat like the account which follows. A *custos rotulorum* or a principal justice is named by the king when he approves the whole membership of the commission. The *custos* notifies the sheriff of the county about the date and the place; and fifteen days before the session, the sheriff issues writs to all who should attend: the constables, bailiffs, the jurors from all over the county, the stewards of manors, the undersheriff and his clerks, a multitude of suitors, all the persons bound by recognizance to appear, attorneys, scriveners, and many others who have business with the court.

In 1536, when the jury system was being introduced into Wales and, as a result, we have more complete records, about four hundred people were summoned to the town of Caernarvon. But the number who actually came was much smaller: two or three or a half dozen justices, twenty to twenty-six bailiffs and constables out of a possible forty, and about seventy jurors. Even these would be enough to transform a quiet town into something like an agitated county fair, with tradesmen and innkeepers doing a thriving business.

The justices assemble at the principal inn and are then ushered to the shire hall or meeting place of the court by the undersheriff "attended by bailiffs bearing their white wands." At the hall, the justices take their place on the bench and court is formally opened. The justices and other officials deliver any inquisitions, recognizances (obligations drawn up before a magistrate for attendance or other actions), or examinations they may have. Two kinds of juries are sworn in—a county or grand jury, and juries of hundreds or boroughs. Bills of indictment are drawn up; each bill goes to the grand jury, to hear evidence and to mark it *Billa vera* or *Ignoramus.* A true bill goes to a petty jury of the freeholders who are present.

While the grand jury is working, probably the court is handling matters of civil administration—bridges, decayed jails, other public buildings, and highways. Next, perhaps, indicted persons are tried, some cases are postponed, and those convicted are sentenced. Cases of poor people and bastards are handled, orders are issued for the repair of highways and bridges, general petitions are considered, and victuallers or other tradesmen are licensed. The *custos* or his deputy receives the calendar of people to be punished and pronounces sentence against those convicted. The court hears grievances if there are any, the crier makes his proclamation three times, and the session ends. It may have lasted several days or less than a day. After the tumult has died and the crowds have departed, the clerk must complete many records, get the signatures of the justices, and arrange the handling of finances.[26]

The power of the justices of the peace appears in the fact that they could investigate and punish, when necessary, mayors, bailiffs, stewards, constables, jailers, and sheriffs. They could also appoint a high constable for each hundred and a petty constable for each parish, except in situations where leet jurisdiction was still alive. But the justices themselves were subject to controls. Any subject, rich or poor, might complain about any justice to other justices; if that failed, to justices of the assize; and if that failed, to

the king or the chancellor. The common law courts, and at
times the Council or Star Chamber, also had control because they could order the justices to take action or to explain action they had already taken.[27]

The plan for commissions of the peace worked well in
the early Tudor period in spite of the growing burden it
put upon the landed gentry. A major reason was that these
men were interested in upholding law and order in their
own areas. (But when their own interests and the demands
of the central government were opposed—for example, in
1521, when they were directed to restore enclosures and
rebuild houses—they did not act as government agents but
as private citizens.) Also the plan worked well because
these men knew local conditions, commanded the respect
of local people, and drew their own livings from property
involved in their decisions. It worked well also because
of a small population: "There was hardly a county and
certainly not a town, except perhaps London, where one
man could not know of his own direct knowledge all that
a government would care to ask about every inhabitant
who was of any political or administrative importance."[28]
Since few men had either the background or the leisure
for such work, these few carried the burden.

Certain larger results came from the plan for commissions of the peace. Because noblemen and gentlemen
worked together in these groups, the noblemen were concerned with peace and its products, instead of centering
their energies on war, like noblemen in many Continental
countries. Also the men who worked on these commissions
were getting a training that later made them efficient members of Parliament.[29] Thomas Elyot was among those who
served in Parliament some years later.


During the twelve years from 1510 to 1522 Thomas
Elyot certainly had a personal life, but as usual, he kept it

underground, like a hidden river. He must have continued his study of the classics. Since a worshipful physician, who must certainly have been Linacre, had read medical works to him before he was twenty years old, we may safely assume that he had a good foundation in Greek by 1510. Probably he continued his reading and his translating of Lucian and Plutarch, following the interests of More and Erasmus, using their methods, and perfecting his skill in both Latin and Greek. It would be strange if he did not read More's *Utopia* and Erasmus' *Institutio principis Christiani,* in 1516, when they appeared. We do have the solid evidence that he praised Erasmus' *Institutio* highly in the *Governour,* saying that every gentleman should read and value it for its "sentence, eloquence, and vertuous abundaunce," and that it cannot be praised as much as it deserves. Perhaps in these years a hope of writing something like the *Governour* began to take shape in his mind. If he never expressed enthusiasm for *Utopia,* the reason may be rooted in a preference for realism over ironic fantasy and his frequently expressed dislike for any suggestion about holding all things in common.

Since we have the records of association between the fathers of Thomas More and Thomas Elyot as serjeants-at-law from 1503 and the statement of Stapleton that Elyot belonged among the younger friends of More in the study of polite letters, it would be strange if Elyot did not at some time listen to the talk of Erasmus at More's house— he was too reticent and inexperienced to be a talker himself—in this period between 1510 and 1522. From 1509 to 1514 Erasmus spent most of his time in England, writing *The Praise of Folly* at More's house, working with Fisher at Cambridge, and returning at intervals to London. He also returned to England for brief periods in 1515, 1516, and 1517.[30]

These were probably the years when Elyot had a chance to observe More's household school. Because More and the other humanists believed in starting children early on their Latin, that school may have started about 1510, when Margaret was five years old. More had definite theories about making grammar easy for little minds, as he indicated in his statements for John Holt's grammar before 1500; thus he may have given some time to Margaret's education himself before he was drawn into public affairs. Elyot may owe something to More's school for his discussion of early education in the *Governour;* he writes there with sureness and a glow of enthusiasm. The period about 1515 to 1522, when William Gonell, John Clement, and Richard Herde were students and teachers in More's school also seems a reasonable time for Elyot to follow their work informally. Since Stapleton tells us that Elyot's wife studied literature in More's school, she may have done so shortly after her marriage, about 1521 or 1522.

Thomas Elyot's marriage to Margaret Barrow, daughter of Sir Maurice Barrow, of Ivychurch near Salisbury, belongs in this period, about 1521. When Sir Richard Elyot wrote the first part of his will, in October, 1521, he gave his son's wife a broad gilt cup with a cover and a low foot, and also his best gold ring. But he did not name her, though his will was full of other personal names. Though the omission of her name might create a doubt whether the marriage had taken place by October 21, we have other evidence in the will of Sir Maurice Barrow, dated February 9, 1521. He willed to his daughter, Margaret Elyot, a gilt cup with a cover. Thomas Elyot was thirty-one or thirty-two years old by this time; and since girls usually married at sixteen in the period, there is some reason to suppose that he was considerably older than his wife.

In the period from 1510 to 1522, there is further evidence of governmental and business connections between the Mores and the Elyots. From 1510 to 1518 the Hampshire commissions of the peace contain the name of a Richard Elyot who becomes Sir Richard about 1517, and the name of a Thomas More who is probably the future chancellor.[31] Also a property transaction which has not been noted before seems to indicate an early business relationship between Thomas More and Thomas Elyot in connection with Hertfordshire property. The item, in the feet of fines for 1516–17, names, along with others, Thomas More, esquire; Thomas Daubridgecourt, esquire; Thomas Elyot, esquire; George Puttenham, knight, and Alice his wife. The property rights involve the manors of Long Marston, Gubbilcote, and Tring.[32] Probably the Thomas Daubridgecourt named here was a half brother of Thomas Elyot, since there is evidence that Sir Thomas and his wife Alice had a son Thomas, who married a Dorothy Puttenham.[33]

With the death of Sir Richard Elyot, who rode the Western Circuit and carried his other governmental responsibilities up to the very end of his life, this chapter in the life of his son comes to an end. Sir Richard dated the first part of his will October 9, 1521, and the second part October 12 of the same year. His will was proved May 26, 1522. His only son and heir, Thomas, was his executor.

By 1522, Thomas Elyot was about thirty-two or thirty-three years old. Most of his services to the government had been carried on in association with his father. At this time he had not gained any appointment at court, and he had not published anything to indicate that he wished to earn a place in the world of literature. Even *Hermathena* and the preface to Edward Powell's *Propugnaculum*, by Papyrius Geminus Eleates, if they were really the work of Clerk Thomas Elyot, were published in 1522 and 1523, after the death of Sir Richard Elyot. Perhaps he had been too dutiful a son, following his father's wishes instead of his own desires. Whatever the reason, his real future was still before him.

# CHAPTER VI

## General Problems.
### Clerk of the Council. ca. *1522–1530*

ROM the death of his father in 1522 to his becoming a knight in 1530, Thomas Elyot led a busy but a comparatively unrewarding life. He had much legal business to settle, because he was the sole executor for his father's will as well as one executor for a clerk of his father, Henry Pauncefoot; he also had a difficult and expensive legal battle to gain possession of property that had been willed him by Sir William Findern. Besides serving on various commissions for the government, he acted for six and a half years as clerk of the king's Council, without pay and without receiving the position of greater honor that Wolsey promised him.

In settling his father's will, which was probated in 1522, he had to look after the torches, black gowns, and doles for the funeral; to pay priests and clerks connected with the burial, the month's mind, and year's mind; to give money to friars in many places and to send gifts and small sums to religious houses for women. He was responsible for much movable property to be delivered to relatives, friends, clerks, and servants. He had to see that John Fettiplace the elder received his property at East Shefford and had his chance to buy certain sheep and cattle, and that the Fettiplace children had the seventeen score of ewes

provided in the indenture made by his father and his step-
mother. If his sister, Eleanor Elyot, the nun at Shaftesbury,
was still living, he had to look after her personal gifts and
arrange her annuity; and if his stepsister, Eleanor Fettiplace, had not yet entered the religious life, he arranged for
her admission into Syon House.[1]

Elyot's work as executor for Henry Pauncefoot, with
two other men, and with Henry's wife Alice as overseer,
was a comparatively small task. Probably this was the
Pauncefoot who was admitted to clerks commons at the
Middle Temple, at the instance of Master Elyot, serjeant-
at-law, about the time Thomas Elyot entered there. In his
will Pauncefoot identified himself as being of Fulleston
St. Peter's in Wiltshire, thus furnishing other evidence
about connections of the Elyots with that county.[2] When
Richard Elyot willed each of his clerks a gilt spoon and a
black gown, he named Pauncefoot among them; but since
Pauncefoot's will was proved in January, 1522, and Elyot's
in May of the same year, he was one clerk who never enjoyed his bequest.

Thomas Elyot's most difficult legal business in the
1520's resulted from the wills made by his father and by
Sir William Findern. Sir Richard had provided that his
manor of Long Combe and other Oxford property, if the
Elyots died without heirs, should go to young Thomas
Findern, whom he described as his cousin and the lord of
the manor of Carlton, Cambridge. And Findern, whose
will was proved in 1517, had provided that if his heir, who
was his grandson Thomas, died without heirs, the manor of
Carlton, land at West Colville, and other property, should
go to Thomas Elyot. (It has been suggested that Findern
meant the manor of Little Carlton, called Loppams, since
Elyot later purchased the manor of Carlton cum Willingham from Thomas Cromwell.) Young Thomas Findern
died in 1523, but Thomas Elyot did not possess the specified properties without opposition. Another Thomas

Findern from another branch of the family brought suit to recover the Cambridge property. His son George had married a daughter of Sir John Port. Port was a prominent member of the Inner Temple, where he had held many offices and had been a reader in 1507; he had also been the king's solicitor at his coronation, and was named a serjeant-at-law in 1521. Hence he was a formidable opponent.[3]

Writing to Thomas Cromwell, December 8, 1532, Elyot summed up the circumstances of this legal conflict:

> although my lord Cardinal, whom God pardon, knowing my title to be perfect and sure, as having it enrolled before him, and at the first beginning hearing himself the mutual covenants between my father and my cousin, Sir William Findern (whose father was my mother's uncle) by his good justice gave me good comfort, yet then having against me many great personages by the means of Mr. Port, the justice, whose daughter mine adversary's son had married, I was constrained to retain so many learned men and so to apply my business that the said suit, continuing one year and a half, stood me above one hundred pounds.[4]

A historian who has examined the Chancery records reports that certain deeds were detained, probably through the influence of Port, and that Elyot had to petition twice to get a hearing.[5] Elyot finally was awarded the property; but as he said later in the same letter to Cromwell, Doctor Naturess claimed the profits of the estate for the period when he was executing the will, and for this service he had to pay him £348.

Elyot had said nothing in his letter about the executors named in Findern's will but there were four of them altogether: Sir Richard Elyot; Sir John Cutt; Robert Clayton, a parson of Honey Lane in London and a sometime fellow of Lincoln College; and Edmund Naturess, a fellow of Clare Hall, Cambridge. Elyot and Cutt were to have ten pounds each for their work, and the others three pounds each. Perhaps Elyot and Cutt had been expected to carry the burden of the work, while the other two looked after the bequests to colleges and the church. But Elyot had died in 1522, and the will of a Sir John Cutt, of Cambridge, Essex, and other places (probably the one Findern had named), was probated in 1521.[6] Richard Elyot was a shrewd man, trained in the English common law, of course; judging from his background, Cutt was probably trained in the same law, but if at the Middle Temple, before the extant records began in 1500. If Naturess and Clayton had law training, it would probably have been in civil or canon law. Thus the death of two executors created an unfortunate situation; it was only by paying the large and unexpected sums of £100 for court costs and £348 in executor's fees that Thomas Elyot gained possession of the Findern properties in Cambridge.

During this period of his life, Thomas Elyot served for six and a half years—the estimate is his own—as the clerk of the king's Council. As he may have been dating the end of his service with the fall of Wolsey in 1529 or with the issue of a patent to the Edens in 1530, we can only estimate that he began the work about 1522 or 1523. Since this part of his career is both strange and revealing, it seems necessary to inquire how definitely the Council was organized at this time, who the members were, what sort of work Elyot did, why he served, and especially why he continued to serve without pay.

Elyot served a Council that was organized, even if somewhat loosely; as yet there was no formal privy council. Since the Ellesmere extracts or the minutes from the 'Acta Consilii' have now been carefully studied, we can be sure that a Whole Council planned to meet during each of the four law terms, on about fifty of the hundred days in those terms; but the members did not hold rigidly to the rules they made. Between 1509 and 1527 "a minimum of 116 men actually attended one or more of forty-nine meetings. . . ." On one of these days as many as fifty-five were present, and on another day only two. It is difficult to distinguish the work of the whole from the work of the parts because the parts were drawn from the whole, and at times the parts did the same things that the entire group might do. But the attendance lists show the membership of the Whole Council; they indicate that formal meetings were held with some regularity, that various functions of government were performed at them, that there were some definite methods of procedure, and that the clerk who recorded the attendance at each meeting was keeping records for a definite institution.[7] Probably the group remained slightly amorphous because the king, in the 1520's, disliked systematic work and because Wolsey worked like a powerful, well-oiled machine but made many high-handed decisions.

Elyot's work for the Council gave him a chance to observe and hear all the great men of the kingdom—and some who were not so great. Probably the men named as the Council in the so-called Eltham reforms were bona fide members, whether or not those reforms were ever put into effect.[8] The Whole Council included all principal officers of state, some lesser officials, courtiers who helped with formal ceremonies or had parts in jousts or tourneys, some churchmen attached to Wolsey; men who had special administrative, religious, or diplomatic work; and men who were considered experts in civil, canon, or English common law. Five men were consistent attendants at all meetings: the chancellor, Wolsey; the treasurer, Norfolk; the lord privy seal, Cuthbert Tunstal; Robert Brudenel, Chief Justice of the Common Pleas; and Sir John Fineux, Chief Justice of the King's Bench to 1526, when he was followed by Sir John Fitzjames. Probably there were many times also when the king, like any modern executive, called in a few men for informal or emergency discussion. For example, in 1521, he called four lawyers from his Council to discuss the problem of a new deputy for Ireland: Sir Thomas Neville, Sir Thomas More, his father Sir John More, and Baron Broke.[9]

Elyot's position as clerk was as indefinite and loose as the organization of the Council itself. We have evidence that he once signed as clerk of the Council meeting in the Star Chamber, for an Act of Parliament begins by citing a decree of the Star Chamber signed by Thomas Elyot as clerk and then bases a new statute on the decree.[10] Perhaps he acted also as clerk of the Court of Requests. In his letter to Cromwell he says that about this time matters were taken from the Star Chamber and assigned to the Council in Wales and the Council in the North; that those remaining were mainly the complaints of beggars; and that he set low fees, in spite of his clerks, to avoid picking a living from the misery of others. These details perhaps suggest the Court of Requests, which was instituted about 1493, and dealt with the suits of poor men and of the king's personal or household servants. Like the Star Chamber, it used the privy seal and its process; but it exerted an equitable jurisdiction similar to that of the Court of Chancery.[11] Perhaps Elyot kept the records for both courts but did not separate them clearly in his letter. It is unlikely that Elyot was present when the king summoned a small group of men for informal discussion.

Elyot's position as clerk for the Council does not become much clearer when we consider his additional statements about his work. He served the king not only in the Star Chamber, as he said in his letter to Cromwell, but in some things pertaining to the clerk of the crown, some to the secretaries, and other labors which he would not stop to rehearse. He did not even receive from the king the thanks he deserved, he added, if his grace had been fully informed about his work and had seen the drafts which he

made for Wolsey.[12] Perhaps it would not be far wrong to
assume that Elyot acted as a clerk for any part of the Council when Wolsey wished a record of what was done—and
Wolsey wished to know nearly everything—and that he did
other work for the king or for Wolsey when either needed
his help. If these conjectures are correct, his work was
even more amorphous in this period than the work of the
Council.

Why did Elyot continue to serve the Council for six
and a half years without receiving the salary due him?
Wolsey had advanced him to the position, we learn from
his letter to Cromwell; and this was done, he says, without
his own desire or request. Then, through the solicitation
of other men still living, Wolsey persuaded him to give up
his position as clerk of the Western Assize, so that he could
attend meetings of the Council at any time. Wolsey also
promised to use his influence with the king to promote him
soon to an office with more profit and honor. Elyot felt that
he must follow Wolsey's suggestions to keep him as his
good lord. At the end of a year Elyot sued to have the
patent confirming his office. The patent was issued, he
heard, but he could never get it because Doctor Cleyburgh
and others kept it from him. Then he sued for the fee of
forty marks a year, as he had heard, but he never received
it. So for six and a half years of work he had nothing—
nothing but the colic, the stone, and almost continual
rheums. After Wolsey's fall, a former patent was found,
and Elyot's was called in and cancelled. He received no
reward except the order of knighthood, a position both
"honorable and onerouse," and he had even less to live on
than he formerly possessed.

Elyot's account is either supported or supplemented
by the official records of the clerkship. In 1509 a French
secretary, John Meutys, was appointed. About 1512
Richard Eden was appointed in place of Meutys, for life
and during pleasure, at a salary of forty marks a year. While

Elyot was doing the work, the accounts show that Eden was paid more than twenty-six pounds; and a Mr. Lee was paid twice in 1527, the first time an unstated amount, the second time forty shillings. A document vaguely dated about 1528 granted Thomas Elyot the right to be clerk of the Council, with forty marks a year and the usual summer and winter livery "on a conditional surrender of the patent . . . granting the office to the said Richard Eden." The final end to any hopes by Elyot came in June, 1530, when a grant was issued to Richard Eden, clerk, and to Thomas Eden in survivorship, of the office, on the conditional surrender of the earlier grant to Richard Eden alone.[13] Elyot was made a knight, an act that cost the king nothing but seems to have given Elyot the feeling that he should maintain a better household without additional income.

The facts certainly seem to mean that Richard Eden, an archdeacon of Middlesex and a chaplain of the king, was willing to hold an office and to accept salary for it while another man did the work. According to A. F. Pollard, they mean that Wolsey had pushed both Richard Lee and Thomas Elyot into office by high-handed acts and by promises that were ignored after his fall.[14] The urging and the promises together seem to indicate that Thomas Elyot was a faithful and a competent clerk, that Wolsey could rely on him, and that nothing else mattered to Wolsey as long as he was handling the king's affairs efficiently.

Elyot's service to the Council also suggests other qualities, in addition to his faithful competence and his refusal to set high fees that would make him seem to pick a living out of the misery of others. When he discussed the clerkship in his letter he reminded Cromwell that he always refused the extra payments from suitors so that he might live "out of all suspicion" while he was serving his king. These payments were ones that many officials accepted and took for granted in the time, when payments from the government were parsimonious. His integrity in refusing fees is like

that of Sir Thomas More as Roper explains him. More
was accused of taking a "faire gilted cup," as a bribe from
a suitor. He admitted taking the cup in his hand, but immediately he called his butler to fill it with wine; then he
drank to the health of the woman who offered the cup and
returned it to her as a New Year's gift for her husband.[15]
Elyot's sympathy for the poor who appealed to the king
through his Council is like that of More as he expresses it
in the first part of *Utopia;* and it may be worth noting that
More's first position on the Council, according to Roper's
apologetic account, was as master of the Courts of Requests, dealing with poor men's causes.

The characteristics of Thomas Elyot that led him to
work six and a half years without pay or other reward except a title seem less certain. Perhaps he expected the reward for efficient service to come automatically. Perhaps
he did not have the force and the self-confidence to demand,
either directly or indirectly, what he deserved—though that
might have been hard to do with Wolsey. Or perhaps an
idealistic honesty kept him from making political bargains.

During the six and a half years of Elyot's clerkship,
while More was a prominent member of the Council, the
two men acted together in asking an office for a certain
William Marshall. The information comes from Wolsey's
letter to Henry and Robert Dakers, in 1527, suggesting
that Robert, now a clerk of the assize, should be willing to
give up his post as secretary of the compter. Both More
and Elyot, Wolsey wrote, had made intercession to have
the latter position for William Marshall.[16] Thus the evidence of some connection between the Mores and Elyots
continues, from the time that Richard Elyot and John
More became serjeants-at-law together in 1503.

While Thomas Elyot was acting as clerk of the Council he was named another time in a document connected
with the Court of Requests. The date was 1527; in this
year the king ordered Sir Edward Thame, Sir Walter

Stoner, knights, and Thomas Denton and Thomas Elyot, esquires, or three of them, to examine disputes between two men and their tenants at Sarsden and Lyneham in Oxford.[17] In this situation Elyot was perhaps acting only as an Oxford gentleman familiar with conditions in the county.

About 1528 Thomas Elyot bought from the king the wardship of Erasmus Pym, son and heir of Reginald Pym of Somerset, for the sum of eighty pounds. With the purchase Elyot acquired custody of the manor of Brymmore, at Cannington near Bridgewater, and of a third part of the manors of Exton and Hawkridge near Dulverton.[18] The boy became the king's ward because some of his lands were held by knight's service under the feudal theory that the king was the original owner of all land, that he granted its use to lords for their military service, and that they exacted service or rent in turn from their tenants. When a man who held land by feudal tenure died, the lord who lost his service while his heir was a minor might take the profits of his land, train the minor heir, and arrange a marriage in his own interests; or if the heir were a girl, he could choose for her a husband not hostile to himself. He could not compel an heir to marry the person he selected, but he could exact a heavy fine for a refusal. Instead of handling all these wardships himself, the king sold them to others. To get revenue, both Henry VII and Henry VIII sought out and enforced these old feudal obligations.[19]

Men had various motives for buying wardships: to make a reasonable business investment; to squeeze out every possible penny for themselves; to arrange a marriage enhancing their own families; or to protect a ward who was a relative by acting as a trustee for him. As early as the twelfth century, Glanvill had stated theories of the trusteeship, adding that if the property involved came from the mother, the guardian should be the nearest relative on the father's side; if it came from the father, he should be the nearest relative on the mother's side. Thus the guardian could not further his own claims to the estate.[20]

Thomas Elyot's motives may also have been various— we do not know. Probably he expected to make a reasonable profit. He could hardly have been planning a marriage to enhance his own family since he was childless after some seven years of marriage. He may have been protecting a relative; for the mother of Erasmus Pym was Mary Daubridgecourt, who seems to have been a daughter of Elyot's mother by her first marriage.[21] Perhaps the childless Elyots hoped for some personal happiness from having the boy with them. Though men of this period do not generally seem sensitive to the paternal role, Elyot had More's example as an affectionate father, and he was responsive to the friendship of other men.

It is possible also that Elyot had known Erasmus Pym from his infancy and had developed some fondness for him. When Thomas Elyot rode the Western Circuit from about 1510 to 1525, with Somerset as a part of that circuit, the Pym manors were near important towns, and men on such commissions stopped whenever they could at gentlemen's houses. It would be natural for them to go a few miles out of their way if necessary for the hospitality of kinsmen. It is even possible that Elyot, who admired the writings of the great Erasmus, gave the boy his Christian name. He is more likely to have done so than any known resident of Somerset. However these are speculations, not facts.

How Elyot educated the boy is uncertain. Probably he was past the age, when he became a ward, to be a good subject for educational theories about the early years. We know that he took over the control of his own property in 1539, when he must have been at least twenty-one, and he may have been older. Sometimes the process itself of receiving the livery of his lands, as it was called, took several years; for if the applicant made even one small error in citing the details of his possessions, he had to start over again.[22] If Pym was only twenty-one in 1539, he would have been eleven years old when Elyot became his guardian, and he may have been several years older. But it is still possible that Elyot read with the boy himself in a kind of informal tutoring and that a part of the zest infusing the conventional ideas in the *Governour* came from his supervision of Erasmus Pym. No facts seem to be available about the boy's later education. His name does not appear in the records of any Inn of Court, though his son and heir entered the Middle Temple in due time, and he is not named as a graduate of either university.[23] We know only that Erasmus Pym seems to have led a blameless and undistinguished life, was still holding his Somerset manors when he died about 1582,[24] and through his son Alexander, became the grandfather of John Pym, the great Parliamentary statesman.[25]

If one motive of Elyot in buying the wardship was to make a reasonable profit, he apparently succeeded in this aim. According to a historian who has examined the Chancery records he received profits of more than forty pounds a year.[26] Since he held control of the Pym properties from 1528 to 1539, his total profit, when one subtracts the £80 he paid the king, exceeded £360.

Thomas Elyot also served on a number of commissions for the government from 1522 to 1530. Though his name did not appear on the lists for the assize of the Western Circuit after 1525, it did appear on commissions for Wiltshire and Oxford, places where he held properties inherited from his father, and commissions for Cambridge, where he held properties inherited from Sir William Findern. In July, 1522, his name began to appear on the Commission of the Peace for Oxfordshire; about the same

time Long Combe in the same county became his chief
country home and continued so during the 1520's. In
August, 1523, he was a member of a commission to collect
the subsidy in Wiltshire; and in November he and another
man turned in their list of forty-nine persons in a hamlet
of the Hundred of Kingsbridge. In April, 1526, he and
John Ernley and several others were listed among those
from Wiltshire who had paid for the second loan to aid the
war with France the sum of £2,566. In January, 1525, and
again in 1526, Elyot was named under Cardinal Wolsey on
the Commission of the Peace for Oxfordshire, and in February, 1526, for both Oxfordshire and Wiltshire. In November, 1527, the king chose him from three nominees as
sheriff of Oxfordshire and Berkshire.[27] His term of office
was for one year, 1528.

While Elyot was sheriff in 1528, there were complaints
about his being overzealous, the same complaints that accompanied many efforts to enforce the law in this period.
In June, 1528, John Knolles, writing from Calais to a
certain Chamberlain, said he understood that Elyot had
made a riot out of the business when Chamberlain and
Elyot met at Woodstock; and he had also heard that Elyot
was ruining the poor men of Woodstock by forcing them
to come to London at their own cost. When the servants
of Chamberlain were taken into custody by order of
Wolsey, this letter was found.[28] Probably more serious
matters than the criticism of Elyot were involved, but the
letter does not make them clear.

Elyot was also involved in the affair of the abbot of
Bruerne, a Cistercian house in Oxford, about this time,
but it does not seem certain whether he was acting on
knowledge that he gained as sheriff or on his interest as a
resident of Oxford. In March, 1529, the abbot, John
Chaffcombe, wrote to Cromwell stating that Elyot's late
letter to Sheriff Harcourt (his successor in that office) had
been wrong, that his enemies had boasted about evicting

him if the action cost them a hundred pounds, and that he would pay Cromwell a sum of money to let him continue. When Chaffcombe had become abbot about 1527, we learn from other sources, he had given Wolsey 250 marks in money and had promised him 280 of the finest oaks on the grounds of the monastery for the building of his new college. Though it seems a large bribe, such offers and payments were commonplace while Wolsey was in power. Chaffcombe was busy repaying the money to himself from the revenues of the abbey. No action seems to have been taken at this time, but later the number of his women friends became an open scandal. About 1532 the neighboring gentry persuaded the Duke of Suffolk through the king to compel a visitation by the heads of the order. Men appointed by the king and some Cistercian reformers eventually held a formal court session in the chapter house at Bruerne. Though the abbot tried to evade the court because proceedings had been instigated by the crown, his prior and many of his monks testified against him: he had wasted the timber, sold jewels and chalices, diminished the sheep and other livestock, and misused £1,200 of money belonging to the abbey. At another session of the court the abbot failed to appear, and he was ousted a few months later by the Cistercians themselves.[29]

Thomas Elyot's part in this affair is interesting because he had reported it long before the neighboring gentry took concerted action, and he made his report to the king's representative, Sheriff Harcourt. One who has followed Elyot's record of loyalty to his church and his king through his life might conclude that he was interested in saving his church by helping to remove corruption wherever it appeared, not by protecting an abbot who was a disgrace to his order. Also he applied his standards of integrity to both state and church.

Elyot was named again in January, 1529, on the Commission of the Peace for Wiltshire. In June, 1530, he was

named on a Commission of Gaol Delivery for Cambridge
Castle, along with Giles Alington (the husband of Sir
Thomas More's stepdaughter), and six or seven others.
About the middle of 1530 he was named on a small commission (also with Giles Alington again) to find out what
property Wolsey had owned in Cambridgeshire. Since the
attainder reached back to 1523, Wolsey had vast possessions, and the commissioners must ask men to certify their
knowledge under oath, the inquisition must have taken
both time and patience. In December, 1530, he was named
in the group headed by Sir Thomas More on the Commission of the Peace for Cambridgeshire. In February and
again in May, 1531, he was named on similar commissions
for Oxfordshire.[30] These commissions, especially the inquiry into the possessions of Wolsey, would not have left a
conscientious man like Elyot with much spare time on his
hands, even when he ceased to work as clerk of the Council in 1529 or 1530. It seems a fallacy, then, to assume that
he suddenly wrote the *Governour* because he was free from
duties to his government for the first time in years. Probably he had been planning, collecting material, and doing
some writing on that monumental work for years, even
from 1516, when Erasmus published his *Institutio principis
Christiani.*

Though Elyot received the honor of knighthood about
the middle of 1530, when his tentative patent as clerk of
the Council was recalled and a new patent was issued to
the Edens, there is no precise record of time and place—as
usual with men who received the honor for civilian service.
About this time Elyot began to be listed in official documents as a knight or as Sir Thomas. When he described
the title as both honorable and "onerouse," or burdensome,
in his letter to Cromwell, he apparently felt that a knight
was expected to maintain a grander household than a man
with no title and that six and a half years of work without
the usual salary had not prepared him for a new scale of

living. But to refuse the title, even if he had been inclined, would mean a loss of favor for the future and the payment of a heavy fine. Fines had been established not long after December 7, 1500, when the king issued letters patent to sheriffs to proclaim that each man with a clear income of £40 should assume knighthood. Apparently the response was insufficient. In December, 1503, the proclamation was ordered again, but a penalty for refusal was fixed at £200.[31] So far as the records indicate, such a penalty was still in force under Henry VIII. With the property Elyot was beginning to accumulate before 1522 and with his inheritance from his father and from the Findern holdings, he could not claim exemption because he lacked income. Though some men tried to beg off because of family, he had no sons to educate and no daughters to provide with dowries. But Wolsey had promised him a salary of forty marks a year and promotion to a position with more money and greater honor. These promises were not carried out. He was about forty years of age. He had published nothing, at least under his own name—nothing important. He had no position at court. His real achievements were still in the future.

In his six and a half years as clerk of the king's Council Elyot had been given an incomparable chance to watch the leading men of England—churchmen and laymen, the great and the near-great—as they made decisions that might shake the world. But his own motivation was completely different from that of typical Tudor courtiers, and one doubts if he ever fathomed fully the complex tapestry of desires and the means to accomplish the desires as they appeared before him. Probably he never understood the plot-weavers of the court, such as Thomas Boleyn, his daughter Anne, or the Duke of Norfolk, "the ponderous, cold-hearted, chicken-brained Duke, moving sluggishly in the mists of the feudal past like some obsolete armored saurian. . . ."[32]

He may have come nearer to understanding Wolsey as the years moved on and the promises to him were empty air. When Elyot reported to Sheriff Harcourt in 1528 or early 1529 on the abbot of Bruerne, he must have known that the great oaks surrounding the abbey were falling in a disgraceful payment to Wolsey. And the love of power with the pomp was obvious: Wolsey marched in state with silver pillars and pole-axes carried before him; he flaunted his regal residences and his household of a thousand men, including four hundred personal servants and many servants of his servants,[33] until his fall pulled others down with him. Elyot's comment on him later was the simple phrase in his letter to Cromwell, "my lorde Cardinall, whome God pardone. . . ."

Perhaps he understood More—or at least three-fourths of that brilliant complexity. In their sense of justice, compassion for the poor, devotion to the church, and a desire to serve their king, and country but to live above all suspicion in the service, Elyot and More had much in common. But so far as one can judge, Elyot never understood the quicksilver part of More: his pleasure in the translation of amoral Greek epigrams, his delight in Lucian, or the free play of mind that led him to write *Utopia*.

Perhaps he never understood Henry VIII as More understood him but still worked with him, trying, where he was allowed, to make things good, or at least to make them less bad. Once, before the troubled times began, the king made a surprise visit to Chelsea and was both familiar with More and gracious to him. As soon as the king had gone, Roper congratulated his father-in-law because he stood high in the king's favor. More agreed that Henry did "as singulerly favour" him as he favoured any subject. But he added, "if my head could winne him a castle in Fraunce . . . it should not faile to goe."[34] More had realized early and fully the cold egotism and ruthless will under the affability. If Elyot had understood, could he have continued to address his king in terms of admiration and affection that he used during the 1530's—even when allowance is made for courtly compliment? Could he have come from his audience with him in 1532, on his return from the embassy to the emperor, thinking that his remonstrances had been effective?

# CHAPTER VII

## Authorship. Doubtful Works.
## *The* Governour, *1531*

HEN Sir Thomas Elyot published the *Governour,* in 1531, he became known for the first time as an author. As he was past forty years of age, it is somewhat strange that no work under his name had appeared earlier; but he was a reticent man, not overconfident, and early struggles with the English common law had perhaps lowered his self-esteem. Possibly Sir Richard Elyot was not friendly to his only son's literary ambitions if he knew of them, and the son's plans to publish serious work may have begun only after his father's death.

So an earlier suggestion, developed by Constance W. Bouck in 1958, that a certain Papyrius Geminus Eleates, who published *Hermathena* in 1522, was Clerk Thomas Elyot, is interesting.[1] *Hermathena* came from the press of Siberch, the first printer at Cambridge; his establishment at that place had been furthered by Richard Croke, Henry Bullock, and others who valued the classical languages. The ten books Siberch printed at Cambridge include Bullock's Latin oration welcoming Wolsey to the university in 1520; his version of Lucian's *Dipsades,* dedicated to Bishop West, a diplomat at the king's court; and Pace's Latin version of Bishop Fisher's sermon against Luther.[2] Three of them, the two by Bullock and the *Hermathena,*

as E. P. Goldschmidt has pointed out, were published by men who wished to display their skill in Latin and Greek and thus to gain academic, court, or diplomatic positions.[3] The Latin version of Fisher's sermon by Pace, also, may have been a sort of vanity publication by a busy man who wished recognition as a classicist.

The suggestion that Elyot wrote *Hermathena* has been excellently supported by Miss Bouck, but for completeness it will be summarized here. Elyot's definitions in his *Dictionary*, 1538, contribute to his identity. Perhaps with tongue in cheek, he defines *Papyrius* as the name of a noble Roman, although the literal meaning *paper* suggests clerk; *Geminus* as the number two, a twin, one of many at a birth, or the name of a man which in Hebrew is *Thomas;* and *Eleates* as a man of Elea, a city in Lucania, a country belonging to Naples. Eleates also suggests *Elyot,* though he is careful not to say so. At any time between 1510 and 1529 or 1530, Elyot had a right to call himself a clerk. Eleates also twice dedicated his *Hermathena* to Richard Pace. The dedication at the beginning is dated from London, February, 1522; the one at the close, from Comi, September, 1522. If *Comi* means Long Combe, Oxford—not Como, Italy, or Combe Bissett, Wiltshire, other suggestions that have been made—this change in place fits perfectly with the fact that Elyot's father died early in 1522, that the son inherited Long Combe in Oxford from his father, and that he made it his chief residence to the end of the 1520's.[4]

Elyot's connections with Pace, which seemed doubtful to others who have discussed the *Hermathena,* are also clear. While Pace was the king's secretary, about 1516 to the end of 1521, Elyot knew him well enough to take him the leaf from the book of vellum which the workmen had found at Ivychurch, and to receive his report on it after he had given it a careful examination.[5] Some years later, when a proclamation had been issued calling in forbidden books,

Elyot reported to Cromwell that he did have a copy of Fisher's sermon in the Latin translation by Pace; he had bought it, he explained, not for the subject matter or the author, but because of the translator.[6] About this time Pace had great influence with the king—so great that Wolsey wished to separate the two, fearing that his own influence might be diminished. Hence he sent Pace to the Continent on a diplomatic mission in December, 1521, and managed to have him there on other important missions for several years. To Elyot, doubtless ignorant of Wolsey's motives, Pace would probably seem an excellent choice for a dedication that might influence his own future.

Two copies of *Hermathena,* printed on vellum and hence meant for gift copies, are now in the British Museum, though one of them was formerly in the library of the Duke of Devonshire. Neither offers any other evidence about the person for whom it was intended; it is possible that one was meant for Pace and the other for Cardinal Wolsey.[7]

Other details also point toward Elyot as the author of *Hermathena.* The address to the reader on the title page has a note of apology because the writer cannot claim any of the Muses as progenitors. The comment is like Elyot's apology in the preface of his *Dictionary,* asking his readers not to consider him a barbarous knight merely because he had no formal education after his twelfth year in his father's house. Another detail in the dedication at the end of *Hermathena* offers additional evidence. Eleates says his work is a preliminary experiment for a history of England which he has begun.[8] Goldschmidt mentions this fact but connects it with John Twyne, when perhaps it should be connected with him and with Elyot. Elyot once told Ascham, who had been in company with him and had asked him about the beginning of archery in England, that he had in hand a work he called *De rebus memorabilibus Angliae* and that he had traced the use of bows and arrows in England back to the first Saxons.[9] But Elyot never published such a work. The work said to be most like it, a history *De rebus Albionicis Britannicis atque Anglicis,* is one that Thomas Twyne published in 1590 as the work of his father, John Twyne. Speculation on whether a manuscript by Elyot came into John Twyne's hands and whether Thomas published it, believing it to be his father's work, soon reaches a dead end for lack of facts. And since either John Twyne (about 1501–1581) or Elyot might have personal memories about Bishop Fox when he was old and blind, or about Vives, the subject matter does not prove authorship.[10] But the ambition to write a history of England, expressed by the author of *Hermathena,* does offer support for the idea that Elyot may have been the author.

Since Bullock and P. G. Eleates hoped to get preferment by their publications with Siberch, it is interesting to know that Bullock soon was made one of the chaplains of Cardinal Wolsey, and a little later he became a vice-chancellor of the university.[11] Thomas Elyot, whether he was or was not Eleates, was chosen by Wolsey in 1522 or 1523 to be clerk of the king's Council.

The subject matter of *Hermathena* also fits with the assumption that the author may have been Thomas Elyot. Like works of Lucian, it deals with a fantasy of gods and personified abstractions, but like Elyot and unlike Lucian, it has no humorous slanting. Wisdom and her daughter Eloquence have been expelled from Rome by Sloth and a group of followers, including some women, some nobility, false philosophers, and quibbling lawyers. After visits to Rome, Athens, the Elysian fields, and after various struggles with the followers of Sloth, Eloquence brings her mother, Wisdom, to England, where both are honored by the people and welcomed by Henry VIII.[12] It seems the sort of work that a youthful Elyot might have written and that Pace or Wolsey would have approved when it came from a young man seeking a position.

Another related question is whether Thomas Elyot was the Papyrius Geminus Eliates who wrote the preface for Edward Powell's *Propugnaculum,* in 1523. The change of one letter in the spelling of the name is certainly immaterial in an age when a man might spell his own name in a half dozen ways. *Propugnaculum* was an attack on Luther which Powell, when he was a favorite preacher at court, had prepared at the king's request.[13] It was certainly reasonable for Elyot to express approval of Powell's ideas at this time and perhaps to cherish them at any time. Possible connections existed also between Elyot and Powell—a fact that seems not to have been noted before. When Thomas Elyot's father made his will and left sums of money to Salisbury Cathedral and to three parish churches in the city, one of the churches he named was St. Edmund's. Edward Powell was connected with both the cathedral and St. Edmund's. He was given a prebend at the cathedral about 1508, and about 1509 he received the living of St. Edmund's in Salisbury. He held the living until 1534, when he disagreed with the king about his separation from Catherine of Aragon.[14] Thus there is a strong chance that Thomas Elyot and Edward Powell, by 1523, had known each other for some years.

Two other facts may contribute to the question of authorship. First, both these works were published shortly after the death of Sir Richard Elyot. He died about February, 1522, we suppose; his will was probated May 26, 1522. *Hermathena* has two dedications to Pace; the one preceding the work is dated February, 1522, the one following it, September 22, of the same year; the preface to *Propugnaculum* is dated 1523. As the evidence about Sir Richard leads to at least a doubt about his favoring a literary career for his son, it is possible that the son planned to begin publication under a pseudonym. Second, though Elyot never acknowledged these works, possibly he considered the *Hermathena* immature and was glad to ignore it, or possibly he did not mention it as his because admitting the authorship of it would involve him in the other. In the 1530's a connection with the ideas of *Propugnaculum* and with Edward Powell was dangerous.

Thomas Elyot began his public career as a literary man in 1531 with *The Book Named the Governour,* whether he was or was not Papyrius Geminus Eleates. As eight editions appeared before 1600—three in his lifetime, in 1531, 1537, and 1544; one during the year of his death, 1546; and others in 1553, 1557, 1565, and 1580—it must have been a rather popular book.[15] But though these editions indicate a continued interest, the book does not appear as often as one might expect in library lists that survive. Perhaps the keepers of the Royal Libraries and such bookish men as William Cecil and Francis Walsingham were interested in preserving French, Latin, and Greek books instead of English ones. The Account Books of William More do list some other books by Elyot and a copy of the *Governour,* without naming the edition.[16] The library of Lord Lumley, as catalogued in 1609, had some other works of Elyot and three copies of the *Governour,* in editions of 1546, 1553 (?), and either 1565 or 1580.[17] No information is available about other copies of the eight editions.

The *Governour* was an ambitious project for the beginning of a literary career. The analysis and organization of ideas, the selection of an enormous number of classical examples, and the writing were no small undertaking. Even more ambitious was the author's plan, to publish another volume on the public weal, as he explained it in I, ii:

> In the fyrste [volume] shall be comprehended the beste fourme of education or bringing up of noble children

from their nativitie, in suche maner as they may be founde
worthy . . . to be governours of a publike weale.

In the sentence he describes with reasonable accuracy
the work that he called the *Governour* and that he divided
into three books, *not* separate volumes.  He will shortly
send forth a second volume, he continues, if God grants
him quietness and peace of mind; it "shall conteine all the
reminant, whiche I can either by lernyng or experience
fynde apt to the perfection of a iuste publike weale. . . ."
He repeats the promise at the close of III, i when he begins the discussion of justice, saying that he will leave
justice commutative "to an other volume, whiche I purpose shall succede this warke, god givynge me tyme and
quietnes of mynde to perfourme it."  The preface of *The
Image of Governance,* 1541, clarifies this mention of a
second volume.  He says there:

> I remembered that in my boke named the Gouernour I
> promised to write a boke of the Forme of good gover-
> nance. And for as moch as in this boke [the source of his
> 1541 material] was expressed of governaunce so perfite an
> ymage, I supposed that I should sufficiently discharge my
> selfe of my promise if I dyd nowe publishe this boke. . . ."

Elyot's statements, when considered together, do not
indicate that he made any change in his ambitious plan;
they promise a separate volume and ten years later he attempted to honor the promise.  Thus the *Governour* deals
with the education and the resulting characteristics,
private and public, of the good ruler; *The Image of
Governance* explains what he does when he has the power.
But some qualities of the *Governour* tend to obscure its
main aim: first, the author's explanations of words and
his use of synonyms to enlarge the vocabularies of Englishmen; second, his use of many examples; and third, digres-
sions to ideas that now seem unimportant.

Elyot's ambition for the *Governour* seems also to be

suggested by his careful revisions for the second edition, in 1537. As a scholar has recently demonstrated, he eliminated naïve personal references, weak repetitions, wordiness, and shifts in structure. His sprawling sentences took form. He also improved his diction; instead of Latin derivatives he had used to enlarge the English vocabulary, he substituted words from Old English or words already established in the language: for *apprehende,* he used *take;* for *facile, easy;* for *perspecuatie and declaration, a playne declaration;* for *pristinate, olde;* and for *semblable, lyke.* He did not try to revive obsolete or obsolescent words. With all these changes he achieved greater simplicity, clarity, and vividness. His work on translations and on his *Dictionary,* giving him a feeling for English words and English idiom, is suggested as an important reason for these revisions.[18]

The main ideas of the *Governour* support Elyot's aim of explaining the education desirable for a man of authority and the private and public virtues that should result from it. The summary that follows presents the bare bones of the book. Elyot begins logically enough, I, i–iii, by explaining that a public weal, not a common weal, is a living body made up of degrees of people and founded on equity and reason. He assumes that monarchy is the best form of government and that degrees are necessary, as there are degrees in heaven, in the four elements, and in the animal and vegetable worlds. From the beginning he assumes that a ruler should use wisdom and virtue and should rule for the good of his people, not for his own pleasure. Any helper of a ruler will be chosen from "worshipfull" men if a sufficient number can be found with wisdom and virtue. Such men have their own revenues, are less prone to corruption, are usually more affable and tolerant, command obedience better even when they are strict, and are likely to be better educated because their fathers have means.

In Book I, iv–xv, Elyot discusses the intellectual

training of the future governor. From the earliest years
he should learn Latin through hearing it spoken perfectly,
and he should live in surroundings with no taint of vice.
At seven he is to continue his education under a tutor, an
ancient, worshipful man, who will try to understand the
child's inclinations and interests, permit him to study
music as recreation, and, if the child is interested, arrange
for him to have masters to teach him painting or carving.
When the child knows well the parts of speech, he should
have a master who is virtuous and chaste in living; he
should either study the authors of both languages together or read Greek authors only while he continues to
speak Latin; his reading should be mostly from the poets.
At fourteen he may begin logic and rhetoric, study geography to prepare for history and for military activities,
and also read history for both utility and pleasure. At
seventeen he may read moral philosophy: Aristotle, Plato,
Cicero, much of the Bible, and Erasmus' *Institutio
principis Christiani*. Elyot takes for granted that the
future governor will study English law, but he wishes him
to devote himself first to liberal studies until he is twenty-
one.

In I, xvi–xxvi, Elyot deals with the physical training
of the future governor, to preserve his health, to increase
his strength, and to prepare him to serve in war or to save
his life in time of peril. He mentions with approval
wrestling, running, leaping, handling the sword and the
battle-ax; he recommends hunting as preparation for war
and concedes that hawking may be used moderately to
keep a man from worse pursuits. In chapters xix–xxv, he
defends dancing, with its harmony, concord, and prudence, and its symbolism of marriage. In xxvi he attacks
dice, tolerates cards and tables [backgammon] if they are
used to teach virtue, and approves chess, especially when
taught with moralizations. In the last chapter of Book I,
after admitting that tennis, bowling, and "claisshe" [a

game now obsolete] may not be entirely bad, and after completely condemning "pynnes," "koyting," and football, he praises shooting with the longbow as the finest of all exercises.

In Book II Elyot analyzes qualities that might be called the personal or the more human qualities of the *Governour,* though any separation into private and political qualities is not clear-cut because he believes that all good qualities are essential for the ideal governor. When called to any position of authority a man should meditate on humility; he should remember that honors come from God, that high position brings increased burdens, that his virtues should increase with his honors, that he should consider the welfare of the people he rules over and live a private life worthy of imitation. A governor may use majesty, not pride, in his manners, speech, clothing, and surroundings; however he must act with affability, placability, and mercy. He must have humanity, which includes benevolence, beneficence, and liberality, though magnificence belongs only to kings. Elyot spends two chapters (II, xi, xii) on friendship, which can exist only between good men with the same studies, tastes, and rank, and which he places above loyalty to family or the loyalty of a man to the woman he loves. He discusses friendship in another chapter on ingratitude, and in still another he contrasts friends and flatterers.

In Book III Elyot discusses the major political virtues: justice, fortitude, temperance, and wisdom. He analyzes justice as distributive and corrective but plans to leave corrective justice for another volume. All justice, he says, depends on reason and knowledge, both self-knowledge and the knowledge of others. Every human being has the same right to own his own body and soul and to benefit from the dew and the sun. The poor herdsman and the mighty emperor have the same freedom of the will. Though degrees are necessary to law and order, the governor or ruler excels others only in understanding. Fortitude, a mean between audacity and fear, is admirable when the aim is worthy, the enterprise is important, and the time and situation are well chosen. Patience is part of fortitude, and magnanimity is its companion, but obstinacy goes beyond reason, and ambition is dangerous. Temperance includes abstinence and continence; it is a mean for regulating the pleasures of the body, especially those of taste and touch. Though temperance is out of fashion, the lack of it causes illness and hinders the conduct of business; it is desirable in many areas, including the punishment of offenders. Wisdom, which considers the causes of things, has its source in God. We draw wisdom from histories—Greek, Roman, and Biblical—but the wisdom from experience is also necessary, and consultation leads to wisdom in action.

The classical sources of Elyot's ideas have been competently analyzed by John M. Major, in *Sir Thomas Elyot and Renaissance Humanism,* with emphasis upon Aristotle, Plutarch, Cicero, Quintilian, Seneca, Isocrates, and Plato. In the *Governour* Elyot uses chiefly the *Nicomachean Ethics,* I and II, from the works of Aristotle. From this source he draws many of his analyses of individual virtues and his definition of virtue as "an election annexed unto our nature, and consisteth in a meane, which is determined by reason, and that meane is the verye myddes of two thynges viciouse, the one in surplusage, the other in lacke. . . ." (II, x) He applies the mean to his analysis of dancing (which was influenced also by Plato, Lucian, and medieval theories of allegory), to other physical exercises, and to such things as a governor's apparel and the furnishings of his house. Elyot also paraphrases Aristotle's *De memoria,* refers briefly several times to Aristotle's *Politics,* and refers once to each of these works: *De anima, Posterior Analytics,* the *Poetics,* and *Historia animalium.*

In the *Governour* also he uses anecdotes from more than half of the fifty *Lives* written by Plutarch; he also follows him closely on the education of young children. He quotes from or mentions Plutarch's *Apophthegmata regum et imperatorum, Apophthegmata Laconica,* and *How to Tell a Friend from a Flatterer.* He also recommends Plutarch as a source of information for the study of patience.

Cicero was a favorite of Elyot, Erasmus, and other humanists because of his success as a statesman at an admirable time in Rome, his eloquence, and his lofty ideas that seemed in complete harmony with the teachings of Christ. Elyot understood completely Cicero's *De oratore,* according to Major, and thus he did not confuse mere cleverness in writing or speaking with the wisdom in genuine eloquence. Though Elyot used a dozen or more of Cicero's works, he was most deeply indebted to the *De officiis.* From it he drew ideas for the virtues of prudence, modesty, placability, patience, moderation, and counsel; and both from it and from the *Nicomachean Ethics* of Aristotle he drew ideas about friendship, justice, fortitude, magnanimity, and abstinence. Cicero's *De amicitia* was another source of Elyot's ideas on friendship; and from the *Tusculan Disputations,* as well as from Pontano, he drew ideas on patience, fortitude, and magnanimity.

Like educators in Italy and Germany, Elyot and Erasmus had both absorbed the spirit of Quintilian's *Institutio oratoria.* Major cites Woodward for the view that Quintilian appealed to the moralist for his insistence on truth as the basis of all education, to the man of knowledge for his demand that the orator be acquainted with all available knowledge, and to the man of affairs for his insistence that his pupils use character and wisdom in the service of the community. Quintilian stressed the early education of the child in morals through virtuous attendants, Major says; the importance of a chaste, learned, and eloquent master; the recognition of individual differences in children; the encouragement by little gifts and praise with no beatings or other harsh treatment; and the beginning of the child's education before seven, with Latin and Greek together or with Greek first because it is harder and with a minimum of formal grammar. (Though Elyot certainly knew Quintilian, it seems reasonable to add that most of these principles had become conventional with Italian educators and with Erasmus many years earlier, and that one of them, the adapting of grammar to the minds of babes, had been emphasized by Thomas More in his contributions to Holt's *Lac puerorum* before 1500, by Colet in his plans for St. Paul's school, and by Erasmus in his treatises on education.)

Seneca exerted a comparatively small influence on the *Governour,* an influence that is harder to measure because Stoical thought had permeated Christian doctrine. The direct influence, according to Major, is almost entirely restricted to the chapters in Book II, on mercy, benevolence, and friendship, with extended quotations from *De clementia* and *De beneficiis.* Stoic sentiment, from Elyot's knowledge of Seneca, Cicero, and Boethius, colors the discussion of such virtues as fortitude, "painfulness," and patience; and for the study of patience Elyot recommends the works of Pontano, Plutarch, and Seneca. *Of the Knowledge Which Maketh a Wise Man* also has a suggestion of Stoicism in its emphasis on the need for controlling the passions and on the view that the universe is governed by providence. (Again it seems that these two ideas might also have come from the Christian tradition.)

"Few ancient authors are closer in spirit to the author of the *Governour* than is Isocrates," Major says. Isocrates was important to the Renaissance for his sane ideas on practical morality, on eloquence, and on the relation between princes and their subjects. His superb style was also an outstanding influence.

To all Renaissance poets and humanists, Plato, or a

body of ideas called Platonism, was "the dominant intellectual force of the sixteenth century." Though there had
never been a break in the availability of his work in some
form, Marsilio Ficino's complete Latin translation of the
dialogues appeared in 1482, and the *editio princeps* of the
Greek text was published in Venice in 1513. His ideas
came into England from two main sources: the *Republic,*
with its emphasis on the good, influencing *Utopia,* the
*Governour,* and Starkey's *Dialogue;* and the *Symposium,*
with its emphasis on the beautiful, influencing aesthetics,
religious mysticism, and English poetry. Elyot's knowledge of Plato did not come from secondary sources; his
work "reveals a high degree of familiarity with the dialogues themselves." Plato's influence was strongest upon
the *Governour, Of the Knowledge Which Maketh a Wise
Man,* and *The Image of Governance,* Major concludes;
but there are traces of it in *The Banquet of Sapience* and
*The Defense of Good Women.* Plato's ideas "thoroughly
affected" Elyot's views of politics, psychology, and ethics,
his use of the Socratic dialogue, and probably some of his
educational ideas. From the *Republic* and the *Laws* Elyot
took his concept of the state as a living body consisting of
classes and ordered by reason and justice, some ideas on
the art of ruling and the qualifications of rulers, the relation between education, virtue, and good government,
and the meaning of nobility. As Elyot uses the general
plan of the *Republic* for the *Governour,* he may have
wished to furnish Englishmen with a counterpart of that
work. Plato ranked first, as certainly as Cicero ranked
second, among the classical influences on Elyot.[19] (Again
it seems reasonable to add, that some of these ideas had
become current coin among Continental and English
humanists and that the *Colloquies* of Erasmus may have
contributed to Elyot's use of the Socratic dialogue—even
though he knew his Plato thoroughly.) It is impossible, of
course, to do full justice to Major's material in a brief

summary; but these were the chief classical sources of the *Governour.*

When we consider the manuals written for the edification of princes, Elyot's *Governour* was no isolated phenomenon. It has distinguished and undistinguished forerunners—not necessarily ancestors—contemporaries, and a multitude of followers who may or may not be descendants. The forerunners, to name a few, include Xenophon's *Cyropaedia;* works of Isocrates; *De regimine principum* by Thomas Aquinas; Hoccleve's English poem with the same title, written for Prince Hal; and even Skelton's *Speculum principis,* written for the boy who became Henry VIII. They include *De l'institution du prince,* by the eminent French humanist, Budé. He is frequently mentioned as a follower of Elyot; but though his treatise did not appear in print until 1547, it was written about 1516 to 1519 for Francis I.[20] Perhaps the forerunners, in one way or another, include such Italians as Patrizi, Pontano, Palmieri, many other fifteenth-century writers on education; Castiglione, with his *Courtier,* and Machiavelli, since his *Prince* was completed about 1513 and was circulating in manuscript. Besides many others not named here, the forerunners include Erasmus, who published in 1516 his *Institutio principis Christiani,* written for Charles V of Spain. If every ruler had heeded his teacher, surely the millenium would have arrived centuries ago!

Of all these forerunners perhaps only a few merit discussion for a possible influence on Elyot's *Governour.* In spite of the claims made by Croft and at one time by Leslie C. Warren for the influence of Patrizi on Elyot's *Governour,* that influence seems to be small. There is very little formal or structural resemblance, according to J. M. Major; but about twenty passages, mainly from the chapters on physical exercise in Book I, are taken almost verbatim from Patrizi. Though the ideas of these passages appear in Plutarch and in works by other classic writers, both the individual words and the phrasing closely resemble Patrizi. Major suggests a convincing reason for the fact that Elyot never acknowledged a debt to him: the passages consist of anecdotes which might be considered common property, and Patrizi was no stylist and hence not one to be cited with pride.[21]

As for Pontano's influence, Elyot recommended his essay *De fortitudine* for the study of patience; the chapter on fortitude and on other related virtues owes something to the same essay and to *De magnanimitate,* though the ultimate source for both is the *Nicomachean Ethics* of Aristotle. Pontano's chapter *De obedientia* furnishes Elyot with an anecdote about a certain Belinger Baldasine, a counselor to Ferdinand of Aragon; and perhaps Pontano's *De principe* has much that contributed to the discussion of majesty, even if Elyot did not follow all of his ideas.[22]

It seems reasonable to suggest Matteo Palmieri (1406–1475), author of *La vita civile,* as an influence on the *Governour,* though we have no evidence that Elyot knew his work. The first edition of Palmieri's treatise did not appear until 1529, but his ideas were in circulation by 1435 or 1440. Palmieri asserted that no life is nobler than that of the citizen who helps unite all classes for the good of the state. Such a citizen learns first to control his own baser instincts, then to act wisely as part of a family, and finally to help govern his state or community with prudence, courage, temperance, and justice. The ideal citizen is also a man of personal culture, whose education includes literature, drawing, singing, and other music.[23] Palmieri's chief sources, it is said, were Plutarch, Quintilian, and Cicero—the sources used by most Renaissance humanists. It is possible that Elyot had some contact with the ideas of Palmieri, perhaps through the treatises written by Italian educators in the last half of the fifteenth century.[24]  Or he may have had oral reports through such Englishmen as Lily, Grocyn, and Linacre. It is also possible, in a time when Western Europe was moving from the concept of education for a knight or a clerk to the concept of education for man as a citizen, with some humane or artistic training, that each writer drew mainly from the classics and from life.

It is true, as Major suggests, that Castiglione puts small stress, comparatively speaking, on the influence of the courtier upon his prince in the direction of good government; the courtier usually wishes to advance himself or to win the favor of the ladies. Perhaps Elyot owed something to the *Courtier* for his ideas on majesty. Possibly Elyot knew and admired Castiglione's idealism, admiration for antiquity, ideas on true nobility, defense of learning, concern for the vernacular, praise of monarchy, and the virtues of a good prince.[25] It is true that both writers agree about the study of singing and of playing musical instruments; that both stress painting and sculpture or similar arts; that both are concerned about physical development. But Elyot had many opportunities also to admire or to follow most of the ideas of Castiglione from other reading, especially from the classics. Perhaps he was encouraged in his natural tact and courtly deference by knowing the *Courtier*. It is true that he had a chance to know the work, for Cromwell, who was a friend of Elyot from 1519 and who was invited to visit him at Combe in 1528, was lending Bishop Bonner an Italian copy of the work about that time.[26] If Elyot did not know Italian, Cromwell did, and could interpret the material for him.

Was Elyot's *Governour* a deliberate attempt to refute More's *Utopia?* The question has been raised by Major in his discussion of sources. The question might mean either of two extremes: first, that Elyot planned and produced his entire work to refute *Utopia* (probably not quite Major's meaning); second, that he was consciously arguing throughout that a good government can exist when men own private property. Or perhaps it might mean something between these extremes. The question should not be confused with the personal relationship between the two men nor does it seem to be affirmatively supported by pointing out that they held many ideas in common, as they did, of course.

Detailed discussion of Elyot's possible intention to refute *Utopia* seems futile (at least to this writer). But a brief look at the problem may be based more soundly when we recall that Plato's *Republic* suggested communal practices and also that the members of the early Christian church held all things in common. Plato was a favorite of the English humanists and of their Continental friends, Erasmus and Vives, who spent much time in England; Colet, Erasmus, and More had turned from the Schoolmen to the teachings of the early fathers in the Christian church. Elyot also often used their ideas as support for his own views. Colet argued passionately for Christian sharing, Erasmus indicated some interest in the problem, and Vives urged that possessions be used for the common good. If Elyot was refuting *Utopia,* he was refuting Christian communism as it was expressed by other humanists; and he was also refuting ideas in Plato's *Republic.*

Also Elyot's attack on communism is only a small detail (even though it was basic and constantly important to him) in a complex book. Probably More would have agreed with most of the other ideas in the *Governour.* Both men had in common one large aim: they wished to improve society and government. Elyot wished to accomplish his aims by educating from infancy all men of authority (both princes and their helpers), in learning, in private and public morality, and in all qualities desirable

in good officials and rulers. Could More have disagreed
with any of these aims?

More was not urging the adoption of communism in
England—in the opinion of this writer, at least. Instead,
he wished to emphasize the ironic contrast between a so-
called Christian civilization and a non-Christian civilization based only on reason. He wished also to drive home
another ironic contrast: the difference between the principles of Christianity and their practice. Attacking strife,
hate, and greed as un-Christian, through his imaginary
Hithloday, More struck at some basic causes of vagrancy
and crime.[27] Thus he produced a great social document
of the early Renaissance.

It is true that More in his *Utopia* and Elyot in his
*Governour* agreed about the honor due to God through
outer symbols (beautiful churches, their decorations, and
ceremonies), and about the danger of heresy to the social
order. They were alike in having a passion for learning
with emphasis on the classics and in believing the aims of
learning to be virtue and service to the state. Both considered justice to be important in the treatment of citizens
and in dealings with other nations.[28] But these agreements
neither prove nor disprove the theory that Elyot was trying
to refute More's *Utopia*. More disagreed with Elyot's
ideas on aristocracy, degrees in government and in life as
a part of the accepted order, and training for war, and
perhaps with his belief that rulers and governors (with
greater understanding and thus with a greater contribution to the public good) should have more honor and
material goods. But these disagreements also prove nothing about Elyot's aim to refute *Utopia*. Elyot's initial
emphasis in the *Governour* is not only logical and sincere
for him but also tactful; he is suggesting that the virtues
he discusses later can be applied in the accepted order of
government.

How much Elyot owes to the *Institutio principis
Christiani* of Erasmus seems difficult or even impossible

to estimate. He apparently took from it, as Major suggests, the seven articles recommended in II, i, for the meditation of men called to receive any new dignity. Without naming Erasmus, Elyot says he did not devise these articles in his own head but gathered them from scripture and "the warkes of other excellent writars of famouse memorie," as those who read good authors in Latin and Greek will soon discover. Elyot also learned, from the same work by Erasmus, that good rulers must also be good men, that goodness can be acquired through education and nurture, and that early education is important.[29] However, it would be strange if Elyot had not absorbed these ideas from Plato and also from Quintilian, Plutarch, and Cicero. Hence, this writer must conclude, when Erasmus and Elyot express the same ideas, that there may or may not have been a direct influence. It is possible, of course, that the *Institutio,* published in 1516, inspired Elyot to write a similar work in English; for there is much evidence both in the *Governour* and elsewhere that he followed closely the work of Erasmus.

In the first edition of the *Governour* Elyot three times praises publications by Erasmus. In I, xi, he says that his *Copia* is sufficient for the man who does not wish to become an "exquisite" orator and that all gentle wits are bound to thank and support him. In the same chapter he wishes that the *Institutio* might be as familiar to all gentlemen as Homer was to Alexander and Xenophon to Scipio: "there was never boke written in latine that, in so lytle a portion, contayned of sentence, eloquence, and vertuous exhortation, a more compendious abundaunce." In III, xi, he mentions the work again for its views on advising princes and adds that the book cannot be praised as much as it deserves. He removed the last comment from the edition of 1537, perhaps as needless repetition. If he overpraises the work, perhaps the cause is his concern for virtuous exhortation.

Elyot's aim in the *Governour* differs in one way from

the aim of his forerunners or contemporaries who address
a prince. He declares his intention to discuss governors
or helpers of a prince (their eyes, ears, legs, and hands),
but much of the time he assumes, either intentionally or
unintentionally, that his remarks apply also to kings and
princes. In I, ii, he says that to write about the office or
duty of a sovereign far exceeds the compass of his learning
and that the hearts of princes are in the care of God. But
as the work progresses, he is unwilling to leave them completely to providence. In I, iii, he says that governors have
their virtues and their education in common with princes.
In concluding his remarks on exercise, I, xxvii, he says
that his discussion applies also to princes and noblemen
and to all who wish to live in honesty and virtue. He begins his discussion of majesty, II, ii, by relating it to a
governor or to a man having "some greatte authoritie" in
the public weal. In II, iii, when he discusses apparel, he
gives examples of a half dozen Roman emperors who used
a discreet moderation in dress; but he concludes that all
Christian men, even those not of the estate of princes,
might do as well. In II, v, wherever he mentions the harm
that princes and their realms have suffered because they
did not encourage freedom of speech, he implies that he
is thinking of rulers; and he uses many examples of kings
and emperors. In II, ix, his discussion of benevolence and
the examples he cites suggest that he is thinking of kings
and other sovereigns; also he names princes and noblemen
who have willingly died for the welfare of their countries.
In III, iii, he discusses self-knowledge and urges it upon
any man who exercises sovereignty over others. In III, vi,
the plea that leagues and truces made by princes should be
kept is clearly aimed at rulers, though Elyot hastily re-
treats by adding, "But lette us leave princes affayres to
their counsailours." Through the whole work he uses examples of kings, princes, and emperors so often that it
would be impossible to summarize all of them. Then he

addresses a tactful Proheme to Henry VIII, asking him to
be both the patron and the defender of the book.

Little can be said here about the followers of the
*Governour,* those that may or may not be descendants. If
dogmatic statements about his sources are sometimes unsound, attempts to prove his direct influence on another
writer about the education of a gentleman are often futile
and a weariness to flesh and spirit. So-called influences
may mean only that ideas were in the air, ebbing and
flowing like an erratic sea. Since Elyot wrote in English,
his effect on men in other countries is less likely than that
of a man who wrote in Latin. Men in England who wrote
later than Elyot continued to read and to cite the classics,
as he had cited them. They also used the increasing number of French and English translations of these classics.
As the years passed, they tended to draw from each other,
instead of returning either to the classics or to Elyot. Even
when the *Governour* may have been a real influence, only
the minor writers tend to betray themselves; writers of
power and imagination, when stimulated by others, choose
their own diction and weave their individual patterns of
thought.

It is interesting, though, to notice briefly the great
variety of the writers who used Elyot, sometimes mentioning and sometimes failing to mention a source. The
anonymous author of the *Institution of a Gentleman* uses
phrasing like Elyot, especially in his discussion of idleness
as the portress who opens the gate of lust; and if the two
were carefully compared, other borrowings might appear.[30] William Cunningham, in *The Cosmographical
Glass,* 1559, without any mention of Elyot, borrows and
enlarges his ideas on the military uses of geography and
on the pleasure of learning it in a warm room at home
without the discomforts of travel.[31] John Bossewell, in
*Works of Armory,* 1572, sometimes cites, sometimes
changes, and sometimes plagiarizes Elyot's statements on

temperance, nobility, chess, the use of the longbow, hawking, and the handling of the wild hobby to kill larks and
quail. He gives credit to Elyot for ideas on the study of
history.[32] John Northbrooke, in *A Treatise wherein Dicing, Dancing, Vain Plays . . . Are Reproved,* 1586, uses
and often cites Elyot to support his attacks on idleness,
dice, and the great oaths and blasphemings that tend to
accompany dice playing. He repeats, often with the same
wording, his ideas on cards, backgammon, and chess.[33]
Apparently he considered Elyot excellent support because
he was a knight.

Nor does Elyot seem to have been a strong influence
on the writers who discussed music for the education of a
gentleman; at least he was not an influence they mentioned. Of course Aristotle leaves little to be said: music
is a pleasure and a relaxation, a purge or an outlet for the
emotions, a means of developing appreciation and judgment, a means of creating in a listener enthusiasm or other
feelings expressed by the music; it should tend to virtue
and character. He recommends ethical rather than passionate music or that inciting to action. He warns against
allowing the use of musical instruments to vulgarize the
body, objecting to the flute because it stops the performer's
speech; and he condemns professional performances or
competitions as unworthy of free men.[34] If Aristotle overlooked anything, Elyot probably could have found it in
Plato. When he recommends music for attaining a better
knowledge of the estates and degrees in the public weal
and their harmony (I, vii) he refers his readers to those
books of Aristotle and Plato that are concerned with the
public weal.

Later writers who discuss an education in music for
the gentleman—at least those whose works are available—
do not usually mention Elyot nor do they pattern their
discussion on his work. They range from the anonymous
*Institution of a Gentleman,* 1555, to Henry Peacham's

*Complete Gentleman,* 1622.[35] The only ones who mention Elyot are two musicians: Thomas Whythorne, whose *Autobiography* was written about 1576, and the author of *The Praise of Music,* presumably John Case. (Peacham, of course, names Elyot in his preface but not for his discussion of music.) Whythorne cites both *The Castle of Health* and the *Governour* in discussing the power of music to lessen "the dolors"; he adds that Elyot rebukes those who misuse it.[36] Case cites almost verbatim several classical examples from Elyot, including one about the desire of Alexander to see the harp of Achilles, with which he sang "nat the illecebrous dilectations of Venus but the valiaunt actes and noble affaires of excellent princes." Those who wish to understand the decent use of music, he says, should consult the eight books of Aristotle's *Politics,* and also the *Governour,* I, vii. From them "he shall sufficiently gather what the proper and sober use hereof is and ought to be."[37]

The poem "Orchestra" by Sir John Davies may owe something to Elyot's discussions of music and dancing, just as both may be indebted to "The Dance" by Lucian, a dialogue in which Lycinus changes the mind of Crato and persuades him to regard dancing as "a thing of utter harmony, putting a fine edge upon the soul, disciplining the body. . . ." Davies' poem suggests that dancing is the rhythm of the spheres, the twin of time, the child of love and music; it changes chaos to order, creating concord and human harmony.[38] Certainly there is a likeness in the poem to Elyot's picture of the dance between a man and a woman (I, xxi–xxii) as the symbol of concord, with the strength of man and the pleasant soberness of woman. Together, Elyot says, they represent all the qualities of nobility: severity, magnanimity, constancy, honor, wisdom, and continence. Davies, of course, does not mention Elyot in his poem.

None of the professional educators whose works are

available mention Elyot for his comments in the *Governour,* though they continue to cite Erasmus, Vives, and Ascham long after the turn of the century. Ascham mentions Elyot in *Toxophilus,* praising him for his learning and saying that he had inquired of him about the origins of archery; he does not mention him in the *Schoolmaster.* Thomas Becon, a writer deeply concerned with education, quotes Lily in his *Catechism,* about 1550 to 1560, as support for virtue in education, but he names no other educational authorities, though he could not have found more earnest support than Elyot. Of the other six or seven writers on education whose books have been examined, every one mentions either Ascham, Vives, or Erasmus; some writers mention all of them; and some mention one or more of them a number of times. Charles Hoole, in *A New Discovery of the Old Art of Teaching School,* as late as 1659 or 1660, names and recommends five separate works of Erasmus for the use of pupils.[39] But neither he nor any other of these writers mentions Elyot for his discussion of education.

Perhaps there are several reasons for the continued naming of Erasmus, Ascham, and sometimes Vives, and for the absence of Elyot's name. Erasmus had tutored some well-known men (Lord Mountjoy and Vives, for example); he had also published books on teaching and other books that were helpful in classrooms. Vives had been a reader at Oxford and had published textbook material. Ascham was known as the author of the *Schoolmaster* and the tutor of Queen Elizabeth. Elyot's theories of education were only a small part of the *Governour,* he published no textbook material, he was not known as a teacher, he served the government as a member of the landed gentry, and he was a knight. His work was not aimed at grammar school teachers, but at young men who wished to become governors, at their parents, the nobles, and the king of England.

The spate of works on the education of a gentleman in the latter part of the sixteenth century seems to indicate a large influence from Sir Thomas Elyot's *Governour,* perhaps an influence on many writers who did not name him at all. (See Appendix I for a tentative list of such works.) Either Elyot inspired other men or he had a remarkable ability to foresee the future. The widespread interest in the training of the gentleman is emphasized by Peacham's address to the reader, 1622, in *The Complete Gentleman:*

> I am not ignorant, judicious reader, how many pieces of the most curious masters have been uttered to the world of this subject, as Plutarch, Erasmus, Vives, Sadoleto, Sturmius, Osorius, Sir Thomas Elyot, Master Ascham, with sundry others, so that my small taper among so many torches were as good out, as seeming to give no light at all.[40]

Peacham's list includes Greek, Dutch, Spanish, Italian, German, Portuguese, and English writers, with a classic forerunner, near-contemporaries or contemporaries of Elyot, and followers. However he does not name Elyot at all in the body of his work.

Other influences were also operating on the education of the gentleman. In early sixteenth-century England Sir Thomas More was exerting a personal influence on the education of women and of noblemen. By the early sixteenth century also, all Western Europe was moving away from the education of young men as knights or as clerks and toward their education as courtiers, soldiers, and scholars.[41]

When we examine specific ideas, such as the education of the gentleman in music, the evidence for the influence of one writer on another seems vague. This is especially true when we consider the views of Aristotle and Plato, remember that Palmieri was including music and other arts in the training of the citizen as early as 1435 to 1440, and recall that Mulcaster and other Englishmen in the long years between Elyot and Peacham had been emphasizing music. Only the musicians name Elyot, and Case also mentions Aristotle. When we consider the professional educators also—those who valued the work of Erasmus, Vives, and Ascham—we discover that they never mentioned Elyot for his ideas on education. Perhaps Elyot's influence will become more apparent when the *Governour* has been compared in detail with other individual works, or perhaps it was cumulative but general.

Elyot does, however, seem to have been a source of ideas for prose writers on other topics than the education of a gentleman in the late sixteenth century. He influenced major poets and dramatists of the Elizabethan period, including Shakespeare. (See Appendix II for summaries of articles.) Also, Elyot's *Governour* was the first work in English to discuss the many-sided education of governors and princes—including their physical, moral and religious, aesthetic, intellectual and classical, courtly, and aristocratic education. Elyot must have exerted a considerable influence (even if it cannot be measured precisely) on Elizabethan literature and Elizabethan life. After all our counting of references and our analysis of parallel passages, we confront intangibles in literature—and in life.

# CHAPTER VIII

## *The* Governour:
## *Individual and English Ideas*

THE importance of Elyot's *Governour* does not emerge from an analysis of its sources or from speculations about its influence on future writers. Instead, it comes from the writer's ideas. Elyot was an Englishman who loved his country; he was writing for other Englishmen. Unlike Castiglione, he was not recalling a happy past or recording the high-class entertainment at a small court or teaching a courtier how to win personal distinction and to charm the ladies. He wrote with the serious purpose of influencing the future government of England and even the character and the life of his king. Though his work has a flavoring of courtly tact and a bias toward aristocracy, he wrote with cumulative emphasis and bulldog tenacity. His minor ideas are often drawn from his own experience or he tends to give them his own emphasis. His persistent stress upon the personal life of the governor or prince, especially upon sexual morality, seems to be something unique in manuals for the education of a gentleman. He demands also the highest standards for the political actions of a governor, relating them to specific virtues. Thus he attempts to circumscribe power by morals and ethics.

Like the other humanists of the period, Elyot had a

king who inherited his position and who might be inclined to wrest governmental controls to serve his own
purposes. Like Erasmus and More, he must have realized
that all talk of an elective ruler or of other systems of
government than a monarchy was merely speculative
philosophy among friends; and that practical idealism, if
one may use a paradoxical term, consisted in taming the
lion, preferably before he realized his full strength, by
teaching him virtue and learning. Elyot's rigorous demands for private and political conduct leave the ruler
little room for unlimited action.

Along with his demands for private morality and
ethical government, Elyot asks also that his governor be
a man of learning because knowledge leads to virtue; that
he be educated in music, and in painting or carving if he
has the inclination for either skill; and that his physical
training prepare him for peace or war. Though Elyot is
tactful, courtly, and aristocratic, he never forgets his
serious purpose. Even his emphasis on aristocracy is modified by his insistence on a certain equality between the
poor herdsman and the powerful emperor. His details
about education in music and other artistic skills, though
they do seem to resemble in some ways those of Castiglione
or other Continental writers, may be a reflection of the
English court or of Elyot's education at an Inn of Court.
Hence it seems fitting to analyze both the individual details and the English elements in the *Governour*.


Elyot's minor ideas often come from his own life
and observations, and often he is concerned with the improvement of English life. He is using his own memories
when he mentions the pleasure that children take in
Virgil's *Bucolics,* adding, "as I knowe by myne owne experience." He is speaking as a man of the landed gentry,
in I, x, when he comments on Virgil's *Georgics,* with

their delight in nature and their details about husbandry;
the author, he adds, had pleasure in horses and a knowledge of them surpassing that of all English breeders,
sellers, or hirers-out of horses. Elyot again speaks as a man
interested in country life when he mentions "shailes" or
"blenchars," used to frighten birds from crops, and when
he pleads, in I, xviii, for the conservation of wild game.
Falcons, he says, should be satisfied with the division of
their prey, as the falcons of Thrace were, instead of consuming the "hennes" of the realm in such numbers. Unless
they are kept to a simpler diet our "familiar pultrie"
(meaning perhaps larks and quails) may soon be as scarce
as our partridges and pheasants have already become. He
is not saying this in dispraise of falcons, he adds—earlier
he had described hawking as "a right delectable solace"
and one that keeps men from worse occupations—but of
those owners who pamper them too much. Perhaps this
is one of the earliest pleas for the conservation of wild
game in England; and though hawking was by no means
restricted to England, Elyot here writes from a knowledge
and a concern about his own country. Elyot's many comparisons to medicine or to the physician, in the *Governour*
(and also in other works) seem also to rise from his individual interest in the subject.

Elyot the scholar speaks, in I, xi, when he says that
the virtues of Aristotle's *Ethics* must be learned from the
Greek original, since the available translations give only
rude and gross ideas of his wisdom and eloquence. Again,
in I, xxv, he mentions the need for English translations of
Greek and Roman wisdom and adds that the English, in
this area, are lagging behind Italians, French, and Germans.

Though Elyot is not the only scholar to speak out
about the difference between rhetoric and wisdom, he
makes specific and many-sided attacks. In the *Governour*,
I, xi, he names Demosthenes and Cicero as the greatest

orators because of their gentle manners and their wisdom, with their eloquence. In I, xiii, he says that the purpose of learning Latin is not mere facility in the language, like a popinjay or a magpie, but the discovery of wisdom. Too many men, even in famous schools and universities, are given to the study of nothing but the language, and when they write epistles they seem like trumpets making a noise without purpose. Rhetoric alone, without wisdom to express, is artificial, like the craft of versifying compared with the philosophy and meaning of true poetry. A similar difference, he says in I, xv, exists between a grammarian who knows only the rules and the teacher who knows philosophy and other wisdom. The man of authority who is a true orator, he explains in II, ii, has a style that is compendious, sententious, and delectable; he adapts his words to the time, the place, and the listeners. Such a persistent and many-sided analysis indicates Elyot's complete understanding of the difference between rhetoric and wisdom.[1]

Elyot's development of the friendship theme in the *Governour* may be considered a minor idea here because his treatment does not quite relate it to the personal qualities of a ruler, unless he has in mind that a ruler should be a good man and that friendship exists only between good men. He devotes two chapters, II, xi, xii, to the explanation of friendship, with the classic examples of Orestes and Pylades and of Damon and Pythias in the first, and with a long, romantic narrative of Titus and Gisippus in the second chapter. The last story had appeared in Boccaccio's *Decameron* and in a Latin version by Beroaldo about 1495. Elyot used the Latin version, it is said, but made such thorough changes that the work is his own version.[2] He follows these chapters with one on ingratitude, using examples of dogs and a lion with more gratitude than most men; then he deplores the absence of true friendship. He adds another chapter on the difference between friends and flatterers. Although one might expect him to emphasize the need for governors to give impartial justice instead of favoring friends, he does not do so.

Friendship, as Elyot develops the theme, is possible only between good men and between those of similar tastes, studies, and rank. The two become one in possessions and in suffering, they come to look so much alike that others cannot tell them apart, and, for the other's happiness, either will renounce the woman he loves or give his life for his friend; but he will not sacrifice his country or commit any other wrongdoing for him. In the story of Titus and Gisippus, Titus falls in love with a girl who is already committed to marry Gisippus; and the love and grief of Titus are so strong that his friend thinks God has destined the girl for him. To save his friend from sorrow, the bridegroom substitutes Titus for himself on the wedding night, lets him loosen the bride's girdle, put his ring on her finger, and consummate his own marriage to her. Though Elyot assumes that no wrongdoing occurs here, the trick is one that only a Renaissance woman, if any, could condone! Various other events follow, in which the two men continue to prove their complete adherence to the code of friendship.

The story of Titus and Gisippus, as Elyot tells it, is vivid, dramatic at moments of tension, free from decorations of style that impede the narrative, and unhampered by extraneous episodes. For its period, at least, it is a close-knit narrative guided by its theme that true friendship of man for man rises above man's love of self or of the woman he plans to marry. It is guided by character in a large and general sense, not in the individualistic psychological sense of the twentieth century, for each man is motivated by his loyalty in friendship. If it did not influence the style in the prose romances of the late sixteenth century it might have done so to their advantage. Apparently its ideas did have a great influence on many

Elizabethans, including Spenser and Shakespeare. (See summaries of articles in Appendix II.) When he discusses friendship, Elyot is speaking for himself, not for Englishmen in his own period; and the four chapters dealing in some way with friendship have only a distant connection with the qualities of the ideal governor.

Elyot's attitude toward religion and toward the use of the Bible in education may now be considered a minor matter, but at the time he wrote, his attitude was related to a climate of controversy in England. His book is primarily a secular one, of course, intended for laymen; it has sometimes been said that he did not emphasize the teaching of the Bible at all.[3] However, in I, xi, Elyot says that when a young man is seventeen and begins the study of philosophy, he should read Aristotle's *Ethicae*, Cicero's *De officiis*, the works of Plato, the Proverbs of Solomon, Ecclesiastes, and Ecclesiasticus; he adds that the nobleman of mature years should read all the historical books of the Bible. In III, xxv, when he deals more fully with the need of his governor or ruler to know history, he names most of the books of both the Old and the New Testament as history. Perhaps he thought that certain actions of men in the Old Testament would not be helpful in teaching morality to younger boys. Apparently he feared also that theological parts of the Bible might be used to teach heresy. In his total work there is clear evidence that he clung to conservative religious doctrines; and when he published the *Governour*, More was defending the teachings of his church against such reformers as Frith, Luther, and Tyndale. When Elyot said, then, in I, xi, that all the historical parts are essential for the mature man of authority, he added that the remainder, including parts of the New Testament, is to be "reverently touched, as a celestiall iewell or relike," and that the interpreter should have a true and constant faith.

Elyot's casual references to art—setting aside for the

time his discussion of it as a part of education—are more frequent and varied than anyone has noted before, though it has been pointed out that he recommended pictures and other physical representations as aids to learning. In his comments on art, Elyot is sometimes the teacher of morals and sometimes the human being with artistic apprecia- tion. Usually the moralist dominates—but not always. In the *Governour,* I, viii, the moralist says that a metal image by Lysippus, of Alexander fighting a lion, inspired those who watched it to gain courage; but the moralist is off guard when he mentions an ivory image of Jupiter made by Phidias, and patterned on a description by Homer. He stresses only its artistic excellence. In III, xix, the teacher is dominant when he compares the lack of constancy in a man of authority to a beautiful portrait that disintegrates because the painter did not use enough sizing; in III, xxvii, when he emphasizes the evils of detraction by de- scribing in detail a painting made by Apelles; and in III, xxvi, where he states the principle that general knowledge must be supported by concrete experience. He illustrates this principle by the incident of Alexander, who tried to discuss lines, shading, and proportion with Apelles, until the painter suggested that the boy who ground his colors for him was laughing at the emperor's ignorance.

In a few other well-developed instances Elyot discusses dancing or painting without emphasizing any moral idea. In I, xx, he says that a philosopher, Demetrius, had always opposed dancing as an art until a famous dancer presented for him without music the story of Venus' infidelity with Mars, Vulcan's exposure of the two for all the gods to see, and the confusion of Venus. Demetrius was delighted, saying that he saw and he heard, and that the dancer spoke with his hands. When the same dancer was performing before Nero, with a strange king present who did not un- derstand the speech of the dancer, the king asked for a loan of the dancer, in order to use him as an interpreter.

In a later work, *Of the Knowledge Which Maketh a Wise Man,* Elyot indicates that he has some understanding of a painter's technique. An artist, picturing a beautiful woman nude and wishing to make the figure seem full and round, as if embossed in metal, timber, or stone, uses a black background.[4] Like the two examples of interpretative dancing, the illustration is completely free of any intent to teach morals.

Elyot is individual in his emphasis upon the private life of a governor or ruler. Perhaps his ideas in this area are more English than Continental, or at least more English than Italian. Certainly his tenacity and his high seriousness have been popularly considered English traits —though any statement about national traits is likely to vanish in quicksand. It is sounder, perhaps, to say, that More, Colet, Erasmus, Vives, and Elyot stress their major ideas with a high seriousness that did not always tend to prevail among Italian humanists—that the English humanists and their friends hoped to reform society by applying classical and Christian principles to contemporary life.[5] But though Erasmus, in the *Institutio principis Christiani,* tried to teach his prince to be a Christian and a good man, he did not harp on sexual morality, as Elyot did; and if one may be permitted to think that Henry VIII was Elyot's concern, his ideas had an immediate application to England.

Elyot demands an education for sexual continence from the child's birth. The child must have a nurse with no vice, lest the child be infected with evil from the milk of her breast, and another woman attendant of virtue, discretion, and gravity, who will not permit him to see any dishonest action or to hear any wanton words. Men, except physicians, are to be excluded. If moral poison infects the child early, he adds in I, iv, it may grow until it causes the complete destruction of the realm. Here he seems to think of the child as a future ruler.

At seven the child should be taken from the company of women, except for one or two attendants who are both serious and old, lest sparks of voluptuousness be fanned, to become later a great fire, consuming reason and virtue. While the tutor, an ancient and worshipful man, is teaching his pupil the elements of grammar, he may let him use musical instruments for recreation, but he must not permit any wanton countenance or dissolute gesture—better no music at all than pleasure leading to wantonness. Among the examples of rulers who guarded themselves against sensuality, Elyot names Alexander; he chose to see the harp of Achilles, who sang the noble acts of princes, not that of Paris, who presumably sang "the illecebrous dilectations of Venus. . . ." (I, vii)

When a master is chosen for the child later, he must be sober, virtuous, and "specially chast of livyng. . . ." (I, ix) In later recreation the young gentleman may use hawking in measure, partly because it will keep him from dalliance and other dishonest occupations (I, xviii). As for dances, he must avoid those that tend to venereal lusts, fornication, and adultery, or those interlaced with ditties of wanton love, ribaldry, or mention of Bacchus and Venus, as if the dances were in memory of them. Elyot adds:

> I wolde to god those names were nat at this day used in balades and ditties in the courtes of princes and noble men, where many good wittes be corrupted with semblable fantasies, whiche in better wise employed mought have bene more necessarye to the publike weale and their princes honour. (I, xix)

Following this discussion, Elyot analyzes the positive virtues that may be cultivated by the dance and uses it as a symbol of concord in marriage.

When he summarizes the seven articles that the governor should think on as he comes to any position of authority (II, i), Elyot begs him to remember that all his "privie daliaunce" or other unprofitable or wanton conditions will become known through the talk of servants; and all the people will tend to imitate him. The verses he translated to follow this discussion stress self-mastery and the conquest of lust. Later, in III, iii, he emphasizes again the obligation of rulers to act as good examples for their subjects; he cites Aristotle to support his belief that men follow the example of their governors into virtue or vice. When he discusses fidelity, in III, vi, he adds that examples of this virtue from the stories about David and Solomon, in tapestry or on painted cloth, would become the houses of noblemen much better than the usual ones dealing with their concubines and voluptuous pleasures.

In the chapters on abstinence and continence, III, xvii, xviii, Elyot limits abstinence to the refraining for a better purpose from such things as money and possessions. Continence (the virtue that keeps man's appetite for pleasure under the control of reason) he limits to forbearing the unlawful company of women and especially to refraining from the act of carnal pleasure when a man fervently desires it or has the opportunity to take it. Continence is wonderful in a nobleman or in any man who has great authority; such a man is not invincible, because carnal desire, called love by its followers, sharply assails men, and continence requires both virtue and wisdom. Elyot's chapter of examples includes Alexander the Great, a King Antiochus of Asia, Pompey, and Scipio—a strong emphasis upon kings and conquerors. (Castiglione also uses the incidents about Alexander and Scipio, but as parts of a lighter discussion on whether men or women are more continent.) Elyot closes his chapter with an incident told by Saint Jerome. The emperor Valerian decided to tempt, rather than torment, a young Christian by putting him into a beautiful garden with an attractive young woman who used all her wiles to seduce him. When the young man was almost vanquished, he began gnawing his own tongue; and the pain he suffered overcame the furious burning of his carnal appetite. (Castiglione uses a similar situation about Xenocrates, but for some reason that worthy philosopher seemed to have no trouble at all about self-control.)[6] Elyot concludes his discussion on continence by saying that he does not mean for men to live forever chaste but to honor matrimony and to take care that sparks of desire do not grow into flames, devouring their wits and all their virtues. Whatever his reason, Elyot indicates that carnal desire is not easily controlled, but the virtuous and wise man can and should succeed in its mastery.

In all this discussion, Elyot seldom indicates that a carnal appetite may cause a king to rule badly, though he does say once that seeds of vice planted during the earliest years may grow wild and produce a poison to destroy the realm. Usually he assumes that the ruler has the duty of setting an example for his subjects by his personal life. Elyot himself seems to have had a continued and deep-seated aversion to adultery and fornication. But it also seems quite probable that in 1531 he was trying to influence the ideas and the conduct of Henry VIII. The conservative nobility who were usually loyal also to the teachings of their church considered that the marriage to Anne Boleyn was incest and a violation of the principle that marriage is a sacrament. Even after the death of Catherine of Aragon many of them resented having a court with Anne as the queen. Earlier or later, they feared that a child of hers might inherit the throne. Just before the king took steps to rid himself of Anne, they were planning to present their views through Jane Seymour if we may trust the report of Chapuys; and even if that ambassador used his facts earlier to the best advantage for Catherine, this time he had no such motivation. There is much other evidence indicating that political and religious conservatives among men, as well as women—and women could not be expected to like the treatment Catherine received—disliked the situation. At least attitudes should be judged in the context of the sixteenth century, not the secular attitudes of the twentieth century.

Thomas Elyot was a conservative in politics and in religious beliefs; he clung to the theology of the old religion all his life. It seems probable then, that his repeated emphasis upon the strength of carnal desires and the need of the governor or ruler to master them had some relation to Henry VIII. No other manual on the education and the resulting virtues of the gentleman, so far as this writer knows, puts such stress upon continence.

When Elyot discusses the political qualities of his governor or prince, he again demands an excellence that sharply limits his conduct. He certainly never assumes the Machiavellian extreme that the duty of a governor is to help his ruler get whatever his heart desires. He never suggests that expediency, concealment, or complete duplicity is necessary in the business of state or that his ideal rulers or governors may have to deal with others who do not operate solely on the principles of reason and justice. He does not encourage absolutism. (Louis XIV is a good example of real absolutism. He had the power to increase old taxes or to levy new ones; to help himself to funds in the public treasury for war, personal gifts, and extravagant living; to sign an order putting a man in prison for any length of time without legal proceedings; and to call before him any case being tried in the courts and then to decide it as he wished.)

Though some scholars have advanced the theory that Elyot wrote the *Governour* to support the absolute power of the king, he does not seem to have in mind that aim. He did not make changes in the first three chapters, after the work had been completed, to support the king's power and thus to please him and Cromwell; nor, in the opinion of this writer, is there convincing evidence that he made any last-minute changes. The plan he mentioned for a second volume has been suggested as evidence—perhaps by those who have not duly considered his statement when he published *The Image of Governance.* His use of tenses in the early chapters of the *Governour* has been offered to support the theory that he made changes for political reasons; but in these chapters he usually employs the future, saying time after time, "I shall, I wyll, or I intende." When he does say once, "I have, with no litle study and labours, prepared this warke," he was probably thinking of his planning and collecting of materials before he wrote. He could hardly have assembled all his examples hastily after he ceased to be clerk of the Council. The fact that Berthelet, the king's printer, published the *Governour,* has also been tentatively suggested as evidence that Elyot intended his opening chapters to support the king. However, Berthelet did not limit the work of his press to orders from his ruler. Actually he published all the works of Elyot and the editions of them that appeared while the author was still living, and some of them were probably indirect attacks on the king.[7]

The most important evidence that Elyot did not change his first three chapters to please Cromwell and the king lies in the limitations he places on the king's power in those chapters. On the first page of the *Governour* he limits the ruler when he defines a public weal as a living body including many degrees of people but ruled by equity and reason. He continues to restrict him when he demands that he have greater understanding than others but use it for the welfare of the people, including all his inferiors, not for his own pleasure. The best government, he says, is that of one ruler, but one who acts only for the weal of his people. Like the sun in heaven (who sheds its brightness on all, as Elyot says later), like the bee without prick or sting who controls the hive for the common good, like God himself, a king should rule with the highest wisdom and justice.

When Elyot comes to grips with the qualities of a governor or other man with authority, in Books II and III (as these men should develop from the education outlined in Book I), he continues his strong emphasis upon their duties and obligations. Discussing majesty, he assumes that the quality is rooted in personality and character. For example, Ulysses the king, shipwrecked and cast naked onto the country of Alcinous, was majestic in his countenance and his speech. A man of authority has the right to proper apparel and to house furnishings that accord with his status; but only a king may sometimes approach magnificence (II, ii, iii, x; III, xxi). After granting these rights to governors or others responsible for government, Elyot continues discussing strict limitations. A king is not above the law, he says, but is obligated to obey his own laws, including those he has instituted for his people. Alexander Severus, the subject of his *Image of Governance* ten years later, is used here, in III, iii, as an outstanding example. Elyot also discusses the duty of rulers to enforce good laws, as it is the duty of a subject to obey them; he supports the idea by a discussion of vagrant lawbreakers. Such persons would not exist, he feels sure, if the laws for the control of idle persons, vagabonds, and those indulging in unlawful games and apparel had been properly enforced (II, vii); he does not consider whether these people are the victims of social or economic causes beyond their control.

When Elyot discusses affability, he makes a strong plea for the freedom of subjects to speak their minds, even to make extreme personal comments; again his examples are kings or other rulers. Both the realms and their rulers have suffered damage where freedom has been curbed. Marcus Antoninus, emperor of Rome; the noble Trajan; and King Phillip (father of Alexander the Great), all permitted men to speak freely to them. The Emperor Augustus, when he was playing a musical instrument in public, heard a poor man say to others in a loud voice, "Seest thou nat howe this voluptuouse lechour tempereth al the worlde with his finger?" Instead of being angry at the man, the emperor tempered his own conduct in future. Alexander the Great and Julius Caesar, in the later years of their rule, might have escaped difficulty or assassination if they had not refused to listen to the free opinions of others (II, v).

When he restates the seven articles that men should meditate on when they assume authority (II, i) he minimizes the honor and privileges and stresses the cares and the obligation to others that rulers assume: all power comes from God and may be taken away again by Him; rulers should consider their cares and burdens, not their honors, and should not treat revenues or treasures as booty; with large domains and greater responsibilities, they will have less time for recreation and personal pleasures; they should try to make their virtues equal to their rich ornaments and garments; and they should not consider subjects as private possessions, like horses or mules. Let rulers remember also that the higher their rank, the more their private behavior is known and imitated. While these ideas are not original with Elyot, he continues to support them with individual details.

Even when Elyot argues in support of nobility he says it originates in virtue and in the service of a man to his country; and the longer it has lasted, the more the virtue is to be honored. When he discusses self-knowledge, in III, iii, as a requisite for any man of authority, he emphasizes a man-to-man equality based on the Bible, the classics, and perhaps some individual thinking. Each man's soul is completely his own, and his body is his own; no one may claim any ownership over either without his consent:

> And of that same mater and substaunce that his soule is of, be all other soules that nowe are, and have ben and ever shall be. . . . In semblable astate is his body, and of no better claye (as I mought frankely saye) is a gentilman made than a carter, and of libertie of wille as moche is gyven of god to the poore herdeman, as to the great and mighty emperour.

Every man also has equal benefit from the dew of heaven or the brightness of the sun. Authority is only a heavy cloak, glittering in the eyes of the partly blind, but heavy to the one who wears it in its true fashion. A man who rules others is mortal, like other men, and his body is subject to the same decay. He is superior only in his understanding.[8] It would be hard to match his eloquent statements in any Continental source, or for that matter in the work of any other English writer at that time, though Erasmus and More might agree with his ideas. In these passages and others, Elyot frequently warns a ruler against pride. In III, xvi, the chapter on the vice of ambition, he says that men of courage and appetite, when they attain authority, tend to think that anything they desire is lawful, and that no one else should contradict, control, or warn them against even outrageous actions.

Elyot points out another duty of rulers when he discusses reverence to God, both the outer signs and the inner feeling, as part of justice. His comment, in III, ii, is tinged with a timely urgency:

> By whiche oppinion they seme to despoyle hym [God] of reverence, which shal cause all obedience to cease, wherof will ensue utter confusion, if good christen princes meved with zeale, do nat shortely provide to extincte utterly all suche opinions.

Elyot does not forget to mention the duty of rulers to observe their commitments to other nations. In III, vi, he cites the example of Joshua who kept his pledge to the Canaanites even though they had deceived him. He concludes:

> By this example it appereth in what estimation and reverence leages and trues [sic] made by princes aught to be had; to the breache where of none excuse is sufficient. But lette us leave princes affayres to their counsailours.

Elyot advises his men of authority to become men of learning. In I, xii, he again deplores their pride and their assumption that it is a reproach to have education or to be called a great clerk. He uses Henry I, called Beauclerk, and other rulers as examples of men whose learning led them to greater wisdom in ruling. He deplores the fact that men of authority in his own time seldom care for learning. In III, xxiv, he asks that men in authority have understanding, the most important part of the soul, he says, the part that is concerned with the causes of things and that analyzes issues with care before deciding on action. Among examples he includes the emperor, Marcus Antoninus, who was called the philosopher but not in reproach. Being already inclined to virtue, he added great learning; as a result he became a wonderful and a perfect prince.

In III, xxv, he continues to explain that learning for rulers is that form of experience which we call history. As he explains it, history includes the actions, counsels, and forms of government of the nations in the past, including the records of the Old and the New Testament, and even anatomy and natural history. But it includes present conditions also, since any governor should travel to all parts of his country and live in each part long enough to investigate conditions, events, and actions of the men engaged in the work of government. As a result, he may be able to reward diligent helpers and to correct or to expel the ineffective ones. A man of learning, whether he is a prince or a helper, will be ready to use good counsel, including all the good counselors who are available—those who are able to view problems objectively. He should realize that many counselors are desirable and should value those who place the public welfare above their personal affairs.

In his discussion of counselors, also, Elyot frequently implies a concern with sovereigns, not merely their helpers. His suggestions that good Christian princes should act to prevent confusion in religious opinions, that all countries should honor commitments between nations, and that carnal indulgence might lead to the destruction of a kingdom are not only aimed at rulers but they often have a timely and an urgent sound.

By the time he wrote the *Governour,* Elyot had a somewhat varied experience in governmental affairs of early Tudor England. His concept of governors included men like his father and himself, civil servants who delivered the gaols, held assizes, and acted as sheriffs or as justices of the peace on the six circuits of England. With experience in such positions as these and with more than six years of service as clerk of the Council, he must have come face to face with varied examples of good and bad government in England. Perhaps he made a sound statement in the Proheme of the *Governour* when he said that he had been continually trained in some daily affairs of the public weal of England almost from his childhood. Since his turn of mind was philosophical, however, he went to the root of the matter as he saw it by stressing education for princes and governors, to develop high ideals for private and public life.

Since Elyot's ideas in the *Governour* about nobility and degrees in government have an aristocratic bias, it seems reasonable to mention again the question whether he had been conditioned somewhat by early contacts with manor life in the West Country, with the degrees in government represented by the manor lord, steward, bailiff, free tenants and serfs. His assumption that nobility is only the praise and the surname of virtue seems a bit naïve, like his implication that the older nobility have displayed a long-continued virtue. But whether the views rise from naïveté or from a desire to be tactful, he limits these ideas in III, iii, by the statements cited earlier that every man owns his own body and soul, that the gentleman is made of no better clay than the carter, that all have the same right to the dew of heaven and the brightness of the sun, and that the poor herdsman and the powerful emperor have the same freedom of the will. Perhaps his religious orthodoxy, also fostered by his early background, and his extensive readings in the classics, led him to these modifications of aristocracy. At least his combination of these ideas seems individual.

In discussing aesthetic education Elyot tends to begin with general ideas and support from reading, but he quickly becomes his own man and writes as an Englishman to other Englishmen. He also mingles the artistic and the practical, like one who understands the temper of his audience. He places the beginning of these pursuits in the early period of the child's life, while he is still under a tutor, but he includes a discussion of their value to mature men. He begins his plea for training in music with an emphasis on the child's need for recreation. When he quickly adds that the music must be used moderately "without wanton countenance and dissolute gesture," he offers as his first support of the idea examples from scripture. He mentions David, whom God has chosen according to his own heart, as one who delighted in music all his life and used his harp to free Saul from the evil spirit. Then he turns to classical examples, continues to warn against sensuality and too much time given to music, suggests that the tutor will teach the child not to give public performances like a common minstrel, and invokes both Aristotle and Plato to support his idea that the understanding of music with its harmony helps in understanding the public weal (I, vii).

When a child wishes to paint or carve (Elyot comments in I, viii), nature is benevolent to him and he should not be rebuked but provided with an excellent master, for the time when he is not engaged in more serious learning. Elyot uses classical support here, perhaps because he lacks examples from scripture. The governor will find the skill useful later in military affairs, such as devising engines of war, improving those already in use, or describing enemy country to show his army or navy the dangerous places. In visiting his own dominions also, the governor will be able to "sette them out in figure" so that his eyes will tell him in future how to employ his resources in safeguarding and developing the country. He adds that the skill in portraiture will be an enticement to all other learning: he will understand and retain better what he reads; and where the lively spirit or grace of the thing is expressed, he will be moved or persuaded more than by oral or spoken words. Of course the gentleman will never display his work to the public like a common painter or carver. But the development of skills will give the governor judgment, not only artistic judgment but wisdom and understanding for other serious studies and affairs. He cites Lactantius for an additional idea that skill results in virtue and that virtue brings happiness. These are large claims. Perhaps one might suggest, since he arranges them approximately in this order, that he is considering his practical English audience. In I, xiv, he talks with frank directness to those English parents who never consult the inclinations of a child but put him early to the study of the common law. In England especially, he says, if children wish to paint, carve, engrave, embroider, or practice any other art that is "commendable concernyne invention," the parents are displeased and hurriedly apprentice them to tailors, weavers, fullers, or even cobblers. As a result, he says, we English suffer the loss of many good wits, we are inferior to all other people in the arts, and when we wish to have any work done in arts or crafts, we must employ aliens.

Though Elyot does turn his discussion of painting and carving, with other related arts, to the reproach of Englishmen, it seems more likely in this area that he might have been influenced by Castiglione. There is an emphasis in the *Courtier* on the military uses of painting and drawing and also on its more artistic merits. It is followed by a long discussion on the relative merits of painting and sculpture,[9] and in this comparison of the two arts Elyot does not follow Castiglione.

Elyot certainly wrote for and about Englishmen when he discussed the study of law, using ideas, as he told us, that were partly drawn from his experience. He suggests that the future governor continue liberal studies until twenty-one and then begin study of the common law, to avoid the risk of confusion, boredom, loss of self-esteem, and an urge to escape into improper pastimes. Elyot is also deeply concerned with the language used in law and law pleadings. Instead of the "barbarous" law French, he wishes England to adopt either English, Latin, or correct French. Later, when the king appointed Nicholas Bacon and others to investigate education at the Inns of Court, he asked the members of the committee to suggest ways in which the students might become better learned in Latin and French while they were studying law. In their formal report to him the committee recommended that inner barristers plead in Latin, that others plead in standard French, and that all do whatever they could to banish the corruption of those tongues. As a help to this improvement they suggested that readers be found, one with an excellent knowledge of Latin and Greek, and one with a solid knowledge of French; these men were to read to the law students some oration, book of rhetoric, or book on government, to further their knowledge of these languages. The readings should be given every Monday, Tuesday, and Wednesday, except on festival days, both in term time and in the vacations.[10] One cannot argue with certainty that the committee made the recommendation because of Elyot's comments in the *Governour,* though it is possible that his words had some influence. But it is certain, whatever else may be doubtful, that Elyot's discussion of law concerns mainly the English common law and that he is talking to English readers.

Elyot had only to look at English life to find encouragement for his suggestions that the young gentleman learn dancing, singing, and performing on musical instruments. Of course he had read Aristotle and Plato; he may have heard Palmieri's theory that the ideal citizen is also a man of personal culture, with training in literature, drawing, singing, and other music; he may have known Castiglione's ideas on literature and languages, dancing, drawing and painting, singing, and performing on musical instruments. If Elyot knew the *Courtier,* he was completely able to reject the emphasis on these skills as a means to making the gentleman an ornament at court and a center of attraction for the ladies.[11] It also seems reasonable to suppose that with the help of Aristotle and Plato, Elyot might have said much the same things without Castiglione.

The court of the young Henry VIII and Catherine of Aragon would have given him inspiration about music and dancing, assuming that he merely heard reports of royal activities. King, courtiers, and the young Catherine loved music and dancing, as Mattingly tells us when he describes her part in the festivities at her first meeting with Henry VII and Prince Arthur:

> After supper she invited Henry and his son to her chamber, where minstrels had been summoned . . . Catherine and two of her ladies danced one of the stately dances of Spain. Catherine loved dancing and was proud of her skill in it. Next she and a partner danced a rapid dance, as gay and furious as the other was langorous and slow. . . .[12]

Probably the tastes of the young Henry VIII need little documentation. Mattingly comments that the king's pastimes in the early years were innocent enough; he loved especially tournaments and masks, followed by dancing. He was also a musician who encouraged musicians:

> The English school of music bloomed, and Italian virtuosi hurried towards a land where excellence was rewarded with a fortune. The king himself was a passionate musician, played the organ and the virginals, was a master hand on the lute, and composed some charming pieces. He was a keen, discriminating, sometimes relentless critic of every kind of musical skill. . . .[13]

Elyot's training at the Middle Temple probably furthered his emphasis on music, dancing, and courtly behavior, even if he could find plenty of comment on these skills by other writers. As we have seen in earlier chapters, Fortescue told us in the fifteenth century that both the lesser inns and the Inns of Court are "a kind of academy of all the manners that the nobles learn. There they learn to sing and to exercise themselves in every kind of harmonics. They are also taught . . . to practice dancing and all games proper for nobles, as those brought up in the king's household are accustomed to practice." These activities and their purpose are confirmed by the records

of the Inns of Court; by William Herbert, who was concerned with the time of Henry VIII; and by the so-called
Bacon report in the later years of the reign of Henry VIII,
containing the comment that the Christmas feasts were
kept only that the young men might learn "how to use
themselves."[14] Thomas Elyot did not need the inspiration
of Castiglione, or other Italians, even if he knew their
work, for his emphasis upon music and dancing.

     Elyot's discussion of archery and the longbow in the
last chapter of Book I is thoroughly English, except for a
brief mention, at the beginning, of Cicero, Alexander
Severus, and of Galen's ideas on exercise. Elyot's discussion owes nothing to the earlier French work *Lart
Darcherie;* for that, at least in its available form, consists
of technical directions on making and handling bows and
arrows.[15] Elyot owes nothing to Castiglione, for he does
not mention archery in the *Courtier* as a sport for young
gentlemen. It owes nothing to any available work by any
other French or English writer. Elyot's ideas come direct
from English life, and the *Governour* appeared fourteen
years before Ascham's *Toxophilus.*
     Archery excels other exercises, Elyot says, because it
uses the muscles of both the upper and lower parts of the
body; it also enables the archer to develop his strength by
gradually choosing larger bows, and to measure his exercise by himself and not by an opponent. In some of these details and in his discussion of shooting at butts and at rovers
or pricks, Elyot speaks as if from firsthand experience.
Archery is the strength of the English in wars, Elyot says
with an outburst of patriotism which he did not borrow
from any foreign writer. It is useful in hunting deer and
other game, and thus it brings both pleasure and profit.
The longbow is superior to crossbows or handguns; these
have been introduced into England by the cunning of our

enemies, so that they may destroy us. Elyot then laments
the decay of archery. We make ordinances, laws, and
statutes to further the use of the longbow; but we mock
ourselves by failing to enforce them, just as we fail to enforce other good laws.

Elyot's ideas on archery echo his own times, as one
can see by looking at the statutes of Parliament. From
about 1285 or earlier, laws were being passed in the reigns
of many different kings to encourage archery and the use
of the longbow. A statute of 1511–1512 will illustrate
English thinking before the *Governour* was written. The
statute begins by reciting these details: the longbow has
been our defense both at home and abroad; crossbows
should not be used; however we lack good bows of yew,
and many men are not able to maintain the cost of archery.
So the law provides that all subjects under sixty years of
age, except clergy and high justices, shall practice the use
of longbows and keep them in their houses. Fathers and
others in charge of youth shall provide bows and arrows
for those between seven and seventeen and shall "induce
their use." For young men who are servants, masters shall
"abate" from their wages the cost of bows and arrows.
Youths older than seventeen shall provide equipment for
themselves. The justices of gaol delivery, of the assize, and
of the peace shall inquire into these matters and commit
those who fail to observe the law. They are also to see
that butts are placed in all towns and in other places where
people might use them. The law includes other details
about the making and the sale of bows. It provides that
mayors, bailiffs, and sheriffs must make proclamation
about these laws.

In 1533–1534 members of Parliament again attempted to limit sharply the use of crossbows and handguns. In 1541–1542 there were new provisions against the
violation of previous laws and also some new statutes.
These statutes began by deploring the decay of archery,

and the main provisions of 1511–1512 were repeated with additions, to further the use of the longbow. Thus Elyot in the *Governour* was emphasizing ideas on archery which were the concern of the English Parliament.[16]

Elyot may have been spurred to the discussion of archery in the *Governour*, also, because his king was an enthusiastic archer or a supporter of archery through much of his life. In 1515, Pasqualigo reported that the king "draws the bow with greater strength than any man in England, and jousts marvellously."[17] An account of the king's archery at the Field of the Cloth of Gold rests upon the word of Paulus Jovius, but his details seem authentic. According to his account, Francis asked for an exhibition of the English king's skill. As a result, Henry, with a group of his nobles, appeared in the forest garb of England, with a bugle horn of gold, an embroidered case of arrows, and a longbow of fine Venetian yew. Time after time the king shot into the center of the target, and his skill drew bursts of admiration from the spectators.[18] Whether this happened or not, it is clearly what should have happened!

The king's continued interest in archery is proved beyond doubt by the list of expenses relating to the privy purse. In 1529–1532, for example, there are payments to a fletcher, sums spent to buy archery equipment for Anne Boleyn, other amounts for bows and arrows, and a record of payment for a crossbow.[19] (The statutes cited earlier did not forbid crossbows for men of high income but discouraged them for others.) The king encouraged archery and other forms of shooting in August, 1537, by granting a patent to four men of his privy chamber, giving them the right to organize a fraternity of St. George for so-called artillery and to concern themselves with handguns, crossbows, and longbows.[20] Later the organization became the Honourable Artillery Company. The king also took an interest in shooting with the longbow at one time when he was keeping his court at Windsor; he is said to have named the winner in archery contests there the "Duke of Shore-ditch" from the man's birthplace. Later he commended a group of archers who called themselves Prince Arthur's Knights.[21]

Elyot's recommendation of archery as the finest sport for gentlemen, then, is no echo from his reading. At the time archery was becoming obsolete as a practical means of defense because other weapons were superior to the bow and arrow; but Parliament supported it by legislation and Elyot defended it partly for patriotic and military reasons. It was being encouraged for the common people and was in high favor as a sport for gentlemen. Elyot's discussion, one may conclude, reflects the interest in archery of the members of Parliament and the king himself. That interest was expressed years before Roger Ascham published *Toxophilus,* in 1545. Even in the age of Elizabeth, as late as 1590, Sir John Smythe, a first cousin of Edward VI through the Seymours, when he published *Certain Discourses Military,* continued to argue for the superiority of the longbow over firearms.[22]

The reflections of Elyot's own life and individual preferences in the *Governour* tend to indicate that he was writing a book for and about Englishmen, not merely a book in English instead of in Latin. When he uses memories of childhood and country life or pleads for conservation of small birds, he is thoroughly English. In his plea for more translations of the classics by Englismen, his varied comments on rhetoric and wisdom, his discussion of friendship, and his shifts from moralist to appreciator when he uses examples from the arts, his ideas have something individual. His demands about the private life of rulers or governors, especially his reiterated demands for sexual morality, are at least individual if not English; it is probable that he hoped to affect the private life of Henry VIII. His demands about the public life of a man of authority are so stringent that they might be considered individual, but even more individual is his combination of respect for a monarchy and for aristocracy with an unusual emphasis on the equality of peasant and emperor in the ownership of soul and body and in freedom of the will. When Elyot discusses aesthetic education and also legal education he talks from English life direct to Englishmen. He would not have found it necessary to go to the classics, to Italian writers, or to other books for his inspiration about dancing and music—though he certainly read the classics and pershaps some of the other books. He might have found his ideas in his own training at the Middle Temple and in what he heard about the court of the young Henry VIII and the young Catherine of Aragon. As for archery, sources outside England do not seem to exist; and his discussion of it is thoroughly English, based on English history, his observation of life, the statutes of Parliament, and the recreation of Henry VIII. Thus the author of the *Governour* may be rightly described as Sir Thomas Elyot, Englishman.

## CHAPTER IX

### *Ambassador to the Emperor.*
### *1531–1532*

SOMETIME in the autumn of 1531, the king sent Sir Thomas Elyot as ambassador to the court of the emperor, Charles V, the nephew of Catherine of Aragon. Chapuys, who sometimes seemed to know the king's plans almost as soon as he did, was writing the emperor on September 10, 1531, about the new ambassador; he said that Elyot had formerly been in the service of Cardinal Wolsey, but he reported, somewhat erroneously, that he now belonged to the party of the Lady, or Anne Boleyn.[1] Elyot knew of his mission in late August, at least; for the first part of his will, drawn on August 29, assigned thirteen shillings and sixpence extra to every servant who went overseas and remained there with him. The king's detailed instructions to his new representative were dated October 7; perhaps Elyot started about that time. He returned to England near the first of June, 1532. Presumably he had guided the *Governour* through the press of Berthelet before he started to the Continent, but we do not know the exact date in 1531 when it appeared.

Many questions have been raised about this embassy. What training or previous experience fitted Elyot for the post? Why was he chosen? Why was he at the court such a brief time? What kind of ambassador was he? Why was no effort made for some years to repay his financial losses? What was his own attitude to the chief problem of his embassy?

The first question can be answered definitely: he had no previous experience as an ambassador, and he was not sent again. This was his only trip to foreign lands. The theory that he was at the court of the emperor in 1535 has been disproved, though William Roper, early biographer of his father-in-law, recorded a talk between Elyot and the emperor as if it had taken place shortly after More's execution. But the facts seem to be different. On February 21, 1531, Chapuys wrote the emperor that More, he understood, wished to resign his office. While Elyot was at the emperor's court in late 1531 and early 1532, the two must have discussed More's wish to resign: probably at that time the emperor said, "we wold rather have lost the best city of our dominions" than to part with such a counselor. Sometime in 1532, after Elyot's return to England, he reported his talk with the emperor to Margaret Roper, the Clements, and the Heywoods. Roper apparently suffered an understandable loss of memory concerning the time of the talk, since he was writing some twenty years later in the reign of Queen Mary, when it was safe to make records of More's life. Other evidence indicates also that Elyot was in England in 1535, at the time of More's execution; and no other facts support the claim that he was with the emperor in 1535.[2]

The idea that Elyot was at the emperor's court a brief time must be related to the length of time other men, before and after Elyot, served. About 1527–1529 Edward Lee and Jerome de Ghinucci seem to have been the chief representatives of the king to the emperor, though in this period he had so many men coming and going that it is hard to speak with certainty. Like the others, Lee sometimes needed more money, but as a churchman, he appealed to Wolsey or to another as if matters had already been arranged. Like others, he sometimes wrote that it would be a great comfort if he might return home. Both Lee and Ghinucci were churchmen.[3]

In November, 1529, the king sent Sir Nicholas Carew, long his familiar friend and at this time the master of his horse; and with him, Richard Sampson, dean of the royal chapel. They were a layman and a churchman; both were experienced ambassadors. Within a month they were asking the king to help them with the excessive charges or they would not be able to continue. Their stay ended in February or March, 1530.[4]

The next ambassador to Charles V was Sir Nicholas Harvey, a layman, without any previous diplomatic experience; he went alone. Perhaps he was better paid than others; besides his twenty shillings and a daily reward of 6s., 8d., he had the same amounts for his brother later in his stay, at least; and in accounts for 1531, he was granted £57, 16s., as ambassador to the emperor. But Hacket, who relieved him in February, 1531, was heartily welcomed by one who was "werry glad to be dyschargyd of his commyssyon."[5]

Sir John Hacket, Harvey's replacement, had had experience at Antwerp as president of the "English House," if not in regular diplomacy. Like Harvey, he was a layman working alone. But Vaughan, a royal agent in the Netherlands, was soon warning Cromwell that the emperor's men were "the polytikist fellows in all this lond," and that Hacket, though discreet, was not one to reason a matter of great weight. Accounts indicate that Hacket was allowed twenty shillings a day for diets and a lump sum of £15 for sending letters. He served from February to September, 1531, about six or seven months.[6]

If we estimate Elyot's time from November first to June first (and he may have gone sooner) he spent about seven months on the Continent. Part of his time at the last, however, was spent in the Low Countries, in a vain effort to get Tyndale back into England.

After sending the three laymen, Harvey, Hacket, and

Elyot, the king returned to churchmen for a time. Thomas
Cranmer, who followed Elyot, near the middle of March,
1532, had proved himself useful because his early suggestion about consulting theologians and universities on the
marriage had come to the king's ears at the right time. He
was being replaced in the autumn. The emperor acknowledged his recall in a letter of November 18, 1532, but
Cranmer delayed his return to England for other reasons.
Having gone to the Continent with a group of men in
1530, he had had some previous diplomatic experience.
He did not complain about expenses, but he had already
received preferments and was archdeacon of Taunton.
Also the Boleyn family, with whom he had been living at
Durham House, probably saw to it that he did not suffer
financial difficulties.[7]

In the early autumn of 1532, the king was asking
credence at the emperor's court for Sir Nicholas Hawkins,
a churchman trained in civil and ecclesiastical law. He
was paid 30s. a day instead of 20s., and given more than
£447 in advance. But he was concerned because all other
ambassadors had their "meat vessel for their tabul all of
silver," and he disliked to offer his guests pewter or tin.
So he asked permission to have some of the king's silver
made into articles more useful to him—at his own expense.
He made other complaints about lack of funds; he also
reported to Cromwell in August that he had done his best
but these men were immovable. He was one ambassador
who never returned: in January, 1534, he died in the village of Balbase, Aragon.[8]

In November, 1533, arrangements were being made
to send another churchman, Richard Pate, to the emperor,
with elaborate instructions about defending the king's
marriage to Anne Boleyn and his treatment of "the Princess Dowager and the Lady Mary." Pate's financial affairs
were looked after by his uncle, John Longland, Bishop of
Lincoln, who wrote Cromwell asking about the arch-

deaconry of Lincoln for him while he was on his embassy. The bishop explained that Pate's "great charges at this time are beyond what his income will bear."[9]

About April, 1537, Pate was succeeded by Sir Thomas Wyatt the elder, poet, student of foreign literature, and experienced diplomat. Though he had wisdom and insight, as well as an understanding of the emperor, authorities say that he had small success. But by this time the period of acute crisis for Henry VIII was over. (When Catherine of Aragon died, January 7, 1536, he was freed of his worst fear—that a foreign invasion supported by Englishmen might attempt her reinstatement as queen.) Wyatt knew well the fact that embassies are hard on the purse, as he indicated in a poem which is a conversation with Sir Francis Bryan; but he continued to serve the king, even if his money disappeared "like water in a sieve."[10]

Elyot's term as ambassador to Charles V was not brief, comparatively speaking, for the early 1530's. Carew and Sampson had served about six months or less, Harvey perhaps seven months, and Hacket about six months. Cranmer may have served about seven months, though he lingered on the Continent and delayed his return. Elyot was with the emperor at least five or six months; he spent additional time at the king's command in trying to get Tyndale back to England, making a total of seven or eight months.

The question, then, is the reason for the short terms, not merely for Elyot's short term. And why were laymen—Harvey, Hacket, and Elyot—each sent alone between 1530 and 1532? Was Henry so engrossed in his passion for Anne Boleyn that he neglected his own interests? Did he feel that laymen could talk more boldly about questions of marriage? Had all the arguments based on theology and the canon law been exhausted, at least for a time? Was the king playing for time, unable to make up his mind about a future course of action?

Perhaps there is no single and no absolute answer. But Henry was a shrewd and a determined man. During these same years he was carefully drawing the church into his power, persuading Convocation to declare him head "so far as the law of Christ allows," threatening to withhold the first fruits, and using these and other actions like moves in a game of chess. It is hard to believe that he was neglecting his own interests. He may have been playing for time. At least these short-time appointments of laymen came when he was most uncertain about his future course of action, most fearful about a complete break with Rome, and still hopeful of getting what he wanted without separating from the larger church and without war. The intentions of Charles V were probably not as clear to Henry then as they now seem to historians who look back with a larger perspective.

After August 23, 1532, when Archbishop Warham died, Henry began living with Anne Boleyn as if she were his wife. Some kind of marriage ceremony was performed, perhaps in January, 1533; and she was crowned queen on the first of June.[11] If these are the facts, as they seem to be, the record is a remarkable one for a king who was not given to patience. He had waited five or six years for the fulfillment of his passion for Anne. Probably he was trying to find an ambassador who could give him assurance that the emperor would not make war, and he was impatiently calling each man back to question him in person.

Such an aim is certainly emphasized in the instructions to Elyot, summed up in Chapter I: "Trusty and right well beloved, we greet you well, and thinking it expedient to fish out and know in what opinion the Emperor is of us, and whether despairing of our old friendship toward him, or fearing other our new communication with France, he seeketh ways and means that might be to our detriment or no. . . ." That is, does the emperor intend to wage war? Then, when Elyot reported to the king, on his return, the king questioned Elyot in great detail, even on things that had already been reported fully in the dispatches. If or while he was playing for time, perhaps laymen, each staying for a brief period, could serve him well. But when he had crossed his personal Rubicon by acknowledging Anne as his wife, he could let his ambassadors stay longer.

Elyot himself had also been trying to make his short term shorter. He must have asked for a recall about February, 1532, or sooner. When he wrote to the Duke of Norfolk on March 15, he thanked him for presenting so benevolently to the king his own desire to return to England. But the king, he said, had ordered him to remain in Brussels for the apprehension of Tyndale. The details seem to imply that Elyot had made a request, that the Duke had answered him, and that Elyot was now thanking the Duke for his answer—a suggestion that some weeks had passed.[12] There is also evidence that Elyot's wife had appealed to the king about her husband's return home. Chapuys wrote the emperor reporting the recall; he had asked the king about the reason. He adds, "the king told me that he had been recalled merely on his wife's application."[13] Though this phrase has been interpreted to mean the wife of the king and though the ambiguous pronoun might mean that grammatically, other considerations make that interpretation improbable. In 1532, the king, when speaking officially, had no wife. Especially in talk with the ambassador of the emperor, he would have called Catherine of Aragon the Princess Dowager. He was steadily trying to persuade the pope and the emperor that he was a bachelor who had been living in sin through no fault of his own! Early in 1532 he would not have called Anne his wife, to Chapuys or to anyone else. Nor would Chapuys have used the word *wife* of either Catherine or Anne. Usually in his letters to the emperor he spoke of Catherine as "the queen," and of Anne Boleyn as "the lady." Sometimes he called Anne "the king's lady," or "the king's mistress"; or when moved to unusual wrath, he referred to her as "the concubine," or "this cursed Anne." But when the phrase is interpreted as Elyot's wife, it becomes completely natural. Margaret Elyot may have backed her husband's request by appealing to the king; and even if she had not done so, the reason was a tactful one to offer the emperor's ambassador.

Why was Elyot chosen as an ambassador at all? He was not named because he supported the absolute power of the king by some hasty changes in the opening chapters of the *Governour;* for even in those chapters he carefully limited the power of a ruler by insisting that he rule with wisdom and justice, for the good of the whole people, not for his own pleasures. Certainly he was not sent because he was known as a literary man on the Continent at this time; for he had just published the first book to appear under his name. It was in English, not Latin.

Elyot may have been selected because he had been a friend of Cromwell for years, because he was well known to Sir Thomas More, or even because he was known to the king through his six and a half years of work as clerk of the Council. Elyot did have some qualifications. Though he was without training in canon or civil law, so far as we know, he was imbued with knowledge of the Greek and Latin classics, and presumably was capable of using good Latin. Also he had practical experience from years of service on many government commissions and from his observations of the king's Council. Elyot was a far better man to send than Nicholas Harvey, unless Harvey had some concealed qualifications. Probably he was a better ambassador than Hacket, in spite of Hacket's experience on the Continent; for as a reader and a philosopher Elyot surpassed Hacket in reasoning "a matter of great weight." Elyot's training at the Middle Temple had also prepared him for the same behavior that the nobles used at court, and the aristocratic tone of the *Governour* may have helped the king to the belief that he would make a good ambassador. It is also possible that the Proheme of the work served to remind the king of Elyot's faithful service in the past.

One might surmise, also, that Elyot had a recognized ability to use tactful and even persuasive language. This skill appears both in the Proheme and in the *Governour* itself, and the book was probably available to Cromwell and the king before Elyot was selected for the emperor's court. Evidence that he had tried to use such a skill and thought he had succeeded appears in his letter to Cromwell, November 18, 1532, the first of the two in which he asked reimbursement for his financial losses. He had really been able to affect the emperor, he said:

> God is my judge that in my replications I have seen him change countenance, which, as they know that have been with him, is no little thing. . . . awaiting opportunity and using . . . silken words, as was the counsels of King Darius' mother, I attained with him such familiarity in communication, that he used with me more abundance of words than (as some of his Council confessed) any ambassador before me had found in him, which I marked diligently and provided the better to serve my master according to his expectation. . . .[14]

Elyot seems to be arguing here on the basis of the persuasive qualities that he had been expected to use; other parts of the letter indicate his disappointment that the king's opinion of him had diminished and he had not been called to membership in the Council.

What kind of ambassador was Elyot? Judging from his own accounts, he worked hard at his job, spending his own money so that he and his servants might make an appearance worthy of his king, giving sums to get information about the emperor or about Tyndale, and securing a real response from Charles V. The only available comments from others are also favorable. As early as December 9, 1531, Stephen Vaughan, in sending Cromwell a letter Elyot had written at Tournai, suggested that Elyot had been without letters a long time; since he was inexperienced in these parts, he wished answers from the king. Vaughan added that if he had a little help he would "soon do right well." In May, 1532, Augustine de Augustinis, formerly Wolsey's physician and at this time a sort of informer for Cromwell, wrote that Elyot had left the emperor's court, "to the great regret of all."[15] But whether Henry was satisfied with Elyot or any other ambassador in these critical years is another question. Apparently he expected his diplomats to accomplish the impossible—without spending reasonable sums of his money.

What was Elyot's real feeling about the chief problem of his embassy? He pursued the hard road later of trying to serve both Catherine and the king, or, rather, as he might have said, to serve the king truly by working for Catherine. Nor is it realistic to suppose that he had been seduced into this opinion after he reached the emperor's court. Thousands of people in England remained loyal to Catherine. If Henry had tried to imprison her in the Tower, thousands of Londoners would have risen to her support, from emotional devotion to her as a person, from aristocratic preferences, from religious attitudes, or from all of them together. Elyot tried to remain loyal to the religious principles that Catherine held (though he also tried to avoid getting into trouble when he explained those principles to Cromwell); and he consistently supported the aristocracy. Though his known attempts to further the cause of Catherine of Aragon were made after his embassy, it seems reasonable to suppose that his sympathies had always been with her.

Some agreement about terms seems necessary in order to discuss the religious differences of this period. We cannot speak of people as Catholic or non-Catholic; for even those who advocated sweeping changes in doctrine probably still thought of themselves as Catholics. We cannot use the terms *Church of England* and *Protestant,* since they were not yet in common use; and we cannot accurately evaluate ideas of the 1530's and the 1540's with those established by the Elizabethan compromise. We cannot speak of a loyalty to Rome without qualifications, since the doctrine of papal infallibility belongs to a later era; and to Sir Thomas More, the basic guides were the decisions of general councils.

Through this work the term *a conservative* (or a follower of the old religion) will be used in contrast to *a reformer* (or a follower of the new religion). A conservative usually regarded the Pope as the earthly head of a universal church of Western Europe, wished to follow the decisions of general councils, and defended the theology of that church against the reforms advocated by such men as Frith, Luther, and Tyndale. An intelligent conservative believed in the seven sacraments (with emphasis on the Mass and the doctrine of transubstantiation), in Purgatory, in the celibate life for priests and for others who had made it a mature choice, in worship of the ideas represented by images but not of images, in worship of saints as the good servants of God but not as God, in some pilgrimages and miracles, in fasting, in the need for contrition or satisfaction as a part of penance, and in the right of a priest only, not a lay man or woman, to receive confession or consecrate the elements. A reformer opposed some or all of these views.

The intelligent religious conservative believed that the way to study scripture is to use reason, virtue, prayer, and all secular learning; to consider the comments of the old holy doctors—Jerome, Augustine, Basil, Ambrose, Cyprian, Gregory—and to test ideas by the articles of the Catholic faith received through the church. If a text seems to

oppose an article of the faith the reader should know (as
Saint Augustine said) that there is a fault in the writer or
translator; and in later centuries there may be a fault in
the printer. An intelligent conservative refuted the view
that all religious truth is contained in scripture and that
every man, with only the help God has promised him—
without learning or the use of human reason and without
the help of teachers approved by the church—may be his
own interpreter of scripture. He denied that faith only,
with baptism but without good works, is sufficient for
salvation. He believed that man has freedom of the will,
with the grace of God, to move toward his own salvation,
instead of letting destiny determine his actions and his
salvation or damnation.

A conservative, if intelligent and informed, believed
in eliminating corruption, immorality, extravagant display, and perhaps some unessential formality, within the
existing structure of the church. However, he might defend ceremonies as a means of increasing reverence, such
as an early hour for service, appropriate clothing for attendance, worship in churches and not the mere feeling
of worship in the heart; he suggested the use of candles,
the crucifix, other ornaments, including costly gold chalices, and beautiful churches, because men should honor
God with their best possessions.

Sir Thomas More, an intelligent and informed conservative, supports these ideas in his *Dialogue concerning
Heresies,* or *Dialogue concerning Tyndale,* as he refutes
the views of Frith, Luther, and Tyndale. Elyot defends
most of these views, and when he defends one of them it
seems safe to assume that for the time and in relation to
that idea, he is a religious conservative. So far as circumstances permitted, he remained a conservative about essential doctrines.

As a religious conservative, what did he admit to the
emperor in private talks? When he spoke frankly, did he

admit that he considered the marriage between Henry and Catherine as one of the seven sacraments of the church? Did he admit that he considered any sexual relationship between the king and Anne Boleyn not only as a vicious passion but as incest, because Anne's sister had earlier been his mistress? We do not know what he admitted, but if truly a conservative in religion, these were the things he believed while he was at the emperor's court and after his return.

Actually we have little information about Elyot's embassy or about his reactions to foreign lands. Though he and his wife must have exchanged letters, in the months of his absence from England, not one scrap of such correspondence remains. His only extant comment appears in his letter to the Duke of Norfolk, written from Ratisbon, in March, 1532. He had promised the king, he says, to write to the duke about Nuremberg, especially religious conditions there. But first he makes brief comments on Worms and Spires. The majority of the people in Worms are Lutherans or Jews, with a few other indifferent ones under a bishop who sees little and drinks much. Spires keeps the faith but carries a little too far the *sanctorum communionem;* lovers with their paramours sitting beside them ride about in horse-drawn vehicles, the horses being decorated with bells that jangle loudly, and the women having their heads uncovered except for embroidered chaplets. This display seems to be the triumph of Venus or of the devil—or both.

Nuremberg, a well-populated city, Elyot describes as the best-ordered public weal that he had ever seen. The food supply is abundant, and though the townspeople openly eat flesh, his party was supplied with fish. Elyot was not permitted to have his own chaplain sing Mass for him but was compelled to attend the public one in a church. He describes in some detail the differences between this service and the English one as he knows it, including the fact that these people may take communion without first going to confession. Elyot and the French ambassador left, to avoid taking communion, and the people were astonished at their departure. The priests have wives, the fairest ones in the city, a situation that Elyot professes to like, though his comment is probably intended to be humorous; and all the women here, they tell him, are gentle in spirit. Elyot also reports on the excellent equipment for horsemen and the weapons ready for war, the amazing supplies of grain, and the success with which they keep grain in storage for many years.[16]

These are not the comments of an adventurer who enjoys the customs of strange lands. Instead, Elyot is eager to be home again and expresses the hope that he may soon be talking with the duke in person. His comments are religious and moral or they are the practical details about a well-managed public weal.

As a religious conservative and a political conservative as well, or a defender of the old aristocracy, Elyot naturally felt loyalty to Catherine of Aragon. Shortly after he reported to the king on his embassy, he told Chapuys on June 3, 1532, of the arrangement he had made to furnish a certain De Puebla with a report in cipher of his talk with his ruler. That talk, he added, had been "greatly to the benefit" of the emperor, the queen, and "principally of the king his master." He had spoken frankly, and he believed that his words had had a beneficial effect. Chapuys' letter also carries the suggestion that Elyot had remonstrated with the king. Again in May, 1533, and in January, 1534, there is evidence that he was reporting to Chapuys in an effort to help Catherine. Again, in 1536, he was giving information to Chapuys in an effort to help Catherine's daughter in her wishes then and to further the chances for an heir that conservative religious people would consider legitimate.[17]

It is the considered judgment of this biographer—

though there will be skeptics, of course—that Elyot's frank talk with the king in June, 1532, was an effort to persuade him to give up Anne Boleyn and to take back Catherine of Aragon as his queen. In December, 1530, Reginald Pole had passionately and spontaneously made a similar appeal, though when he asked for an interview, he had planned to tell the king that he had found a way to support his separation from his queen. Other conservatives in religion were concerned about the conscience and the soul of their monarch in a way that is difficult for secular-minded twentieth-century people to understand. When More begged Chapuys not to visit him, about April, 1531, he explained that such a visit might deprive him of the liberty he had always used in speaking boldly about matters concerning the emperor and the queen, but also about "the welfare, honor, and conscience of his master, and the repose of his kingdom." The phrases, though they are a translation of a report by Chapuys, carry a sense of a religious obligation quite different from a chancellor's duty to be the king's conscience in making legal decisions. Bishop Fisher continued to receive the emperor's messages through a third person but not direct from Chapuys; in January, 1531, he asked that messages be sent to him only in cipher, and he promised his services to the emperor. More and Fisher were both conscious of a double loyalty, to England and to the larger church. No one has accused either of a lack of integrity, and perhaps no one will successfully do so. Until we find positive evidence of a lack of integrity in Elyot, then, it seems better not to assume without evidence that he was perhaps getting a material reward from the emperor.[18] Why should we not believe that he was honestly trying to follow his religious principles and hoping to serve the emperor, the king, and the queen?

Perhaps if Elyot made an effort to influence Henry about his marriage in June, 1532, he would never have undertaken it if he had not been outside England for some months and if his reception at the emperor's court had not given him a greater sense of power than he actually possessed. However, his whole character also—his admiration for his king, his lack of a sense of humor and a sense of proportion, his sense of duty, moral rectitude, and religious attitudes—seems to make such an effort possible. Perhaps those who reject the theory that he asked Henry to take back Catherine should suggest what else at this time might be considered a benefit to the emperor, the queen, and to the king himself. In the early 1530's the crux of Henry's diplomacy was the marriage to Catherine.

Why was Elyot not compensated for the extra expenses of his embassy? A basic reason, perhaps, is that the king permitted the same thing to happen to other men in the diplomatic service. Wyatt's complaint in verse, mentioned earlier in this chapter, points up the usual situation. But Elyot's sense of justice or of property and the amounts he had spent trying to achieve the expected goals led him to write his complaints to Cromwell. In the letter of November 18, 1532, cited earlier, he says that he had spent money to furnish himself and his servants in a manner befitting the ambassador of a king, both at his own table and in other entertainment of strangers, "thereby fisshing oute some knowlege that doing otherwise I sholde have lakkid." The king allowed him twenty shillings a day, but he had to spend forty shillings and sometimes four marks. Since he received the king's money in angels, also, he lost 14d. sterling on every angel. Also he gave many rewards, both to the emperor's servants and to various people who might help him apprehend Tyndale, in the hope of getting information. He was greatly in debt as a result of the embassy, having spent almost six hundred marks above the king's allowance and having borrowed one hundred marks of the king. In the same letter he reported that he had been nominated as sheriff of Cambridgeshire and Huntingdonshire. He begged to be excused from serving; for if chosen by the king, he would have to spend a large sum in that office. He was chosen. There is no record that he received any recompense for some years, and no note appeared in Cromwell's Remembrances to ask the king about money for him. Cromwell often made such notations about other men, such as the one for October, 1533, "To remember Mr. Hackett's diets, and to make suit to the king for the same." The item was also repeated in a second list.[19]

There may have been reasons for the failure to pay Elyot besides the basic one that the king was always slow in paying, if he paid at all. It is possible that the king learned of his report in cipher to the emperor's chaplain, even if he did not find out the contents; but it seems unlikely, because the penalty for it would probably have been positive, instead of negative. At this time, too, the representatives of the emperor were skillful in transmitting information. Chapuys, the persistent, middle-class man, Swiss by birth and Flemish by education, who quickly became Catherine's champion, made intelligence his chief concern. He organized Catherine's former servants, including those of several nationalities; he sometimes used doctors of divinity and doctors of medicine; he listened to courtiers and weighed their motives; he made friends with merchants of several countries; he had a silent Fleming who attended him everywhere, because of his gout, he said; but the valet had unsuspected skill in languages. Chapuys knew all the ways of getting letters delivered without using diplomatic pouches, one of the best messengers being a trusted merchant who had never come under suspicion. If Elyot needed help in 1532 to send his cipher message, Chapuys could have assisted him. In 1532, also, Thomas Cromwell had merely begun to build up a secret service which became good eventually, and he did not break Chapuys' code until 1535.[20]

Another possible reason for the treatment of Elyot is that he did not succeed in getting Tyndale to England. When Stephen Vaughan had failed to accomplish the same thing, Henry had accused him of having Lutheran sympathies himself, and Cromwell had warned Vaughan to be careful. The king had been much interested in Tyndale's doctrine of obedience to the temporal power, as he had presented it in 1528, and then outraged by his attack in 1530 on the plans for a separation from Catherine. Elyot no doubt did his best to capture Tyndale; but as he said in his letter to the Duke of Norfolk, Tyndale was as quick in his wit as he was nimble in escaping pursuit.

Another possible reason for the king's failure to recompense Elyot is that he resented, after he thought it over, Elyot's frank remonstrance with him about his own conduct. Although his account of the talk caused Chapuys to write the emperor, "it is a long time since the king has been remonstrated with in this manner," and Elyot carried away with him the belief that he had had a desirable effect, the king's resentment may have grown after Elyot left him. Future events, of course, indicate that Elyot's talk did not change either the king or the course of history.

Elyot's cipher report to Gonsalvo De Puebla about his talk with the king on his return from his embassy has been noticed before, of course, but it has not been related to the other activities of the emperor's man about this time. Gonsalvo was the son of the former ambassador to England, Dr. Roderigo Gonsalez De Puebla, the patient, astute, and long-suffering diplomat who had managed affairs for Catherine of Aragon before her marriage to Henry. The son was given denization papers in 1508; his status was confirmed by letters patent March 9, 1509, when he was described as the son of Doctor De Puebla, deceased. In a letter to his new father-in-law, Ferdinand,

July 17, 1509, Henry reported that his "chaplain and pre-
centor of St. Paul's . . . Gundisalvus Ferdinandus, son of
the late Spanish ambassador," was now going into Spain.
As he had witnessed the funeral of Henry VII, the marriage of Henry and Catherine, and their coronation, he
could give Ferdinand a full account of them. Henry
recommended him to the care of Ferdinand, calling him a
virtuous man and a member of the English clergy.[21] Apparently he stayed in Spain; for in 1513 he was deprived
of a fourth part of his benefices by a ruling of a previous
Convocation about foreign clergy; and further details
about his activities in England do not appear.[22]

In 1529, Gonsalvo De Puebla was the chaplain of
the emperor. He became of interest to Edward Lee and
other Englishmen when they discovered that he had a
complete file of papers on his father's activities in England,
"a better file than the government possessed, among them
one document of the first importance, a brief of Pope
Julius II, bearing the same date as his bull of dispensa-
tion, and likewise dispensing for the marriage." The brief
assumed that Catherine's marriage to Arthur had been
consummated but it permitted the marriage to Henry
VIII. To Henry and his advisers, this brief was embar-
rassing.[23] We shall never know whether Elyot saw it or
not, but the presumption would be that his sympathies
were already with Catherine, partly because of his association with More but mainly because he remained loyal
to the old religion.

Perhaps the most interesting activities of De Puebla
about this time concerned his efforts to make a firm military alliance between Charles V and the Earl of Desmond
in Ireland. The emperor's instructions, in February,
1529, charged his chaplain, De Puebla, to inquire carefully
about the earl's motives, his powers, his plans for waging
war, and the help he expected from the emperor. In April,
1529, the earl promised to bring into the field 16,500 in-

fantry and 1,500 cavalry, gave exact lists of the additional forces that his relatives and adherents would contribute, reported that a firm league existed between him and Scotland, and asked for ships and large guns to batter walls and breach castles. De Puebla had been instructed to tell the earl that the emperor accepted his services, that he would sign no treaty which did not include him and his people, and that he did intend to wage war on the king of England.[24]

Thomas Elyot was by no means the only Englishman involved at this time in plans against Henry VIII. It has been estimated, with documentation, that a number of groups were ready to join against the king if the emperor had sent troops and if there had been an effective leader in England to fuse them into united action. A northern group included Lord John Hussey, Lord Thomas Darcy of Templehurst, Yorkshire, Lord Dacre of the North, the Earl of Derby (Thomas Stanley), Lord William Sandys, and perhaps Henry Percy, Earl of Northumberland, though there was doubt about Percy. In 1534, for example, Darcy told a trusted representative of Chapuys that 600 earls, knights, and other gentlemen were of his opinion, and that he would himself lead 8,000 men. Such definite statements can hardly be explained away as a momentary fit of temper. A western group was headed by Lord Abergavenny, a son-in-law of the unfortunate Duke of Buckingham; and Sir James Griffith ap Howell was ready to bring in half of Wales. George Talbot, Earl of Shrewsbury, had been frank about his dislike of the king's policies; and Chapuys believed he would either join the rebellion or withhold help from the king. South of them, other men were led by Henry Courtenay (Marquess of Exeter and one of the nearest in succession to the throne); he was encouraged by his wife, the daughter of William Blount, Lord Mountjoy, who had been the chamberlain of Catherine of Aragon. In this group were Sir Thomas Arundel, Sir Henry Parker, Sir George Carewe, and the members of the Pole family— Henry, Lord Montague, and his brother, Geoffrey Pole. In the south and east near London, Lord Edmund Bray reported that twenty peers and a hundred knights were ready to take military action for the queen. These included Sir Thomas Burgoyne, another son-in-law of Buckingham; Thomas Manners, Earl of Rutland; Sir Thomas Kingston, Constable of the Tower; and Sir Thomas Elyot. Even the Dukes of Suffolk and of Norfolk were at times considered possibilities.[25]

Allowing for a certain proportion who might have withdrawn in the face of real danger, these men were a formidable array. The lack was a leader who could fuse them into unified action. If Reginald Pole, who was near in succession to the throne, had returned from the Continent and assumed leadership, Catherine and the Princess Mary were willing to arrange a marriage between him and the princess—or so Chapuys believed at one time. At times there was talk of marriage between Mary and James V of Scotland, an able young man of the right age, who had a valid claim to the English throne. Chapuys could not lead, of course; he could only listen and encourage. Catherine of Aragon could have led, as Henry himself said when he refused to let the Princess Mary move into her mother's quarters when the girl was seriously ill. The queen, he said, is "a proud and intractable woman"; if she decides to act in favor of her daughter, "she might well take the field, raise assemblies of men, and carry on war," just as her mother Isabella once waged successful war against her enemies. But Catherine, who had been moving more and more toward a pacifist position—partly through the influence of More, Erasmus, and Vives—refused to take the leadership or to sanction the outbreak of hostilities. With the exception of situations where her conscience compelled her to disobedience, she refused to disobey the man who was both her husband and her king.[26]

A natural question to ask is why Henry did not take action against men who were technically guilty of plotting treason. In 1534 the king tried an accusation of treason against Lord Thomas Dacre of the North, Warden of the West Marches. The evidence against him was stronger, it is said, than the evidence used to convict Buckingham in 1521, and he was less popular than that unfortunate duke. But though the king had already seized Dacre's property, expecting a verdict of guilty, the accused defended himself so ably and Henry's course was so unpopular that the trial ended in unanimous acquittal—something that had not happened before in the memory of man.[27] After this event, Henry probably found it unwise to start other legal action for fear the indictment of another great man, as long as Catherine was still living, might trigger open rebellion.

But some other procedures may have been an indirect handling of rebellious spirits. For example, Henry detained Dacre after his acquittal, secured from him a confession that he had concealed two letters, and pardoned him only after he had made a cash payment, and had given bond for completing a payment of £10,000 and for his future behavior.[28] Cromwell's dealing with Lord Edmund Bray may be another example. In March, 1535, Bray had asked Chapuys for a cipher so that he might communicate with him safely. About the same time, Cromwell had Lord Bray brought before him for the felony of "multiplying." In June, 1535, Cromwell's Remembrances included the item, "Lord Bray, who is contented to pay."[29] The timing of these events may be a mere coincidence—and it may not.

Later many of these conspirators were tried and executed. In 1537, Lord Thomas Darcy and Lord John Hussey were convicted of treason and beheaded. Though Percy, Earl of Northumberland, avoided indictment, his

brothers, Sir Thomas and Sir Ingelram, were attainted
and executed the same year. Lord Abergavenny had died
a natural death in 1535. Henry struck hard at those who
were near the succession to the throne; he executed Henry
Courtenay, Marquess of Exeter, and Henry Pole, Lord
Montague, on the same day, in December, 1538. Because
Sir Geoffrey Pole broke under torture and gave some
evidence, after trying first to commit suicide, his life was
spared. Margaret Pole, Countess of Salisbury, on little
evidence of guilt, suffered a long imprisonment, with
insufficient clothing in severe weather, before she was
finally executed in May, 1541. By keeping her in the
Tower about two years under hardships the king may have
hoped to bring about the return of her son, Reginald Pole,
from the Continent. Minor conspirators escaped trial,
either because they were unimportant or their attitudes
were never revealed. After the death of Catherine in
January, 1536, ended the thought of action for her sake,
some former plotters, such as Lord William Sandys and
George Talbot, Earl of Shrewsbury, again gave the king
their loyal support. Talbot's courage and fidelity in
raising forces against the rebels in the north, it has been
said, "perhaps saved Henry's crown."[30]

The conflicting loyalties in the early 1530's—adherence to the old religion, desire for revenge when a
member of a family had been unjustly convicted of treason, reaction against the growing arrogance of Anne Boleyn
and her family, scorn for the upstart Thomas Cromwell,
sympathy for Catherine of Aragon and the Princess Mary,
reason and conscience versus allegiance to a king—make
an intricate pattern. Sir Thomas Elyot was one of a large
and powerful company. If he differed from others who
were willing to rebel, it is possible that he was trying
without motives of revenge or personal gain to influence
the king for the sake of the king himself. On his return
from the court of the emperor, he had the courage to talk

firmly and, he thought, persuasively to his sovereign. When he published *Pasquil the Plain,* in 1533, without his name, and *Of the Knowledge Which Maketh a Wise Man,* with his name, in 1533, he was still trying to persuade the king to change his course of action. He may have justified the words he used in his letter to the Duke of Norfolk, in March, 1532, "I am all the Kinges except my soule. . . ."

# CHAPTER X

Pasquil the Plain. Of the Knowledge Which
Maketh a Wise Man. *Events, 1532–1533*

FTER Elyot returned from his embassy in 1532
with a desire to influence his king, life was
apparently a series of disappointments. He was
not called to Council; he was not given any other position
of importance. His name did not appear for several years
on commissions where we might expect it because he was
a member of the landed gentry; at times he was left in
uncertainty about the attitude toward him of Cromwell
and the king. Our information about Elyot in 1532 and
1533 comes mainly from letters he wrote—three to Cromwell, one to Lady Lisle, and one to Sir John Hacket.
Other records of his thoughts and feelings come from two
works he published: *Pasquil the Plain,* 1533 (unless a 1532
copy unexpectedly appears); and *Of the Knowledge Which
Maketh a Wise Man,* also in 1533. In both, he continued
his indirect efforts to influence Henry VIII.

On November 18, 1532, Elyot wrote the first of his
letters to Cromwell because he wished to avoid an appointment as sheriff. He had learned that he was one of the
three from whom the king would choose a man to serve
during 1533 for the counties of Cambridge and Huntingdon. Parts of this letter have been cited in earlier chapters, since it is a main source of information about him

during these years. He begins the letter tactfully: he rejoices at the king's safe return (from Calais, where he had been meeting with Francis I); a fear of some misfortune to his sovereign had made him sleepless. He is happy to know that Cromwell, day by day, is growing in royal favor. Then using the bridge that he has built to his own problems, he says that Cromwell has power to overcome false reports against those who have served the king well; and his own services to the king have not been recognized. Others who have not acted with the same loyalty or have not spent their money for the king have been preferred before him; he has not been made a member of the Council, and his standing with the king is below the favor he enjoyed when he served as a clerk of that body. With these ideas he interweaves a report on his efforts as ambassador and the financial troubles which have come from his embassy. Since he had borrowed from the king, he asks that the king either forgive him his debt, allow him his losses on extra fees and rewards and on the exchange, or give him time to make repayment. He also asks that he may not be the one chosen as sheriff. Cromwell knows, he says, that he does not take any questionable fees while he holds an office; and a sheriff loses about a hundred marks during a year of service. If the king appoints him, he says, he will "never be able to serve him nor to kepe my house. . . ." He is unfitted for the office in these counties, since he knows only an area of three miles or so around his own home.[1] His plea about not knowing the territory is based on the fact that Carlton, Cambridge, had become his chief residence about 1530, when he was knighted, and he had spent some seven months of 1531–1532 on the Continent.

The king did "prick" the name of Elyot for sheriff. So Elyot wrote Cromwell again on December 8. This second letter begins with thanks to Cromwell for the wise counsels he had sent through Elyot's loving friend, Mr. Raynsford. (It would be interesting to know what these

counsels were, but we have no record.) If Cromwell knew
the full situation, and if his "olde gentill nature" has not
changed, Elyot says, he would sympathize and not blame
him. His own devotion to the king does not stem from
hope of reward; he is really faithful to his allegiance and
has a genuine admiration for the king's person and the
qualities of his mind. He summarizes again his difficulties
and financial losses from the Cambridge inheritance, from
his work as clerk of the Council, and from his embassy.
Again he reminds Cromwell that he refuses the fees some
men collect, so that he may live with no suspicion against
him while he serves the king. Since acting as sheriff will
mean a loss of more money and a loss of the esteem in
which people hold him, now that all justice has become
odious, he pleads again to be relieved of the office. But he
does not reproach the king. He is sure that his sovereign
has not been fully informed about his services.[2]

In spite of Elyot's pleas he served the year of 1533 as
sheriff of the two counties, like other landed gentry who
did not dare refuse. As we have seen in earlier chapters,
the office of sheriff was still essential in county government; but as Holdsworth says, it had declined from its
"former magnificence," when the sheriff ruled his county.
But all royal writs came to him: "He had . . . become
the agent to set in motion the complicated process of all
the royal courts, criminal and civil, central and local."
He was responsible for the appointment of an undersheriff, bailiffs of the hundreds, and other essential officials
for county government; and since he was accountable for
their misdeeds, he must be a man of property. He had
charge of the elections of knights of the shire, counted the
ballots, and certified the election of those chosen by the
majority of the freeholders. He saw to it that proclamations were cried or affixed in public places.[3] Thus the
work included clerical duties of a high order, calling for
decisiveness and responsibility, but they were legal admin-

istration. They would not appeal to an ethical philosopher who had hoped to become a member of the Council and to influence the private and public conduct of Henry VIII.

While Elyot was serving his term as sheriff, in April or May of 1533, he wrote Cromwell another letter that indicates his concern for others and his sense of justice. His undersheriff had recommended for knighthood a certain Wawton. Later Elyot found from reliable sources that Wawton did not have an income from his lands of forty pounds a year and that he was educating many sons and arranging marriages for a number of daughters. Hence he begged to have him excused.[4]

Another event in Elyot's year as sheriff may have pleased him. At Michaelmas, 1533, the town of Cambridge made him a payment of 53s., 4d., for the friendship he had shown.[5] Perhaps his sense of rectitude did not keep him from accepting this token of appreciation.

Elyot's letter of December 5, 1533, to Lady Lisle at Calais, is unimportant except as it shows some of his characteristic attitudes. If the lady was Honor Granville, whose first husband was Sir John Bassett, as Croft indicated, she was perhaps a distant connection of the Elyot family. In the letter Elyot thanks her for being a good lady to her servant, Thomas Raynsford, a brother of his friend, Mr. Raynsford, a gentleman usher; he asks her to continue her kindness. Though Thomas has been guilty of wasting his substance at dice, he has thoroughly repented; if he should slip again, a sharp reproof will be effective.[6] Elyot's dislike of dicing and his belief in helping a friend were certainly constant qualities in his life.

Elyot's letters to Cromwell suggest much about the character of the writer: his trust in Cromwell's friendship, his belief that competent service should be rewarded, his efforts to practice justice and other qualities he discussed in the *Governour,* and his loyalty to his king. Perhaps they also suggest an unwordly view of king and court—as if the teachings of the Christian religion and the wisdom of the classical philosophers were the bases of government. Those who use the term Christian humanist might well, it seems, include Thomas Elyot in that select group. Perhaps the second letter to Cromwell also indicates that Elyot was too persistent in asking favors and repayment of funds; he did not remember that he had been permitted in 1528 to buy the wardship of Erasmus Pym and was deriving from it a reasonable profit. But whatever a modern reader may think, so far as we know, Cromwell gave no sign of irritation about his friend's requests.

Certain public events of 1532 and 1533 seem essential background for understanding Elyot's letter to Sir John Hacket and Elyot's literary works published in these years. On August 23, 1532, Archbishop Warham died—just as he had found the courage to word a spirited defense against his indictment for praemunire. On September 1, Anne Boleyn was created Marchioness of Pembroke. In October, Cranmer was summoned home from the Continent to become the new archbishop; he delayed his return partly because he had married a wife in Germany and partly because he was reluctant to accept the office. The pope issued the necessary bulls, and on March 30, 1533, Cranmer was formally consecrated Archbishop of Canterbury. On May 23, he declared that the marriage of Henry and Catherine of Aragon had been void from the beginning. On May 28, he announced that he had investigated the marriage of Henry to Anne Boleyn (though he did not say when, where, or by whom the ceremony had been performed) and that he found it valid. On June 1, 1533, Anne was crowned queen of England.

Seven days after the consecration of Cranmer as Archbishop of Canterbury, on April 6, 1533, Elyot wrote from London to Sir John Hacket, ambassador in the Low Countries, answering a letter that Mr. Raynsford had brought him from Hacket. The important parts of the letter are these sentences:

> We have hanging over us a great cloud, which is likely to be a great storm when it falleth. The king's highness, thanked be God, is in good health. I beseech God continue it, and send his comfort of spirit unto him, and that truth may be freely and thankfully heard. For my part I am finally determined to live and die therein; neither mine importable expenses unrecompenced shall so much fear me, nor the advancement of my successor, the bishop of Canterbury so much allure me, that I shall ever decline from truth or abuse my sovereign lord, unto whom I am sworn . . . I know that there is a God, and he is all truth, and therefore he will grievously punish all falsehood. . . . Ye shall hear, ere it be long, some strange things of the spirituality. . . . Some do say that they digged the ditch that they be now fallen in, which causeth many good men the less to pity them. . . .

The letter closes with the phrase, "Your son and assured friend. . . ."

Elyot included greetings to many other men. According to Croft, these were the Archbishop of Palermo, who was Jean Carondolet, President of the Council of the Low Countries; the Duc de Soria, or Philippe de Croy, who held offices in Hainault under Charles V; Antoine de Berghes, who was made Count of Walhain and Marquis de Berghes about this time; Philippe de Lannoy, Seigneur de Molembais, the Grand Master of Artillery under Charles V; another who may be Adrien de Croy, the Comte de Roeulx, and also his "good bedfellow," whose honesty, patience, and gentle entertainment he never ceases to bring to the notice of English women. These greetings give us our only information about the friends Elyot made on the Continent.[7]

Elyot's use of *importable* (meaning unbearable, unendurable) for the expenses that have not been repaid to
him, seems significant. So does his resolution not to let
either that situation or the advancement of his successor
to the see of Canterbury allure him from the allegiance he
has sworn to his king. The truth in which he is determined to live and die may be the doctrines of the old
religion or his duty to his king or both. Cranmer, of
course, followed Elyot at the court of Charles V; and as
one letter tells us, he had arrived there before Elyot left.
These words about his successor are interesting because
one who must state a resolution against an action has
been tempted, though ever so slightly, and his emotions
have been aroused. Seldom does the conflict between
Elyot's loyalties appear as clearly as it does in this letter.

The ceremonies connected with the coronation of
Anne Boleyn, June first, and Elyot's part in them probably
did nothing to calm his emotions. Elyot and also Sir Giles
Alington, stepson-in-law of More, are both in the list of
many "Knights and gentlemen to be servitors." Alington
is named again twice: in the list of "Servitors from the
dressers for the queen," his name appears; and in the list
of "Noblemen admitted to do service according to the
tenure of their lands," the notation is added, "Sir Giles
Alington to bear the first cup to the queen." Elyot is
named again as the first person in the sublist, "For the
Archbishop."[8] Although Sir Thomas More had refused
to be present at the coronation, apparently Elyot attended
and carried out the duties assigned to him. Judging from
Elyot's letter to Hacket, serving Archbishop Cranmer at
the coronation banquet must have been a humiliation.
But was it a mere accident in a long-delayed coronation?
Or was it both a test and a planned humiliation for the
man who had dared, a year earlier, to speak frankly to
his king?

Early in May, between his letter to Hacket and his

serving Cranmer at the coronation of Anne, Elyot was again trying to do what he could to further the cause of Catherine of Aragon. When Chapuys wrote to the emperor on May 10, he told him that the English people had a great love for him and for the queen—and to Chapuys the queen was always Catherine—but that efforts were being made to give them false information and to change their loyalties. He added that he had this information from others and from the ambassador, Elyot.[9]

*Pasquil the Plain* and *Of the Knowledge Which Maketh a Wise Man,* both published in 1533 so far as our present information goes, deal indirectly with English affairs and were attempts to exert influence on Henry VIII.

There are two editions of *Pasquil;* one in 1533 was issued without the name of the author and with a prefatory statement addressed only to the gentle readers. Toward the close of the work (fol. 29) Pasquil refers to the merry month of May as a time when men are likely to take merrily any words spoken against them; at this time he dares to speak boldly. Whether Elyot meant to suggest in this phrase a date of writing or of publication seems uncertain but possible. Thus the work may have been completed after Elyot wrote his letter to Hacket and before he acted as a servitor to Cranmer at the coronation of Anne Boleyn. *Pasquil the Plain* was published again in 1540, after the tumult and shouting about the king's second marriage had died; this time the author admitted his work by means of a preface, "Thomas Eliot, Knight, to the Gentile reders."[10]

Since there are no available literary references in England to the Pasquil tradition before Elyot's work appeared, he may have learned of it while he was on the Continent. Or he may possibly have seen the dialogue sent by Bishop Bonner to Cromwell, December 24, 1532. In his letter about the gift Bonner said that Cromwell would certainly remember the great statue of Marforius in Rome and also "Mr. Pasquillus."[11] However it seems somewhat more likely that Elyot learned of Pasquil on the Continent, that he began his own work in the latter half of 1532 or the first part of 1533, and that he published *Pasquil* before he began *Of the Knowledge Which Maketh a Wise Man.* These surmises are based largely on the tone of the two works and their ideas.

In the Roman tradition, Pasquil might be a shoe-maker, a schoolmaster, a tailor, or a barber.[12] Once a year, any person had the privilege of lampooning any other, no matter how high his rank, by attaching his comments to the old statue of Pasquil. In his anonymous work, then, Elyot is claiming the privilege of speaking out freely—a principle that he had defended with some feeling in the *Governour.*

*Pasquil the Plain,* Elyot's first use of the Socratic dialogue, so far as we know, uses the classical form to emphasize English subject matter. The main theme of the work is that counselors should speak frankly to a master instead of agreeing with every opinion he utters or every plan of action he proposes to undertake.[13]

The center of the discussion is a master who is clearly a king: there is mention of privy chamber and gallery, but more important, of the fact that Pasquil could be called to court if he would only follow the advice of the others; and when the talk ends, the other two counselors are hurrying back to court. The master has a tendency to wrath and to dishonest affections (appetites, passions, lust, according to the *NED*); thus his mind and his soul are in peril. Since avarice, tyranny, and beastly living will make both man and God hate him, his reputation is also in danger.

The dialogue is carried on by three men. The first,

Pasquil, holds the philosophy of warning his master before it is too late, but of selecting the proper time and place, when the passions are somewhat mitigated, and of speaking reverently with tokens of love toward him. From his childhood, Pasquil has never spoken in earnest to either master or friend anything that he did not believe. Throughout the discussion he insists on his right to free speech and free thought.

Gnatho, the second speaker, uses words to agree with the master in everything, never saying anything that will not be pleasantly received. He is strangely dressed; Pasquil suggests that he has walked late at night and stolen his tippit from some learned doctor. He carries with him a copy of Troilus and Cressida and a New Testament; he picks out detached statements from the Bible and uses them to prove almost anything that he wishes, and he recommends the method to Pasquil as a means to success at court. Pasquil's response to the plan is to say that he couldn't have found a craftier knave to learn from between this place and Jerusalem. Like Erasmus and other humanists of the period, Pasquil is not objecting to the possession or use of the New Testament but to its misuse. In contrast, Erasmus studied a work of scripture as a unit written by a specific human being for a definite audience at a specific time and place, and for a specific purpose—just as he tried to understand a Greek or a Latin play. He, as well as More and Colet, attempted to apply the total meaning of Christianity to daily living. Likewise Pasquil complains that Gnatho's life does not reflect the spirit of the Christian religion. The third character, Harpocrates, a churchman, who is the master's confessor, agrees with him in everything but does so by looking his approval and keeping silent.

The main Socratic questions are these: At what time and place should counselors speak frankly? Would you warn your master or friend if someone were at his back ready to kill him with a sword or were handing him a poisoned cup? Would you, in such circumstances, wish to be warned? How long would you wait to warn? What do you mean when you say you would wait till danger is imminent? Suppose you know the danger only on hearsay or on suspicion? Suppose the danger is withdrawn and thus your master is not convinced that he owes you reward or gratitude? Is your own life or the rewards you might receive to be placed above the welfare of your master or your country? Is the death of your master's soul less important than the death of his body? Doesn't a surgeon sometimes use words as well as deeds in dealing with a patient? Isn't the confessor of the master a physician to the soul? If counselors fail to act, what is left but the grace of God? Will grace enter unless false opinions and vicious affections are first removed by good counsel?

By these Socratic questions Pasquil lifts the discussion from smaller to larger ideas and from the concrete to the moral and spiritual issues. Pasquil uses other concrete illustrations not implied in the preceding questions. For example he concedes that time and place must be carefully chosen for any effective warning to the master. When battle is being joined, when men are already in the heat of a dice game, when men are eating and drinking with pleasure, or when young men and women are banqueting or enjoying other recreation together, we do not then deliver them lectures on what they are doing. Likewise, we should not try to speak frankly to a master while he is angry or when he is becoming wanton. Gnatho compares Pasquil, who is getting no results with his talk, to a miller who keeps on grinding after he knows that the meal will only fall on the floor and be wasted or may fly into his own eyes and perhaps make him blind. Gnatho again illustrates his philosophy of agreement with his master by telling Pasquil to remember that the tenor bell is always in tune, no matter how it rings; if it jars somewhat, he cannot hear it because the sound is so great and his ears are so small. If others find fault he should tell them that what they are hearing is only "a quaver in musike, and became the bell if they had the witte to perceyve it." Such earthy comparisons are a part of the Socratic tradition.

When the clash of opinions is over, with Gnatho and Harpocrates eager to return to court, Pasquil has lost in his efforts to persuade the two counselors that they should be frank with their master. The reason lies in the fact that they cling to their basic motives of personal advancement, trying to persuade their opponent also to cease his vain babbling and thus be called to court. Pasquil adheres to his basic principle that personal position is less important than the condition of church and state and the welfare of the master's soul.

When Pasquil emphasizes through the dialogue the decay in the church, his charges include the decrease in offerings to monasteries with the resulting lack of hospitality that they are able to offer, the small number of pilgrims who go to shrines, the tendency of confessors to adjust rebukes to the amount of money they receive, and the scorn for prelates, saints, and miracles. He deplores the revolt against the church in Germany. He mentions as another result the tendency to despise laws and statutes and to disregard officers of the law, the growth toward subversion of the commonweal, and the possible destruction of the kingdom.

The differences in the *Governour* and in *Pasquil the Plain* are greater than one might expect to find in works written within so short a space of time by the same author. Instead of being courtly and aristocratic in tone (even while being uncourtly about ideas), *Pasquil* is earthy, satiric, bitter; it aims at specifics and at timely situations. It also uses many ideas which Elyot had emphasized in the *Governour*. Besides the right of any subject to speak freely, which he had there defended with many examples, he had put great emphasis on the private life of a ruler, stressing especially sexual morality. At the close of the work he had given several chapters to the need of the ruler for consultation or good counsel. No good counselor, he said, should be passed over, the reasons of each should be heard fully, with every reason expressed being "rightwise," good, and honest. When asked for opinions, a counselor should be free of hate, friendship, or pity. A great number of advisers is an advantage, but each of them should be able to place the general welfare above any private interest. These ideas are basic also in *Pasquil the Plain.*

The timely quality of *Pasquil the Plain* has already been suggested in the serious results that have come about or are threatening because counselors have lacked frankness. Further immediacy is indicated by the fact that Pasquil is Elyot himself—and not only in the arguments he uses. In his letter to Cromwell, November 18, 1532, Elyot had made a comment, tinged with disappointment, on his not being called to Council. Pasquil has not been called; the reason is that he speaks too frankly. As Elyot had remonstrated frankly with Henry VIII, about the first of June, 1532, when he returned from his embassy, it seems fair to suggest that he too was in political eclipse because of his frankness. In the preface to the first edition of his work, the anonymous Elyot identifies his views with those of his chief character when he asks his readers, if they believe that Pasquil speaks truly, to defend him against venomous tongues and "overthwart" wits.

The master himself certainly seems to be Henry VIII. Those who clung passionately to the conservative religion considered the connection with Anne Boleyn as both a vicious affection—a passion, lust, according to the *NED*— and also as incest. That Elyot clung to the conservative teachings of the church is clear from the record of his life and writings. His efforts to help Catherine of Aragon, as long as she lived, suggest his attitude toward Henry's relationship with Anne Boleyn. Perhaps it was fortunate for Elyot that he did not use his name with the first edition of *Pasquil the Plain*. If an enemy had known that the work was his and had accused him of indirectly attacking Henry VIII, it seems doubtful whether he would have been able to clear himself of the accusation.

Though Elyot perhaps had many counselors in mind as he developed Gnatho and Harpocrates, one target may have been Thomas Cranmer, whom Elyot had certainly met at the court of Charles V. In March, 1532, he was writing to Norfolk that neither he nor his successor could have an audience with the emperor, who was suffering because of a fall from his horse. At that time Elyot had a chance to form opinions about Cranmer's views and his pliancy. He had also emotional reactions to Cranmer's appointment as Archbishop of Canterbury and to his own failure to become a member of the Council. However, any surmise about the identity of a counselor is unimportant compared with Pasquil's major concerns—the welfare of the church, the status of the kingdom, and the soul of the master. About this time Sir Thomas More, at least as he is reported to us by Chapuys, had some of the same concern for Henry VIII. When More begged the ambassador not to visit him, about April, 1531, he feared that such a visit would deprive him of "the liberty he had always used in speaking boldly," not only about affairs of the emperor and the queen, "but also for the welfare, honor, and conscience of his master, and the repose of his kingdom."[14] Thus More and Pasquil-Elyot had some of the same concerns.

*Pasquil the Plain* is a complex work and perhaps a more serious work than some scholars have considered it. Perhaps Elyot's concept of Pasquil as an image of stone at the marketplace in Rome, becoming rude and blunt from listening to the chatter around, or perhaps the satirical bitterness (not lightness) at the beginning when the false counselors are introduced may somewhat obscure its meaning for modern readers. But such details may have made it possible for Elyot to issue the work at all.

*Of the Knowledge Which Maketh a Wise Man* was published first in 1533, but probably later in the year than *Pasquil,* since Elyot's emotional control and his greater success with the Socratic method suggest a later date. A second undated edition was published probably about 1534; the title page carried the notation that the material was a Platonic discussion. One or two other editions appeared after the death of Elyot. The author acknowledged his work in the first edition by a Proheme of Thomas Elyot, knight.[15] The treatise has been reprinted twice in this century: by Kurt Schroeder in his book on Platonism, in 1920; and in an edition of 1946, which its editor describes as a "page-for-page reprint of the first extant edition of 1533."[16]

In the preface to the first edition, Elyot mentions his two constant desires: to get knowledge and to serve his country. So he reads all the Latin and Greek books he can come by and then expresses in English whatever might help others to virtue. But men criticize him because he uses strange terms and because he censures the things they commend by their actions. They even divine that he is attacking some individual and then try to stir against him some man in authority. How different from these critics is Henry VIII! When he read the *Governour,* he saw Elyot's desire to augment the language and his method of clarifying his strange terms. He did not take offence at ideas but commended the author for rebuking vice in every estate. (One may wonder, for several reasons, how thoroughly Henry read the book.) Elyot protests that he is not attacking one man more than another:

> For there be Gnathos in Spayne as well as in Grece, Pas-
> quilles in England as well as in Rome—Platos be fewe,
> and them I doubte where to fynde. And if men will aske
> for them in Englande, whiche I sette in other places, I
> can not lette them.

But where, he asks, does one find wisdom? Men disagree
about the answer, but the reply that Plato made to
Dionysius seems to contain wisdom. He closes with ideas
from the book of Sapience: knowing the Lord is justice,
justice and virtue are the roots of immortality, and therein
is true wisdom.[17]

It is hard to determine whether Elyot was being
naïve or clever in this praise of Henry. Perhaps he was
applying Erasmus' theory of the panegyric: praise rulers
and other powerful men, hoping that they will shape
themselves by the praise. And when he mentioned Pasquils
and Gnathos, was he admitting authorship or trying to
draw a red herring across his trail? So far as we know,
Henry remained oblivious; perhaps he was engrossed in
his successes—the confirmation of Cranmer, the coronation of Anne, and the prospect of a male heir.

Some of the minor ideas in *Of the Knowledge Which
Maketh a Wise Man* seem thoroughly English. Plato and
Aristippus talk casually of dogs, horses, and sheep as the
landed gentry in England might do. When they are speaking of Sardanapalus, who became as wanton as a beast,
Aristippus mentions his old horse that still hastens to join
a group of mares, but when he reaches them, can do nothing but neigh and kick. The details bear some resemblance to Shakespeare's description of horses in *Venus
and Adonis*, but probably each found his material in
country life. At one point Plato mentions a dog taken
from his master and confined for six months; but when
freed, the dog is able to find his way over forty miles of
strange roads to his master's house. Plato also speaks of dogs
that leap for joy at preparations for a hunt, and when the

hunter blows his horn, "they doo all ryse, and with one voyce doo make a greate noyse as if they consented to that solace." He knows that horses accustomed to battle begin to snort and prance when they hear the trumpets. He compares the fat sheep with much wool and the thin ones with little wool as if he had known the flocks belonging to Elyot's father.

Other minor details are interesting for different reasons. One passage suggests Friar Lawrence's soliloquy in *Romeo and Juliet,* II, 3, on vice as virtue misapplied. Nothing in this world is so good, Elyot says, that it may not bring damage to some man:

> Finally that under the region of the Moone is nothing so good that it is not mixt with some yll, but . . . one is better than an other and be never yll but by disordre. . . ."

Of course there may be other versions of this idea. Plato emphasizes again the difference between mere rhetoric and wisdom—an idea that Elyot had mentioned often, with many-sided applications, in the *Governour.* He and Aristippus agree that the ability to argue well is not wisdom; Plato comments also that Dionysius did not know the difference and did not recognize the teacher of wisdom as the greater authority.[18]

*Of the Knowledge Which Maketh a Wise Man* seems a simpler, more effective, and more mature form of the Socratic dialogue than *Pasquil the Plain.*[19] Elyot had used English subject matter and a Roman setting in *Pasquil,* with almost no classical examples. *Of the Knowledge Which Maketh a Wise Man* is based on a classical situation with classical characters but with strong implications about English affairs. Plato and Aristippus, meeting by chance some time after they had been together at the court of Dionysius, carry on the dialogue. Plato explains that Dionysius, who had once held him in such high regard that others could scarcely get a chance to speak to their ruler, became proud and intractable. When he asked Plato to define a true king, Plato answered that he is a perfect image of God who rules for the good of his people, but a tyrant is one who rules for his own welfare. As a result of Dionysius' anger, Plato had been twice threatened with death and twice sold into slavery but now he had been set free. Thus Dionysius was a tyrant who not only banished his favorite philosopher from the court but threatened him with death.

Elyot deals with three major questions in the work: What is the difference between a king and a tyrant? What kind of knowledge does a wise man have? Why does God permit suffering and adversity, and especially why does he permit a good man to meet these evils?

With the first question partly answered, Elyot goes on to the second. The man of wisdom knows himself, knows that he is made in the image of God. Because his soul only is immortal and immutable, he is inferior to God. His understanding is perfect when it contemplates the divine but imperfect when it is joined to bodily desires. If the soul rules these desires, treating them as servants or slaves, with understanding as a chief counselor and free will as a secretary, the desires are virtues. If the senses rule the desires, only to satisfy the body, they become vices, the soul loses her dignity, and thus she sinks to the level of brutes. When this happens, man has broken the links in that chain of goodness which binds him to God. Disorder results. Elyot seems to suggest here the idea known as the great chain of being, that disorder in the life of a ruler will cause disorder in the kingdom. Thus he implies a philosophical basis for his concern in the *Governour* and in *Pasquil the Plain* about the private life of a man in authority.

In Dialogue V Elyot applies his definition of wisdom to the distinction between a true king and a tyrant. The true king is one whose soul dominates his senses and whose emotions or desires obey his understanding. He is an example to his subjects to set their own souls in order and thus become kingly and Godlike. Because such a king has self-knowledge he understands others. In contrast, Dionysius is inclined to all vicious affections (a repetition of the charge against the master in *Pasquil*), his appetite is corrupt, and he is impatient and cruel. Plato had to speak the truth when asked to define the true king or he would have proved himself a coward and a fool. Since his speaking caused Dionysius to act as a tyrant, he was thus given a further chance to know himself.

Answering the question why God permits suffering and adversity, Elyot says that God, who loves man as the part of creation most like himself, has arranged these things as obstacles in his path to give him self-knowledge and to cure him of stubbornness, pride, ambition, and other vices. Such obstacles include diseases, poisonous herbs, serpents, and scorpions. Among adversities Elyot names the loss of friends, of promising children, of a constant and patient wife, or the loss of a prince's favor, of great authority, possessions, movable riches, and other temporal benefits.

Elyot attempts an answer also to the question why God permits a man to suffer when he is already good. Since no man is perfect, he suggests, most men can improve through adversity. If a man is unusually good already, God may wish to bring him to great honor. To do this he must give him either an unusual affliction or a powerful adversary. Also since wisdom is self-knowledge, man cannot truly know himself until he has proved himself in action. The ideal man of wisdom is so armed against adversity that, no matter what the body feels, the soul is never "unquieted."[20] Unlike the author of the Book of Job, Elyot attempts a complete and an orthodox answer. As a result, his work lacks the profundity of the Bible narrative and of other artistic works that dramatize powerfully the insoluble mysteries.

Though Elyot is continuing here, from the *Governour*

and *Pasquil the Plain,* his assertion that the good king
must be also a good man, able to control by reason his
carnal desires, he rises above the satiric bitterness of
*Pasquil,* achieving calmness of tone with a philosophic
basis. Pasquil fails in his effort to convince his opponents,
but Plato succeeds in convincing Aristippus. The change
in him is developed steadily from the comment of Plato
that he is pleased to find his listener so reasonable, to the
parting, when Aristippus says that he would not have
missed the talk for the horse he is riding and that he has
somewhat changed his old opinion. But Aristippus, who
has been given to carnal appetites himself, seems a straw
figure, set up merely that he may be knocked down. The
reader, or at least this reader, does not quite believe in him
or his changes; thus the real drama achieved by Erasmus
in the best of his colloquies, is lacking, though the
Socratic reasoning is well developed. Also, as compared
with *Pasquil the Plain,* Elyot adds a new emphasis about
the contrast between the tyrant and the true king. Through
his choice of Greek characters and a situation from classical literature he presents a tyrant who has parted from
his favorite philosopher and has even threatened him with
death. Thus *Of the Knowledge Which Maketh a Wise
Man* places emphasis upon the master or ruler and also
upon the philosopher.

Are Elyot's ideas, which are orthodox and conventional in their abstract form, related to conditions in England about 1533?

On his return from his embassy, in June, 1532, Elyot
had remonstrated frankly with the king, for the good of
others and the king himself, just as Pasquil-Elyot wished
counselors to be frank, and as Plato had spoken the truth
to Dionysius. Elyot doubtless used tactful language in his
talk with the king, but his remonstrance may have had implications either about dishonest affections or the need of
the soul to govern the senses.

Henry VIII had parted with his favorite philosopher, Sir Thomas More; and though the resignation, based on a plea of ill health, had seemed to be amicably accepted, it shocked Christendom. An interesting parallel appears in the talk about Dionysius' loss of Plato and Henry's loss of More. Plato offers to prove that the providence of God is often excellent where people think it is lacking. If he can do that, Aristippus says, he will grant that Dionysius was unwise to part with him, "For he hadde bene better to have gyven to hym sixe the best cities in Sicile than to have departed from suche a consayllour."[21] Months earlier, when Elyot and Charles V had talked about the rumor that More wished to resign, the emperor had said that he would rather give up the best city of his domain than to lose such a counselor. Others have also noted the likeness between Plato and More as favorite philosophers.[22]

In 1533, also, whom would Elyot have been thinking of when he discussed the uses of adversity in making men better, or if they were unusually good, preparing them for singular honor?

Elyot thought that he had suffered injustice, and he may have been trying to reconcile himself. He had not received the regular pay for his years of work as clerk of the Council; he called the expenses of his embassy, beyond his allowance from the king, unendurable. He saw Cranmer, who followed him on his embassy, preferred to the highest office in the English church while he was a servitor to Cranmer at the coronation of Anne Boleyn. He was not called to Council. But if he thought of himself, as he discussed adversity, perhaps he was modest enough to realize that others had suffered more and to believe that he might need to become better.

Since Elyot kept trying to aid Catherine of Aragon and the Princess Mary, he could hardly have written his discussion of the way God sends trouble to the good without thinking of them. The mother and daughter were separated; and when Archbishop Cranmer, in May, 1533, declared Henry's marriage to Catherine invalid and his marriage to Anne Boleyn valid, even before Parliament took action, Mary was no longer considered legitimate or the heir to the throne. Catherine, now called the princess dowager, was reduced almost to penury and was a virtual prisoner in the custody of her chamberlain, Lord Blount. She had lost her property, her power, and her position as queen.

Elyot must certainly have thought of Sir Thomas More when he wrote of the adversity God sends to the man who is already good. After More gave up the chancellorship, he had an income of little more than a hundred pounds a year, but he tried to keep together all the members of his family. He cut down his household, providing places for his fool and for the servants he must dismiss; and as Stapleton tells us, he sold his silver plate, worth more than £400, lest it be seized later for the royal treasury.[23] To Elyot, with his thrifty eye for property, such changes would be adversity. Of course More had also given up great authority. Probably More had refused to attend the coronation of Anne Boleyn before *Of the Knowledge Which Maketh a Wise Man* came from the press, though we cannot be sure. But when Elyot wrote to Hacket in early April, 1533, a sense of impending trouble was in the air. Whether he knew that More's life was in danger we do not know, but it seems possible that he surmised it when he represented the tyrant as threatening to kill his favorite philosopher.

Elyot's ideas and their relation to England appear in bolder perspective when the *Governour*, *Pasquil the Plain*, and *Of the Knowledge Which Maketh a Wise Man* are compared for some of their major ideas. In the *Governour* Elyot was concerned with the private morality of the ruler, emphasizing sexual continence, with public ethics and public virtues, with the right of the humble subject to free speech for the public good, and with the need for many frank, unbiased, wise counselors. In

*Pasquil the Plain* the center of concern is a master whose vicious affections are poisoning his mind and soul. Pasquil argues, without having a positive effect on his listeners, that self-seeking counselors should speak frankly to the master. His physician-confessor is especially obligated to warn him, since there is still hope of healing him. The master is a king. The dialogue stresses the evil results from lack of frank speech—not only the peril to the soul of the master but the decay of the church in England and in Germany and the danger of subversion to the state. Whether Elyot had in mind a philosophic concept or the actual plots in England when he warned against danger to the state seems uncertain. In the third work *Of the Knowledge Which Maketh a Wise Man* the ruler has become a tyrant, not a true king. He has been yielding to desires of the body, not of the soul. Through his failure to attain knowledge of himself he has broken the links in the chain of goodness that binds him to God. Thus he has endangered the kingdom. Plato's frank answer when asked to define the true king causes his dismissal as the favorite philosopher, with slavery and the threat of death. Through the three works there seems to be a cumulative development based on Elyot's effort to influence his king and conditions in England. But in the third one he has become hopeless about the ruler and has shifted his concern to the philosopher who is out of favor.

When Thomas Elyot attended the coronation dinner for Anne Boleyn, June 1, 1533, and led in the serving of Archbishop Cranmer, he must have realized with sharp finality that his efforts had failed. His frank remonstrance with his king about June 1, 1532, based on the principles advocated by Pasquil, and his writings had neither improved his own position nor affected the conduct of Henry VIII. But he had done his duty as he saw it, persistently and stubbornly, for king and for country. That fact may have been some consolation.

# CHAPTER XI

## A Sermon of Holy Saint Cyprian
### *and Pico's* Rules of a Christian Life. *1534*

URING 1534 there is no convincing evidence that Thomas Elyot made any effort to influence Henry VIII. However, Elyot and other Englishmen were trying to persuade the emperor to take action on behalf of Catherine of Aragon.

According to a letter from Chapuys to the emperor, January 29, 1534, Catherine herself had asked that men of influence be sent to speak for her in the English Parliament. Though Chapuys doubted whether they could get permission to speak, he was transmitting the information because the queen had made the request and because "many worthy persons of this kingdom, including Mr. Elyot, who certainly has not been the last to ask for them in his own name and in that of several others highly placed here" had made the same request. "Although the said Master Elyot does not rank among the principal lords of the kingdom," Chapuys continued, "I have . . . singled him out because Your Majesty knows him well. Even members of this Parliament have sent me messages the last week to the effect that should anyone come to England on behalf of Your Majesty . . . they will hold out . . . in hopes that a large majority of good Christians, indignant at the way the Pope is treated in this country, will vote with them." The king had countermanded those who might oppose his views, Chapuys added—for example, the Archbishop of York, the Bishop of Durham, and the Bishop of Rochester. Thus he would probably be able to carry any measure that he chose.[1]

The statutes passed by Parliament between January 15 and March 30, 1534, indicate that the king, whatever the reason, was mainly successful. The first of those with a bearing on the discussion here was a bill of attainder against Elizabeth Barton, the Nun of Kent. Among the six other persons named with her for the death penalty were Sir Thomas More and Bishop John Fisher. When the bill was read for the third time, their names were still included among those marked for death. If it had been passed in that form, both could have been executed without a trial. But a message went to the king asking whether they might be tried in the Star Chamber. He refused but finally consented to a private examination before a committee composed of Cranmer, Audeley, Norfolk, and Cromwell. More handled his defense so well that the king became even more anxious to have his name in the bill. When he was told that the bill with More's name in it would be defeated, he offered to come himself and see that it passed. Finally Audeley went down on his knees, it is said, and begged the king not to risk such a defeat in Parliament. The king allowed More's name to be removed, but Fisher's remained for imprisonment and loss of goods. Those named in the bill were accused of spreading information to the fathers and the nuns of Syon House, to the Charterhouse monks in London and Richmond, and to the Friars Observant at Greenwich, Richmond, and Canterbury.[2] It is true that More had gone to Syon House to talk with Elizabeth Barton, because the fathers wished to know his opinion of her and that he had talked with others about her; but his explanations in his letter to Cromwell, March, 1534, should have freed him from any blame. In the days when the bill was being debated, rumors about Fisher and More must have spread about London like a forest fire in dry timber.

The bill also provided for a proclamation under the king's great seal, to be made known in every shire, city, borough, town, and liberty. "It shall be proclaimed," the statute says, that every person with copies of any of the feigned miracles of Elizabeth Barton in his keeping shall deliver them within forty days to the lord chancellor or to one of certain other officials who were named, under a penalty of fine or imprisonment. As no copy of this actual proclamation is available, we do not know whether it included also a demand that sermons by Fisher or books defending the authority of the Pope he turned in. Another bill on heresy at this time included the declaration that speaking against the pretended authority of the Bishop of Rome is not heresy, since the present Pope and his predecessors have made many ordinances only for their worldly glory and ambition.

During the month of March, Parliament passed other measures separating the church from its center at Rome, though some of these statutes merely confirmed provisions already adopted as permissive. Convocations, canon laws, and visitations to religious houses were placed firmly under the royal power. Peter's pence and first-fruits or annates were not to be sent to Rome, nor any bulls and briefs to be procured from there. Archbishops and bishops were to be elected without reference to any foreign power, since the king had no superior under God, and subjects were to obey him, not the "lawes of any foren Prynce, Potentate, or Prelate," and any churchman nominated by the king was to be elected within twelve days or the electors would be charged with praemunire (prosecuting in a foreign court a suit that belonged under the jurisdiction of an English court).[3] While no other extant proclamation deals with forbidden books at this time, another calling in books that supported papal power would have been eminently reasonable.

The same Parliament passed the provisions known as the Act of Succession. By these laws the marriage of Henry to Catherine of Aragon was declared invalid, and her title in future was to be the Princess Dowager. The marriage to Anne Boleyn was declared valid, and the king's issue by Anne lawful issue and consequently heirs to the throne. To slander the latter marriage by "writing, print, deed, or act" was declared high treason. An oath to uphold the succession was required of every subject who was of age; but at this time the exact form of the oath was not provided by statute, and hence we do not know whether every subject confronted exactly the same wording. However, the statute included the declaration that the marriage to Catherine was invalid because she had been "carnally known" to Arthur (an allegation that she steadfastly denied) and because man's power "which is but usurped" cannot dispense with God's law.[4] More was doubtless asked to subscribe to the whole statute, since he refused but was willing to support the theory that Parliament could determine the succession. All of these statutes connected with the bill of attainder, the separation from Rome, and the succession to the throne must have given conservative Catholics, loyal to the old religion, a sense of dismay or terror, even if they did not know the methods by which the legislation had been secured. Henry dominated Parliament by countermanding his opponents, letting his views be known, and discussing his views with legislators outside formal sessions. He was furthering government by Parliament, from a desire for support in achieving his ends.

About March 23, 1534, a week before the English Parliament ended its session, Pope Clement issued his declaration that the marriage of Henry VIII to Catherine of Aragon was valid.[5] For Catherine, the verdict came at least two years, possibly even seven years, too late.

With the acts of Parliament as his instruments, the king stepped up his campaign against those who opposed him. Many of his opponents were connected with the religious houses named in the bill of attainder against Elizabeth Barton, the Nun of Kent: Syon House, the Charterhouse, and the Friars Observant. All the men and women in these houses were passively or actively refusing to accept the king's marriage to Anne Boleyn.

About April, 1534, Richard Reynolds, the Father Superior or General Confessor at Syon House, was declaring that Henry was not the head of the church and that Catherine was still the true queen. But he was not imprisoned until a little later and was not executed until May 4, 1535. Richard Whitford, earlier a chaplain and confessor to William Blount, Lord Mountjoy, an intimate friend of both More and Erasmus, and now a member of Syon House, was being reported for his stubborn opposition in the summer of 1534.[6] The views of both men must have been known early that spring to members of Syon House and their friends.

On April 12, 1534, Sir Thomas More was cited to appear before the commissioners, and after some efforts to persuade him into taking the oath, was committed to the Tower. About April 16, Bishop Fisher was arrested and sent to the Tower. On April 20 or 21, Elizabeth Barton, the Nun of Kent, and others named in the final form of the bill of attainder against her were executed at Tyburn. Fanatical and foolish as she may have been, she was used in efforts to implicate those who were both great and wise.

About May 1, 1534, Prior John Houghton and Proctor Humphrey Middlemore of the London Charterhouse, having scruples about the oath, were sent to the Tower, where they remained in foul lodgings with short rations for a month. Leading churchmen finally persuaded them to take the oath in some form, probably with reservations; but when they were released, Houghton seems to have known that they had not seen the end of the business. On June 17, two cartloads of Friars Observant from Greenwich and Richmond were taken to the Tower. Later in the summer all seven houses of the order were cleared; the remaining residents were taken to other religious houses, where they were to be ill treated and kept in chains.[7]

Some time in 1534, probably in February, Thomas Abell, a chaplain of Catherine of Aragon, who had written an answer to her opponents on the question of her marriage and had secured for her a notarized copy of important papers in Spain, was lodged in prison again.[8] Father John Forrest, Catherine's confessor, seems to have gone to prison early in 1534 for denying the king's supremacy, if the letters between him and the queen are correctly assigned to the early part of 1534. Edmund Powell, who may have been an early associate of Elyot through St. Edmund's at Salisbury, was opposing the king's policies and was being carefully watched and reported on in 1534; but his imprisonment came later.[9]

While these events were moving forward, with a threat hanging over Syon House and with More a prisoner in the Tower, Thomas Elyot was preparing for the press his little volume containing the translations *A Sweet and Devout Sermon of Holy Saint Cyprian* and Pico, *The Rules of a Christian Life*. He dated his preface July 1, 1534, and the colophon gives 1534 as the date of publication. The work was issued again in 1539, after the fury of these political events had subsided.[10]

The prefatory material is of special interest. Using his own name instead of hiding behind anonymity, Elyot addresses the preface to "my ryghte worshypfull suster

Dame Susan Knygestone," and asks her to share the work
with "our two susters religiouse, Dorothe and Alianour."
He does not call Susan Kingston a religious sister. He
asks all of them to join in their prayers for him, that he
may be constant in the service of God, and also that he
may perform well such other works as are in his hand to
the honor and glory of God. He values Dame Susan, he
says, because of the family connections, but even more
because she perseveres in virtue and in works of true faith.

Elyot begins the main part of his preface by saying
that the wise person who is subject to fever, catarrh, or
other bodily illness will try to care for himself so as to
reduce the severity of an attack. In the same way every
reasonable creature should try to be ready for death at any
time or for "the toyes of fortune or the crankes of the
world." The method of preparation is to have a pure and
constant faith with wisdom and patience—a union of
Christian and classical virtues, though Elyot does not himself say so. Saint Cyprian (whom he calls the holy doctor
and martyr) prescribed such remedies in a time of pestilence and persecution. Many people, Elyot continues, are
as negligent as he has been in these affairs, in spite of the
fact that they "have beholden men and women of every
astate whiche have dyed eyther before they looked for
death, or in some other wyse than they vouched saulfe, or
else forsaken of fortune have lyved in povertye." So he
has translated this little book for their instruction as well
as his own.[11]

Elyot's preface to the *Saint Cyprian* takes on a new
meaning when we realize that three of his Fettiplace sisters, Susan, Eleanor, and Dorothy, were probably all
living at Syon House. Dame Susan Kingston, a "vowess,"
dedicated to chastity and permitted to wear the robes of
the order, was boarding there with her servants. Probably
she had gone there after the death of her husband, in
1514. When her uncle, Sir Thomas Fettiplace, made his

PLATE I. Sir Thomas Elyot. Drawing by Hans Holbein the Younger. From the Collection of Her Majesty the Queen at Windsor Castle. (*Crown Copyright reserved*). *ca.* 1532

313

PLATE II. Henry VIII. Portrait perhaps by Joos van Cleve. From the Collection of Her Majesty the Queen at Hampton Court. (*Crown Copyright reserved*). Dates suggested range from 1528 or 1530 to 1535–1536.

PLATE III. Henry VIII. Portrait of the School of Holbein. From the Collection of Her Majesty the Queen at Windsor Castle. (*Crown Copyright reserved*). *ca.* 1537?

PLATE IV. Henry VIII.　Line engraving by Cornelys
Matsys. British Museum. 1544?

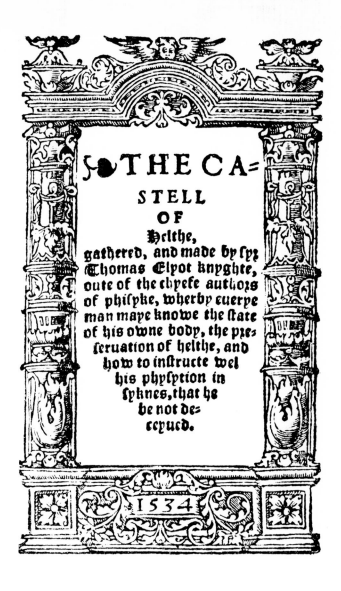

**THE CA=
STELL
OF**
Helthe,
gathered, and made by fyr
Thomas Elyot knyghte,
oute of the chyefe authors
of phifyke, wherby euerye
man maye knowe the ftate
of his owne body, the pre-
feruation of helthe, and
how to inftructe wel
his phyfycion in
fyknes, that he
be not de-
cyued.

1534

PLATE V. Title page of the first edition of *The Castle of Health*, Historical Library, Yale Medical Library, Yale University. 1536–1539?

# Cooperus Lectori.

ELIOTA vir clarissimus, & præter omnium, quos
ego ex Equestri ordine noui, consuetudinem,
bonarum literarum studijs mirificè deditus, primus
hac nostra memoria, Dictionarium Latino Anglicum,
in gratiam studiosorum composuit. Quod opus ille
vocauit BIBLIOTHECAM *suam*. In cuius labores,
postquàm illum mors immatura præripuisset, ego
pertractus amicorum præcibus successi, & BIBLIO-
THECAM illam pro mea tenui facultate, iterum atq;
tertiò auctiorem reddidi, donec tandem Thesaurus
hic noster in lucem prodijt. Istud ego in hoc loco præ-
figendum putaui, ne vel memoria tam inusitatæ viri
Nobilis industriæ, per immutatam Tituli rationem,
periret, vel ego meritò à nostris hominibus ingratus
existimer, cum omnibus constet, me illius laboribus
ad hunc Thesaurum congerendum non mediocriter
adiutum esse.

The Lady Eliot.

PLATE VII. Lady Margaret Elyot. Drawing by Hans Holbein the Younger. From the Collection of Her Majesty the Queen at Windsor Castle. *(Crown Copyright reserved). ca.* 1532

ᴀᴛᴇ VI. Tribute of Thomas Cooper to Sir Thomas ᴏt, from Cooper's *Thesaurus*, 1578. (English para-ᴀse is on page 293 of this work.)

will in 1524, he described her as being at Syon House. Apparently she stayed on when danger threatened; for in accounts of 1537, the cellaress, Dame Agnes Merritt, recorded the payment of a bill by "My Lady Kyngeston" for the board of herself and her servants.[12] As the members later made some kind of submission to the king's will, Syon House was not formally dissolved until 1539. When Dame Susan died in 1540 and was buried in the church at Shalston, Bucks, where her sister, Anne Purefoy, lived, the brass effigy placed for Susan commemorated her life at Syon House. "She wears a mantle, veil, and wimple," the county historian says, "and a ring on her right hand."[13] The mantle shown in a picture of the effigy seems to be the same as the one worn by the nuns at that house.[14]

Eleanor Fettiplace, the stepdaughter whom Sir Richard Elyot provided for in his will, entered Syon House as a regular nun, according to the evidence reported in an earlier chapter. The Dorothy Codrington on the pension lists of the same house was probably a Fettiplace, since James Yate later collected her pension along with that of other members of the family.[15]

The basis for Elyot's concern at this time seems to lie in the fact that the king was determined to secure the submission of Syon House. The place was a double house of sixty nuns and twenty-five men (including thirteen priests, four deacons, and eight lay brethren) presided over by an abbess who ruled both temporals and spirituals. It belonged to a modified order of St. Augustine as reformed by St. Bridget of Sweden.[16] It was important to many devout people besides members of the Delamere, Bessils, and Fettiplace families, several of whom had expressed a wish to be buried there. In the happier days of the 1520's Catherine of Aragon often traveled there for prayers. Once when Vives was still a welcome guest at the English court, she had taken him with her; and as they

came back by barge on the late afternoon tide, they had
spoken of the sudden changes from good to bad fortune
that occur in human lives.[17]

> The flourishing condition of Syon, its excellent observ-
> ance, its aristocratic connections, and the intellectual dis-
> tinction and virtue of Reynolds and Whytford and others
> made it something unique in Tudor England. . . . When
> the divorce was mooted, Syon was all but solid in its
> opposition. . . . The various negotiations and stratagems
> employed to persuade the two families of Syon [the men
> and women of the double house] to take the oath can be
> seen only by glimpses. . . . These are, however, numerous
> enough to show that Syon, though ultimately yielding at
> last a tacit consent, struggled long . . . that both the
> king and Cromwell set great store by its submission, and
> that to achieve their end, they were willing to go through
> a long and torturous process of persuasion, oppression,
> and intimidation.[18]

In the earlier part of 1534, or before July first, when
Elyot was preparing his *Saint Cyprian* for the press, it was
not yet clear what steps the king might take to secure the
submission of Syon House. The fate of its residents, including Susan Kingston, Eleanor Fettiplace, and Dorothy
Fettiplace Codrington, was uncertain. Hence it is not
surprising that Elyot suggested a comparison between the
threat to members of the religious houses at the time
and earlier troubles in the period of St. Cyprian. He lived
in a time of pestilence, political pressures, and persecution
for his religion. As the first bishop in Africa to become a
martyr, he was a model for others in his refusal to seek out
martyrdom, his giving his executioners many pieces of
gold (inherited from his wealthy family) as a sign of his
complete forgiveness of them, and his calm acceptance of
death.[19]

His sermon emphasizes ideas for a time of trouble.
Now that difficulties are upon us and the end of the world

seems at hand, Saint Cyprian says, stand fast in the Christian faith. Do not think that God has forsaken us. These trials test us for the glory of the future life. Do not sorrow for the death of others. Look forward to your own death as you would look forward to firm land if you were on a ship tossed by terrific storms.

The ideas in *The Rules of a Christian Life* are similar but less urgent, less definitely aimed at weathering a period of trial and persecution. The writer urges the Christian to be steadfast, to use his wordly possessions well and to dispose of them charitably, to remember the sufferings of Christ, to fight against temptations, to be ready to fight again, and to arm himself against the sin of pride.

When Elyot published the *Saint Cyprian* and the Pico in 1534 he clearly wished to hearten the Fettiplace sisters at Syon House, to strengthen himself through their prayers, and to encourage all who wished to remain loyal to the faith. If he had meant his material for the Fettiplace sisters only, he might have sent it to Dame Susan Kingston in manuscript and asked her to pass it on to Eleanor and Dorothy. But he chose to publish it under his own name. It has been suggested that Elyot published it to encourage Sir Thomas More in his resolution.[20] But More had made his choice—even though he had chances later to change his mind—and he was already a prisoner in the Tower. Probably Elyot would not have had the presumption to think that he, the younger and the less stable man, needed to encourage his senior, though he may have had private thoughts about Saint Cyprian and More as martyrs. More had been under threat of an earlier execution, of course, while his name remained in the bill of attainder against Elizabeth Barton. It is interesting also that More thought of Saint Cyprian in relation to his own execution, according to Roper. The lieutenant persuaded him not to wear his best apparel to the scaffold, saying that the executioner was only a worthless fellow. But More said that he wished to follow the example of Cyprian, who gave his executioner pieces of gold; and out of the small sum in his possession, he finally sent him an angel of gold.[21]

Perhaps Elyot, in the first half of 1534, really thought of refusing the oath of supremacy himself, when he asked the prayers of his sisters-in-law that he might remain constant. But if the spirit was hopeful at that time, the flesh became weak.

Elyot had probably been familiar for some years with the work of Saint Cyprian and of Pico della Mirandola, since his own translations and some of his other work tended to follow an interest of More or of Erasmus. He may have known something about Pico from about 1510, when More had published his translation of the life of that great Italian. About that time, according to his great-grandson, Cresacre More, More had chosen as a pattern for his own life "a singular layman, John Picus, Earl of Mirandola."[22] Elyot had perhaps become familiar with Saint Cyprian in 1519–1520, when the edition of his work by Erasmus came from the press of Froben.[23] Perhaps he had worked on the translations of both authors earlier, when he was teaching himself the classical languages. If so, he had them at hand for use in 1534.

The Parliament meeting in November, 1534, passed a number of new acts, some of which seemed to be small additions or repetitions. The king as head of the church, one new statute asserted, had the power to punish offences against the church or to correct heresies. Parliament also provided a form for swearing allegiance to the king and to his lawful wife, Queen Anne, and for renouncing any other allegiance. A refusal to take the oath was to constitute a lawful indictment, as if the person refusing had been indicted before twelve men at the common law. To attempt bodily harm to the king, the queen, or their heirs, to deprive them of their titles, or to call the king a heretic

—any or all of these things were declared to be high treason. An act of attainder was passed against a number of men, including Edward Powell. An individual act of attainder was passed against Thomas More also, for his refusal to accept the king as head of the church on earth.[24]


No record about Thomas Elyot appears in any available material from July 1, 1534, when he dated the preface for the *Saint Cyprian* and the Pico, until the end of the year—unless a letter he wrote from Combe to Cromwell, dated only on the Vigil of St. Thomas, belongs here. The arguments for assuming that it was written in 1534 are not overwhelming—but neither are the arguments for a later year. Elyot is concerned about the king's proclamation calling in seditious books, and he mentions having some books which support the authority of the Bishop of Rome and a sermon by Bishop Fisher. But his details do not fit precisely with any extant proclamation. Henry probably issued a proclamation calling in copies of the feigned miracles of Elizabeth Barton, as Parliament directed in the bill of attainder against her, early in 1534, but no copy of it remains. The action of Parliament, also early in 1534, declaring that it was not heresy to speak against the pretended power of the pope, would have given the king both reason and authority to call in any books defending the papal power if he had wished; but we lack evidence that he took action at this time. On June 9, 1535, he issued a proclamation against the defense of papal authority, one that considered alone, would make December, 1535, seem a valid date for Elyot's letter. On January 1, 1536, he issued one calling in the books and sermons of Bishop Fisher, with specific details about the time allowed and the officials who were to receive them.[25] But no extant proclamation seems to fit all the statements in Elyot's letter, since he is concerned about works of

Fisher and books supporting the papal power. By 1535 and 1536 there are signs also that Elyot was coming back into favor, or at least into acceptance. On January 1, 1535, he was named on a commission to collect taxes in Oxford and Oxfordshire. By the middle of 1536 a letter to Cromwell that certainly seems to belong under that date contains the report that Elyot was visiting monasteries according to the king's command and he was also asking some financial help from a pension or from the monastic lands. In the same letter he says that on his last visit to the Rolls, Cromwell comforted him with gentle words. By November, 1536, also he was being named on the Commission of the Peace for Oxfordshire. (See Chapter XIII for these details about 1535 and 1536.)

By contrast, the letter under consideration here has a remote sound as if Elyot were completely out of touch with the court and Cromwell, or as if he had only vague reports of a proclamation but had also a sense of legal guilt about several kinds of books in his possession. Since proclamations, too, were ephemeral things, and since the king certainly had the right to base a proclamation on any statute of Parliament, it seems reasonable to suppose that the king issued one about books supporting papal power in 1534. Admittedly, these suppositions are not proof. But December, 1534, still seems the most reasonable date; December, 1535, is possible; and December, 1536, is apparently eliminated by outer events. A long illness in the latter part of 1534 at least fits with the fact that we have no other records of Elyot between July, 1534 and the beginning of 1535, though we also know little about him in the latter part of 1535. So the letter, dated only on the Vigil of St. Thomas, will be discussed here.

Whatever the date may be, Elyot begins by humbly admitting his duty to call on Cromwell for exact instructions about the king's proclamation concerning seditious books. But since he has been very sick and has not yet fully recovered, he is writing. He hopes that a letter will not be distasteful to Cromwell, whom he has always considered one of his best friends because of their common interest in studies, the most perfect foundation of amity. As Cromwell knows, he has a great many books, especially about humanity and moral philosophy:

> But concerning holy scripture I have very few, for in questionists I never delighted; unsavory glosses and comments I ever abhorred; the boasters and advancers [Elyot's word is *advauntars*] of the pompous authority of the Bishop of Rome I never esteemed. But after that by much and serious reading I had apprehended a judgment or estimation of things, I did anon smell out their corrupt affections, and beheld with sorrowful eyes the sundry abuses of their authorities, adorned with a licentious and dissolute form of living, of the which, as well in them as in the universal state of the clergy, I have oftentimes wished a necessary reformation; whereof hath happed no little contention betwixt me and such persons as ye have thought that I have specially favored, even as ye also did, for some laudable qualities which we supposed to be in them. But neither they might [his word is *mought*] persuade me to approve that which both faith and my reason condemned, nor I might dissuade them from the excusing of that which all the world abhorred, which obstinacy of both parts relented the great affection between us and withdrew our familiar repair.[26]

As for the prohibited books about the Bishop of Rome's authority, Elyot continues, he does have some of them, joined in one great volume or perhaps two volumes at the most, but he never found the leisure to read them. He will gladly bring them in if the king and Cromwell wish him to do so. As for the works of John Fisher, he has only the little sermon that Mr. Pace translated into Latin eight or nine years ago; and he bought that because of the translator, not the author or the subject matter. (Apparently this was the sermon against Luther, the one Siberch had published about 1522 or 1523. Even in 1534, if that was the date of Elyot's letter, Pace's translation had been published eleven or twelve years earlier.) If this sermon and the other works should be turned in, Elyot hopes he may be allowed more time to recover from his illness and then to travel to his widely separated houses and to find them. He will search diligently as well as follow any directions he is given. If Cromwell does not have time to write instructions, will he please ask Mr. Peter Vannes or Mr. Augustine to write his advice for him. Then he reminds Mr. Secretary that from their first acquaintance, "which began of a mutuall benevolence," he had never been guilty of stubborn opinion or dissimulation; but a natural simplicity not well managed might cause men to suspect that he favored hypocrisy, superstition, and vanity. But if Cromwell could see his thoughts, he would find him a reformer of these things. In closing he wishes Cromwell prosperity, honor, and long life.

The letter is a masterpiece of evasion or of tact, depending on the point of view. Elyot has said nothing against any fundamental doctrine of his church. He desires reform, but he does not go as far as Erasmus often went when he did not have life and possessions at stake, and Erasmus considered himself loyal to his church. Even the younger Thomas More, before the years when he had his back to the wall defending his church, might have made these same comments—as scholarly Catholic priests whom I have consulted suggest. More never insisted on papal infallibility even about doctrine, but accepted a general council of the whole church as his authority.[27] Some, including the editor who first published Elyot's letter, have considered Elyot's statements as proof that he held "Protestant" principles, but perhaps they oversimplify the situation.

The letter contains other puzzles without definite solutions. We do not know how long Elyot was ill or the cause of the illness. Remembering his emphasis on heaviness of mind in *The Castle of Health,* Third Book, chapters 11 and 12, one might wonder whether events of the time contributed. Perhaps a minor cause of the illness was the king's ingratitude in failing to repay the extra expenses of his embassy or to give him a place on the Council. Perhaps major causes included the break with the church at Rome, the imprisonment and impending death of many whom he respected, the threat to other religious houses and to his sisters-in-law at Syon House, the need to take the loyalty oath, and the failure of his own efforts to influence the king. These conjectures about causes might also apply if the letter were written in 1535, after the execution of More. Nor is it necessary to assume an intimate personal friendship between More and Elyot—only the fact that his king had behaved like a tyrant and executed a great statesman and philosopher. The causes, considered alone, might also be applicable, though less so, in 1536.

Another puzzle lies in Elyot's reference to his wish for reformation in the church and the resulting contention between him and "such persons as ye have thought that I have specially favored, even as ye also did. . . ." Is he using a plural because he does not wish to name a specific person, as we often do today? Is he referring to More when he says that disagreement had reduced the affection between them and stopped their familiar association? Probably he meant More. (In a later letter to Cromwell, about February, 1537, he named More and asked Cromwell to put aside the memory of that friendship; he insisted that the friendship had never had any effect on his loyalty to the king.) In the letter discussed here he is skillful in drawing attention to the fact also that Cromwell had once had a high regard for the person or persons that he believed Elyot had favored.

Perhaps it is difficult for people of the twentieth

century to agree on what Elyot's religious views really were or to understand the conflicts between temporal and spiritual loyalties in an age when the latter were strong. Also, though people today, as in the past, yield to the pressure of circumstances, they sometimes tend to expect consistency in historical characters. However, Elyot did change some of his views—not his belief in what he considered essential doctrines—and a biographer must record these changes. So far, one thing seems clear: Elyot was not the man to become a martyr.

# CHAPTER XII

## *Other Translations*, ca. *1530–1535*

EVERAL other translations, some known and some surmised to be the work of Thomas Elyot, came from the press of Berthelet about 1528–1530 to 1535. Only two of the four volumes to be discussed in this chapter were published under Elyot's name; and when he listed his books in the preface of *The Image of Governance* in 1541, he did not claim as his any of the anonymous translations. Publication by Berthelet does not prove authorship, of course, even though all editions of all Elyot's works that appeared in his lifetime came from that press; but neither does Elyot's failure to acknowledge them later prove that he was not the translator. One of the anonymous volumes contained two works: *How One May Take Profit from his Enemies,* a free translation from Plutarch, and an additional six-page compilation, *The Manner to Choose and Cherish a Friend.* Another translation from Plutarch, *The Education or Bringing Up of Children,* carried Elyot's name. A translation from Lucian with the title *A Dialogue between Lucian and Diogenes* was published without a name. These were all translated from Latin into English, it is said. A fourth work by Isocrates, *The Doctrinal of Princes,* translated from Greek into English, carried Elyot's name.

It is suggested here as a reasonable hypothesis that all

these translations were probably the work of Thomas Elyot, that most of them were begun much earlier than any possible date of their publication, and that a number of them were exercises begun when Elyot was training himself in the use of Greek and Latin.

The hypothesis seems reasonable because translation, especially double translation, was a common practice for learning a classical language in the period. The method was recommended by Cicero, Pliny, and Quintilian; hence it was available to all as a theory. The pupils in More's school almost every day turned English into Latin and then translated the same material from Latin into English. Erasmus, when he found that the available teachers of Greek were unsatisfactory, taught himself the language, partly by translating the *Hecuba* of Euripides from Greek into Latin; and he recommended that pupils turn Greek into Latin before beginning original composition. Vives also recommended translation from the mother tongue into Latin and then into the mother tongue again; and though he added that the same exercise could be applied to Greek, he considered it better to translate from the Greek authors. Roger Ascham suggested a little later several plans for double translation, including the turning of Ionic into Attic Greek for the one who wished to attain perfection.[1] So Elyot must have translated from both languages as exercises, while he was gaining skill. Though it is possible that one or more of these translations appeared before 1531, they were mainly given to the press after Elyot had had a chance to gain confidence from the publication of the *Governour*. If they were exercises, he probably did not wish to acknowledge them when he listed his major works in 1541.

The writers who furnished most of the material for these translations—Plutarch, Lucian, and Isocrates—were highly esteemed by the other classicists of the period as well as by Elyot himself. Erasmus was praising Plutarch years before Elyot published anything. In November, 1512, Erasmus wrote More from Cambridge that he was translating his work on the difference between a friend and a flatterer; later he gave a copy of his work to Henry VIII. About January 1, 1513, he sent John Yonge, Master of the Rolls, a manuscript copy of Plutarch, *De tuenda bona valetudine;* later that year he published the work at Louvain. Early in 1514 he gave Wolsey a manuscript copy of Plutarch on making use of one's enemies, with praise of Plutarch's learning, charm, exact knowledge, and power of expression. In 1516 he included this work and the one on a friend versus a flatterer with Froben's publication of *Institutio principis Christiani.*[2] More also paid tribute to Plutarch, apparently as a philosopher, when he said that his Utopians valued him highly.[3] Vives cited Plutarch some seventeen times in one work and used his ideas in many other passages; when he discussed imitation and moral philosophy he suggested the use of Plutarch, and he recommended both the *Lives of Famous Men* and the *Morals* to the teacher of languages.[4] Elyot cited Plutarch in other places. In the *Governour,* I, ii, he referred to Plutarch as support for his theory of kingship, and in the same work he drew upon the *Lives* for many of his incidents and examples.[5] Perhaps these men valued Plutarch because he united philosophy with action, emphasizing the idea that one should not shirk any public duty.[6]

As for Lucian, he was the delight of both More and Erasmus, who translated many of his works from Greek into Latin. More translated *Menippus, Philopseudes,* and *Tyrannicida,* as well as the *Cynicus.* Both More and Erasmus wrote replies to the *Tyrannicida.* About 1506 Erasmus translated *Toxaris,* a discussion of friendship, *Alexander, Gallus,* and a number of other short dialogues. The translations of both men were published by Bade in 1506. Eventually Erasmus translated eighteen short dialogues and eighteen longer pieces by Lucian; some of them, often with those of More, were published about forty times between 1506 and 1550.[7] All these were turned from Greek into Latin.

Elyot discussed Lucian as a part of his program of study, but with reservations. In the *Governour*, I, x, he suggests that a good teacher may select quick and merry dialogues of Lucian, ones without ribaldry or too much scorning, or he may prefer the comedies of Aristophanes. He is sure of one thing: it is better for a child to have no Lucian than to read all his works. Elyot was probably indebted to Lucian, *De saltatione,* for some of his ideas on dancing, in I, xx; and in discussing detraction, III, xxvii, he says once that he is using almost the words of Lucian.

Erasmus was early an admirer of Isocrates, as well as of Plutarch and Lucian. In 1501 he was sending to a friend both Euripides and Isocrates (he was not specific), probably in a Latin translation.[8] In 1516 he published a Latin translation of Isocrates' *Oratio* to Nicocles with his *Institutio principis Christiani,* mentioning it in his dedication of the *Institutio* to the young prince who became Charles V; and probably he based some of his ideas on Isocrates. However, he carefully stressed the fact that Isocrates was a pagan philosopher instructing a pagan prince, but he was a Christian philosopher teaching a Christian prince.[9]

Elyot also gave Isocrates high praise in the *Governour,* I, xi. His discussion on the training of orators, Elyot said, is extremely profitable, with almost as many wise statements as he has words; he is also so sweet and delectable to read that after him others seem unpleasant and tedious. He persuades both princes and private persons to virtue, and every one should read and keep in his memory the oration to Nicocles and the work addressed to his friend Demonicus. Later in the same chapter he cites sweet Isocrates, who exhorted the king to leave behind him not images of his body but the memory of his actions written into history.

These facts about the interest of the classicists in Plutarch, Lucian, and Isocrates perhaps strengthen the probability that Elyot was the translator of all these works, and they add to the evidence that Elyot, like many other men, tended to follow the trails blazed by Erasmus.

To turn to the translations themselves, the volume including the Plutarch *How One May Take Profit from his Enemies,* and the six-page compilation, *The Manner to Choose and Cherish a Friend,* was perhaps published about 1533.[10] The work is undated, but Berthelet describes himself as the king's printer, an appointment he received in 1530.[11] The compilation includes opinions on friendship from Cicero, Scipio through Cicero, Gellius, Seneca, Theophrastus, Epicurus, and Terence; these ideas, we are told, are used to fill space that would otherwise be empty. Hence it seems certain that the same person translated the Plutarch and prepared the compilation. It has often been assumed that Elyot was the translator of *How One May Take Profit from his Enemies.* In 1883 Croft said that the work has usually been attributed to him.[12] In 1933 Lathrop stated that Erasmus had translated the work, of course from Greek to Latin, that his Latin was turned into English about 1535, that Elyot did not list the work as his, and he knew of no evidence that he was the translator.[13] A recent biographer gave good reasons for believing Elyot to be the translator: the style is like his, and he was familiar with the other parts of Plutarch's *Moralia.*[14]

The translator follows Plutarch's main ideas but uses freedom, as one may see by merely comparing it with an exact translation. He has retained effective comparisons, including the one to wild beasts. Primitive men were happy to keep wild beasts from harming them; later, men learned to use them for food, clothing, medicine, and even armor. Now men know how to take profit from misfortunes, diseases, and even enemies. We profit from enemies because they have keen eyes for our faults, like vultures scenting carrion; they impel us to improve our lives. Since friendship has lost its power to speak freely, love is blind, and flattery has too much tongue, enemies are the only ones who warn us. We profit if we ask ourselves why each charge was made and what we have been doing to cause wrong impressions, if we learn to control our emotions when our enemies chide, and if we praise them when they deserve praise and thus decrease our own envy. We improve ourselves if we avoid deceit in dealing with enemies, and we gain when we try to surpass them in their virtues.

Elyot's translation, assuming it to be his, has an easy flowing style as if the translator has considered the whole sentence and is expressing the thought in English idiom. His diction is simple; his sentences are clear and well formed, with much balance and parallelism. For example: "These thynges do folde up a tonge, as sayth Demosthenes, these do shutte and close up the mouth, these do stoppe the throte, these cause silence, these cause the [thee] that, as sayth Pyndarus, thou dareste not ones hisce." Again: "But if he cal the unlerned, aplye thou thyself to studye, and quicken thy endevour; if he calle the cowarde, styrre thy corage and the redynes of thy mynde; if he calle thee unchast and vicious, chace out of thy mynde the desyre of luste, if any suche printe, unaware to thee, styche in thee." His short sentences are often firm: "For there is nothinge to be wondred at or notable that groweth from dishoneste."[15]

In the pages of the compilation, *The Manner to Choose and Cherish a Friend,* the ideas clearly resemble those on friendship that Elyot expressed in his known works. One comment is especially interesting: "But yet he that is a good man shal do nothing for his frendes sake that is either against the common welthe or else agaynst his othe or fidelitie. For the offense is not excusable to say, thou dyddest it for thy frendes sake." The passage says, in different words, what Elyot wrote to Cromwell about his friendship for More, that he had never placed it above his oath of allegiance to his king. Another passage pays a high tribute to friendship: "O howe great is the goodnes whan the breastis be prepared redye, in to the whiche all secretenes maye surely descende, whose conscience thou dredest lesse than thyne owne, whose talkynge easeth the grefe and hevynes of thy harte, the sentence gyveth redy and quicke counsaile, the chere dassheth the inwarde sorow, and the very regarde and beholdynge deliteth."[16] As Elyot expressed similar ideas in the *Governour,* in his personal letters, and in other works, one may say that these few pages add to the evidence that he was responsible for the little volume containing *How One May Take Profit of his Enemies* and *The Manner to Choose and Cherish a Friend.* The sentences and the diction in the latter work are also firm and sure: "And he that maketh and proveth his frende festynge at the table doth fayle." This dependent clause also is effective: "But for bicause there be certayne businesses the whiche custome maketh secrete, make thy friende priuie to all thy cares and thoughtes."[17]

The title page of *The Education or the Bringing Up of Children* tells us that the work was translated from Plutarch by Sir Thomas Elyot, Knight. The preface is headed, "Thomas Elyot to his only entierly beloved sister, Margery Puttenham." Though the book is not dated, the colophon tells us that it came from the press of Berthelet, the king's printer.[18] It could not have appeared earlier than 1530, since Berthelet's official appointment and the knighting of Elyot both came about 1530.[19] Both 1533 and 1535 have been suggested as dates of the publication.

The prefatory statements tell us more about Elyot

than the ideas from Plutarch do. The words he uses about Margery indicate that his sister, Eleanor Elyot, the nun at Shaftesbury, had died earlier; other records support this view. It would be a greater grief, Elyot says, to have degraded and vicious children than to have none. After stating that the ideas from Plutarch will be marvelously instructive to his sister, he tactfully corrects himself: they will confirm her own wisdom. He states that his translation is not literal; he has declared some things at greater length, and he has omitted much that is found in both the Greek and the Latin because it is strange to the present time or because the vices Plutarch is reproving should not be stated in the vulgar tongue. He hopes that none will compare his style with that of classic writers because he has done this work as a mere pastime. It will be sufficient reward if his sister trains his little nephews in virtue, so that they may attain honor, be a comfort to friends and parents, and be a profit to their country. (If we may judge from the details that are given about the later lives of Richard and George Puttenham, Elyot was not completely rewarded.) As she succeeds in the training of her children, his love for her will be augmented.

Elyot's wording implies that he had used both Greek and Latin versions of Plutarch. Both were available; the Aldine edition of the Greek text of the *Moralia* had appeared in Venice in 1509, and many Latin versions of parts of his work had been appearing, a favorite selection being the essay on the education of children.[20] Elyot's statement that his translation was not literal can be easily substantiated by comparing it with a modern translation. For example, in chapter xi, he translates Plutarch's material about Antigonus, a king with one eye, and then amplifies by adding the story of Polyphemus.

It seems highly probable that this work especially, as well as the other translations discussed here, had been prepared some years before it was published, perhaps as early as 1524 or 1525, given to Margery Puttenham in manuscript, and then issued in print after the *Governour* had established Elyot's literary reputation. A minor and perhaps a doubtful reason for the assumption is that Elyot does not call himself a knight in the prefatory statement to his sister, though he tended to do so in such instances after 1530; however, the word does appear on the title page. Another minor reason is that his comment in the preface on the lack of children seems somewhat conditional: "For as god shall iuge me, the lacke of children shuld nat be to me so payneful as feare of having succession of heires in whom shulde be lacke of vertue and lerning." Since he had been married ten or twelve years, so far as we can estimate, when the book was published, he must have known his childlessness then as an inescapable fact. Still another minor reason is that his ideas on education are similar to those in the *Governour,* with less individuality and charm. It seems more reasonable to consider them an early preparation for the *Governour,* not a work translated after that *magnum opus* had been given to the public. At any time after 1531, he could have sent his sister a copy of the *Governour,* asking her to read I, chapters iv–xi.

A major reason for supposing that *The Education or the Bringing Up of Children* was prepared for Margery Puttenham some years before it was published lies in the facts about the birth dates of the Puttenham boys. In 1546, when Elyot's will was probated and Richard was declared the next heir after Elyot's wife, that young man was twenty-six years old. Hence he was born about 1520. George Puttenham was perhaps a year or two younger. By 1535, the date usually suggested for the publication of the translation, Richard was fifteen and George perhaps fourteen, the ages for entering a university. Even if the work came out in 1533, Margery Puttenham would have gained little at that time from Plutarch's ideas on parentage, procreation, the duty of mothers to nurse their own children, and the formation of early habits related to nature, reason, and custom. She might have taken some profit from them in the early 1520's. Elyot's suggestion in his preface about Margery's fertility is supported by the pedigree of the Puttenham family. There were four sons, though two of them apparently died early, and three daughters. When Elyot wrote his preface, possibly there were three or four little nephews whose education was a concern to their uncle.[21]


*The Dialogue between Lucian and Diogenes,* a translation from Lucian of some twenty small pages, appeared without date or name of translator, though the editors of the *Short-Title Catalogue* inserted Elyot's name in brackets.[22] There were no other editions. In 1932 Lathrop listed a translation of Lucian's *Cynicus* as the work of Elyot, adding that the translator used More's Latin version.[23] In 1948 Wortham made the same statement, including the use of More's Latin version.[24] In 1960 a biographer of Elyot suggested a date about 1528 or 1530 because virgules are often used instead of commas; he also suggested that it may be the earliest English version of Lucian.[25] Though the use of virgules may have had other reasons, it is true that Berthelet, who published the work, did not describe himself in it as the king's printer. Hence it may have appeared before 1530 or early in that year.

The ideas in the *Dialogue* might appeal to Elyot. Diogenes assumes that virtue consists in avoiding pleasure and that morality lies in a return to simplicity. Lucian accuses him of leading a life like a beast. He answers that his life is desirable: his feet perform well their function of walking, his body is strong, he sleeps well on the ground, and his old cloak is warm. Lucian argues that God has given us fat sheep, sweet wines, meats, money, soft beds, beautiful houses, and their furnishings for our enjoyment.

Diogenes answers that these things are secured with the labor, peril, and death of other men; that many who lie on soft beds are sleepless; that much food weakens the body and causes sickness; and while he walks, men like Lucian travel in litters and use other men like beasts of burden. Those who need many things—children, women, and sick men—are the weaker beings; but Theseus, Hercules, and the gods have few needs. Though Lucian is carried by his desires as if by a stream or a wild horse, Diogenes' own way of life, he says, protects him from the foolish and the un-learned and allows him to choose the company of temper-ate and wise men. Diogenes dominates the discussion throughout, and he has the last words.

Elyot's sympathy for a life without excesses or luxu-ries brought from overseas appears in his other acknowl-edged works. One example is *The Castle of Health,* Sec-ond Book, chapters 19 and 26; another is the simple life of Alexander Severus in *The Image of Governance.* It seems reasonable, then, to consider him the probable translator of *A Dialogue between Lucian and Diogenes*; and so far, no one has suggested a more likely person. If he began it early, to teach himself Greek and Latin, and if he taught himself partly by comparing his work with that of More and with other translations from Lucian by Erasmus, it seems reasonable for him to omit his name in publication and to avoid naming it in 1541 with other published works. These same ideas may apply also to the other anon-ymous translations.

In praising Elyot as a translator who used methods similar to those of Erasmus but did not necessarily pattern work on his, James Wortham mentions Elyot's *Cynicus* as a "sprightly colloquial piece, close to the original in sense, and with an English flavor in its diction." Before Elyot, he says, there were two methods of translating into Eng-lish: first, taking each phrase as a unit and perhaps adding synonyms but keeping them within the phrases; second, interpolating freely, adding phrases, clauses, and whole sentences. Elyot considered whole sentences as units. He realized the characteristic structure of the two languages he worked with, or the differences in idiom; and he was faithful to the original thought. In translating the dialogue he was able to suggest the difference between individual speakers.[26] Since the translations of Erasmus were from Greek into Latin—he never learned enough English to converse well in it or to write it—Elyot's work as a translator into English stands high as an individual achievement.

*The Doctrinal of Princes* carries Elyot's name as the translator and adds that he translated this work of Isocrates from Greek into English. The work appeared in three editions, two of them perhaps in 1534 and the third conjecturally assigned to 1538 or even 1548.[27] It has been described as the first work in the Renaissance to be translated directly from Greek into English; but Gentian Hervet translated Xenophon's *Oeconimus* from Greek to English by 1532, and there may have been an earlier edition. Hervet, a French scholar who had studied with Erasmus, was also a good translator, skillful in the use of English idiom.[28]

Elyot's own interest in Isocrates had probably developed many years before his translation appeared. It may have begun as early as 1516, when Erasmus published a Latin version of the oration to Nicocles, since Elyot tended to follow the translations and the other work of Erasmus. Since Isocrates was trying to influence a ruler, also, his work is a kind of remote ancestor of Erasmus' *Institutio* and Elyot's *Governour*. In the translation Elyot represents Isocrates as telling the young prince that he does "prescribe rules to them that be governours," implying that the prince and his helpers should have the same virtues.

The preface, as well as the title page of the work, tell us that Elyot translated the work from the Greek:

> This little booke . . . I have translated out of greeke, not presumying to contende with theim whiche have doone the same in latine: but to thintent onely that I wolde assaie if our Englisshe tunge mought receive the quicke and propre sentences pronounced by the greekes. And in this experience I have founde (if I be not muche deceived) that the forme of speakyng, used of the Greekes, called in greeke, and also in latine, Phrasis, muche nere approcheth to that whiche at this daie we use, than the order of the latine tunge. I meane in the sentences, and not in the wordes. . . .

He believes that his judgment will be supported by those who know well the three languages and who read his translation with good understanding.[29]

Elyot's forthright statement carries conviction, though a scholar has recently spoken with doubt about his knowledge of the Greek language.[30] Perhaps the scholar had not seen this preface or an article, cited later in this chapter, by James Wortham. There is other evidence that Elyot had a good knowledge of Greek. In London, during the first decade of the century, when More was learning Greek with the help of Grocyn, Linacre, and Lily, he had a wonderful chance to learn the language. In the preface to *The Castle of Health* (1541) he told us of the worshipful, renowned physician who had read medical works to him in Greek before he was twenty years old. His comments in the *Governour* on the need for translations support his own knowledge. Aristotle's *Ethicae,* he says in I, xi, must be studied in the Greek, for the translations that we have so far are a mere shadow of the author's eloquence and wisdom. In I, xxv, he says that Englishmen, compared with French, Italians, and Germans, have been slow in translating the wisdom of the Greeks. Ascham's praise of

Elyot's learning in *Toxophilus* seems evidence that he knew Greek since Ascham was one of two or three outstanding Greek scholars of his period.[31] He does not mention Greek, to be sure, but he says that for his many kinds of learning, Elyot brings much worship to all the nobility of England. More was living and may even have been still a free man when Elyot published his first edition of *The Doctrinal of Princes*. Nothing that we know of Elyot's character gives us the right to call him an empty boaster; and even if he had been inclined to play fast and loose with the truth, he would not have risked the unfavorable judgment of men like More and Ascham.

Perhaps Elyot chose to publish *The Doctrinal of Princes* because Isocrates was highly regarded in the Renaissance both for his thought and his style. He wished to give his readers pleasure in a work as artistic as he could make the form of a prose oration. Since Isocrates influenced first the Greeks, then Cicero, and through Cicero the entire western world, perhaps he was the most important influence on style in the Renaissance. Though he used the term *oration*, he did not mean a speech but a written discourse, a political pamphlet intended to mold public opinion. Probably he never delivered a speech in his life because he lacked the voice and the confidence and because he loved a quiet life. His ideas on a sane and practical morality also passed from the Greeks to the Romans and then to the Christians.[32] Of course Elyot was always glad to take an opportunity to teach a few more ideas on good government.

The ideas expressed in *The Doctrinal of Princes* seem conventional enough to the modern reader, at least to one who has been following the work of Erasmus and of the other humanists in the period. Elyot himself had stated most of the ideas of Isocrates in the *Governour*, and he would state many of them again in the *Image of Governance*. An early sixteenth-century humanist was never afraid of repetition; he accepted it as a cardinal principle of education. A ruler should further peace, Isocrates said, keep the country wealthy if it has wealth, study hard, secure wise counselors, take care of his people, change bad laws and ordinances, make good and universal laws, love his people, do nothing in anger and nothing cruel, consider as loyal not the ones who praise him for everything but the ones who tell him his faults, dress well enough to look like a ruler but be continent in other living, follow himself the rules he gives his children and his servants, and hold consultations before he decides on a course of action.

Elyot was not making any special and conscious effort to influence Henry VIII in *The Doctrinal of Princes* about his attitudes to Sir Thomas More. Of course he probably penned any comment on government with the pious hope that it might have an influence on his beloved England. But this particular work has nothing that is either timely or urgent. It is not dedicated to Cromwell or to the king or to anyone else in the government, if one may use negative evidence; and if Elyot really wished to influence Henry VIII to clemency, standard procedure suggests that it would have been dedicated to him, with praise for his clemency! Though Elyot does praise the wisdom and brevity of the work beyond anything except scripture, he moves quickly to the fact that he has translated directly from the Greek and that he has discovered interesting relationships between the English and the Greek languages.

If the ideas of the whole work and of the preface do not indicate an urgent desire to influence the king about More, the same thing may be said of the phrases in the margin and of the "Addicion to fill up vacant pages." The marginal comments (beginning with the avoiding of injuries and hurtful traditions and establishing laws for the universal welfare, continuing with warnings against crafty flatterers and false detractors, and concluding with the usual emphasis upon a good counselor) have nothing timely or urgent. The "Addicion" of about two pages, it has been suggested, deals with clemency. So it does, after other general comments from scripture on kings. But clemency is specifically related to a king's concern with widows, the fatherless, and all oppressed people; to his duty about tempering severe laws, and to his conduct in wars. A king should not wage war if he can avoid it; if he must go to war, let him spill as little human blood as he possibly can, and end the war quickly. Clemency in war receives emphasis both by space and by terminal position. Such ideas have as little relation to Sir Thomas More as a man could devise if he wished to stress clemency.

Probably Elyot was not recognized as a great translator in his own time or even in the latter part of the sixteenth century. Many comments on him in that time are praise, but vague praise like that of Nash, in his preface to Greene's *Menaphon*, when he says that his "elegance did sever itself from all equals."

But in the twentieth century, H. B. Lathrop and James Wortham have given Elyot high praise for his achievement, both as a stylist and as a translator, in *The Doctrinal of Princes*. Isocrates guided him, it is said, to an excellent English prose:

> [It was] not only accurate in syntax, but made, so far as he could make it, flowing in movement, and given a pattern after the ideas of Isocrates. Roger Ascham is generally given the credit for inaugurating the influence here attributed to Elyot; but Elyot is half a generation earlier . . . he [Ascham] had before him the encouraging example of the older writer.[33]

Elyot used all the methods Erasmus had used in translating from Greek into Latin, Wortham says, and he succeeded in his translation from Greek into English. He weighed whole sentences for their meaning, instead of counting words or translating a phrase as if it were a unit. He reproduced variations of tone, figures of sound, and even the texture of the original. He remembered idiom. He attained brevity and conciseness, or what he called a "compendious" style. He also considered something that Erasmus did not undertake: the prose rhythm. He reproduced rhythm, phrasing, and the *schemata verborum,* using balance and antithesis. He used clauses of equal length, a series of words with the same endings or similar ones, an antithesis of words and ideas, a repetition of the same word with different inflections, other effective repetition, and alliteration. "Each of the short paragraphs into which he divided the work forms a rhythmical unit consistent in itself and coming to a rather stable conclusion in a sort of cadence." At times, Wortham says, Elyot's translation of Isocrates goes beyond craftsmanship "and becomes art by virtue of his own control of diction, rhythm, and melody." Wortham concludes his encomium with the statement that he has examined all the prose translations of classical works printed before 1580 and that he has found "no other which seems to fulfill all the principles recognized by Elyot."[34] Thus his estimate is not only high praise but also sound praise.

Such a translation probably would not develop in a few weeks or a few months. If Elyot began reading Isocrates when Erasmus published his Latin version of the *Oratio* to Nicocles. even if he began translating it at that time as an exercise, he may have worked at intervals for more than fifteen years on the version he finally published. We do not know about his influence on other translators. But it seems safe to conclude that before 1580 Sir Thomas Elyot ranks highest as a translator from Greek into English because of his *Doctrinal of Princes.*

# CHAPTER XIII

## The Castle of Health, *1536–1539*
## *(1539, 1541)*.
## *Events, ca. 1535–1536*

HE years 1535–1536 must have continued to be difficult ones for Sir Thomas Elyot. After he had acted as sheriff for the counties of Cambridge and Huntingdon in 1533, in spite of his two letters of protest to Thomas Cromwell, his name seldom appeared on governmental commissions. He had not been paid for his past services, nor had he been appointed to any office of importance. He was waiting perhaps to see whether he would be condemned by Cromwell or Henry VIII for guilt by association with Sir Thomas More. Several letters to Cromwell seem a defense against such an accusation, whether it had been made or whether he merely feared that it would be made; and in a later letter he begged Cromwell to put aside the memory of his friendship for More. Thus the fear continued to haunt him. In January, 1535, he was appointed on the Commission for the Tenths of the Spiritualities, for Oxfordshire and the Town of Oxford—a group of eighteen or twenty men with four of them starred as auditors.[1] Perhaps his appointment was a test of his willingness to collect these taxes, since the king had become head of the church in England, or perhaps the appointment was mere routine. Apparently he did his part of the work on the commission.

If Elyot was a man of normal sensitivity, as he seems to have been, he must have suffered, both as a friend and an adherent of the old religion, at some of the executions and the other deaths in the period. On April 29, 1535, a verdict of guilt on an accusation of treason was returned against John Houghton, the prior of the London Charterhouse, three Charterhouse priors in other localities, and Richard Reynolds of Syon House. The first verdict, it is said, was an acquittal; but after Cromwell had threatened the jury if they refused to convict, they reluctantly pronounced the men guilty. On May 4, the condemned churchmen were executed in the robes of their orders, instead of being degraded first, and the executions were the ultimate in brutality. On June 19, seven Charterhouse monks were drawn on hurdles through London to the place of execution and then hanged and quartered. On June 22, Bishop Fisher, whose sentence as a traitor had been eased from hanging and disemboweling at Tyburn, was beheaded on Tower Hill. On July 1, Sir Thomas More was condemned as a traitor; and the king's carefully arranged program of terror having failed to shake his resolution he was beheaded July 6 on Tower Hill.[2] Though Elyot was a younger associate of More, not the other self that Erasmus had been by maturity and temperament, he must have been shocked at the execution of a friend who had once been so powerful.

On January 7, 1536, Catherine of Aragon died in the isolation of Kimbolton Castle with only Chapuys and Lady Willoughby (who had been Maria de Salinas, her Spanish attendant) to visit her in her last days. As Elyot had taken risks in trying to support her cause, her death could not have left him unmoved.

On January 29, the day of Catherine's funeral, Anne

Boleyn gave premature birth to a dead child, the son Henry had desired. On April 24 Cromwell formed a secret commission to try Anne as soon as evidence against her could be collected. On May 2 she was taken as a prisoner to the Tower. On May 17, Cranmer relieved the king from the stigma of executing his queen by declaring that the marriage to Anne had been void from the beginning. On May 19 Anne was beheaded on Tower Hill. Next day the king was formally betrothed to Jane Seymour, and ten days later they were married in a private ceremony at York Place.[3]

Through the events that immediately followed the death of Catherine, Elyot continued his efforts to exert some influence. As early as April 1, 1536, Chapuys reported a visit from a Mr. Gelyot, doubtless Elyot, who gave him the first news that the king was courting a young woman named Seymour. Later the news was confirmed by a marchioness, perhaps the Dowager Marchioness of Dorset. The conservative nobility planned for Jane Seymour to tell the king in their presence that many of his subjects considered the marriage to Anne Boleyn "abominable and incestuous" and they would support her declaration.[4] But as Henry had tired of Anne, their plans were not necessary.

Elyot and the other conservatives were probably acting as Catherine of Aragon would have wished them to act after her death—so that Henry might have a legitimate heir to the throne, perhaps a son. At this time the Princess Mary was said to be willing to give up any claim to the throne if her father had other children that she could consider legitimate. Elyot was thus continuing to act with loyalty to Catherine and her daughter and also with loyalty to the conservative religion. He must also have been watching with great shrewdness; for the dates indicate that he was reporting the king's interest in Jane Seymour almost a month before Cromwell organized his secret commission to find evidence against Anne Boleyn. Also he must have taken some risk in his talk with Chapuys, since that careful ambassador reported such details to the emperor, and Cromwell had broken his code about 1535.[5]

Some other public and governmental actions were surely not entirely pleasing to Elyot. On January 25, 1535, the king issued a commission to Thomas Cromwell, his vicar-general as head of the church, for a general visitation of churches, clergy, and religious houses, in accordance with an earlier act of Parliament. The visitors were to inquire into the lives and morals of those who lived in such houses, remove and punish the guilty, receive resignations offered them, give pensions, appoint successors, and take oaths of fealty to the king.[6] These aims probably would not have troubled Elyot. Many Englishmen, like Erasmus and More, who saw the need for reform, were conservative about doctrine. But Elyot would not have approved the methods of the two prominent commissioners, Richard Leighton and Thomas Leigh, who were pompous, insolent, brutal, receptive to bribes, determined to discover damning evidence, and inclined to cover territory like animated whirlwinds.[7]

If Elyot approved the action of Parliament, in March, 1536, giving to the king and his heirs all monasteries not having a clear annual revenue of £200, he would probably not have been completely happy at the results. The act contained words about "manifest sin, carnal and abominable living," and a declaration that many great and solemn places in the realm were not guilty of these excesses. But when the skirmishes were over and the smoke had cleared away, some of the houses left standing were those gravely accused by Layton and Leigh. About 376 houses were dissolved; the crown received new revenues estimated at £32,000 a year, in addition to plate, jewels, and other movable property.[8]

In the latter part of May, 1536, Reginald Pole sent

the king his treatise *Pro ecclesiasticae unitatis defensione.*
He had formulated his views, as the king requested. But
instead of supporting Henry, he attacked his separation
from Catherine and his assuming a position as head of the
church; and he defended the unity of the church.[9] He pru-
dently declined an invitation to return to England. So
far as one can judge, Elyot remained in sympathy with
some of Pole's views.

Lest previous statutes might be insufficient to cover
details, the Parliament which began its session in June,
1536, abolished all authority of the Bishop of Rome.[10]

In July, 1536, Convocation endorsed the Ten Articles
of religious faith given them by the king, though the details probably owed something to the persuasions of Cromwell and Cranmer. Religious truth, the articles stated, is
contained in the Bible, the three creeds, and the decisions
of the first four councils; three sacraments are necessary—
baptism, penance, and that of the altar; penance includes
confession, absolution, and amendment, with prayer, fasting, and alms; justification is based on both faith and good
works; images may be permitted as symbols, and saints are
worthy of honors and prayers; vestments, holy water, and
lights may be continued but have no power to remit sins;
prayers for the dead are worthy of praise but the belief that
pardons or Masses can deliver a soul from purgatory is a
superstition.[11] The articles had been carefully worded as
a bid for German support. That Elyot was not in complete sympathy with them becomes clear when one examines his effusive praise of the king in 1538 for a return
to greater orthodoxy.

About the middle of 1536 (if a letter from Elyot to
Cromwell is correctly assigned to this year, as it seems to
be) there were signs of a thaw in the relationship of Elyot
to his superiors. Like other letters of Elyot, it carries no
year date; Croft's reasons for placing it earlier have now
been disproved; and the editors of *Letters and Papers* . . .

have assigned it to June, 1536. Events occurring before
and after that year make the date seem probable. These
are the pertinent parts of the letter:

> Sir, where it liked you at my last being with you at the
> Rolls to minister unto me most gentle words to my great
> comfort, I have often times since revolved them in my
> remembrance, setting in you only all my whole confidence,
> and so do persist. Where late I have traveled about the
> surveying of certain monasteries by the King's command-
> ment, wherein my pains should appear not unthankful, if
> opportunity might [Elyot's word is printed as *mowght*]
> happen for me to declare it. If now, sir, it might [mought]
> like you in approving your benevolent mind toward me,
> wherein I do specially trust, to set forth with your gentle
> report unto the king's highness my true heart and diligent
> endeavor in his grace's service, to my importable charges
> and unrecuperable decay of my living, unless his highness
> relieve me with his . . . gracious liberality; and therewith
> it might please you to devise with his highness for my
> convenient recompense toward my said charges either by
> lands now suppressed or pension, I shall not only take
> comfort of your approved fidelity and the same advance
> unto your honor, but also in such wise order me toward
> you as ye shall deem me not unworthy your gentle re-
> membrance. . . . I would [have] awaited on you as my
> duty had been, but that I dread to find you occupied with
> great affairs, which of late hath caused me to make many
> vain journeys when I have been right desirous to see you,
> not for my necessity only but to have communicate with
> you some tokens of hearty friendship. . . .[12]

Perhaps Elyot's work in surveying certain monasteries
at the king's command had furthered the thaw in his treatment, though he could hardly have refused without grave
risk; and perhaps his suggestion that he might receive
some of the suppressed lands further pleased both Cromwell and the king. Whatever the reason, Elyot was emerg-
ing from political limbo. In November, 1536, he was on
the Commission of the Peace for Oxfordshire, and he con-

tinued to be named with the group for some time in the future.[13]

Elyot prepared his first edition of *The Castle of Health* to aid Cromwell in his illness—a fact that seems natural enough when we consider the way Elyot depended on Cromwell to further his fortunes. The first edition came from the press some time between 1536 and 1539. Since Elyot addresses Cromwell as lord privy seal, 1536 is the earliest possible date. The only extant copy known is in the Historical Collections of the Yale Medical Library. It is one of the five editions appearing in Elyot's lifetime. In 1539 both octavo and quarto versions were issued, in 1541 a quarto version, and either in 1541 or 1544 another octavo edition. Some nine others appeared before 1600 and another in 1610.[14] Judging by the number of editions, *The Castle* was one of the most popular of Elyot's books.

Perhaps *The Castle of Health* became popular for two reasons. First, Elyot himself was gaining a sure position as a writer. Second, during the Renaissance people in all Europe as well as in England were vitally interested in information about medicine and health. Perhaps the second is the more important reason. In this period physicians, scholars, and other laymen were furthering a many-sided growth of medical knowledge and practice. Scholars were reading the classical works on medicine in the original Greek, writing commentaries on them, and instead of using earlier versions through the Arabic, translating them directly from Greek into Latin. Laymen, instead of ecclesiastics, were taking up the practice of medicine in growing numbers. Physicians were drafting requirements both for the study of medicine and for licenses to practice the art of healing. Students of medicine were using dissection to learn anatomy and new facts about the organs of the body. Sixtus IV, pope from 1471 to 1484, issued a bull authorizing the use of cadavers for dissection; and Clement VII, pope from 1523 to 1534, confirmed the authorization. Especially in Italy, hospitals and pharmacies were being established. Students of natural science and botany were discovering new uses of plants and herbs as medicines. Writers in various countries developed a literature of medicine and personal hygiene aimed at helping the layman in his growing desire to improve his health.[15]

In England, Thomas Linacre, with his medical degree from Padua, his lectures on scientific subjects, his translations from Galen, his establishment of a college of physicians in London with standards for a license to practice, and his plan for lectureships in medicine at the universities, apparently fostered his own interest in other people.[16] Because Linacre helped More with his Greek, as we know (and without any reasonable doubt was the physician who read Galen and other medical works to Elyot), the interest in medicine spread through the More household. In the early years of the century Erasmus wrote a *Declamatio* in praise of medicine; he published it in 1518, and it appeared in an English translation about 1530.[17] More himself learned enough medicine to suggest to the doctors the glister which led to his daughter Margaret's recovery from an almost fatal illness. At one time he expressed the hope that she would study medicine and thus prepare herself for the whole scope of life—a healthy soul in a healthy body. Margaret Gigs, More's foster daughter, once diagnosed More's illness from her reading of Galen. John Clement, who was connected with More's household and his school and who later married Margaret Gigs, gave up his Greek readership at Oxford to study medicine, and became a distinguished physician. Richard Herde, student and tutor in More's school before his early death, also became a physician. Without the influence of Linacre, probably Elyot would not have been prepared to write *The Castle of Health*.

Many other writers about this time were publishing books to help the average citizen care for his health. Judging from the title, one was directed to poor men; one, at least, concerned the pestilence. Sometimes a single work ran through as many as fifteen editions. As books on childbirth and anatomy appear in the lists, the reading public must have had an appetite for varied medical knowledge. In 1528 Thomas Paynell ventured to publish a translation of the *Regimen sanitatis Salerni,* a medieval work which had circulated through Europe for generations, with some 200 separate editions including Irish, Bohemian, Provençal, and Hebrew. The original recommendations in verse had been amplified here and there by comments in prose; and, for the times, it is said to have been a useful and a sensible work.[18] Thus Elyot's *Castle of Health* was only one of a great company of works on medicine.

References to *The Castle* in the sixteenth century indicate that it made an appeal to the public, and some readers valued it for other reasons besides its concern with health. Thomas Whythorne, a musician, whose autobiography was written about 1576 but published in 1961–1962, apparently considered it a favorite book. His editor suggests that he followed Elyot's analysis of the ages of man with only one variation: Elyot names four periods—adolescence to age 24, juventute from 25 to 39, senectute from 40 to 60, and age decrepit from 60 to death. Whythorne divides the first period into two parts: childhood to age 15, and adolescence from 16 to 24. Whythorne seems also to follow Elyot in his assumptions about the effect of borage; he tells the story of a gentlewoman who fell in love with him but did not win him over because he refused to commit adultery. When she could not sleep at night, she took borage to make her heart light.[19] Elyot had said of borage: "Comforteth the harte and maketh one merye, eaten rawe before meals, or layde in wine that is drunke. . . ."

Whythorne did not mention Elyot in connection with these details, but his modern editor points out the parallels.

In his discussion of the power of music to ease the dolor of the mind, Whythorne does mention *The Castle of Health* as well as the *Governour,* with Elyot's reproof of those who misuse music.[20] Apparently he had in mind the Third Book, chapter 12, of *The Castle,* where Elyot suggests that one avoid being angry, studious, or solitary, and that he rejoice with melody.

In *The Haven of Health,* 1584, Thomas Cogan paid his respects to Elyot and informed his readers about his own methods:

> If they [the readers] finde whole sentences taken out of Maister Eliote his Castle of Health or out of *Schola Salerni,* or anie other author whatsoever, that they will not condemne me of vaine glorie . . . as if I meant to set foorth for mine owne works that which other men have devised, for I confesse that I have taken *Verbatim* out of others where it served for my purpose, and especiallie out of *Schola Salerni:* but I have so enterlaced it with mine owne that . . . it may be the better perceived. And therefore, seeing that all my travaile tendeth to common commoditie, I trust everie man will interpret all to the best.[21]

The popularity of Elyot's *Castle of Health* is suggested also by the Household Account Books of William More. Though his library, about 1600, had only a copy of *The Defense of Good Women* and no copy of the *Governour,* except in a list under a later date, there were three copies of *The Castle of Health.* The third time when the maker of the inventory noted the title he added, "Agayne the Castel of Helthe."[22]

Elyot's prefatory statements for the early editions of *The Castle* are perhaps the most interesting and revealing parts of his work, for the general student. The first edition (1536–1539); the one of 1539; and the quarto edition of 1541 have three entirely different prefaces.

In the first of these editions, addressing himself to Thomas Cromwell as lord privy seal, Elyot stresses the idea of giving with goodwill and promptness to one who is worthy to receive the gift. About two months earlier, when he went to Cromwell's house to salute him, he says, servants told him that Cromwell was suffering from some illness or disease. He realizes that a man who carries great responsibilities must sometimes experience a failure of his bodily powers. He thinks of Cromwell's many great qualities and of the times that Cromwell "advanced moste gentylly" Elyot's own poor reputation with the king and also with other worshipful people. Cromwell has also assisted him in various pursuits. Because of these things, he has gathered from the most ancient and noble authors the necessary information on medicine, for those who love virtue; and he gives it to Cromwell as one who is worthy to receive it. Since emperors and other great men have not only studied but also practiced medicine, he defends his own right as a knight to explain the principles of good health. In closing he says that Cromwell is "the principall and fryste occasion" that moved him to begin this honest enterprise.[23]

The preface of the 1539 edition is also addressed to Cromwell. Because of Cromwell's illness or disease, he says, he had made such speed in getting *The Castle* ready for him that there were imperfections. Thus he makes clear that he is issuing a revised edition. As his membership in the lower house of Parliament has given him little leisure, there may still be errors. He can see Cromwell with the eye of memory as clearly as those who sit with him daily at meals are able to do. He does not choose his friends in order to follow fortune, as swine follow a girl who carries a pail of milk on her head but forsake her if the pail falls or is empty. The moderate person who loves a friend possessing virtue and authority will continue to love him if he loses the authority. (One wonders about this comment, but surely he would not have made it if he had feared the fall of Cromwell, which came the next year.) He apologizes for speaking much of friendship, but it is a treasure more precious than anything contained in the mountains of Ethiopia or the rivers of India; and he wishes to recall the friendship to one who has little leisure to think of it. His *Castle* is a monument to his long-continued affection for Cromwell, and he will pray for Cromwell's continued health and fortune.[24]

The preface of the 1541 quarto edition is not addressed to any individual. Cromwell had been executed in July, 1540. Instead, Elyot strikes back at his critics. Since even Galen, the most excellent physician, feared to lose his labor because people in his time did not care for the truth, Elyot thinks that he should not be grieved by the reproaches of his countrymen. They say that a knight who is not a doctor might be better occupied than in trying to write on medicine. Again, his labors have been "taken without hope of temporall rewarde, onely for the fervent affectyon whiche I have ever borne toward the publike weale of my countraye." In the past, kings and emperors have helped advance medicine, and a king of England asked for the *Regimen sanitatis*. He hopes that Henry VIII, "who dayly preparith to stablyshe among us true and uncorrupted doctrines" and who "hath not dysdained to be the chief authour and settar fourthe of an Introduction in to Grammer, for the childerne of his loving subiectes," will act to advance the study of medicine.

Elyot refutes his critics by explaining this time that he has a considerable knowledge of medicine: a worshipful physician, one of the most renowned at that time in England, had read to him, before he was twenty years of age, works of Galen *De temperamentis* and *De naturalibus facultatibus,* also Johannitius, and some *Aphorisms* of Hippocrates. Later, by his own study, he continues to explain, he had read, "in order the more parte" of Hippocrates, Galen, Oribasius, Paulus Celius, Alexander Trallianus, Celsus, both Plinys, and Dioscorides. He had even read the Canons of Avicenna, the commentaries of Averroes, the practices of "Isake," Halyabbas, "Rasys," and Mesuë, and also "the more part of them which were their aggregatours [adherents] and folowers." Physicians should not be angry with him: he wrote his book to help people prevent illness by watching their diets, and when they become ill, to analyze their own symptoms and report them more accurately to their doctors. Thus he wrote his *Castle* to help doctors, not injure them. Physicians should not be angry with him because he has put medical information into English: "let theym remembre that the grekes wrate in greke, the Romanes in latyne, Auicena and the other in Arabike, which were their owne propre and maternal tonges." If these earlier physicians had been as envious and covetous as some in his own day, they would have used some strange cipher to conceal their knowledge. He closes his preface by saying that his own motives are not glory, reward, or promotion, but the desire to give others profitable information. His material is sound because it comes from the best writers on medicine, and it will not harm doctors who use Christian charity.[25]

Several of these ideas from the 1541 preface of *The Castle* call for further discussion or explanation. When he says that the king "dayly preparith to stablyshe among us true and uncorrupted doctrines," he probably has in mind the Six Articles of 1539, when the pendulum was swinging back to religious conservatism and the subsequent efforts to enforce these doctrines. The account of Henry as the author and setter-forth of a grammar may be based on the fact that he did issue a proclamation requiring that a certain textbook be used by all teachers of the subject within the realm.[26] This grammar was a compilation by Colet and Lily, and was emended by Erasmus. So far as we know, the king never wrote a grammar. If Elyot was referring to his proclamation about a textbook, he was carrying courtly compliment to the extreme outskirts of truth or he was uninformed (as he may well have been since he was not a teacher, and the multiple authorship was confusing).

Elyot's defense of English as a language for medical information echoes, in ideas and phrasing, More's defense of the Bible in English. Though More's position is often misunderstood, he insisted in the *Dialogue concerning Heresies* that the clergy should not keep from the people all English Bibles and had not done so in the past. But because Wycliffe and Tyndale were heretics he hotly opposed their translations. He suggested a version translated by a good Catholic with learning or by a group conferring together, a version approved by the bishops, and distributed by the bishops' deputies to those capable of using it wisely. No good thing should be withheld from all because a few might abuse it:

> Nor I never yet heard any reason layd why it were not convenient to have the byble translated into the englishe tong but al those reasons . . . myght . . . as wel be layde against the holy writers that wrote the scripture in the Hebrue tongue, and against the blessed evangelistes that wrote the scripture in Greke, and against all those in likewise that translated it oute of every of those tonges into latine, as to their charge that would well and faithfully translate it oute of latine into our englishe tong. For as for that our tong is called barbarous is but a fantasye . . . there is no doubte but it is plenteous enough to expresse our myndes in anye thing wherof one man hath used to speke with another. . . . For scripture . . . was not writen but in a vulgare tonge, suche as the whole people understode, nor in no secrete cyphers but such common letters as almost every man could rede.[27]

The parallels or perhaps the common points of view between More and Elyot seem obvious.

The differences in medical details and even in the arrangement of material in the various editions of *The Castle of Health* are of interest only to the specialist in the history of medicine. In the discussion that follows, about details which are of interest to the biographer and the literary student, the 1541 quarto edition will be cited because it is Elyot's revised version and is accessible in a modern facsimile.

Elyot's concern with the English vocabulary appears often in *The Castle*, as it does in his other works. Introducing his list of remedies to purge superfluous humors, in the Third Book, chapter 6, he names the five doctors from whose books he has gathered them: Dioscorides, Galen, Paulus Egineta, Oribasius, Aëtius, and other late writers; he adds that he has been unable to list everything because we do not have the English words to express some of the details. In the Fourth Book, chapter 1, also, he uses the words *crudity* and *lassitude,* explaining that they are words he has made from Latin because no English terms are available, but he hopes to explain them well enough so that they could henceforth be used in English. In such examples his approach is completely practical. He is not adding synonyms, as he did earlier, merely to augment the language.

Elyot's style in *The Castle* is remarkably simple, and he uses some highly effective figures of speech. In the Second Book, chapter 25, when he advises old men to eat often but to take a little food at a time, he compares them to lamps in which the light is almost extinct. If one pours a little oil at a time into the lamp, the flame will burn well; if he pours in a quantity of oil, he will put out the flame. In chapter 28 of the same book he uses well an elaborate figure of Gluttony in his glorious chariot called welfare, driving us before him into his dungeon of surfeit.

There we are tormented with catarrh, fever, gout, pleurisy, and other sicknesses; and we are put to death either in youth or at least in a pleasant time when we would gladly live. The nobility are especially liable to enter this dungeon and thus to shorten their own lives. In the *Governour,* some years earlier, Elyot had stressed medical ideas and comparisons. He had compared evil opinions to sores and diseases, recommended sobriety in diet, said that governors, who should cure the ills of the public weal, are physicians to the state, and in their need for consultation they are like physicians, who should not prescribe medicines until they have learned the nature of the illness.[28] In *Pasquil the Plain* Elyot compared the confessor, responsible for a man's soul, to a physician who heals the body.

Using the ideas on excess as a springboard, Elyot leaps into another favorite topic, the need to make and then to enforce good laws. We have sometimes made laws against vain expenses, especially of the common people, he says, but we have not enforced them. The topic of law is a favorite, not only with Elyot, but with Colet, Erasmus, Vives, John Rastell, and More; the Utopians, for example, were dominated by law. In the intellectual climate of the period, at least of the humanists, two means were stressed for the regeneration of society: education, and good laws strictly enforced.

The foods that Elyot mentions in *The Castle* are interesting, since they indicate what an Englishman had available to eat about 1535 to 1540, though perhaps not what the average one was really eating. Under meats he discusses swine's flesh, mutton, kid, veal, hare, cony, and red and fallow deer. Of fallow deer neither Hippocrates nor any other old writer speaks, he says, because there are more of them in England than in all the rest of the world together; they consume much of the best pasture and are good for nothing except leather. In discussing birds he mentions hens, capons, chickens, pheasant, partridge, quail, larks, plover, blackbirds, sparrows, woodcocks, pigeons, geese, ducks, cranes, bustards, heron, bittern, and shovelers. Under parts, he names the common ones such as liver and gizzard, but also includes tripe and chitterlings. Some of his specific comments are interesting: beef makes a good food for healthy Englishmen but it engenders melancholy; sparrows are hard to digest and their brains especially stir up Venus; five or six almonds eaten before meat will keep a man from drunkenness.

Under the heading of fruits he discusses the desirable and undesirable qualities of melons, pepons [pumpkins], cucumbers, dates, figs, grapes, raisins, cherries, peaches, apples, quinces, pomegranates, pears, medlars, walnuts, and many other fruits and nuts. Under the heading of herbs to be used in pottage or eaten, he includes enough herbs and vegetables to make up a modern seed catalogue. Though he mentions the sow-thistle and the dandelion [his word is *dentdelyon*] he does not recommend them for well people because of their bitterness. Under the heading of spices that grow out of the realm, those used in food or drink, he mentions pepper, ginger, saffron, cloves, mace, and nutmegs; he also names at some time coriander seed and cinnamon. Other foods, medicines, or seasonings that he knows are spinach, pulse, mushrooms, mustard, rue, citron, yreos [iris], and elecampane [later known as horseheal]. He is concerned, of course, with the relation of all these foods or seasonings to health.

Elyot's simple, clear explanation of the four elements in *The Castle of Health* (also in the beginning of the *Governour*) may have influenced later sixteenth-century writers, including Shakespeare, even if they were able to find statements in other sources. In the first chapter of *The Castle* he defines the elements as "those originall thinges unmyxt and uncompounde, of whose temperance and myxture all other thynges, havynge corporall substaunce, be compacte. . . ." Of the four elements the earth is the heaviest, and in its own nature it is cold and dry. Water is subtler and lighter than earth but heavier than air and fire; in its own nature it is cold and moist. Fire is absolutely light and clear, is the purifier of other elements if they are corrupted, and is properly hot and dry. Mortals do not usually see or feel these elements in their pure form but so mixed and corrupted that they are earthy, watery, airy, and fiery, not absolute earth, water, air, and fire.

These elements, Elyot says, are mingled in the body of every human being, and though each person has some of all four, yet the complexion results from a combination of two of the four elements in one body. Thus we have the sanguine, the phlegmatic, the choleric, and the melancholy man. The sanguine man is one in whom heat and moisture have sovereignty and air has the pre-eminence. The choleric man is hot and dry; in him fire is dominant. The melancholy man is cold and dry; the earth rules him. Besides the complexion of the whole body, each member of the body has its proper complexion also, and any distemperature there results in sickness of that member. Thus the treatment of diseases becomes an effort to bring the body or the member that is out of balance back to the proper proportion of these elements. Hippocrates had used these ideas in part and Galen was a major source for them, but if Elyot did nothing more he at least gave a clear exposition of them in English, one from which Elizabethans might continue to draw. Readers of Shakespeare will recall the Dauphin's horse in *Henry V;* Cleopatra's comments, as she prepares to kill herself, about becoming air and fire; Petruchio's reasoning about foods in *The Taming of the Shrew;* the melancholy Jaques in *As You Like It,* and other similar ideas.

Elyot's discussion of melancholy may have contributed to the Elizabethan emphasis on the melancholy man. In the First Book of *The Castle* he analyzes melancholy or black choler, as natural and unnatural, with the unnatural tending to violence and murder. In the Third Book, chapter 18, he analyzes effects and suggests remedies. Natural melancholy in moderation, he says, helps the wit. Melancholy adust or burned melancholy harms the wit and judgment; in one stage it makes men mad; in another stage it makes them fools, forgetful and dull. In some forms of it the victim may seem to be asleep, needing a spur to prick him forward; in other forms he may be given to sudden fury, lack of control over his tongue, paleness, fearful dreams of darkness, deep pits, the death of friends, and everything black. As remedies Elyot suggests certain foods; but above all, the person afflicted should use moderate exercise and diet and seek good company, mirth, and gladness.

In the Third Book, chapters 11 and 12, Elyot deals with the effects of the mind, specifically with anger, grief or heaviness of mind, and joy. In this connection he quotes scripture and the classical philosophers, but he also points out the physical effects of the emotions and prescribes foods that may be helpful. He spends most of his space on heaviness of mind, naming among the causes ingratitude, death of children, loss of goods, lack of promotion, and the chances of fortune. In discussing ingratitude at length, he says that he does so because in this grief he has had "sufficient experience."

In the sixteenth century it is fitting that the last chapter of *The Castle of Health* should be concerned with the pestilence. Elyot discusses the bodies most susceptible to the infection, placing first the sanguine, then the choleric, the phlegmatic [his word is "fleumatike"], and then, as the least likely of all, the melancholic person. In suggesting diet, he cites Marsilio Ficino. He also recommends cleanliness of body and prescribes the pills "invented" by Rufus, probably Rufus of Ephesus, who had written the first descriptions of the bubonic plague.

One of the most interesting facts about *The Castle* is the amazing number of authorities, medical and non-medical, that Elyot cites. As he is writing for laymen and including suggestions on self-control, he mentions such philosophers as Plato and Seneca. He also refers to Apollodorus the philosopher; Appianus, a Greek historian of Alexandria; Aristoxenus, who was a disciple of Aristotle, a musician, and the writer of the earliest extant book on music; Pliny the Younger, whom he names as if he were a medical authority; Theognis, a Greek poet of Megara; and Titus Livius. Since he is a moralist and a Christian philosopher, he often mentions Ecclesiasticus and other books of the Bible as authorities.

Elyot's medical authorities range from the earliest physicians mentioned in the history of medicine up to his own time. His explanation, in the Proheme of the 1541 edition, cited earlier in this chapter, indicates that he had read widely, both with his renowned physician and later on his own initiative. Throughout the work he continues to name, either in the discussion or in the margin, outstanding authorities from the Greek, the Latin, the Byzantine, the Mohammedan and Jewish or Arabic periods, the late Medieval period, and a few contemporaries. Often his citations are specific: for example, Dioscorides, book 2, chapter 106; Hippocrates, *Aphorisms,* 13, li. 1; Galen, *De sanitate tuenda,* the first book. His comments and references certainly sound as if he had been reading these works in the original, not in some compendium, though to many people it would seem unbelievable. It is possible that he borrowed books from Linacre, who probably had during his active life the best medical library in the British Isles.

Elyot is certainly somewhat selective about those he cites. Though he had read Avicenna and Averroes, he names Avicenna only once, for the minor detail that hens are better when roasted in the belly of a kid or a lamb.

He does not cite Averroes at all in the 1541 edition from which this material is drawn. Histories of medicine give some possible clues to his reasons. Avicenna, a court physician to several caliphs, died early because of his own sensual excesses. His canon, according to Garrison, was a pernicious influence because he confirmed people in the belief that ratiocination is better than firsthand investigation and because his own use of cautery instead of surgery stopped medical progress.[29] Averroes, better known as a philosopher and a freethinker than an authority on medicine, tried to base a system of medicine on the neoPlatonic modifications of Aristotle.[30] Hence Elyot perhaps did the English people a service by not perpetuating the errors of Avicenna and Averroes.

The physicians or medical writers whom Elyot cites frequently were highly respected in their own day and are still praised for their contributions by those who write the history of medicine. They include Hippocrates, "perhaps the greatest of all physicians," Soranus Ephesius, Diocles of Carystus, Oribasius, Galen, Aëtius, Alexander of Tralles, Isaac Ben Solomon or Isaac Judaeus, Paul of Aegina, Mesuë the Older, Johannitius, Rhazes, Haly Ben Abbas, and many others who were influential for their practice or their writings. Elyot often cites Hippocrates, but his high favorite is Galen, whom he mentions either in the margin or in the text more than fifty times. He must have had a strong feeling for men like Cornelius Celsus, who was not a physician but loved medical science and wrote valuable books on both theory and practice. (See Appendix III.)

Elyot's medical authorities near or in his own time include Guainerius, "a new practiser," who was a fifteenth-century medical writer of Pavia and one of the best in his period. He mentions Doctor Augustine as a person and a friend, as well as a physician, saying that he is worshipful and well learned and by his manners he declares the gentleness of his ancient blood. He praises Linacre, as he had done in the *Governour*, when he cites his work *De sanitate tuenda* in his discussion of exercise. He adds that the work had been translated from Greek into Latin most truly and eloquently by Linacre, "late phisition of most worthy memory to . . . Henry the eighth."[31]

Elyot made an individual contribution in *The Castle of Health* through various qualities of his work. One of these qualities was the emphasis on exercise—an emphasis that one might expect from the author of the *Governour*. But the purposes have shifted from the achievement of courtly grace and of military prowess to the effects on health. In the Second Book, chapters 31–35 he classifies exercises as 'fricasies,' diverse exercises, gestation, and vociferation. Fricasies are rubbings of the body (after it has been washed clean), with a coarse linen cloth, first softly and easily, then roughly and swiftly, up-and-down and then around, until the flesh swells and becomes ruddy. He cites Hippocrates, Galen, Paul of Aegina, Oribasius, Aëtius, and "some other late writers," but concludes that for suggestions on rubbing, the incomparable authority is Galen. In the chapter on diverse exercises he mentions digging in heavy clay, carrying burdens, climbing hills, climbing up a rope, and stretching the arms up or out at the sides as exercises to increase strength. He mentions also running, playing with weapons, tennis, throwing a ball, using plummets, dancing the galliard, walking, and football. In contrast to the *Governour*, he makes no derogatory comment on football, and only one of these exercises, dancing the galliard, might be considered primarily graceful. But in 1531 he was writing as a courtier; in *The Castle* he writes as a practical man concerned with health.

Gestation is any form of exercise, he says, in which one is moved by another object—being carried in a chair, riding horseback, or traveling in a boat. It is good for people with palsy, gout, the stone, or various other forms of illness.

Vociferation, an exercise of the breast and the organs of the voice, includes singing, reading, or shouting. It is good for persons short of breath and those who cannot draw breath without holding their necks upright. As a morning exercise, Elyot suggests that a person begin speaking with as low or as bass a voice as he can manage; and while he is walking, that he begin singing louder and louder but still in a bass voice, paying no attention to sweetness or harmony. Perhaps Elyot had plenty of space in his manors and also a household without sensitive ears; for a modern masculine tendency to sing in the shower seems inoffensive compared with vociferation.

Another individual quality of Elyot's work is the amount of emphasis he gives to a simple and moderate life—simple diet and medicines, little drinking of wine, and a reasonable amount of sleep. In the Second Book he protests against the avarice of merchants who import spices and exotic foods to please wanton appetites. In the Third Book he applies moderation to the control of the emotions, such as anger, sorrow at the loss of property or children, other tricks of fortune, or the heaviness of mind caused by ingratitude. In the Fourth Book, chapter 2, he attacks the excess at banquets and all other forms of overeating or overdrinking, and also the excess in fashionable dress. Many men, even young boys and serving men, wear too many caps. Priests use velvet caps embroidered with lace, as if they were ashamed of the crowns which are the token of priesthood. He wonders that bishops, especially those with leisure to read the works of Saint Cyprian, Saint Jerome, Saint Chrysostom, and Saint Ambrose, or the sundry decrees made by the old fathers, will permit priests to wear such finery. This preference for a simple primitive Christianity and for the fathers of the early Christian church is one that Elyot shared with both More and Erasmus and that he expressed in other books; perhaps attention has not been called to it because his usual subject matter did not impel him to express the preference often or at length. His details recommending life without extravagance in food, drink, or dress, and with simplicity in religious dress present a complete philosophy of moderation in living.

Another outstanding quality of Elyot in *The Castle of Health* is his realism. He is not a believer in astrology as a help to healing; he never recommends charms or even prayers to saints. As a religious man, he does mention the power of God, which is wonderful and merciful, preserving or striking certain people with the pestilence in a way that is beyond human understanding. But he does not rely on prayers to saints or to God as a means of cure. He differs from Arnold of Villanova, for example, a thirteenth-century physician who opposed scholastic dogma and was a pioneer in classifying diseases, but did suggest prayers to saints as a method of relieving disease.[32] Like More, Erasmus, and Vives, Elyot also had a realistic attitude to other areas besides medicine.

Elyot was also the kind of realist who followed the simple inductive method of experimenting on himself with diets and remedies and then reporting the results. For example, Doctor Augustine had given him a remedy for crudity or indigestion, fine rhubarb chewed with raisins of Corinth. He had never found anything better, and when necessary, he continued to use the prescription. Though Galen recommended the feet of swine, he had proved also by his own experimenting, he said, that the feet of a young bullock, soused for two or three days and then eaten in the evening without other meat first and without drink, would produce good digestion and sleep. Also he recommended sorrel for preventing infection; he had learned it from Guainerius but had proved the principle in his own household. He had found from his own painful experience that choleric persons like himself should avoid a long abstinence from food. For certain conditions of the stomach he had found a good remedy in fresh milk boiled a little with honey or sugar and with three leaves of spearmint. For rheum, which he had complained of in other connections, he found that his practice had been wrong and that Galen's advice was good. As a result, he threw away his quilted cap and other close bonnets, lay in a thin coif only, and wore a light bonnet of velvet. As Galen had advised, he made concoctions with oxymel; he also tried roots of parsley, fennel, endive, chicory, and betaine, all boiled in vinegar. Using these remedies and forming new habits, he had improved his condition of sixteen years earlier, as his long-time acquaintances could testify.[33] Such instances indicate that he did far more than read widely in medicine—though one might venture to conclude that he had read more medicine than any other layman of his time in England and perhaps more than any doctor except Linacre. He was also an assiduous experimenter who worked to improve his own health and then to give others the benefit of his reading and experience.

# CHAPTER XIV

## Dictionary, *1538 (1542, 1545)*.
## *Events, 1537–1538*

So far as outer events are concerned, the years 1537–1538 continued fortunate for Thomas Elyot. He was named on many commissions, he acquired valuable property from Cromwell, and he was offered the king's help on his *Dictionary*. Though he may have given some time to *The Castle of Health,* he probably used most of his literary energy on the *Dictionary,* published late in 1538.

But some public events must have been painful to him. One was the execution of two leading noblemen of the north, Lord Darcy and Lord Hussey, in June, 1537.[1] They were tried for treason as an aftermath of the Yorkshire rising in favor of the old religion and found guilty by a unanimous judgment of their peers, but perhaps they received the sentence of death partly because they, like Elyot, had been willing earlier to support Catherine of Aragon.

On October 12, 1537, the prince who was to become Edward VI was born to Henry VIII and Jane Seymour. Though the mother died about twelve days later, the king had a male heir whom his most conservative subjects considered legitimate. Elyot probably rejoiced at the birth of a prince but cherished an unhappy loyalty for the Princess Mary, who was still branded as a bastard.

Toward the end of 1537 the surrender of religious houses, more often the richer ones, was speeded up a little. In January, 1538, a new visitation, with Layton and Leigh still in charge, was begun. Though Elyot admitted the need of reform, he probably disapproved of their methods.

In May, 1538, John Forrest, former prior of the Observants at Greenwich and also friend and confessor of Catherine of Aragon, was executed as a heretic for denying the king's supremacy as earthly head of the church. A fiendish form of slow torture was devised for his death.[2]

In August or September, 1538, the shrine of Saint Thomas à Becket at Canterbury was stripped, furnishing the king with many wagonloads of gold and jewels.[3] Though the Catholic world outside England was outraged, it is difficult to judge Elyot's attitude. He was probably familiar with the colloquy of Erasmus on pilgrimages and shrines; its appearance in an anonymous English translation about the time when Cromwell began his work of destroying the religious houses could scarcely have been an accident.[4] Elyot expressed his preference here and there in his secular writings for the simple primitive Christianity of the early church, and he made a positive declaration in 1538 that his king was earthly head of the church. Hence he may by this time have considered the stripping of shrines unimportant compared with adhering to the essential doctrines of the church.

On November 16, 1538, John Lambert, or Nicholson, was tried in Westminster Hall before the secular peers and the bishops. The king presided as head of the church. Lambert was accused of heresy because he refused to accept the doctrine of transubstantiation, wished to interpret scripture according to his own reason and the views of teachers not approved by the church, and held other alleged heretical beliefs. After he had stood and debated against the king and ten bishops for five hours, he became silent, perhaps from complete exhaustion. Cromwell pronounced sentence against him, and a few days later he was burned to death at Smithfield.[5] Thus both Cromwell and the king upheld conservative doctrines. Elyot's pleasure in the king's support of these doctrines appears in the prefatory statements of his *Dictionary.*

On December 9, 1538, Lord Montague (Henry Pole) and also the Marquis of Exeter (Henry Courtenay) were executed for treason. They had been involved earlier in plans to support the emperor if he landed troops on behalf of Catherine of Aragon. Reginald Pole's indictment of the king in *Pro ecclesiasticae unitatis defensione,* 1536, and his refusal to put himself in the king's power by returning to England, no doubt fanned the royal anger against the Pole family. The plan of certain plotters earlier to arrange a marriage between Reginald Pole and the Princess Mary and to put the two on the throne, if the king knew of the plan, would have given him another cause for violent anger. The Poles and Henry Courtenay were also guilty of having royal blood and some rights of succession to the throne.[6] Like Elyot, they had wished to support Catherine of Aragon and to cling to the conservative religion.

Again Elyot was surviving, while others of higher rank and similar opinions were executed. At times, in spite of Cromwell's friendship, he must have feared for his property and his life. Even if the common people led a placid life, the period must have been one of grief and soul-searching for many. In an age of loyalty oaths, guilt by association, and accusations that might be motivated by fanaticism and malice, no one but an ignorant man, an unimportant one, or a thick-skinned knave could have remained unmoved.

Early in 1537, Elyot and others met a fanatical accusation from a lawyer named John Perkins, a man about the same age as Elyot. Perkins was an Inner Temple man and had once practiced in London; but, if rumors were true, he had been banished from Westminster Hall. He had published in law French a book on conveyancing; it was valuable enough to be translated into English in 1555 and then to be reprinted about fifteen times by 1600. At this time Perkins had been doing business for some of the religious houses in Oxfordshire.

Late in 1536 Perkins began efforts at blackmail and extortion against John Burton, abbot of Osney. A little later he accused him and Anthony Dunstone, or Kitchen, abbot of Eynsham, another Oxfordshire house, of inciting unlawful assembly and failing to show respect for the king's commissioners. On January 13, 1537, Burton sent Perkins' letters to Cromwell, who took the affair to the Council. On January 18, a commission headed by Sir Simon Harcourt and including the mayor of Oxford and other appropriate officials was appointed to investigate. Before the commission could act, Perkins was sending accusations against Elyot to William Fitzwilliam, Lord High Admiral then, and also to Cromwell. The abbot of Eynsham had told Perkins, the latter said, that Cromwell had Elyot at supper, and saying that Elyot had once done him a good turn, he called him aside and warned him not to be too friendly with abbots. Perkins attempted to show, it seems, that the warning had not been heeded. Elyot had once told the abbot of Eynsham that the emperor never spoke of the Bishop of Rome without doffing his bonnet; whenever Elyot was in these parts, he and the abbot "were but little space asunder"; Elyot sometimes rode a mile to Handborough from Eynsham for nothing except to drink there with the parson, Doctor Holyman. Undoubtedly, Perkins added, Holyman was a secret supporter of the Bishop of Rome; he was also "marvellous familiar" with the abbots of Eynsham and Reading and with Doctor London, the warden at New College, Oxford.[7]

The mental condition of Perkins is illuminated, perhaps, by the detailed plans he had submitted for reorganizing the whole kingdom and by his "politic" scheme for handling the northern rebels. Let men loyal to the king pretend to be sympathizers with them, penetrate their ranks, separate them into small groups, and then kill them all. Meantime other troops of the king would burn their homes and slaughter their wives and children.

Unfortunately for Perkins, when the commission headed by Harcourt met at the Oxford Guildhall, January 22, 1537, he was unable to produce evidence for any serious charges. He was sentenced to Bocardo prison till next market day, when he was to be exhibited with a sign declaring that he had been guilty of false accusations. If he remained in Oxford after February 3, he was to be put in the pillory. After he failed to produce evidence, the commissioners treated the accused abbots as friends. There is no reason to believe that the commissioners considered seriously any accusations against Elyot. Perhaps, as one member of the commission told Perkins, he was not well in his mind.[8]


The events that we know about Elyot's personal life in 1537–1538 include important and unimportant ones. An unimportant one concerns a property transaction of February, 1537. A William Dale was pardoned for alienating without license the manor of Tikingcot, Rutland, to Sir Thomas Englefield, Sir Thomas Elyot, and others. Eventually the manor was to be assigned to the use of Alexander Fettiplace and his wife, Anne.[9] The item suggests, perhaps, Elyot's continuing interest in the people with whom he was connected by his father's second marriage.

Elyot's appointment on commissions seems to indicate that he was accepted again as one of the landed gentry who carried the work of the government to the counties of England. In June and again in November,

1537, he was named on the Commission of the Peace for Oxfordshire. With him were named such men as Sir Simon Harcourt, who had headed the group named to investigate Perkins; Sir John Port, his opponent in the earlier struggle for the Findern property; a Will Raynsford, perhaps the friend Elyot named later in his will; and a John More who may have been the husband of Jane Fettiplace.[10]

Elyot's name was not in the list of those present at the christening of Prince Edward, October 15, 1537.[11] But since we do not know why he was absent, speculation is unwarranted.

Perhaps the most important appointment Elyot held during 1537–1538 was his position on a Commission of Oyer and Terminer, in July, 1538, for handling treason cases in the counties of Bedford, Buckingham, Cambridge, Huntingdon, Norfolk, and Suffolk and in the city of Norwich.[12] It is difficult to tell how much work was involved in the position and whether membership on the commission was routine or whether it was a test of Elyot's own loyalty.

Some time in 1538 Elyot acquired property, an event that must have given him satisfaction, since the records of his life indicate that he valued lands and manors. He purchased from Thomas Cromwell the manor of Carlton, presumably Carlton cum Willingham, adjoining Little Carlton or Loppams, which he had inherited from Sir William Findern. Elyot was offering £750 at first, as Cromwell's agent, Henry Polstead reported to him, and that was £24, 5s. less than the asking price. Perhaps Elyot thought the asking price too high because a farmer, Gilbert Claydon, had a patent for a fee of forty shillings and also an acre of wood assigned to him for fuel, and Elyot had to continue honoring these rights. Later Polstead wrote that he had concluded a bargain with Elyot and had told a clerk to make out the deeds. Cromwell kept the patronage of Carlton church with Willingham chapel annexed and had a yearly pension of two shillings from the parson there. He was to have another pension also of two shillings and sixpence from the parsonage of Weston Colville but not the patronage; Elyot was to name the incumbent and Cromwell was to present him. Cromwell was to have also two portions of tithe, one amounting to thirteen shillings, fourpence, and the other twenty shillings a year. Though these may seem small sums with complicated arrangements, in actual purchase power the values were much greater than they are now. Elyot acquired the new property at a price considered favorable, at twenty years' purchase, or twenty times the annual rent from the land.[13]

Perhaps the most revealing idea in the property transaction just explained is that Elyot's friendship and the gratitude to Cromwell, which he was expressing in a letter dated probably a little earlier, did not overcome his desire to bargain when he bought property. Like his father and the other landed gentry of the period, he struggled to acquire land. He also felt keenly the injustice when money he considered his due was not paid him.

Elyot's problems, however, were not over when he concluded the purchase of Carlton from Cromwell. He had trouble getting Gilbert Claydon to vacate properties. Finally Claydon petitioned the king in Star Chamber, asserting that Elyot and other "riotous" persons, "with bills and swords," had entered forcibly and taken possession of these and other properties. Petitions with these same conventional phrases were commonplace at this time, when titles were unsettled and men were eager for land. Elyot had entered, Claydon asserted, against the decision of a group of arbitrators headed by Sir Edward North. Claydon appealed for justice in Star Chamber as a poor man unable to bring suit at the common law. In reply Elyot granted that Claydon's father had held four acres by copyhold and that he himself had leased the manors from Cromwell; but Claydon had confused the terms freehold and copyhold, refused any service to the lord of the manor, and had been guilty of other illegal actions. When Claydon had agreed to let Audley settle the differences in Chancery, he had later refused to abide by Audley's decision. Next he had wished to have a local group decide; but when that group agreed that Elyot should pay Claydon 100 marks and that the latter should give up the manors immediately, he had refused. Though we do not know what was decided in Star Chamber, since decisions are not recorded, the historian who has investigated these records suggests that the suit must surely have gone in Elyot's favor.[14] Such were the difficulties about acquiring property in the early sixteenth century; but judging from the property Elyot owned at his death, such difficulties did not deter him.

Elyot's fears, growing from his conflicting loyalties, apparently extended into 1537. A letter discussed in an earlier chapter, one written to Cromwell perhaps in 1534 or even in 1535, had merely suggested his feeling that he was being judged on past associations. A letter to Cromwell in this period, written probably in February, 1537, states definitely the same fear. Since this letter may be related to his work on the *Dictionary*, it seems worthwhile to quote it entire:

> My most special good lord: Whereas, by your continual exercise in weighty affairs, also frequent access of suitors unto your good lordship, I could not find opportunity to give to your lordship due and convenient thanks for your honorable and gentle report to the king's majesty on Wednesday last passed in my favor, I am now constrained to supply with my pen my said duty. Offering unto your lordship all hearty love and service that a poor man may owe and bear to his good lord and approved friend, which although ability lacking in me I cannot express by any benefit, your wisdom notwithstanding (which I have alway honored and trusted) will, I doubt not, accept my good

intent, being, I thank God, ever sincere and without flattery or ill dissimulation. I wishing unto your lordship the honorable desires of your heart with the continual favor of God and your prince. My lord, for asmuch as I suppose that the king's most genial communication with me, and also his most comfortable report unto the lords of me, proceeded of your afore remembered recommendations, I am animate to importune your good lordship with most hearty desires to continue my good lord in augmenting the king's good estimation of me. Whereof I promise you before God your lordship shall never have cause to repent.

And when I perceive that ye suspect that I savor not truly holy scripture, I would God that the king and you might see the most secret thoughts of my heart. Surely ye should then perceive that, the Order of Charity saved, I have in as much detestation as any man living all vain superstitions, superfluous ceremonies, slanderous juggling, counterfeit miracles, arrogant usurpations of men called spiritual, and masking religious, and all other abusions of Christ's holy doctrine and laws. And as much I enjoy at the king's godly proceeding to the due reformation of the said enormities as any his grace's poor subject living.

I therefore beseech your good lordship now to lay apart the remembrance of the amity between me and Sir Thomas More, which was but *usque ad aras,* as is the proverb, considering that I was never so much addict unto him as I was unto truth and fidelity toward my sovereign lord, as God is my judge. And where my special trust and only expectation is to be holpen by the means of your lordship, and natural shamefastness more reigneth in me than is necessary, so that I would not press to the king's majesty without your lordship's assistance unto whom I have sundry times declared mine indigence, and whereof it hath happened.

I therefore most humbly desire you, my special good lord, so to bring me into the king's most noble remembrance that of his most bounteous liberality it may like his highness to reward me with some convenient portion of the suppressed lands, whereby I may be able to continue my life according to that honest degree whereunto his grace hath called me. And that your lordship forget not that neither of his grace nor of any other person I have fee, office, pension, or farm, nor have any manner of lucre or advantage besides the revenues of my poor land, which are but small and no more than I may therewith maintain my poor house. And if by your lordship's means I may achieve good effect of my suit, your lordship shall not find me ingrate. And whatsoever portion of land that I shall attain by the king's gift, I promise to give to your lordship the first year's fruits, with mine assured and faithful heart and service.

This letter I have written because I heard that your lordship went to the court. And as for my first suit, I shall at your lordship's better leisure recontinue it, trusting also in your lordship's favor therein. Written at my house by Smithfield this Monday. Yours most bounden, Thomas Elyot, Knight.[15]

There are two main problems about the letter. First, when was it written? Second, what was the substance of the honorable and gentle report to the king, which Cromwell had made on the preceding Wednesday, and also the "comfortable report" which the king made to the lords about Elyot?

As to the date, a biographer has suggested that it was written early in 1537 and has related it to the accusations by Perkins.[16] Elyot also addressed the letter to Cromwell as lord privy seal, an appointment he received in 1536. This fact fits with the assumption of a date about February, 1537. But surely the accusations by Perkins alone, with their lack of any genuine evidence, could not have impelled the king to communicate with Elyot and to make a report to the lords. Perhaps there was an additional and a better reason: the same date, early in 1537, would be about right for the report that Cromwell, aided by Antony Denny and William Tildsley, made to the king about Elyot's *Dictionary*. News of it might cause the king to write Elyot and to tell the lords about the forthcoming work; and we do know from Elyot's preface that the king offered him help. Hence it seems reasonable to suggest that Cromwell's report was mainly concerned with the *Dictionary.*

There are also other problems about the letter: Elyot's request for financial help, even for a part of the suppressed property or the monastic lands; his comment on his friendship for More; and his expression of religious views.

Elyot's request for a grant of some kind seems pertinacious, ill-timed, and a little too close to the heels of his gratitude. But he does refrain from repeating the details about his work for the Council without pay and the unbearable expenses of his embassy. Though it may seem strange that he could ask for a grant from the monastic lands, it is possible that Erasmus and some of the English humanists of the time would have understood, at least in part. They believed that true religion, based on love of man and God, is an inner feeling expressing itself in the sacraments and other worthy action. Elyot agreed with them that corruption and materialism had harmed the church; and details in several of his works emphasize his preference for the simplicity of the early church. One does not know whether he also became so adjusted to the climate of opinion about him that he thought only in terms of his personal finances.

Elyot's comment on More in the letter has been interpreted in various ways, and no doubt disagreement will continue. One must consider first, it seems, that More had been executed many months before this letter was written, and nothing that Elyot might say could either help or harm him. Probably Croft was right in relating the comment to one of the *adagia* of Erasmus: *usque ad aram amicus sum,* or "up to the altar I am your friend."[17] It was the answer attributed to Pericles by Plutarch when a friend asked that he help him by giving false testimony. Elyot is saying, then, that friendship for More has not caused him to break the allegiance he has sworn to his king. When Elyot discussed friendship in the *Governour* and in other writings he said many times that a man should never do wrong or act against his country and try to justify himself by saying that he was helping a friend. Here he was merely applying his own precepts. He was not seeking a useless martyrdom. If he was a coward—so are we all.

As for the religious views in the letter, Elyot is not expressing "Protestant" views, though Sir Henry Ellis made that suggestion when he published the letter more than a hundred years ago. He does not deny any conservative belief; and he uses his adjectives so skillfully that he merely seems, if superficially considered, to talk like a follower of the new religion. He does not even deny superstitions but "vain superstitions," "superfluous ceremonies," and "counterfeit miracles." He says nothing about papal power directly; he detests "arrogant usurpations of men called spiritual." But if he does not believe that the pope is arrogant or that he is usurping any power, then he has said nothing at all. If he really wished to stand up and be counted as a reformer, he would deplore the "usurped power of the Bishop of Rome," or use similar phrasing. He is walking a tightrope with consummate skill, hoping to remain a conservative but to sound like a reformer. These statements are not meant as an attack or a defense of Elyot; they are made merely in an effort to understand him.

We cannot know completely, of course, what Elyot thought and felt during his period of uncertainty about 1532 to 1537, and we do not know when he took the oath of allegiance to the king as head of the church. Certainly he must have taken it—just as all the adult members of More's household took it at some time. Nor do we know how he justified his action to himself. Human minds react in different ways when they confront immovable complexity. Some reluctant ones who submitted argued that the king's command absolved them; some, that an act of Parliament removed individual responsibility. Others, like Bishop Tunstal, recommended "passive obedience" to temporal authority. Others argued themselves into thinking (as Henry VIII did without difficulty when he needed the thought) that lack of inner consent to an action cleared away all problems of conscience. Still others took the oath after long resistance and then applied to the pope for absolution from the sin of perjury.

The attitudes of Lord Darcy may help in the understanding of conflicting loyalties at this time. Darcy had objected to Henry's separation from Catherine of Aragon and the break from the church at Rome, and he had suggested to Chapuys that the emperor land troops in the north of England. Later he found the spoiling of the monasteries so intolerable that he moved against his king. When he was in the Tower waiting for his execution, he told Latimer, "and I had seen his grace [the king] come against us, I would have lighted from my horse and taken my sword by the point and yielded it into his grace's hands." Darcy, aristocrat, religious conservative, and political loyalist, had a not uncommon tendency to blame others instead of the king for actions he deplored. During his examination he had said to Cromwell:

> it is thou that art the . . . chief causer of all this rebellion and mischief, and art causer . . . of the apprehension of us that be noble men . . . I trust that or thou die, though thou wouldst procure all the noblemen's heads within the realm to be stricken off, yet shall there one head remain that shall strike off thy head.[18]

Earlier, aristocrats who were loyal to the old religion and to the king accused Wolsey and then Anne Boleyn of causing trouble. Later they blamed Cromwell or talked vaguely of the king's advisers. Of course Elyot did not criticise his friend, Cromwell; he refused to blame the

king even when he was unrewarded, saying that the king
had not been informed; and in *Pasquil the Plain* he
blamed the self-seeking counselors who did not speak with
frankness. Conservative men of property, like Elyot and
the other landed gentry, of course felt impelled to support
a strong king; and when they were also conservative in religion they were likely to feel keenly a conflict in loyalties.
Perhaps it is not surprising, then, that Elyot maintained
his equivocal position on matters of religion, as he did in
this letter to Cromwell about February, 1537, and that he
did not describe his king as earthly head of the church until late in 1538.

Meantime Elyot was making progress on his Latin-
English *Dictionary,* is spite of public and private events,
membership on commissions, and conflicts in loyalties. It
was the chief work that he published in 1537–1538. The
first edition appeared late in the year, since the preface
describes the trial of John Lambert, which was held November 16, 1538. New editions of the dictionary were
published in 1542 and 1545 also, the 1542 edition being
much enlarged, and both of them having a new title:
*Bibliotheca Eliotae: Eliotis Librarie.*[19]

Elyot's influence developed from these three editions
that he published himself, from Thomas Cooper's revisions
of his work in 1548, 1552, and 1559, and from four editions of Cooper's *Thesaurus,* in 1565, 1573, 1578, and
1584.[20] In the *Thesaurus* Cooper continued to use freely
material from his revisions of Elyot and from Elyot himself; thus the influence of the one who had originated the
work went on to the end of the century. But the editions
of 1538 and 1542 are the important ones for this discussion.

In the preface of the 1538 edition Elyot explains a
new relationship between him and his king. Thus he

lends support to the theory that Cromwell's "honorable and gentle report" was concerned with the *Dictionary*. Elyot begins by addressing the king and describing him as "supreme heed in erthe immediately under Christe of the churche of England." The position of a king, as one next to God, he continues, is to be honored, loved, and feared in incomparable fashion. God is called a king, and there is a likeness between him and an earthly king. Then, instead of dwelling further on majesty and power, he adds that the office of a king is to distribute justice, keep people in a quiet, honest life not guided by bestial appetites, and to help them win eternal life. Thus he restates ideas that are important in the *Governour, Pasquil the Plain,* and *Of the Knowledge Which Maketh a Wise Man.* Such a view of kingship is a large order for any ruler—and for Henry VIII. Those who rebel against kings are enemies of God, seeking to destroy natural order and providence. Taken out of context, this last comment might sound like absolutism; however, it says that people should not rebel against efforts to keep them in a virtuous life and in the hope of immortality.

Kings reigning with justice, Elyot says, seem to have "a Divine influence or sparke of divinitie." That Henry has this influence is apparent to all who saw him sitting as supreme head of the church under Christ at the trial of that detestable heretic, John Lambert. The king was the perfect image of kingly majesty, made up of true religion, sapience, justice, and mercy. All men rejoiced at the king's clear declaration of faith, his forceful arguments against abominable heresies, his just reproof of the perverse opinions Lambert had drawn from his teachers and his own wit, not from holy scripture and the learned doctors, his patience with the tedious objections of Lambert, and his Christian charity in trying to persuade him to give up his heresies. Hearing the spirit of God speaking in the anointed king, his subjects shed tears of joy.

Continuing his preface, Elyot relates the story of the help and encouragement given him by the king on his *Dictionary*. When the book was about half printed, the king heard of his work from Cromwell and from two others, Antony Denny of the king's privy chamber, and William Tildsley. (Elyot describes Tildsley as the royal librarian, though elsewhere he is called a groom of the wardrobe.) When he heard their reports, the king offered to help with such books as he had and Elyot lacked, and also with his counsel. As a result, Elyot says, he received an increased understanding, for kings do amplify the natural powers of those who come into their presence. (His phrasing seems to suggest, of course, that he had one or more face-to-face talks with Henry.) As a result of the king's help, Elyot asked the printer to stop his work; then he began with the letter M and worked to the close with new diligence. After that, he returned to the first letter of the alphabet, revising that part with renewed energy.

Now, Elyot says, he has about a thousand more Latin words than had appeared in any dictionary when he began his work. He has compared the phrases or forms of speaking used in English and in Latin, added words used in law and medicine, words used for English herbs and for fish found in English oceans and rivers, and words for weights, coins, and measures used by the Greeks, Romans, and Hebrews. The latter details will be useful to those who read histories, the orations of Cicero, scripture, and the books of ancient physicians. He has also included such *adagia*, or other quick sentences, as he thinks should be remembered.

Discussing dictionaries in his preface, Elyot says he has discovered that all of them have been drawn from one another, but each omits some words that others have. He names Festus, Varro, Nonius, Nestor, Tortellius, Laurentius Valla, Perottus and his *Cornucopia*, Friar Calepine, and Nebressensis. Often he adds some critical comment:

that Valla wrote only of words called "elegancies" but is excellent in those; that Perottus included almost all that had been in earlier dictionaries but is too brief in treating compound words; that Friar Calepine has only made worse what others had gathered; and that Budé is exact in giving the meaning of both Greek and Latin words but spends too much time comparing words from the two languages. Nebressensis is learned and diligent, as he can judge from some words explained in Latin; but since most of his explanations are in Spanish, Elyot does not have a complete opinion of him. Elyot discusses these dictionaries as if he had examined them himself in detail.

Though Elyot has studied other dictionaries, he fears his own lack of ability; but remembering the king's encouragement, he has set up the sail of good courage and completed the work. If the king is doubtful about a word, let him consult the Additions or the Table of Corrections following the preface. He gives the king hearty thanks for being the "chief author" of the book. It will help men learn Latin better in six months than they have previously been able to do in three years. He closes the preface with other courtly compliments.[21]

Elyot's desire to be loyal, both to the conservative religion and to his king, is never more apparent than it is in this preface. By this time he seems to have decided that the essential theological doctrines were more important than the material property of the church or the nominal headship on earth. Since his king is defending publicly such doctrines as transubstantiation and the authority of the church over the interpretation of scripture, he is giving his king praise that seems fulsome to modern ears. Perhaps, like Erasmus when he used the panegyric, he hoped that the praise would help to keep Henry in the paths of rectitude. Thus his preface may be another skirmish in a long war to influence his king in personal conduct, ethical principles of government, and the essentials of religious conservatism. Elyot had changed since 1534, when he wrote the preface to the sermon of Saint Cyprian, and when he asked the prayers of his Fettiplace sisters at Syon House that he might remain constant. But he did not explain for us the causes of the change.

Elyot's statement in the preface about stopping the printer when the king offered his help is supported by an examination of the *Dictionary*. It has about 71 large leaves from A to M, about 98 from M through Z, and 34 or 35 pages of Additions, mostly used to define other words coming before M. The number of marginal references also increases in the latter part and in the Additions. The amount of actual help, in addition to his encouragement, that Henry gave must remain uncertain; but it does not seem out of character for him to fancy himself as a helper in scholarship and even to talk with Elyot personally about the problems of his *Dictionary*.

Perhaps Elyot learned of Nebressensis, the Spanish grammarian, through the writings of Vives or even in personal meetings with the latter at More's home. Though Vives mentioned Nebressensis often, he considered him not comprehensive enough and more useful to beginners than to advanced students.[22]

The space spent here in discussing the preface seems justified by the fact that it contributes more than the body of the work to our knowledge of Elyot. Then a biographer cannot hope to say much that is new about the *Dictionary* itself but only to summarize and to give due credit to D. T. Starnes, *Renaissance Dictionaries*.

Elyot did not forget Cromwell, even though he addressed the preface of the *Dictionary* to the king. A gift copy, now in the British Museum, carries on the flyleaf Elyot's Latin letter to Cromwell. He congratulates Cromwell on his position, suggesting that God has sent him to the people of England; he mentions Cicero's views on friendship, adding that no crime is worse than harming the reputation of a friend or failing to protect him when he is in danger. He is a loyal friend of Cromwell, as the latter may judge for himself if he recalls their first meeting nineteen years earlier.[23] Again Elyot is suggesting that there was something unusual about that meeting, but we have no definite facts—only the vague possibility that he was able to do something for Cromwell because of his connections with Pace and More.

In the *Dictionary* itself, Elyot's marginal references help to reveal his aims and methods. Plautus, Cicero, and Terence were his chief sources, judging from the fact that he cites Plautus some 600 times, Cicero some 275 or 280 times, and Terence about 250 times. Thus he indicates his concern with nonutilitarian literature. But strangely enough, he mentions Pliny about 100 times. He names Virgil some 85 times, usually the *Georgics* or *Bucolics* and seldom the *Aeneid*—facts that may be related to his comment in the *Governour* about the delight children take in Virgil's accounts of country life. In the margins Elyot refers to Caesar, Suetonius, Livy, and Sallust about 20 to 60 times each. He mentions Columella 39 to 40 times; he explains him in the body of the *Dictionary* as one who "wrate of husbandry moste eloquently." Columella was also considered a great naturalist and a patient observer.[24] He mentions Erasmus by name in the margins only 15 or 16 times, but he sometimes refers to him within his definitions; and such details are not itemized here. Since Elyot had a distaste for stories of carnal love, like the other humanists of the period, perhaps it is not surprising that he cites Ovid only about 10 times. He names Vitruvius and Catullus several times, and Seneca and Aristotle about 4 times each. Because his emphasis is on humane letters, he mentions Galen only 2 or 3 times. These figures are approximate and comparative only, since the intention of Elyot's abbreviations is not always clear and exact totals are difficult to estimate.

Elyot cites occasionally many other sources—Pomponius Mela, Plutarch, Martial, Herodotus, Josephus, and Boethius. He knew the mathematical work of Cuthbert Tunstal; he mentions him when he explains the term *denarius* in his Additions. He mentions many different books of the Old Testament from time to time. Again he gives evidence of a genuine interest in the fathers of the early Christian church when he cites Tertullian, Origen, Ambrose, Jerome, and Augustine.

Elyot's chief sources for biographical information, according to Starnes, were Diogenes Laertius, *Lives and Opinions of Eminent Philosophers,* in a fifteenth-century Latin edition, and Walter Burley, *De vita et moribus philosophorum.* Most of his biographies concern classical figures, not those in or even near his own time. For proverbs and what he called "quick sentences" he used Erasmus, both the *Adagia* and the *Apophthegmata,* though he does not cite him in the margin as often as one might expect. Among other dictionaries, perhaps Calepine's *Dictionarium,* 1502, was his chief help, as Starnes suggests, since he followed him in the general plan of his work, named the same references in his preface, and apparently turned Calepine's Latin into Elyot's English for a number of his definitions.[25] However, he cited Calepine and Suidas only two or three times each in margins, but he cited Nonius Marcellus about 30 times, Varro some 35 times, and Pompey Festus 70 to 75 times.[26]

Because of some details in his *Dictionary,* Elyot has a claim to be considered a botanist and a discerning bird watcher, according to those who write the history of English naturalists. Of course he uses pseudo-naturalism from Pliny and other sources, but occasionally he adds details from observation: *"phoca,* a sea-calfe, it may be supposed to be a seale"; and *"trigla,* a fishe, I suppose it to be a sore mullette such as ar taken in Devonshyre and Cornwal." He defines one bird thus: "attagen, or attegena, a byrd, whiche is found in Ionia, and beynge at large, is always syngenge or chatteringe; whan he is taken, he maketh no noyse . . . They are deceived that take hym for a woodcocke." As a botanist, also, he starts with traditional material but sometimes defines from his own knowledge. Elyot and Turner, an English naturalist who published *Libellus de re herbarii novus* in 1538, "use the same English names for plants too many times for us to suppose that the cause is accident. And Elyot is a real and independent student who gives names not found in the *Libellus* and some which Turner never mentions at all. . . ."[27]

Occasionally Elyot writes in a bit of social comment when he defines a term; an example is *suffibulum*. It is an article that the nuns of Vesta wore on their heads when making sacrifices, he explains; it resembles the bonnets that the women of London formerly wore, and that became them much better than the recent bonnets of velvet. With the latter, they imitate ladies and gentlemen "and thereby doo gette the name to be callyde Maskynge ladyes." This satirical comment on feminine fashions is not added to the definition of *suffibulum* in later editions of the dictionary.

Elyot's second edition of his *Dictionary,* published by Berthelet in 1542 as *Bibliotheca Eliotae: Eliotis Librarie,* is greatly enlarged. The leaves are approximately the same size; but excluding the Proheme, a Latin address to readers, and a leaf of errata, it has about 280 to 285 leaves, compared with about 140 in the earlier edition. The title page gives the place and date of publication; the colophon gives place, date, and Berthelet's name as the printer, with his sign of Lucrece.[28]

The Proheme, addressed to Henry VIII, states that a king who governs for the welfare of his country has the power to increase the abilities and thus the performance of competent people. Elyot himself has received incredible comfort and encouragement from the king's help on his dictionary. As a result, he has worked with more exactness and has enlarged his material. For this new edition he has assembled all the necessary authors, examined every word or phrase that might cause any doubt for a reader, and corrected it by these authors. With new courage received from the king, he has made an alphabetical list of all notable countries, cities, mountains, and rivers, and has explained each. He has included the terms for important beasts, fowls, serpents, and fishes; for herbs, trees, fruits, gums, precious stones, and metals not before tranlated into English; the names of diseases and their causes; and the names of important men from Adam to 300 A.D., with details of their lives. He has included the fables and inventions of the pagans, as a help to understanding the poets. He has named detestable heretics and explained their heresies to warn people against them since they tend to mix their heresies with Christian doctrine. He has determined the time, before or after Christ, when men lived. He has explained ancient coins, weights, and measures, comparing them with those commonly known, quoted and explained important *adagia,* included terms used in physics and surgery and in other sciences and arts; and he has even defined some Greek words derived from Latin.

His successful completion of the work, he says, has been due to the king's encouragement. Repeating the idea that rulers have the ability to stimulate the learned as well as the valiant, he adds that when such men achieve more, they are advanced to new dignities, "many enriched, none unrewarded." He also manages to suggest that he be allowed both the freedom from work requiring more physical energy and also the financial means to carry out other enterprises similar to his dictionary. He closes with the usual compliments to the king as the bulwark of his own wealth and comfort and the guardian for the welfare of all England.[29]

Whatever the reason may be, the flattery has been toned down; the king is no longer called the "chief author" of the book. Elyot manages to suggest also the idea of "new dignities" and to speak plainly his hope of relief from other labors and of financial help to carry out more literary labors. Such boldness is quite different from anything he had said in other dedications to the king.

The method of work that Elyot describes in his preface may seem incredible at first glance, since his list of necessary authors following the Proheme includes 119 or 120 men. He has carefully classified them as historians, cosmographers, philosophers, sacred writers, authorities on law and medicine, authors of fables, and miscellaneous writers. He also gives many marginal citations. "My interpretation," says Starnes, "is that he did actually verify, correct, and extend the number of illustrative phrases of his first edition. In the Calepine, his pattern, he would find many specific references to his authorities. Having the books open before him, he would need only to turn to the passages specified by Calepine for verification. Incidentally he would accumulate additional illustrations in the process."[30] Thus he could use and correct Calepine, who had guided both form and content for the 1538 edition, but as he thought later, had sometimes led him astray.

Elyot also used a number of other new sources for additional words he defined, for biographical and geographical information, and for details on the lives of Latin poets.[31]

Items in the dictionary support Elyot's prefatory statement about warning his readers against heretics, and he found a surprising number of these unbelievers. For example, he describes Averroes as an enemy to Avicenna and also to Christ; but instead of stressing Avicenna's religious aberrations, he mentions his errors in interpreting Galen and also his useful comments on medicine. Cerdon, another heretic, insisted, he says, that Christ was not born of woman, that he had no flesh and suffered no passion but merely pretended to suffer. Eunomius was a great heretic of the sect of Arrius, but he added of his own malice that the Son is unlike the Father in everything, that the Holy Ghost had "no medlynge" with either Father or Son, and that people who kept the faith he taught would be saved, no matter what sins they committed. In many such items the man who struggled to maintain conservative doctrines of his church fulfilled his promise to warn his readers against heresy.[32]

Many of Elyot's definitions have an interesting relation to opinions he expressed elsewhere or to the subjects of other books. He says of Alexander Severus:

> By his vertue, prudence, and continyual iustyce, reduced it [Rome] unto a perfecte publyke weale . . . and so hated corrupted judges that he dyd not onely put theym to tourments, but whan any came in his presence, he was redy with his two fyngers to put out theyr eyes.

Though he does not list Eucolpius as a main item, he does mention under *Origen* the supposition that the bishop converted Alexander Severus; he adds, "Whereof ye may reade in the boke whiche I translated out of Eucolpius, and called it the Image of Governance." Perhaps this comment was thoughtlessly worded. In *The Image* itself and in the preface to it, he had avoided speaking of the work as a translation. Instead, he carefully cited other sources within the work and in the margins and called it a compilation.

In his biography of Aristotle, Elyot admits that the philosopher excelled in sharpness of wit and the knowledge of many sciences, but as the source for his high general praise, he cites Quintilian. In the biography of Plato, Elyot seems to speak for himself when he describes him as "the prynce of all philosophers, in wisdome, knowlege, vertue, and eloquence fer excedynge all other gentyles. . . ." He adds that Plato is called divine for his excellent teaching which, as Saint Augustine said, is in accord with holy scripture.

In 1538 Elyot had explained America only as a land late found in the east by "Amercum Vesputium"; but in 1542 he describes it as one lately found in the west part of the world "by Americus Vesputius the yere of our lorde a thousand foure hundred lxxvii." He explains Hippocrates concisely as "the name of a physician most excellent." As one might expect, he gives much space to Galen, calling him a noble physician, and adding:

> This man in the arte of phisike excellyd all other before his tyme and sens, in so moch as in his ministration, counsell, or doctrine he never had reproche, as he hym selfe writeth.

In explaining King Arthur, under *Arthurus,* Elyot proves himself a realist in interpreting English history. He describes him as a man of great prowess who conquered and drove out the Saxons in fifteen great battles and who also subdued Scotland and Ireland, countries that were well inhabited and in a state of culture. The fact that Arthur kept an honorable and somewhat magnificent house "gave occasion to frenchemen and Spanyardes to exercise theyr wyttes in the advauncynge of Arthurs maiestie with incredible fables. . . . Al be it this Arthur was a very noble and famous prince, yet of them which wrate hystories about his time he was unremembered. He floryshed about the yere of our lorde 510." Also under *Britania* [his spelling] he attacks the theory that Britain had been founded by a descendant of the Trojan Aeneas

named Brut. The words *Brut* and *Britain,* he says, do not
seem closely related; he adds other reasons for rejecting
the theory. He relates the story of the book of vellum
found in a hollow stone at Ivychurch and the single defaced leaf from which Pace could make out only one word,
*Prytania,* for *Britania.* (See Chapters II and VII for a more
complete account.) He deduces that the Greeks had made
early expeditions into the sea near England and were interested in metals there. Whether he was right or wrong
(and scholars now are finding new evidence for such ideas),
he is reasoning to new conclusions based on his own experience. He is nearer the truth, he thinks, than the in-
ventors of other stories have been; and if anyone before
the time of Bede or Geoffrey of Monmouth can confute
his story, he will gladly yield.

Elyot's 1545 edition of his dictionary, issued by
Berthelet under the same title *Bibliotheca Eliotae: Eliotis
Librarie,* is dated on the title page. But it seems to have
been set up from a copy of the 1542 edition; and when
the printer came to the colophon, habit took over, and he
copied the date he saw before him.[33] Comparing copies
of the two editions superficially, one finds that the
Proheme, the list of essential authors, and the Latin address to the reader are similar. The leaf of Errata has
disappeared from the edition of 1545, and at least some
of the errors have been corrected. Following the early
pages through the two editions, one finds small variations
in space. Perhaps Elyot merely corrected errors in a copy
of the 1542 edition, with some other small changes, and
then sent a printed book to be reset. But a final judgment
on the differences must wait until a monumental work,
now under way, to edit the whole body of Elyot's work,
has been completed.[34]

After the death of Elyot, Berthelet asked Thomas Cooper to continue the dictionary. He issued a revised and augmented edition in 1548; one the "second tyme inriched," in 1552; and one "the third tyme corrected and enriched," in 1559. In an address to the reader Cooper said that he might expect to be lashed by those who found some little error, as Elyot had been, and that the work demanded more breadth and skill in languages than he possessed. But Berthelet had reassured and persuaded him, telling him that such gifts as a man had he should use for the common welfare.[35] So Cooper undertook the work. Apparently he was well qualified.

When Cooper edited and published under his own name the four editions of his *Thesaurus,* he continued to use freely in all of them material from Elyot or from his revisions of Elyot. As a result, some critics brought against him unwarranted charges of plagiarism. Something of Elyot still lived in all these versions, even of the *Thesaurus,* and the work became the "great monument of the English language in the Tudor period," before English dictionaries had come into existence, and an outstanding influence upon the great writers of the Elizabethan Age.[36] Without Elyot, too, it seems probable that none of these editions would have developed. Elyot and Cooper, through the ten editions of their work, were certainly the dominant influence upon Latin-English dictionaries from 1538 through the Elizabethan period and an important but not a dominant influence on English-Latin dictionaries. Perhaps they had also an indirect influence on English dictionaries when such works finally began to appear.

In the 1530's Elyot probably had reason for planning and publishing a Latin-English dictionary. At that time there were no dictionaries of the English language and no dictionaries in England with a vocabulary of Renaissance Latin words. There were publications with the vocabulary of medieval Latin used by the church, in scripture and in canon law, and by all teachers of formal learning. The *Promptorium parvulorum* was an early one of those, with manuscripts dating back to about 1440. Among the later ones was the *Vulgaria,* 1508, by Stanbridge; it was reprinted at least seven times by 1529.[37] Such works were adapted to use in grammar schools.

Many developments in England and in Western Europe had created a demand for dictionaries of classical Latin. Pagan philosophy had been revived; the classics of Greece and Rome, including poetry and drama, were appearing in new editions and translations; numbers of people were reading because printed books were available; diplomats, especially at the papal court and in Italy, found that the ability to speak classical Latin was an asset; and the physical world had been expanded by voyages and discoveries.

Pagan philosophy did not appeal to Elyot unless it agreed with Christian doctrine, but the two were often in harmony. Elyot and other Englishmen, comparatively speaking, had not been affected much in 1538 by the expansion of the physical world. But Elyot was writing for the new reading public, and he and other English humanists were greatly concerned with new editions and translations of the classics. Probably Elyot's own studies had been reminding him for years of the need for a Latin-English dictionary emphasizing classical Latin. The king, who had been trained in classical scholarship, probably knew that such a work would sometimes be useful to him. Certainly Vives recognized a need about 1531, when he suggested the use of a good two-part dictionary, with one part giving the Latin word and its meaning in the vulgar tongue, and the other part giving the word first in the vulgar tongue and then its Latin equivalent. Analyzing the problem as it affected teaching, Vives said that we lack such a dictionary; meantime the teacher must make notes from his own reading and supply his pupils with lists of words.[38]

Perhaps Elyot had been indirectly influenced toward his Latin-English dictionary by the example of John Palsgrave, whose *Lesclarcissement de la langue francoyse* had been published at least eight years earlier. After dealing with pronunciation, conjugations, other changes, and finally with the way words are arranged in sentences, Palsgrave follows this material with an extensive English-French dictionary arranged by parts of speech, with an a, b, c order under each part of speech. As Palsgrave says in his dedication to the king, he wishes to serve the realm and the nobility and to make it easier for people to learn another language. He had taught the king's sister Mary her French, at the king's command; she and her husband, the Duke of Suffolk, had thoroughly "visited" his first two books, and he has their approval. Just as the king offered his counsel and the loan of his books to Elyot, so he issued letters of privilege protecting Palsgrave for seven years against the printing or the sale of competing books in England.[39] Elyot had become aware of French grammar years before he published his own dictionary; for he said in the *Governour* (I, x) that "pure French" had been "broughte in to as many rules and figures and as longe a grammer as is latine or greeke. . . ." The most likely source of that awareness was *Lesclarcissement de la langue francoyse* by John Palsgrave.

As Elyot's dictionary was meant for mature people rather than schoolboys, it is not surprising that a teacher, much later, expressed a need for a source of words. John Barret, who published the *Alvearie* in 1573, has told us that he and his students made a dictionary, so that they would not have to keep running to him for words. At that time, he says, he knew of no dictionary to help them

but Sir Thomas Elyot's *Librarie,* which had come out a
little earlier:

> I appoynted them certain leaves . . . to write the English
> before the Latin, and likewise to gather a number of fine
> phrases out of Cicero, Terence, and Livie, and to set them
> under Tytles, for the more ready finding them againe at
> their neede.

In a year or two they had enough for a great volume.
Friends began borrowing the material and urging him to
publish it. So he asked former students, now at the Inns
of Court, to take their old work and to put it into good
condition. He also employed others to help him. The result was the *Alvearie,* so named because his boys had been
like busy bees, gathering wax and honey.[40]  Whether one
accepts all his explaining as the essence of truth or not—
and some doubt has been cast on his details—he emphasizes
the need a generation later for dictionaries to be used by
schoolboys and also the importance of Elyot's work.


   The popularity of Elyot's dictionary is partly indicated by the freedom with which others helped themselves
to his material. Thomas Palfreyman, for example, in his
revision of William Baldwin's *Moral Philosophy,* took
eighteen biographical sketches almost verbatim from the
*Bibliotheca.* William Alley, in 1565 and in 1571, freely
borrowed biographies and other items for his *Ptochmu-
seion.* Stephen Batman, adding to Bartholomew's *De
proprietatibus rebus,* drew heavily upon Cooper.[41] Copies
of some version appeared in various libraries, of course.
When Archbishop Parker bought gifts in 1562 for the
Norwich Grammar School, he included a copy of Cooper's
revision of the *Bibliotheca;* a copy of the same work also
belonged to the Stratford Grammar School and was presumably used by the young William Shakespeare.[42]

The popularity of the dictionary is indicated also by the tributes to Elyot later, though he never received in his lifetime the recognition that his work deserved. Four years after his death, Richard Sherry, in dedicating *A Treatise of Schemes and Tropes* to Master Thomas Brooke, praised Elyot. Many have complained that the English language is barbarous and lacks eloquence, he says, but many English writers have proved this opinion untrue. After naming Chaucer, Gower, Lydgate, and others, he adds special praise for the right worshipful knight, Thomas Elyot, "which first in hys dictionayre as it were generallye searchinge oute the copye of our language . . . hathe herbi declared the plentyfulnes of our mother tounge, love toward hys country, hys tyme not spent in vanitye and trifles."[43]

John Leland, the antiquarian, gave Elyot high praise in a twenty-four-line Latin poem, *"Ad Thomas Eliotam, Equitem Ornatiss.,"* a part of his *Encomia illustrium virorum.* As Leland died in 1552, the poem may have been written while Elyot was living, but it was not published until many years later.[44] Rudolph Waddington, who published a Latin-English dictionary in 1575, mentioned in his preface the learned knight, Sir Thomas Elyot, who "trode the first path" to the making of such a work.[45]

Thomas Cooper also paid a special tribute to Elyot in the 1578 edition of his *Thesaurus.* Praising his learning and his devotion to good letters, he says that he was the first to compose a Latin-English dictionary. After his untimely death, Cooper succeeded to his labors and directed the *Bibliotheca* through three revisions before he began his own *Thesaurus.* He would be ungrateful if he did not bring to the attention of all the extraordinary industry of Elyot; for his collections made a contribution, and no mediocre one, to the *Thesaurus.*[46]

In the seventeenth century Elyot was remembered and praised for his dictionary. Philemon Holland, a

medical man who published a *Supplementum* to a dictionary by a certain Thomas Thomas, in 1615, comments on
the useful work done by Linacre, Elyot, Cooper, and
others. In 1664 Francis Gouldman, in his *Copious Dictionary in Three Parts,* described Elyot as an able lawyer
and a famous scholar, who "first brake the Ice as to our
English Tongue, with great pains Compiling a Latine
and English Dictionary, called his Bibliotheca," and
dedicating it to Henry VIII.[47] About 1668 or 1669, a
gifted schoolboy, Peter Bold, writing from Repton Grammar School to his patron, the Earl of Huntingdon, asked
for a specific edition of the dictionary:

> This, I suppose, is called Eliotes Dictionary, though by
> Cooper amended . . . it is indeed the original of the
> other, but it is so abundantly enlarged and enriched with
> very many most useful phrases that it looses its own name
> and is called by ye name of its augmentor.[48]

Though none of these tributes extending over more
than a hundred years came while Sir Thomas Elyot could
enjoy them, they make clear that his work was not forgotten. His achievements as the compiler of a dictionary
were varied and important. He was the first Englishman
to analyze the need for a comprehensive Latin-English
dictionary and then to spend hours of careful labor in
filling the need. He was the first to use Continental dictionaries both as models and as sources of words. He extended the boundaries of definition to include personal
reminiscences, such as the giant skeleton that he and his
father saw at Ivychurch and the leaf of vellum about the
early history of Britain that he and Pace could not decipher. He was an innovator who added to Pliny and the
pseudo-natural history of the medieval bestiaries details
from his own observation. He was a realist who rejected
the myths that had attached themselves to history when he
discussed Brutus and Arthur. He included terms from

mythology, proverbs and *adagia*, biographies in brief form, and other historical material. He used quotations from standard Latin authors to support his definitions, and he cited authorities. He was the first to attempt a dictionary of classical Latin explained in the English idiom of his own period. He did not completely realize his plan to define only classical Latin words, for medieval Latin words did not disappear entirely from dictionaries of classical Latin until the eighteenth century. But his use of English idiom was an important influence upon the great Elizabethans—Spenser, Marlowe, and Shakespeare.[49]

These things are a solid achievement.

# CHAPTER XV

The Banquet of Sapience.
The Defense of Good Women. *Events, 1539–1540*

HE years 1539–1540 continued to be mainly fortunate ones for Sir Thomas Elyot. Probably he felt satisfaction when Parliament passed the Six Articles in 1539, perhaps with his help as a member of that body. He remained in favor with his king, as we know partly from the appearance of his name on commissions but mainly from the advantages the king gave him in acquiring property. His literary work prospered, at least in the quantity of publication or republication. At this time he was about fifty years of age; and according to his own analysis he had reached the period when the powers diminish, but he was not yet in age decrepit. However, in the death of his friend, Thomas Cromwell, through imprisonment and execution, he probably suffered a great grief.

The Six Articles, giving renewed emphasis to conservative religious doctrines, were described as an act to establish uniformity. On May 16, 1539, Norfolk brought to the lords some articles which he asked them to discuss and then to adopt a statute carrying penalties. "Reaction was in the air," says one historian; "the temporal peers were determined to curry favor with the king, to avenge themselves on Cromwell, and to exhibit their abhorrence of dogmatic novelty." The king gave every sign of favoring the conservative side. Some had noted his behavior on Good Friday, when he observed the ceremony of creeping to the cross; and at Mass he himself had served the priest, "his own person kneeling on his grace's knees." Others reported that he received the holy bread and the holy water every Sunday.[1]

Eventually Parliament passed articles with these tenets: first, a belief in transubstantiation must be accepted; second, since either the bread or the wine contains both the body and the blood of Christ, communion in both kinds is not necessary for the laity; third, priests may not marry, and those who are cohabiting with women must put them away; fourth, vows of chastity or of widowhood, if made to God advisedly, are to be kept; but a person should be twenty-one years old before making such a vow; fifth, private Masses (those celebrated without a public congregation, as in a private chapel) may be continued; sixth, auricular confession is both expedient and necessary. Reformers in the period had been opposing these doctrines. For example, Cranmer had married a wife while he was in Germany, had continued to live with her secretly, but found it expedient to smuggle her back to the Continent after the adoption of the Six Articles.

At first the penalties for violation of the articles were severe. A person who refused to declare his belief in transubstantiation was to be burned for heresy and his goods and lands were to be forfeited. If he refused to accept any other article, he was guilty of a felony for the first offense, with imprisonment and loss of goods; and for a second offense he was sentenced to death. We have no sure way of knowing how Elyot felt about these severe penalties though he did not suggest any regret a year earlier about the execution of the heretic, John Lambert. However, opinion began swinging like an erratic pendulum after the adoption of the Six Articles; and Parliament soon modified the penalties. But the statements of doctrine remained.[2]

Elyot was probably not pleased by the alliance between Henry VIII and William of Cleves, for the House of Cleves held religious opinions that to him were heretical. Negotiations leading to a marriage between the king and Anne of Cleves were signed in September, 1539. Elyot was one of many knights named to attend the king when he welcomed his bride to England.[3] On January 1, 1540, near Rochester, Henry saw the lady for the first time—and felt immediate distaste for what he saw. She was not young, she was not beautiful, at least in his eyes, and she was not educated in languages or in music. But for political reasons, the king proceeded, and they were married on January 6.

For a time Thomas Cromwell, who had a large part in the negotiations leading to the marriage, seemed to remain in favor. He was made Earl of Essex and lord great chamberlain; he continued his efforts to destroy the conservative bishops and the old nobility. But on June 10 he was suddenly arrested and imprisoned. By nightfall his possessions had been inventoried and assigned to the royal treasury—usually a sign that the prisoner would be condemned. On July 9 the Convocations of York and of Canterbury declared the marriage of Henry and Anne of Cleves void because of a precontract, a lack of inner consent by the king, and a failure to consummate the union. On July 12 Parliament annulled the marriage. Anne made no trouble. She seemed to prefer two residences and a good income to a position as the wife of Henry and queen of England. Perhaps there is something to be said for her preference!

Cromwell was beheaded at Tyburn on July 29, 1540. Since Elyot placed the devotion of a man to his friend above all other loyalties except his adherence to moral principles and his allegiance to king and country, he must have had troubled thoughts about the execution. He had expressed his ideas on friendship many times in his writings, and for more than twenty years had considered Cromwell his friend and protector. Now for the third time in about ten years he witnessed the public disgrace and death of a powerful man with whom he had been associated— Wolsey in 1530, More in 1535, and Thomas Cromwell in 1540. But with his usual reticence he has left us no record of his reactions.

Though the friendship between Elyot and Cromwell seems strange, Cromwell was many-sided, and a summary of the facets in his personality may help to explain the relationship between the two men. Cromwell could be completely ruthless if the goal he had in mind for himself or for his king demanded that quality. When he was building his new house in Throgmorton Street, he ordered fences to be moved back so that he might take twenty-two feet from the land of other men for his own grounds. Stow, who reports this fact, says that his father, one of those whose land was taken, could never get satisfaction but had to continue paying rent on the land Cromwell had seized. But Stow tells us also that Cromwell fed daily at his gate two hundred poor people, with sufficient bread, meat, and drink. In affairs of government Cromwell could organize a secret commission to find evidence for the destruction of Anne Boleyn when the king tired of her; he could use physical torture to break a weak and possibly an innocent lute player to a confession of guilt. In the trial of Richard Reynolds and others he could threaten jurors until they violated their consciences with a verdict of guilty.[4]

Another strange contrast in Cromwell concerns his religion. He had a reputation for being irreligious or for holding the ideas of the reformers. But in his will, made

about 1529, he provided £46 for a priest to pray for his soul,
the money to be divided into seven annual payments; and
at his death, it is said (though this is more doubtful), he
declared his belief in the doctrines of the old religion.[5]
When Elyot referred to the friendship between himself
and Cromwell he usually stressed an interest in similar
studies as the basis, without mention of religion. But
since he stated later that identical religious views are the
best possible basis, one might infer, it seems, that he did
not consider Cromwell a religious man.

Perhaps Elyot was drawn to Cromwell by some of the
qualities that Chapuys grudgingly admired:

> Norfolk and Henry both set Chapuys' teeth on edge.
> . . . But Thomas Cromwell, though he might be an un-
> mitigated scoundrel . . . never told unnecessary lies, and
> did not feel obliged to begin a policy of deception by de-
> ceiving himself. . . .
> Besides, the two men [Chapuys and Cromwell] had
> more in common than a preference for realism. Both were
> of the middle class; both had been touched by the Italian
> Renaissance. They like to ride hawking together, to dine
> together, to lend each other books, and sometimes to slip
> away together from the wrangles of the council table to a
> garden by the river and let the talk wander from world
> politics to scholarship, the goldsmith work of Antwerp,
> ancient intaglios, sculpture, painting, and reminiscences
> of the Italy they both had loved. Chapuys believed that
> Cromwell was a conscienceless scoundrel . . . Cromwell
> judged Chapuys an inveterate intriguer . . . resourceful
> and dangerous. . . . But they enjoyed each other's com-
> pany.[6]

The Cromwell whom Chapuys enjoyed at intervals may
have been the kind of Cromwell Elyot knew. Elyot, the
idealist, believing that friendship is possible only between
good men, may have been unable to see a possible scoun-
drel back of the golden talk and the kindness to him.

Elyot was not the only man whose friendship Cromwell was able to hold from his obscure days to the end of his life. Others, some of them literary men, were Stephen Vaughan, William Marshall, John Palsgrave, Thomas Starkey, and Richard Morison. A recent biographer says of Cromwell: "He was certainly loyal and generous toward people who had helped him in his struggling days."[7] As we have only the details mentioned in earlier chapters, we do not know whether Elyot was in a position to help him—possibly through More or Pace—when he was still unknown. When Elyot said once that the friendship began in a mutual benevolence, he may have meant either feelings of goodwill or actions to promote each other's welfare. At least the friendship lasted. If Elyot needed protection, Cromwell protected him. It is certain that he sent him advice. And about 1537, Cromwell's report to the king on the *Dictionary* won for Elyot the king's favor.

Elyot may have been saddened in 1540 by two other executions, unless he had won immunity through the execution of many men whose views were like his own. One victim was Edward Powell, whom he had probably known at St. Edmund's in Salisbury, and for whom he may have written a preface for *Propugnaculum*. The other was Thomas Abell, former chaplain and friend of Catherine of Aragon. Abell had acted for Catherine with courage and wisdom on a mission to the emperor's court earlier and had written a tract against the king's marriage to Anne Boleyn. After years in prison, the two men were executed for refusing to accept the king as head of the church.[8]

Elyot had mixed feelings, perhaps, about his appointment on commissions—satisfaction from being accepted as one of the landed gentry, and reluctance about taking time from his literary work. In November, 1539, he was listed on the Commission of the Peace for Cambridge, and in

February, 1540, on the same commission for the Norfolk Circuit.[9]  In September, 1540, he was named in a group of about 125 men called the Commission of the Sewers, for the seacoasts and marshy lands in Lincoln, Cambridge, Huntingdon, and Northampton Counties.[10] Especially on large commissions such as this, membership might be nominal; thus it is possible that Elyot had the recognition without much responsibility.

Elyot was fortunate in acquiring property in 1539 and 1540, and the fact must have given him satisfaction. A desire for lands, perhaps fostered by his father and other landed gentry in the West Country or perhaps by the general desire for land as a basis of citizenship and rank, manifested itself through his life.  In September, 1539, Elyot was listed in Augmentation Accounts as one of many who bought lands from the king.  In December, Thomas Elyot and his wife Margaret were granted in fee for £437, 15s., and 4d., the manor of Histon Eynsham, Cambridge, and all the appurtenances of the manor and rectory, formerly belonging to the suppressed monastery of Eynsham, Oxford. The grant named properties in Histon Denny, Oakington, Impington, Girton, Wilton, and Land-beach.[11] According to the historian who has investigated the records, Elyot gave the Court of Augmentations an annual rent of four pounds. In 1546, at the inquiry into Elyot's property, these lands were said to be worth annually £40, 10s. As the usual price for lands was twenty times the income they yielded, Elyot seems to have acquired these properties at a low rate.[12] Ironically enough, what he received at a low price, not as a gift, had once been under the control of the abbot of Eynsham, with whom John Perkins had accused him of being too friendly. After years, then, Elyot was compensated for his work as clerk of the Council and for the extra expenses of his embassy. We do not know whether the king had these old debts in mind, or was rewarding a literary man, or had other reasons for the favorable price.

How did Elyot reconcile his support of the old religion with his inspection of monasteries for the king, his request for a part of the suppressed lands, and his purchase at a low price of former monastery land? Perhaps no one can be certain. But though he was mainly a secular writer, he frequently spoke for a simple, primitive Christianity, citing as his authorities the fathers of the early church. Apparently he believed that true religion has little connection with pomp, pride, and material possessions of the church.

In March, 1540, Elyot had the satisfaction of acquiring additional property from Thomas Cromwell. While the latter still seemed to be in favor with the king, he was licensed to alienate to Thomas Elyot, his wife, and their heirs, additional rights to Cambridge lands. The transaction concerned the manors of Carlton and Willingham, the advowsons of the parish church of Carlton, with the chapel of Willingham, and of Weston Colville, with yearly pensions from Weston Colville and Carlton, all tithes and portions of tithes of Barbedors, and other lands in Carlton.[13] Whether Cromwell assigned to his friend his remaining interests in these properties because he foresaw his own fall, which came in June, is a possible question. But again, no answer is available. It is possible also that Cromwell would have acted earlier to compensate Elyot for the losses which he complained of so often and so bitterly, but that he had to wait the king's pleasure.

When Cromwell was arrested and his property was forfeited to the king, the lands he had sold to Elyot were included. But in August, 1940, the king granted in fee to the Elyots all that they had bought from Cromwell. It was noted in the grant that Cromwell had sold these possessions for a little more than £789, and about £489 remained to be paid.[14] Perhaps after ten years Elyot could support that station in life to which the king had called him when he made him a knight, and perhaps the increased income did not come too late to give him satisfaction.

With these events, public and private, Elyot was continuing his literary work. In 1539, he published a second edition of *The Castle of Health,* and according to his preface, he had done much revision. In the same year he issued again the *Sermon of Holy Saint Cyprian* and Pico's *Rules.* In 1540 he published again *Pasquil the Plain,* this time under his name. Though the editions of these two works have never been carefully compared, there is little reason to suppose that he did much revision on them. Since his dictionary did appear in 1542, in a greatly enlarged form, he was probably working on it in 1539–1540.

In 1539 Elyot published an edition of *The Banquet of Sapience,* and in 1540 a first edition of *The Defense of Good Women.*

*The Banquet of Sapience* may have been a second edition. It is described on the title page as "newly augmented with dyverse tytles and sentences." But so far, no one has seen an earlier edition. It was issued again in 1542 and 1545. These three editions are definitely dated, the first in the colophon and the others on the title page. After Elyot's death, it was reprinted twice in the sixteenth century.[15] Two reasons seem apparent for its continued popularity: Elyot was widely known for other work, and through the Renaissance people had an enormous appetite for the wise saying. It might be called an adage, an aphorism, a proverb, an epigram, or a "quick saying" (Elyot's term). An epigram might also be "a short poem ending in a witty or an ingenious turn of thought, to which the rest of the poem is supposed to lead up," or a short poem ending in a sententious comment.[16]

Collections of wise sayings in prose may be traced to the third century and to Diogenes Laertius, or even to the proverbs of Solomon. Walter Burley continued the tradition in the fourteenth century; so did Caxton when he published a translation from the French, by the Earl of Rivers, as the *Dictes* or the *Sayings of the Philosophers*.[17] About 1503 and 1504 Thomas More and William Lily were interested in epigrammatic poems. They selected eighteen Greek poems, and each translated all of them into Latin poems. These epigrams were published in several different editions about 1518 and 1520.[18] Some of them had witty and semibawdy endings.

Erasmus also had been whetting appetites for wise sayings with his *Collectanea adagiorum veterum,* in 1500, with about 500 passages from the classics. By 1508 he had more than 3,000; his title became *Adagiorum chiliades,* or thousands of adages. By 1517 he had more than 5,000 passages. In his *Apophthegmata,* published several times between 1531 and 1535, he used stories about great men, with their wise and witty sayings. For this material he was greatly indebted to Plutarch. His collections introduced readers to the ethical side of Greek life, and since they were in Latin, gave help in learning the language.[19]

In 1524 Vives published at Antwerp a collection of wise sayings, *Introductio ad sapientiam.* In 1540 his work was translated into English by Richard Morison, with several editions appearing.[20] Elyot himself, as Starnes has pointed out, used sayings of the philosophers to illustrate ideas in the *Governour* and to support definitions in his *Dictionary.* Prose epigrams in English continued after Elyot in the work of such writers as Nicholas Udall, Richard Taverner, William Baldwin, William Palfreyman, and Timothy Kendall. They did not stop at the end of the century. Polonius, with his ready advice for the departing Laertes, and Iago with his moral comments on reputation belong in this tradition. But in these instances Shakespeare apparently took delight in letting his fools and villains utter virtuous sayings.

In dedicating his *Banquet* to the king, Elyot expands the figure of a feast. Spring after Lent is an appropriate time to hold symposia, he says, like those of the Greek philosophers and to give the king and his counselors refreshment after their work for the public weal. He himself deserves no more praise for his collection than does the one who carries a torch before a course for a feast when it is brought from the dresser. He concludes his dedication with the usual expressions of devotion as a humble servant who owes the king all his study, prayer, service, and loyalty. He beseeches the king to receive the work as a token of his sincere mind and intention, according to the king's usual and incomparable gentleness. In a general introduction also Elyot issues the call of Sapience to all people who are willing to enter her house, where she has prepared for them red wine and fruits more valuable than gold or precious stones.[21]

Though Elyot was not original merely in publishing wise sayings, he was one of the earliest to make and to publish such a collection in English. Some of his details are interesting also. He uses an alphabetical arrangement of headings, beginning with Abstinence, Adversity, Affection, and closing with Vainglory, Virginity, and Wrath. Under each heading he gives one, two, or even seven or eight quotations, usually with his sources in the margin. Under Amity, for example, he cites four church fathers, Solomon, and four classical writers. Under Charity he quotes only a part of the thirteenth chapter of first Corinthians. Under Quiet of Mind, his sources are Plutarch and Seneca. Characteristically he includes a section on diet, with passages from Hippocrates and Galen. Some of his headings represent other human needs or situations, such as Age, Battle, and Sickness. Those who have tabulated his references find that a little more than half refer to scripture and to Christian authors.[22] When he quotes religious writers outside the Bible, he prefers again such early fathers of the Christian church as Augustine and Jerome. He uses no verses and he includes no medieval or contemporary writers. For him the Bible, the fathers of the early church, and the classical philosophers were sufficient sources of wisdom. Elyot's aim, unlike that of Udall and Taverner, was not to teach virtue and Latin to children. He was writing for mature adults like Henry VIII— though he should have known long before 1539 that he could not teach the king his virtue!

Though the editions of *The Banquet* indicate that the work was in demand, few direct references to it appear. But the musician, Thomas Whythorne, who referred to *The Castle of Health,* also told us himself that he used a passage from *The Banquet* as the basis for one of his songs. His editor cites a passage under Hypocrisy, where Elyot says that a man of gentle courage, instead of concealing what is in his heart, tends to show openly his love or hate. This is Whythorne's song:

> It doth belong more of good right
> To such as have courage gentle
> To show forth plain to every wight
> The love or hate they bear them till,
> Than slyly to cloak or closely to hide
> By their dissembling look and cheer
> The good or ill that in their hearts doth bide,
> Wherby their wiles cannot appear.

One who is interested can also find the music that Whythorne composed for these lines.[23]

Elyot received early and generous praise from William Baldwin, like Elyot a West Country man and also an editor of terse sayings. But he did not mention Elyot's *Banquet of Sapience*. In his first edition, *A Treatise of Moral Philosophy . . . the Sayings of the Wise,* 1547, he mentions Elyot's translation from Plutarch on education and calls him "the excellent and famous knyght . . . whose good zeale and love bothe to further good learnyng and to profit his countrey appeareth as well therby as by other many workes, which he hathe payned him selfe to bryng into our language, sheweth well his good affection . . . to the common weale."[24]

Elyot published *The Defense of Good Women* in 1540. Only one copy of this edition is extant, so far as we know; and for many years its existence was unsuspected. It is clearly dated both on the title page and in the colophon. Another edition of 1545 is dated on the title page.[25] Elyot dedicated the first edition to Anne of Cleves but removed his entire preface with the dedication to her from the second edition, substituting for it a brief summary of the book. The work has appeared twice in this century. In 1912 Foster Watson reprinted the 1545 edition in *Vives and the Renascence Education of Women;* in 1940 Edwin J. Howard reprinted the first edition.

Elyot's 1540 preface begins:

> To the most noble and moste vertuouse princesse Quene Anne, wyfe unto the most excellent prynce, our moste graciouse soveraygne lorde, kynge Henry the VIII, Thomas Elyot, knyghte, desyreth all honour.

Continuing the preface, Elyot says that he is anxious to have the life of Queen Zenobia, who was famous for her virtues and her courage, available in English, so that women may be moved to embrace virtue and to use care in bringing up their children. Though many men delight in rebuking women even when they have received benefits from them, or they praise them beyond reason when wanton desire is stirred, he is interested in the reverence that honest men should give to gentle women who are virtuous and good. So he imagines that Zenobia is living now, not in 274 A.D. He has developed a contention between Caninius, who is always barking at women like a cur, and Candidus, who defends them. After the two men have argued, Zenobia enters, confirms the statements of Candidus by her talk, and changes the mind of Caninius.

After this explanation of his aims and methods, Elyot concludes his preface by addressing again Anne of Cleves:

> and so endeth the matter, whiche I doo dedycate unto your hyghnes, mooste noble princesse, humbly desyryng your highnesse in suche wyse to accepte my good wyll and service and this litell warke as your owne, that under your gracis protection and favour it may surely passe through the dangerous rase of dysdayne and envy, and be recevyed thankfully and ioyousely of al good women in this your noble realme, who by the onely example of your excellent maiestie, may be alway desyrouse to imbrace vertue and gentylnesse, wherein consisteth verye nobilitie.

The first edition must have come from the press early in 1540. Possibly the bound copies were already in the hands of the booksellers when Anne of Cleves entered England. If they were not, surely a man of Elyot's rank who attended the king when he met his new queen, would not have used that dedication; it was not a political asset. One might even speculate with reason on a theory that Elyot tried to recall the 1540 copies—though there is no positive evidence. But the theory might help account for the fact that only one copy remains; and until it came up for sale in 1924, it seems to have been unknown.

The preface of the first edition would certainly not turn a reader's mind to Catherine of Aragon, though some

have assumed that Elyot was subtly presenting a defense
of her. Perhaps they had not seen the dedication to Anne
of Cleves. Though it is true that Elyot supported the
cause of Catherine so far as he could until her death, that
proves nothing about his intentions in a specific work of
1540. It is also true that he describes Zenobia as being
from "Surry," with the same spelling in both editions. He
says that she was "late a greate queene and wyfe to
Odenatus, kynge of Palmyry, whiche is a citie and a
countreye in Surry . . . she hath had of our host victory
twise . . . and was taken prisoner by Aurelian the emperor. . . ."[26] Perhaps Elyot meant this to be Syria,
spelling being what it was in the sixteenth century. Even
if he meant Richmond Palace in Surrey, England, the
minds of readers would not infallibly have traveled to
Catherine of Aragon. Like other queens, she had sometimes resided there. But when Henry left her finally, she
was at Windsor. Later, by his orders, she went to the
More in Hertfordshire, to Ampthill in Bedfordshire, and
then to Buckden and Kimbolton, both in Huntingdonshire.[27] If Elyot meant Surrey, England, perhaps he supposed that Anne of Cleves would live there. She was actually residing at Richmond in Surrey during July, 1540,
when she gave her formal consent to the separation from
Henry.[28]

Nor would the qualities possessed by Zenobia in *The
Defense of Good Women* necessarily turn the mind of a
reader to Catherine of Aragon, if that reader knew the
literature and learning of the period. There were general
resemblances, of course: both were queens, were educated
in the classics, were interested in the education of their
children or child, and had other noble traits. Zenobia
avoided even innocent actions that might injure her reputation; she had honored her husband, avoided actions
that might displease him, and had done whatever she
could to make him content. She had reason, constancy,

fidelity; like other good rulers, she possessed justice, fortitude, temperance, and magnanimity.

But by 1540 these qualities were conventional. For a generation, educated Englishmen had been hearing about them both in Latin and in English. Agrippa of Nettesheim, a guest of Colet in England about 1510, had made fantastic claims about the ability of women in public life. By precept and by the education of his daughters More told the English world that women had the capacity and the right to an equal opportunity for a classical education. Linacre and Vives, in the early 1520's, had planned a rigid and unfeminine education for the Princess Mary. Those who did not read Latin had Richard Herde's praise of women's scholarship in his preface to Margaret Roper's translation of Erasmus' *Precatio dominica,* in 1524, and his English translation of Vives, *The Instruction of a Christian Woman,* published perhaps about 1529.

Erasmus also had been teaching the world about the capacities of women. Converted to a new view by knowing More's daughters, he was expressing in his *Colloquies* every shade of liberal opinion about women. Before his death in 1536, probably a hundred impressions of them were in print.[29] Elyot must have known them, since there is much evidence that he followed and admired the work of that great scholar. Since they were used in grammar schools and translated into English, most educated men and women knew them. Of the half dozen or more dealing with the abilities of women, a good example is "The Abbot and the Learned Lady," published first in 1524. Magdalia, who is reading Greek and Latin books and getting from them the wisdom to train her children and endear herself to her husband, needles the smug abbot by telling him that women have also the ability to become bishops and rulers. "The New Mother," 1526, covers thoroughly the physical and spiritual obligations of mothers to children. "Courtship," 1523, stresses virtue,

learning, and a union of minds in a good marriage; Maria
has the poise and saucy teasing of Shakespeare's heroines,
with a warmth of feeling that makes her human.[30]

After reading Erasmus, one cannot avoid feeling that
the ideas in Elyot's *Defense of Good Women* are bookish
and imitative. They have no specific reminders of Catherine of Aragon.[31] Candidus and Caninius consider the
opinions of poets, philosophers, and narrative writers
about women. Candidus persuades his opponent that
reason ranks above physical strength, and that reason includes discretion, judgment, and prudence. Defeated by
logic, apparently, before Zenobia enters, Caninius yields
to her explanations of what learning has done for her in
the past when she was a ruler and the wife of a king and
what it still does for her as a mother.

An interesting minor detail in *The Defense* is the
reference to the Copernican theory. Caninius accuses
Candidus of belonging among the followers of Pyrrho,
who maintain that nothing is the way it seems—that snow is
black, not white, and that the earth is not stable but is
always moving. Candidus denies that he holds any such
vain opinions. In *Pasquil the Plain* the chief character
compares changes in life to the possible movement of the
earth: "Herdest thou never that the worlde is rounde and
therfore it is ever tournynge, nowe the wrong side up-
warde, an other tyme the ryghte, but lette this passe."
Each reference is a mere comparison, not a scientific comment; and though Pasquil seems more inclined than
Candidus to accept the theory, it seems useless to debate
the question whether Elyot changed his mind. Perhaps
he heard of the Copernican theory at the emperor's court,
since statements about it began circulating in manuscript
by 1530, though it was not in print before 1540. But until the theory was proved by mathematicians and by
Galileo with his telescope many years later, it was considered only an interesting speculation. In the seventeenth

century English textbooks were still dominated by Ptolemaic principles. Hence one could not expect Elyot, at any time in his life, to advance seriously the Copernican theory.

In 1539 and 1540 Elyot's literary work was growing, at least in bulk. His revised edition of *The Castle of Health* was important. Probably he was giving much time to the revision of his dictionary, though the new edition did not appear until 1542. His new works, *The Banquet of Sapience* (if it was really first published in 1539) and *The Defense of Good Women* were not his most distinguished ones. However *The Banquet* was well arranged and well documented; it gave wise sayings to those who read English, not Greek or Latin. In writing *The Defense of Good Women* perhaps Elyot was carrying out in perfunctory fashion a promise he had made in the *Governour,* II, vii. There he praised Livia, the empress, for counseling her husband to use patience and mercy, "to whiche counsayle onely they [women] shulde be admitted and have free libertie." He promised to make a book for ladies later and to give ample praise to Livia, but he did not mention her in *The Defense of Good Women.* Considered as an example of the Platonic dialogue also, the work must be rated far below *Pasquil the Plain* or *Of the Knowledge which Maketh a Wise Man.* Fortunately Elyot's literary reputation does not rest upon one book. It has more solid foundations.

# CHAPTER XVI

The Image of Governance. A Preservative against
Death.
*Last Years, 1541–1546*

URING the last five years of his life Elyot apparently
remained a busy man. He held a number of
those commissions through which the local gentry
carried on the government of England, though it seems
impossible to determine how much time and effort he was
actually required to give to these duties. He issued editions of books he had published previously, providing for
some of them changes and new prefaces and for others
substantial revision and enlargement. He also published
two new books in these years: *The Image of Governance,*
1541, and *A Preservative against Death,* 1545. His literary
work alone might have been enough to keep the average
man busy.

In this period perhaps Elyot regarded no public
events with such keen interest as he had given to the trial
of the heretic John Lambert in 1538 or to the adoption
of the six Articles in 1539. Apparently he was not dis-
turbed by the execution of friends or other public men
with whom he had sympathized; for by 1540 the king had
completed any delayed executions (except for Margaret
Pole, Countess of Salisbury) connected with his separation
from Catherine of Aragon and his break with Rome.

Elyot's duties for the government were numerous and varied. In February, 1541, he was named on a special Commission of Oyer and Terminer for the Norfolk Circuit, one of the four or five parts into which all England was divided.[1] Such a commission might be a general one for all crimes in the area, or a special one for a particular crime, or for certain specified crimes. In March, 1541, he was named again on the Commission of the Peace for Oxfordshire.[2]

Elyot began the year 1542 with a small sign of favor from his king. His name appears in a list headed "Rewards given on Saturday, New Year's Day, at Hampton Court, anno xxxij." He was one of a number of knights to receive 13s., 4d., with no indication what each had done to receive these payments. Besides these sums to ladies and gentlemen, certain amounts were given to the heralds, the trumpeters, the pages, the "stille minstrelles," a Mr. Crane who brought the children of the chapel to play before the king, the king's minstrels, and others.[3] It seems uncertain whether Sir Thomas and Lady Elyot were present at court festivities when the rewards were given.

In 1542 Elyot was listed again for certain routine duties of the landed gentry. In June he was named, with Sir Giles Alington and others, on the Commission of Oyer and Terminer for the Eastern Circuit. In August he was named again on the Commission of the Peace for Oxfordshire; in October on the same commission for Cambridgeshire; and in November again, on the Commission for Gaol Delivery of Cambridge Castle. He seems to have been a member of Parliament for 1542, but as the official records for that year are missing, we do not know whether he represented Cambridge or some other area.[4]

In 1543 Elyot was named again, also with Sir Giles Alington, on the Commission of Oyer and Terminer for the Eastern Circuit. In July he was listed among those contributing to the army for Flanders; he and four others

were to send ten footmen each, though Sir Robert Peyton
and Sir Giles Alington were to send twenty each. Elyot
was also mentioned in an item suggesting that he had much
earlier disposed of some Oxford property, probably part
of his inheritance from his father; the crown was granting to a certain Leonard Chamberlain the right to be
keeper of the "chief messuage called Combe," in Oxford,
and of the gardens, ponds, and fishings which had belonged to Sir Thomas Elyot, and after him to Richard
Andrews.[5] In November, 1543, he was one of the three
nominees from whom the king was to choose a sheriff for
Cambridge and Huntingdon counties. In the item under
that date Robert Aprice was "pricked" as the one to serve.
If Elyot held at this time the opinion he expressed in 1532
about the resentment against justice and the expense a
sheriff had to bear, he would have been happy not to be
chosen. However, a later list indicates that he served for
1544, Giles Alington for 1545, and a man named "Tay-
lard" for 1546.[6] It is possible that Aprice was unable to
serve and that Elyot replaced him, but no explanation
appears.

    In 1544 Elyot was named again among those to fur-
nish men for the army against France, but this time his
quota had doubled over the previous year. He, his friend
Sir Edward North, and Sir Giles Alington were to furnish
twenty footmen each.[7] In 1544 and 1545 he was named
several times on the Commission of Oyer and Terminer
for the Counties of Bedford, Buckingham, Cambridge,
Huntingdon, Norfolk, Suffolk, and the City of Norwich,
with mainly the same people each time. In these years, he
was on the Commission of Sewers for Cambridge and
Huntingdon Counties; and in 1545, he was again on the
Commission of the Peace for Cambridgeshire and for Oxfordshire.[8] In January, 1546, he was named in the muster
levies for Cambridge; Giles Alington, Robert Peyton,
Thomas Cotton, and Elyot were to furnish a hundred men

for war.[9] Like his father, then, Thomas Elyot was assigned the duties of government almost to the end of his life.

Elyot's literary work during the last five years of his life included many new editions of earlier work. In 1541 he republished *The Castle of Health,* with rearrangement, other changes, and a new preface. In 1542 he issued the greatly enlarged Latin-English dictionary with the new title *Bibliotheca Eliotae: Eliotis Librarie,* and in 1545 another edition of the same work, which is said to be without significant changes. In 1544 the *Governour* appeared for a third time, probably without changes of importance, though the second edition had been carefully revised. In 1542 and again in 1545 *The Banquet of Sapience* was reprinted and in 1545 *The Defense of Good Women* without its dedication to Anne of Cleves. If he read proof on all these new editions, he must have been busy.

*The Image of Governance,* one of the two new works, came from the press in 1541, as we learn from the title page, though the colophon is dated 1540. Probably the printer set up the title page and the preface last, early in 1541. The work appeared again in 1544, while Elyot was still living, and twice after his death, in 1549 and 1556.[10] Thus it seems to have been a reasonably popular book; and, so far as we know, it met no adverse criticism in the sixteenth century. It is concerned with the deeds and the political philosophy of Alexander Severus, emperor from 222 to 235 A.D.; its purpose is to explain how an ideal ruler manages his kingdom.

In his preface Elyot emphasizes strongly the dedication, first addressing all the nobility of the flourishing realm of England; then returning to the idea later, he says, "I do dedicate unto you noble lordes, gentil knightes,

and other in the state of honour or worship as being moste
redy to be advanced to governaunce under your Prince:
so that your vertues be correspondent unto your fortunes."
Though the *Governour* had been dedicated to the king,
the *Dictionary* had been addressed to him with excessive
compliments and had even been called the king's work,
and *The Banquet of Sapience* had been addressed to him,
Elyot does not include the king in this dedication to *The
Image of Governance*. It is possible that the absence of
the king's name where we might expect it, in Elyot's last
work on government, has some relation to the execution
of his friend, Cromwell. But we do not know. Before he
ends his preface he does assert that learned men have made
good rulers and that Henry VIII is a man of learning.
After this restrained compliment he praises the king because he has "sifted out detestable heresies, late mingled
amonge the corne of his faythfull subiectes, and caused
moche of the chaffe to be throwen in the fyre, also hypocrisy and vayne superstition to be cleane banysshed. . . ."

In his preface, Elyot says also that he has tried to make
the style conform to English idiom and to write with
simplicity not eloquence. With his usual sensitivity to
criticism, he says that in derision men call him only a
maker of books. It may be true that he sets the trees, but
the printer eats the fruits. If he had spent on personal
affairs the time he has given to the writing of books for
the needs of others, he would have more property and
esteem. But remembering the story of the man who hid
his talent in a napkin, he begins to be concerned about his
last reckoning. As evidence that he has used his talent,
he lists eleven works; all of them had been published or
republished under his name. He suggests that all were
written to aid others and thus to help his country:

> *The Governour,* teaching men the virtues that are ex-
> pedient in authority.

*The Doctrinal of Princes,* or the counsels of Isocrates, giving noblemen honest opinions.

*The Education . . . of Children,* a translation from Plutarch, helping men and women to be worthy parents.

*Pasquil the Plain,* teaching servants to be faithful to masters, and masters to detect flatterers.

*Of the Knowledge Which Maketh a Wise Man,* explaining the office of a good counselor and the need for courage in adversity.

*The Sermon of Saint Cyprian,* offering the devout comfort in plague or calamities.

*The Banquet of Sapience,* giving many wise sentences from holy scripture.

*The Castle of Health,* aiding men to keep themselves from serious illness.

*The Defense of Good Women,* refuting evil report against women and counseling wives on their duties.

The *Dictionary* of Latin-English, helping both children and men of learning.

*The Image of Governance.*

Developing further the idea of his last reckoning, he says that though he had never expounded scripture in his writings, he had never offended the conscience of any man, never written one sentence against the commandments of God or "the true Catholic faith," and never given occasion for any man to be stirred to wanton devices. Thus he has refrained from any influence toward evil and has made a positive contribution through many books. Though he does not name here any of the anonymous translations associated with his name, they may still be his. If they were early exercises, used to help him in learning Latin and Greek, he may have considered them not worth mentioning in this final summary.

Elyot also refers to an earlier promise to write a book on the form of good government, apparently made in the *Governour,* I, ii. There he mentioned a plan to write two volumes, the first one on the education from their birth of noble children, so that they may become worthy governors.

He added: "The second volume, whiche, god grantyng me quietnes and libertie of mynde, I wyll shortly after sende forthe, it shall conteine all the reminant, which I can either by lernyng or experience fynde apt to the perfection of a iuste publike weale. . . ." It is important to note that he promised another *volume,* not another *book* that might be considered a part of the *Governour;* and readers who try to relate the statement only to the *Governour* create for themselves a mystery or a change of plan that was probably not in the author's mind. Hence, he says in 1541, he has decided that a work on Alexander Severus might give his readers pleasure and profit and discharge him from the earlier promise.

Discussing the origin of the work, he says that when he became tired from working on his dictionary (apparently meaning the edition of 1542) he was looking about for something to refresh his spirit. He found certain quires of paper he had written about nine years before, on the acts of Alexander Severus. Thus he places these notes about 1531–1532, when he was ambassador to Charles V. The material, he says, came from a life written in Greek by Alexander's secretary, Eucolpius (a historical character, though the form in other references is Encolpius). It was lent to him by Pudericus, a gentleman from Naples. Being "marvelously ravished" by the account, he started translating it into English; but before he had finished, the owner called for his work. As a result, Elyot had to complete his book from other authors, both Latin and Greek. He describes his work as "compiled" from all these sources.[11]

No Greek life by Eucolpius exists, and there is no evidence that it ever existed. But it is quite possible that Elyot did have a manuscript, either genuine or spurious, at the emperor's court. If it was spurious, Elyot, without known experience in handling manuscripts, in an age which had not developed critical tests for them, would have been easily persuaded to believe it genuine. Since the details cited from Eucolpius tend to be concerned with the conversion of Alexander Severus to Christianity, it is possible that a life was forged to support the tradition of that conversion, and that the manuscript did later disappear. It is also possible historically that Origen, who is said to have converted the emperor to Christianity, came to Rome at his request; the two were contemporaries, and Origen made a number of trips from Alexandria to Rome. It is possible too that Elyot met some man named Pudericus while he was on the Continent; a John Mario Poderico, who died in 1525, had been a chaplain of Charles V.[12] But for all these things there is a lack of evidence.

It is also remotely possible that Elyot meant his story of the manuscript to be an innocent fantasy, like More's story of Hythlodaye with the marmoset that had destroyed parts of a book, and other details in *Utopia*. If so, Elyot sailed too close to the shores of realism for his intention, and he is usually taken seriously.

Elyot's statements were not called in question during the sixteenth century, but as the demand for historical accuracy grew, later men dealt with him severely. John Selden, if he is correctly quoted by others, said in *Eutychius*, 1642, that Elyot had a manuscript but it was composed by a modern writer. Pierre Bayle, in his *Dictionnaire*, 1699, said that Encolpius, beloved of the emperor, had written a history of his life but it is not extant, and the author who boasts that he translated *The Image of Governance* from a Greek manuscript "justly passes for an impostor." William Wotton, in *The History of Rome*, 1701, says that Elyot represented himself as translating *The Image of Governance* from a Greek manuscript but that he probably composed the whole book himself.[13] Bayle and Wotton overlook one fact: Elyot said that he compiled the book from a Greek manuscript by Eucolpius and from other sources, both Greek and Latin. But in the

1542 edition of his dictionary, under *Origines,* he did speak, perhaps carelessly, of the book "whiche I translated out of Eucolpius and called it the Image of Governaunce." Perhaps these attacks on him by men in later centuries will seem irrelevant when we consider the main purpose of his work.

Elyot seems to justify his statement that *The Image of Governance* is a compilation. In chapters xi, xxv, xxix, and xxxiv, he gives marginal references to Lampridius, and to Eucolpius. He cites Eucolpius also in his discussion. In chapter xxv, Origen came to Rome, he says, at the request of Alexander Severus; he explained the Christian religion to the emperor, his mother, and others, "of whom I, Eucolpius, was most happily one." Since the emperor did not dare to publish his conversion to the Christian religion, which he, Eucolpius, and others accepted, he let Origen return to his own country. But in his private room he had images of Moses, Abraham, and Christ; and he honored one God, Eucolpius says, "as I my selfe being often tymes secrete with hym dyd well perseyve." Also the emperor continued to study the books of the Christians, to use their sayings, and to make decisions on the basis of the Golden Rule. In chapter xxvi Elyot cites Eucolpius also in giving the emperor's reasons for embracing Christianity: the humility and charity of the Christians in their daily living had done more to influence him than all the persuasions of Origen. In the closing pages Elyot says that he did not have the last part of the book by Eucolpius; so he consulted Herodianus and also Lampridius: the latter had gathered his material from Accolius and Eucolpius, two men who were always in company with the emperor. Thus Elyot not only says in the work that his book is a compilation, but he refers to various sources through the body of the work.

In writing *The Image of Governance* Thomas Elyot may have had in mind one or more of several possible aims.

One aim appears in his own statement that he was fulfilling the early promise of 1531 to write a volume on the form of government. Perhaps another minor aim was to express more fully his long-standing interest in Alexander Severus. That interest may have begun by 1516, when Erasmus mentioned in his *Institutio principis Christiani* the intense dislike that Alexander felt for flatterers and the cruel punishment he inflicted on offenders.[14] Elyot certainly had the interest in 1531 when he used Alexander Severus in the *Governour* as a pattern for rulers. The emperor was one of many who realized that rulers should have learning, he said. He was beneficent in rebuilding houses or cities decayed by age or overturned by earthquakes. He was willing to obey himself the laws that he devised for others. He spared no pains of mind or body in ruling and developing a people who lived moderately, and he consulted with men of great wisdom and experience from all over the world. He used moderation in his titles, his apparel, and the adornments he permitted his empress to wear.[15]

It is possible that one aim of Elyot was to imitate the work of Guevara. There is no documentary proof that he met the Spanish writer at the court of Charles V, but it would be strange if they did not meet. Though Guevara had become a Franciscan monk in 1528, he was a court preacher and the royal historian; he continued to travel with the emperor and to live at his various residences. His *Libro Aureo,* a supposed history of Marcus Aurelius, was romantic fiction; his aim was to place before Charles V "the model of a prince more perfect for wisdom and virtue than any other of antiquity." He pretended to have a genuine history, a manuscript in Florence; but when he was accused of misrepresentation, in 1540, he insisted to the end that all ancient pagan history is romance and that he had the same right to invent as Livy or Herodotus. When Guevara published *Decada de los Cesares* in 1539, he included Alexander Severus among his emperors and gave a highly favorable view of him. This work was not translated into English until about 1577.[16] At least Elyot and Guevara had interests in common.

Guevara's *Libro Aureo* proved popular in England, more popular than Elyot's *Image of Governance,* and it remained longer in favor. In 1533, a few days before his death, Lord Berners finished translating it into English as the *Golden Book.* It was published in 1534 or 1535. Two more editions appeared about 1536 and 1539, and there were eight or ten other editions by 1600. Thus Elyot not only had a chance to meet Guevara at the emperor's court, but three English editions of the *Golden Book* were within his reach before he issued his *Image of Governance.*[17]

Elyot and Guevara also chose emperors who had much in common. Though Marcus Aurelius persecuted Christians for political reasons, he applied his Stoical philosophy to a busy life and wrote appealing records of that philosophy in action. Alexander Severus was reputed to approach perfection as a ruler, and tradition recorded his conversion to Christianity; hence he was the perfect choice for Elyot. Of course Elyot and Guevara had one aim in common: to present a model of good government.

Perhaps Elyot's main aim in *The Image of Governance,* as Miss Lascelles has pointed out, was to write a didactic biography, according to literary conventions that were almost universally accepted in his Age—a statement that remains true whether he was or was not influenced by Guevara. By the rules for this type of writing, the author selected a historical figure as a symbol for vice or virtue. He wrote a sketch that was supposedly historical, but he amplified his material with anecdotes, letters, speeches, or other details that were not historical. Some of the material he added might be his own invention. The test for additions was not whether they were factually accurate but whether they helped to develop and support the ideas the author wished to teach—that is, whether they helped him present his model for good government.[18]

Such a didactic biography is More's *History of Richard III*, with its chief character as a symbol of evil. More dealt with events that happened mainly after he was born and in his own city. Much of his material apparently came from Cardinal Morton, from his own father, or from others who had been eyewitnesses (prejudiced ones, no doubt); and he checked reports circulating in London about the little princes and their murder. But the long, first-person orations of his characters seem to be mainly created: the appeal of the dying Edward IV to the factions in his kingdom for unity and support of his heirs and later the assertions of the Duke of Buckingham that the children of Edward were bastards and that Richard should be king. In the same way Elyot created a first-person oration for Alexander Severus, giving his views on marriage and on children who might inherit his throne.

As Miss Lascelles has pointed out, the didactic biography usually had its constant elements, but writers using the basic pattern gave it alternative developments. For Alexander Severus the constant elements were gravity, diligence, rectitude, and discernment, in both private and public life. But one who wished to support the power of the king could use these constant elements to present him as a reformer of the legislative body, and one who wished to support the power of a parliamentary body could use them for his contention that the legislative body asserted itself under his noble rule. For example, the author of *The Old Parliament,* in 1645, seriously used ideas from *The Image of Governance* to defend the power of the legislative body. In 1683, the author of *A Most Eloquent Speech . . . by a Most Noble and Wise . . . Emperor . . . Alexander Severus* used ideas from the same source

just as seriously to oppose that power.[19] The major aim of
Elyot is summarized in these words:

> He for his part was impelled rather by the desire to con-
> gratulate his sovereign on those qualities which his sub-
> jects wished him to possess and draw attention to the oc-
> casion for their happy employment, than to transmit in-
> formation about the past. . . . So congenial, moreover,
> were both the substance of the *Image* and its manner of
> employing anecdote: so agreeable to learned and popular
> alike . . . that, for a century and a half, this legendary
> stuff continued to serve the purpose of writers various
> in quality and temper, when they endeavored to frame an
> ideal of administrative practice and the character of the
> good ruler.[20]

Perhaps Elyot was also following, either consciously or
unconsciously, the precepts of Erasmus about the panegyric. Praise a prince, he suggested, for the virtues you
wish him to have and he will be persuaded to improvement.[21]

We might also say that Elyot's aim in *The Image of
Governance* was to present an ideal commonwealth, though
he would prefer to describe it as the form of a just public
weal and thus to keep it free from any hint of a com-
munistic plan. Thus his aim was like that of *Utopia,* but
with his type of mind he had to begin with historical
reality and, throughout the work, to move on the plane of
reality. Because his temperament was not ironic also, he
wished to give positive emphasis to a Christian civilization
—not, like More, to demonstrate the tragic contrast between the Christian ideal and its practice.

Many of the ideas in Elyot's work resemble the ideas
of *Utopia,* whether he was conscious or unconscious of the
likeness. Like the Utopians, the subjects of Alexander
Severus lived a simple life with few servants; they were
temperate in food and drink. To conserve health, they
were expected to have only two meals a day, with six

hours between, and to serve only one kind of meat or fish and a limited number of other foods. Even at court, they avoided expensive gold-trimmed garments. Like the Utopians, who treated gold and jewels as toys for children, Alexander Severus sold the precious stones that were given him, or if he could not sell them, put them in the ears of a statue of Venus. He did not tolerate idleness. He encouraged chess and similar games but forbade gambling. If a man tried to play dice, the state took his property into custody as if he were insane or a natural fool until he returned to thrift. Thus authority dominated the individual, as in *Utopia,* for his own good. Every form of education, physical and intellectual, was provided for the young men; but when Elyot discusses the education for young women, he differs from More and also from Erasmus. The girls were to be trained in modesty, humility, and the occupations necessary for a housewife and were not to be seen outside their homes except in the temples for women only, and then in the company of their mothers or those who acted as mothers for them. Libraries and books were provided; but the books were all locked in cases, a reader had only those an attendant brought him, and an attendant examined each book to see if it had suffered damage before he permitted the reader to leave. If a book had been "deformed," the reader was imprisoned and compelled to replace the book or repair the damage.

The emperor, according to Elyot, did not permit merchant-adventurers to enter the country, since they might bring in newfangled wares to tempt people away from the simple life; but merchant strangers and others allowed to enter were treated with courtesy. The government provided public barns to house the stuff which individuals still owned but were not able to house for themselves. Thus Elyot stresses action for the good of all but avoids the communal ownership of *Utopia.* The emperor also arranged that all vile occupations should be turned

328

over to bondsmen or strangers, as the butchers in *Utopia* were bondsmen. But though Elyot emphasizes only an aristocratic aversion to these occupations, More suggests that butchering and hunting wild animals destroys the sense of compassion and furthers warfare.

The emperor is presented as a builder and a developer of public works. He erected many fair houses that he gave to trusted and honest friends. His program of public works included harbors, beautiful meres and pools filled with strange fish, places for exercise, and public baths, to encourage cleanliness and stop the pestilence. He repaired bridges, built beautiful new ones, erected a place to hear civil controversies, put up statues of good rulers with tablets recording their deeds, rebuilt ruined cities, and built a magnificent sports area near his palace. In addition to repairing libraries and having books rewritten, he arranged for books on science, equipment for geometry and astronomy, tables for arithmetic, and musical instruments. He made visits to the common schools and provided good salaries for teachers, as well as for musicians and architects.

To this program of public works the emperor added hospitals, as in *Utopia:* two in the city for those maimed in war, and two outside the city for other people. As the emperor hated flatterers, bribers, extortioners, and usurers, he eliminated or punished them; but all punishments were designed to help the community, not to execute vengeance. He believed that learned men make good governors. He did not desire power himself, but when he had to accept it, he carried out to the extent of his ability the duty of ruling.

All these ideas sound familiar, at least to one who has analyzed the suggestions of More and Erasmus for the reform of society. If Elyot was not consciously following the ideas of *Utopia* but placing it on a realistic basis and eliminating its communism, the result is what we might expect if he had done so.

Elyot also emphasizes some other ideas of his own, in conflict with those of More and Erasmus, but ideas that he had stressed in the *Governour*. He discusses hunting as a preparation for war and he takes for granted that men will continue to make war. Also he presents Alexander Severus as a firm advocate of degrees in government. The emperor was severe with the proud young men who failed to salute him and the senators. He was sad about the base young men who tried to join the gentlemen in their games and would have come to blows with them if the officers had not interfered. He delivered an oration about the commoners, who should not be given any authority but should work at their occupations, execute the laws made by the senate, obey their leaders, and when necessary, give obedient service in war.[22]

It seems fitting that *The Image of Governance,* though it was not Elyot's last work, should be the last new work that he directed to the improvement of this world. In it he conscientiously carried out a promise made ten years earlier to write another volume on the form of government; he expressed more fully an interest in the perfection of Alexander Severus as a ruler; and while he may have followed somewhat the path of Guevara, he avoided the extremes of romance in the *Golden Book,* and developed the principles for a realistic public weal instead of an ironic *Utopia.* In a didactic biography rather than a factual history, he made his final effort to influence English noblemen to virtue and good government.

Elyot's last work, *A Preservative against Death,* was issued by Berthelet in 1545. There were no other editions. The title page has only the name of the book, the place, and the date of publication, arranged within Berthelet's picture-frame design. The preface identifies the author, saying that Thomas Elyot, knight, "to his worshypfull frende, Syr Edwarde North, knight, chancellour of the augmentacions . . . desireth well to doo." The colophon adds a more exact date, July 2, 1545.

In the first sentence of his preface Elyot says that he had sent his friend North the little book, at the beginning of Lent, as a small return for his gentle benefits. This copy apparently was in manuscript, for he adds that he has now caused the book to be printed as a testimony of the hearty love he bears his friend, so that the book may endure longer, and though a private gift, be beneficial to many men.

Again, with his usual sensitivity to criticism, Elyot says some men think knights should leave sermons to priests. But he defends himself by saying that he writes with humility, and since he must often punish men for breaking severe temporal laws, he would like to do what he can to keep them from breaking the laws of God. Again he says that he will face a strict reckoning if he hides his talent. A Christian knight has the obligation to defend his country and his faith with his sword and also to combat vice and error with his wit and learning. He adds, "as muche as I am a sheriffe . . . I thinke my selfe the more bounden to bee thus occupied." If his present tense is accurate, he was writing the preface in 1544, the last time he held the office of sheriff. Probably he sent a manuscript copy to North at Lent, 1545, and then gave the copy to the printer.

"Moreover," he adds, "as often as I doo consyder the temporall pumyshementes and doo abhorre the sharpnesse of theim, I do devoulve in my mynde what horrible peynes are prepared for theim whome the sonne of god shall condemne at his generall iugement. . . ." Here the sensitive man speaks as he had not spoken out before about affairs of government. Then, using the comparison of Mary and Martha, he suggests to his friend that a man busy with temporal things might even read this book during Mass, since meditation and prayer in their nature are one. He trusts that he and North may receive comfort from each other in the present world and the world to come, "whiche is the perfection of amitie. . . ."[23] While this is a striking change from earlier years when he addressed Cromwell and considered a love of studies the perfect basis of amity, it accords with the other evidence about his growing religious feeling and his concern about his last reckoning.

Elyot's work, *A Preservative against Death,* belongs to a great tradition, with many companions in the sixteenth century. An early ancestor, the *Ars moriendi,* about 1450, stressed the things to be done as death drew near, with emphasis upon Catholic ritual. Editions of it continued to appear in Elyot's lifetime.[24] Most of the sixteenth-century treatises were universal instead of stressing the theology of the old or the new religion. Many of the writers were facing martyrdom, and some were consoling family and friends as well as steeling themselves to meet death.

An anonymous author of *The Treatise of the Dying Creature,* about 1507, probably belongs in the tradition but his work is not available for examination.[25] About the same time Richard Whitford wrote a treatise on dying, at the request of Elizabeth Gibbs, the abbess of Syon House.[26] In 1529 Thomas Lupset, an able young man who met an untimely death from illness, wrote his *Treatise Teaching the Way of Dying.* He emphasizes living well as a preparation for dying, and he combines universal Christian beliefs with classical philosophy.[27] About 1533 Erasmus wrote *De preparatione ad mortem* at the request of Sir Thomas Boleyn. Erasmus offers practical comments about making a will and suggests the rites of the church, along with ideas from classical philosophy. Though he also mentions living well as a good preparation for dying, he tends to follow somewhat the older pattern of the *Ars moriendi.*[28] Bishop John Fisher addressed to his sister Elizabeth *A Spiritual Consolation* on death while he was a prisoner in the Tower, waiting execution.[29] Sir Thomas More wrote *The Four Last Things,* a look at life and death, about 1522, while he was a very active member of the king's Council.[30] As a prisoner in the Tower, he faced death in his *Dialogue of Comfort,* his comments on a *Book of Hours,* and his unfinished *Treatise on the Passion.* Some of the religious reformers, such as John Frith, Richard Tracy, John Bradfield, and Thomas Becon, continued the tradition with treatises that tended to be universal.[31]

In writing *A Preservative against Death,* 1545, Elyot does not seem conscious that he is part of a great tradition. He is merely a religious man, putting down ideas for himself, Edward North, and others, who need at some future time to face death. Many of his ideas are conventional and do not belong specifically to the old or the new religion: the temptations of the world (with her two "pappes" of avarice and ambition), the flesh, and the devil; the lesser value of material possessions compared with treasures in heaven; and the worth of worldly dignity only if one comes to authority virtuously and administers affairs so that justice is nourished, necessity relieved, true religion established, vice repressed, and virtue supported.[32] Consistent with his attitude in the *Governour* and other works, he avoids the term *common weal* and uses *public weal.*

Elyot speaks with feeling about the death of vigorous young men:

> But if we consyder daiely how many men we have knowen, beynge of yeres lusty, stronge, and couragious, aboundynge in the giftes of nature and fortune, howe sodaynely above mens expectacion and also their owne, have been attached with deathe, either naturall or violente, that is to saie, beynge either slayne or put to execution by lawes.[33]

By 1545 Elyot might well make the statement from the depths of personal experience.

At times Elyot unites medical comment with his religious ideas as one might expect from the author of *The Castle of Health*. When death is near we should eat and drink less than usual so that our minds may be free, our wits quick, and our memory ready to help us in preparing our last reckoning. He defends exercise and also labor as a worthy part of the human condition, though these ideas seem unconnected with his immediate topic, the preparation for death. Later, in discussing the virtue of patience, he stresses its physical effects, saying that the patient person continues to look young longer, digests his food well, and is less often troubled with illness because he avoids anger, which brings on fevers and other diseases worse than death. Elyot also repeats with some variation a plan for the control of anger that he had given in *The Castle*. Again he cites Apollodorus, saying this time that he taught the emperor, before speaking or acting in anger, to repeat all the letters in the Greek alphabet. As Christian men, he says, we might use the *Pater noster*, in Latin or in English.

Elyot emphasizes doctrines of the old religion more than one might expect him to do in a period when other treatises about facing death tended to be universal. Perhaps as a writer whose work had been largely secular, he wished to leave a final testimony to his beliefs. Whatever the motive, he uses the slanting of the old religion, not that of the reformers, in his discussion of fasting, good works, the danger in permitting an individual to be his own interpreter of the scripture, and the problem of predestination and free will.

Concerning fasting, Elyot says that the devil lies when he tries to persuade us that fasting destroys nature. If we did not have scripture, we still have reason to tell us that fasting, discreetly used, preserves nature but overeating destroys it. Overeating also makes the wits dull, but moderate abstinence quickens the spirit, sharpens wits,

and gives reason its freedom.[34] He spends much space
defending the giving of alms and other works of repent-
ance. He refutes the idea that one may refrain from giving
to the needy because a gift will cause the receiver to live
in idleness. One should not knowingly encourage idleness
or any other vice, but if the receiver misuses the gift without the giver's knowledge, he still is given credit for the
good deed. Alms, an act of compassion toward those in
need of the gift and given for the sake of God, cannot be
wrong. After quoting scripture, he cites Saint Augustine,
who said, "Almesse ded pourgeth synne, and maketh intercession for us unto God."[35] This idea clearly belongs
to the conservative religion.

   Elyot is not usually controversial in handling these
ideas; he does not seem so when he discusses the problem
of interpreting scripture. Instead of trying to convert an
opponent he addresses the believer, but he makes clear his
opposition to the idea of the reformers that every man
should be his own interpreter:

> Humbly therefore and simply reade and heare holy scrip-
> ture, not presumyng that thou understandest every thyng
> that thou dost reade, whiche to other seemeth darke: but
> often tymes, if thou maiest, consulte with theim whiche
> be syncerely exercised therein, or with the bokes of moste
> auncyente and catholike doctours. Or if thou maiest not
> easily or shortly come by the one or the other, ceasse to
> be curiouse, and committe all to god untyl it shall lyke
> hym, by some meanes to revele it unto the. Beware, drawe
> not the understandynge of scripture to thyne affection:
> but slake thine affection before thou appliest thy witte
> to make exposicion. . . . If we wolde applie it unto our
> phantasy . . . we than be striken with the clubbe of wil-
> ful opinion, and our taste and savoure is altered unto a
> false tast and a false smell.[36]

He adds that there are many places in scripture which require for their understanding both a constant faith and

learning. So we should approach scripture reverently and fearfully, lest we be stricken, like the man who put profane hands on the ark of God. His discussion here helps, if such help is needed, in understanding his cautious recommendation about the study of the Bible in the *Governour,* written in a time of acute religious controversy.

When Elyot attacks the doctrine of predestination he becomes more controversial in his tone. He describes the devil as a giant with a great club, saying to any man:

> Presumest thou, ignorant foole, to atteyne to the kingdome of heaven by thy warkes? Thynkest thou that almes dede, fastyng, or prayer, or that foolishnesse whiche thou callest Vertue hath power to brynge thee to any other estate than god hath ordeyned the? Accordynge as he hathe predestinate the, so shalte thou be. . . .

When we are tempted to believe this error, we need to call upon God for better help than our own wits can give us. Later in the discussion he says that from the beginning, God left man in the power of his own counsel or his own free will.[37]

Elyot's authorities in *A Preservative against Death* are never the Schoolmen, not even Thomas Aquinas. He cites scripture, both the Old and the New Testament, many times. Like Colet, More, and Erasmus, he calls upon the fathers of the early Christian church as support: Saint Bernard, Saint Ambrose, Saint Chrysostom, and Origen at least once each; Saint Jerome and Saint Gregory at least twice; and Saint Augustine some eleven times. He also cites classic authors: the "philosopher" twice, and Apollodorus, Aristotle, Cicero, and Seneca at least once each. He puts no emphasis upon making a will, religious ceremonies, or other actions at the time of death—perhaps because his work is for those who are still in good health—but upon living by orthodox principles so that one may be ready to die well. *A Preservative against Death* is the most religious of his works, perhaps his only nonsecular work.

It seems fitting that Sir Thomas Elyot should be listed for many governmental commissions almost to the end of his life. It seems equally fitting that his only new works during his last five years should be concerned with the ideal government and with his religious views in preparation for death. Five years before his death, in *The Image of Governance,* he suggests a deepening sense of religion and a concern about the full use of his talents in relation to his last reckoning. Later, in *A Preservative against Death,* these attitudes persist, mingled with the defense of essential conservative doctrines. To the end of his life, then, Elyot expressed his desire to benefit his country, to honor his allegiance to his king, and to worship according to the old faith.

Elyot's friendship for Edward North, to whom he addressed *A Preservative against Death,* has other interesting facets. The two men were neighbors in Cambridge. Elyot's chief residence from about 1530 was Carlton, seven miles south of Newmarket. North's chief country residence, from about 1533, when he married a widow of property, was Kirtling, five miles southeast of Newmarket. In 1541 when North was knighted and also appointed treasurer of the Court of Augmentations, the two men became equals in rank; and as North did not become a baron until 1554, they remained equals as long as Elyot lived. Queen Mary pardoned North for his brief support of Lady Jane Grey and in 1557 appointed him on her commission to suppress heresy.[38] His loyalty to the old faith helps explain Elyot's dedication to him of his last work.

While Elyot and North were neighbors, North's second son was born, probably about 1535, the one we know

now as Sir Thomas North, the famous Elizabethan translator. Presumably the boy knew Elyot as his father's friend
and neighbor until he was about eleven years old. Elyot
was a literary man with a library, he had probably met
Guevara at the court of Charles V, he wrote a didactic
biography in which he may have emulated that writer
without following him into the thickets of fictionalized
romance, he cited and translated Plutarch, and at his best
he was an excellent translator who produced a work of
art. Edward North, so far as we know, had none of these
literary interests and did none of these things.

Was Elyot a major but early influence on Sir Thomas
North? After perhaps attending Cambridge and then following his father to Lincoln's Inn for a brief stay, Thomas
North gave up everything else for his literary pursuits.
His first book, *The Dial of Princes,* published in 1557,
was a translation of Guevara's *Libro Aureo,* the romantic
and didactic biography. His greatest work, published in
1579 and dedicated to Queen Elizabeth, was a translation
from Plutarch, *The Lives of the Noble Grecians and
Romans.*[39]

Would Sir Thomas North ever have translated *The
Dial of Princes* or Plutarch's *Lives* if he had never known
his father's friend and neighbor, Sir Thomas Elyot? Of
course Shakespeare owed to North's Plutarch his material
for *Julius Caesar, Coriolanus,* and *Antony and Cleopatra;*
he transformed many of North's beautiful prose passages
into blank verse without drastic changes in either ideas
or wording. Without Sir Thomas North and possibly
without Sir Thomas Elyot, would these plays have come
into existence at all? Or would they have been quite different plays?

We know little or nothing about the circumstances of
Thomas Elyot's death. His will had been made first on
August 29, 1531, when he was preparing to go on his em-

bassy to the court of Charles V. It had been witnessed by
Sir John Sharp, curate of Combe, and four others. The
whole will was confirmed by an additional statement dated
March 23, 1546, when Elyot described himself as sick in
body but sound and perfect in mind.

Among the witnesses to the confirmation of the will
were Thomas Elvington, Esquire, and Sir Giles Alington,
the husband of Sir Thomas More's stepdaughter. Alington, a resident of Cambridgeshire, had been named
steadily, of course, on commissions for that county, and
thus often with Elyot. According to the will of Alington's
father, Bottisham and Horseheath were family properties,
and Cambridgeshire maps indicate that both were near
Elyot's Cambridge residence. Bottisham is perhaps seven
or eight miles from Carlton as a homing pigeon might fly,
and Horseheath is perhaps four or five miles away. Elyot's
will was proved July 2, 1546, by Thomas Laughton and
Margaret Elyot. As the will directed, the widow was
named the executor.[40]

Elyot asked to be buried in the Christian burial
ground nearest the place where he happened to die, with
some image or stone set in a wall next to his grave, bearing
in Latin his name and the time of his death. As this direction comes in the first part of the will, he probably thought
that he might die overseas. He left such usual bequests as
a hundred shillings to a hundred bedridden or aged men
and women, money for the marriage of poor maidens, a
black coat for every servant, and more than thirteen
shillings to each servant who went overseas with him and
remained with him there. He willed forty shillings besides his wages to his servant, Thomas Laughton, and the
same sum to a Margaret Restwold, for her marriage. He
asked that his brother-in-law, Robert Puttenham, be dis-
charged of more than sixteen pounds of a twenty-pound
debt, provided that he did not trouble Elyot's wife or executor. He directed that all his books be sold and the

money given to poor scholars who were also good students, 6s., 8d., to each one. All of these bequests, except possibly the sale of his books, seem a matter of simple duty.

Elyot provided for the usual religious ceremonies. In one section of the will be provided a yearly obit at Weston Colville; in another section he directed his wife to keep an annual obit at Weston with ten priests to sing a solemn Mass and nine low Masses for the souls of Sir William Findern, Sir Richard Elyot and Alice his wife, his own soul, and all Christian souls—the usual formula. He directed his wife also to have him "rehersed" and prayed for by name every term at St. Paul's Cross and to give three pence to three poor men every Friday in the year to pray for him and for his father and mother. But the first Parliament under Edward VI dissolved the chantries, saying that prayers for the souls of the dead were mere superstition. Hence Elyot had these prayers for himself and for others only a short time. The residue of his property he left to his wife, charging her to pay his debts and to do deeds of charity for the weal of his soul, as she must answer at the day of judgment. She must have received the profits of the six manors (four in Cambridge, one in Dorset, and one in Southampton) and of their appurtenances, and of other lands, including land in Wiltshire. If he died without heirs, his property, after the death of his wife, was to go to his sister Margery and her lawful heirs; and for lack of them, to John Elyot of Grewer and his lawful heirs. In one item of the will he specified that certain lands, for lack of any of these heirs, should go to John Michell, otherwise called John Elyot, of Frome, in Somerset.

One special gift in Elyot's will went beyond duty: as a gift to his friend William Raynsford he left twenty links of his chain and the best gelding in his stable.[41] This is the only gift that seems to be based either on love or on friendship. Thus his will is quite different from that of his father, Sir Richard, who remembered by name numbers of friends and relatives with gifts of movable property, such as cloaks, gowns, hangings, cups, spoons, and other special belongings. Whether the difference comes from the fact that the wife of Thomas Elyot was still living, from his hurried completing of his will due to illness, from a lack of concern for people, or from other reasons is uncertain. He uses no term of endearment for his wife in his entire will.

Elyot was buried in the parish church at Carlton, Cambridge. A description of the Elyot monument written in 1632 by Layer—probably John Layer, an antiquarian of Cambridgeshire—has survived and was quoted by Croft, but it adds little to our information. Brass likenesses of both the Elyots were erected, it is said, but they disappeared long ago.


There is little evidence about the happiness or unhappiness of the marriage between Thomas Elyot and Margaret Barrow. Though there is reason to believe that she was years younger than her husband—perhaps fifteen years younger—that fact does not prove unhappiness. After Elyot died, his widow married Sir James Dyer, who was born in 1512. Dyer was probably younger than she was and more than twenty years younger than Elyot. There is no indication that he had been married before. They had no children. Dyer attained high position in legal affairs, as a serjeant-at-law, a king's serjeant, a Justice of the Common Pleas, and then a member of the Queen's Bench. He is said to have been a man of intelligence, learning, and integrity. She died in 1560, and Sir James died in 1582. A monument to them in the church at Great Staughton, Huntingdonshire, listed her only as Margaret Barrow, with nothing to suggest that for twenty-five years she had been the wife of Sir Thomas Elyot.[42] These facts, strange as some of them seem, do not tell us whether the marriage of Margaret Barrow and Thomas Elyot was happy or even companionable. Perhaps we shall never know.

Some other questions, keep coming to mind: Would Elyot have ordered all his books sold, with no exceptions, if his wife had been interested in her husband's literary work? (As she had studied in More's household school, one is inclined to expect from her a behavior superior to that of the uneducated wife.) Was she responsible for the fact that no personal letters or papers that were in his possession remain to us? Did she allow one of the Puttenham nephews to have some material on literary criticism—material which made a contribution years later to *The Art of English Poesy?* Did she dispose of an unpublished history of England which, directly or indirectly, came into the hands of John Twyne? Perhaps these questions also must remain unanswered.

# CHAPTER XVII

## *Elyot's Personality and His Influence: Summary*

HEN Sir Thomas Elyot talked frankly to his king on returning from his embassy to Charles V about June 1, 1532, the basis of his motivation was integrity—as his whole life and his writings suggest. Believing that a king should rule by high ethical standards and should be a good man in his personal life, he was concerned both for the kingdom and for the royal soul. As a conservative in religion and in government he wished to remain loyal to king and to church. Perhaps one should not make a judgment about him without remembering that loyalty to the church of Western Europe, for the deeply religious man, was as real as loyalty to king and country and that it had older, deeper roots.

Elyot had probed the ideas of the classical philosophers and of his Christian teachers and had chosen the standards of the early church, with its simplicity and its freedom from corruption and materialism. The result of such probing is not naïveté. Though he could hardly be called bold and he had no continuing appetite for martyrdom, surely he was not naïve enough to think that he took no risks when he remonstrated with his king, especially when the talk must have glanced at the royal passion for Anne Boleyn. It seems clear that he suffered material losses for a time because he dared to speak frankly, to reiterate in his writings the need for kings to control carnal desires and to rule for the common good, and because he gave no active support to Henry in his separation from his queen and from the church at Rome. The same integrity controlled his conduct in the offices he held and in his efforts to aid Catherine of Aragon.

When we analyze other elements in the personality of Elyot, the human being, an outstanding quality is reticence. He has left us little evidence about personal emotions, but the lack suggests reticence. Some other qualities seem clear. He was a serious-minded, almost solemn man, though bits of humor occasionally break through the crust of solemnity. His portrait, his letters, his other writings, and the lack of any tradition about his wit or humor all tell the same story. Except for his feeling toward intimate friends, there is little evidence of warmth or charm. Of course he loved books and the classical literatures, and (as he told us himself) he was by nature prone to knowledge.

Persistence was also dominant in Elyot's personality. He was persistent in personal affairs, especially in his efforts to get payment for his work as clerk of the Council and for the extra expenses on his embassy. At times he must have seemed a nuisance to Cromwell with his requests, but so far as we know that busy official never expressed impatience. He was just as persistent in his efforts to influence his king away from dishonest affections about 1531 through 1533. One may wonder why he did not suffer a positive penalty for the ideas he emphasized in his books. Perhaps Cromwell protected him in case of need. Perhaps he escaped because, unlike More, he was not important enough: the loss of his head would not have helped Henry's "great cause." Then, too, his books, with their indirect suggestions about the behavior of the king, were subtle and philosophical; they were not the sort to inflame public opinion. Elyot was persistent and also consistent in the expression of other ideas. Though some ideas deepen, as the preference for the simple life seems to do, even minor ideas in an earlier work are likely to reappear in later works without change. His desire to honor his allegiance to his king, to support conservative doctrines in religion, to follow the teachings of the early church, to recognize a difference between rhetoric and wisdom, to emphasize exercise and diet for good health, to defend aristocracy with modifications, to stress for rulers personal morality, high ethical principles, and learning with wisdom—in all these ideas he is consistent.

Elyot's feelings against injustice and ingratitude are closely connected with his persistence, since these qualities appear together in his protests about the failure to compensate him for his clerkship and the expenses of his embassy. His letter to Hacket implies a protest against injustice because he had not been named to the Council, though his successor to the court of Charles V had received preferment. In one letter to Cromwell also he mentions the failure to make him a member of the Council. In *The Castle of Health* he discusses ingratitude at length, adding that he has spent space on the topic because he has had experience in this grief.

Elyot lacked an adventurous spirit about physical travel and in the realms of the mind. He preferred to learn his geography at home in a comfortable study, using maps, globes, and perhaps other wonderful new instruments. When he was at the emperor's court, his only venture outside England, he appealed to the Duke of Norfolk and perhaps used the help of his wife about returning home. His letter to Norfolk from the Continent is a dutiful set of observations but is not infused with the zest for exploring new worlds. As for adventures of the mind, a comparison of Elyot's *Image of Governance* with More's *Utopia* will probably lead a reader to conclude that Elyot was not at home on the dizzy peaks of imagination.

Elyot was generally a believer in the simple life for himself, though in 1531 he admitted that magnificence might sometimes be necessary for kings. In *The Castle of Health* he recommends simplicity in the dress of parish priests, according to the rules of the early church, and he emphasizes for all, simplicity in food, drink, sleep, and the control of emotions. In *The Image of Governance* he presents his ideal ruler as one who dresses simply, wears no jewels, and is temperate in food and drink. By 1541 perhaps he had seen too much of magnificence. His belief in the simple life did not keep him from recognizing a certain decorum for a ruler or even for himself. As a knight he wished for enough income to live according to the station of life to which the king had called him. At the emperor's court he felt it necessary to equip his servants and maintain a household befitting the ambassador of a great king. But in all things his personal preference was for moderation.

Elyot was a man of property who believed in acquiring and keeping possessions. We do not know whether he had beautiful movable property, such as silver cups, bowls, and hangings; for he does not mention such things in his will. But his fervent and continued opposition to the theory of holding all things in common and his insistence on the term public weal, not common weal, are evidence of his belief in private ownership. His persistent efforts to get pay for the sums he believed were due him do not indicate an indifference to worldly goods. The six manors and the other lands he named in his will are clear evidence that he acquired and kept property.

Elyot's interest in artistic pursuits has not usually been sufficiently emphasized. His comment in the *Governour* is well known; there he pleads that children inclined to paint, engrave, or carve be allowed to follow their desires. He also emphasizes the study of poetry as few men in his time did, and of course he recommends the study of music and dancing. It has not been noted before, it seems, that in the *Governour* and in other works, when he uses comparisons involving the subjects or the techniques of great artists, his comments are sometimes completely separated from any desire to teach morals.

In the area of human relations Elyot had many facets. He was not the hail-fellow-well-met type. Instead he seems to have had a loneliness of spirit. Though he was about the same age as his king, he surely never felt at home, even in the innocent days of that ruler, in a court where Francis Bryan and the brawny, jovial, unsubtle Charles Brandon belonged. So far as we know, he had no skill in composing songs or playing musical instruments or turning a quick and graceful compliment—even though he had been trained at an Inn of Court as the nobles are trained. He had no taste at all for the flirtatious, the carnal, or the bawdy. He was not the typical courtier.

His attitudes toward women are strange, especially for a man whose wife had studied in More's household school. He never mentioned his wife in his extant letters or referred to her in his other writings. He never made warm, general comments, like those of Vives, for example, about the wives who share and lighten the cares of their husbands—as if he were thinking of his own wife. In the *Governour*, I, vii, when he praises Livia's counsel to her husband about mercy and patience, he adds that women should have liberty to give only this kind of counsel and no other. He followed his account of Livia with a promise to write a book only for ladies and to praise Livia amply; but when he published *The Defense of Good Women* nine years later, he did not mention Livia, and his ideas were remote and conventional. In the *Governour*, I, xviii, he says that hunting hares with greyhounds might be good for women who are not afraid of injuring their beauty in sun and wind and that the sport might cause them to be less idle than they are at home. Though his comment may be true, it does not suggest a high opinion of women. When he mentions women who live in his own world, he prefers them to be gentle. Since his wife studied in More's school, he must have known Margaret More Roper and her sisters; but unlike Erasmus and Vives, who wrote of Margaret with affection and admiration, he gives no sign of friendship for an intellectual woman.

Apparently Elyot had affection for his sister and his stepsisters. In his prefatory remarks for *The Education or Bringing Up of Children* he calls Margery Puttenham his entirely beloved sister, he is concerned about the education of her sons, and he is tactful enough to assume that he is merely supplementing her wisdom. His *Sermon of Holy Saint Cyprian,* published at a time of crisis for Syon House, suggests warmth of feeling for three stepsisters, especially for Dame Susan Kingston.

From time to time Elyot writes almost as if he were giving himself an indirect consolation for the fact that he had no children. In the *Education or Bringing Up of Children* he comments that no children are preferable to ignorant and vicious ones. In *The Castle of Health,* Third Book, chapter 12, he uses the same idea as a consolation to parents who have lost children. In *The Image of Governance,* chapter xxvi, he explains the attitude of Alexander Severus as if it were a personal regret that he tries to consider no regret. The emperor indulges in a long, didactic oration, probably the creation of Elyot, saying that he would gladly lack children because he is more concerned about his benefits to the public weal. He fears that his children, if he had them, would not carry out his ideals. In being childless he is only giving up the doting pleasure of seeing his little son ride a cockhorse or hearing him chatter and speak like a wanton.

Elyot emphasized the friendship of man for man

above other human relations, in the *Governour,* in other
books, and in letters and dedications. He also cherished
men friends, instead of talking in generalities. In 1533 he
treated Sir John Hacket as an intimate friend when he
wrote him about the dark cloud hovering over England
but his own resolution to follow truth and keep his allegiance to his king. He signed himself as Hacket's son
and assured friend. He considered William Raynsford a
special friend for years; and though he did not name personal gifts for other relatives, his nephews, or his wife, he
willed Raynsford twenty links of his chain and his best
gelding. For about twenty years he considered Cromwell a
trusted friend, long before the latter had become powerful.
He wrote him concerning all his problems, asked help, and
eventually received it. While he was dedicating books to
Cromwell he stressed an interest in similar studies as the
basis of friendship. In the last years of Elyot's life, Sir
Edward North was a cherished friend; and as Elyot considered his last reckoning, he stated that the same religious
faith is the best basis for friendship, in this world and in
the world to come.

So far as we can judge from his whole life, how did
Sir Thomas Elyot evaluate his successes and failures in
his earthly life? To modern readers the answer to this
question is more interesting than his reckoning with
heaven. He must have been disappointed in having no
son to carry on his name and inherit his manors. The
modern biographer shares the regret, for a son with an
interest in him might have preserved his library and his
personal papers. He did not receive an appointment to
the Council; as a result he felt a sense of personal injustice
and of frustration because he wished to exert an ethical
influence on the king and the government.

Since it seems fairly certain that Elyot would have
preferred England to remain part of the larger church of

Western Europe he must have been dismayed at the separation of England from that church. Perhaps it is well that he did not outlive his king, to witness the events directed by those who governed for Edward VI. Thus he never saw the end of his plan to have Masses said for the souls of his parents and of Sir William Findern, for himself, and for all Christian souls.

As for larger events outside his personal life, an obvious failure appears in his efforts to keep Catherine of Aragon as queen or to restore her to the throne. Since he tried to help her he must have felt disappointment when she died in loneliness and poverty. Another failure is connected with his desire to influence Henry into becoming a good man without dishonest passions and a king who ruled for the temporal and spiritual welfare of his subjects. Perhaps Elyot persuaded himself that his praise of Henry's orthodoxy in the preface of his 1538 *Dictionary* contributed to the adoption of the Six Articles in 1539. If so, one would not wish to deny him the satisfaction whether it was true or not. But any efforts to make Henry into a good man and a good king, according to his own standards, were a failure.

Perhaps the greatest satisfaction Elyot had in his life resulted from his belief that his books were a rich and many-sided legacy to England. Although estimating his total influence is like trying to count the drops of water in the Thames, he was not wrong about a general achievement.

In the final analysis, why is Elyot important? From the record of his life and writings it seems clear that he exerted little or no political influence. He offered no support to the unlimited power of the king, no help in the separation from Catherine of Aragon or the break from the church of Western Europe, and no aid to Henry's shrewd handling of Parliament in the 1530's to legalize his aims. He did what he could to keep Catherine queen of England and to persuade Henry into the paths of religious orthodoxy and moral and ethical behavior, but there is no evidence that his efforts had any effect. As a member of Parliament he may have had a chance to vote for the Six Articles in 1539, but one vote was unimportant when a high tide of conservatism was rising.

Elyot was not a measurable political influence because his concept of government was an ethical system. Like other humanists of his period in England, he tended to accept a monarchy; he was not one of the bolder spirits who sometimes speculated among friends about an elective system. He was not concerned about the king's power, the controls exercised by legislative bodies, or the conflict between spiritual and temporal power. If a king acted with justice, temperance, and wisdom, and if his helpers or governors did the same, all would be well. Trying to fit Elyot to the political theories or motives of so-called "practical" men, like stretching him on a bed of Procrustes, is a common practice—and a common error.

Since Elyot had little or no political influence, then, his reputation rests on his literary work. As we look back from the twentieth century, works of lesser importance are perhaps *The Castle of Health, The Banquet of Sapience,* and *A Preservative against Death. The Castle,* with its suggestions on watching symptoms, diet, exercise, and experimentation, and its rational approach without magic or charms, doubtless had a desirable effect on the bodies of some Englishmen. *The Banquet,* with its careful organization, classical and Christian sources, and appeal to readers of English instead of Latin, gave men a thoughtful occupation for moments of leisure and furnished them quotable maxims. *A Preservative against Death,* though never reprinted and not widely known, perhaps consoled a few people in a lingering illness. But if these works had never been published, the future of English life and literature would probably have remained the same.

The translations, including two little volumes that may be Elyot's though he never acknowledged them, and two other volumes (*Saint Cyprian* with Pico's *Rules of a Christian Life* and another from Plutarch on education) are not mountain peaks in a general estimate of his work. But *The Doctrinal of Princes,* from Isocrates, carries Elyot's name and a preface stating his discoveries about the English and Greek languages. It has been evaluated by an authority, James Wortham, who examined also all other translations of classical works published before 1580. Elyot used all the methods that Erasmus had used earlier in translating Greek into Latin, he says; and Elyot succeeded in giving the thought concisely and accurately, reproducing the tone and texture of the original, and thus producing a translation that at times was a work of art. It was one of the earliest, if not the earliest, translation from Greek into English, though Elyot may have checked his work by the Latin. The question of his influence on future translators seems to be unanswered, but the individual work was an achievement.

Elyot's Platonic dialogues were an important influence. Though his later *Defense of Good Women* indicated his understanding of the inductive method, the work made no real contribution in 1540 to the Socratic method, to characterization, dramatic skill, or ideas. But *Pasquil the Plain* and *Of the Knowledge Which Maketh the Wise Man* were pioneer work in England. *Pasquil* has an earthy, satiric flavor; *Of the Knowledge* often uses everyday language but rises to large philosophic patterns. Both employ the inductive method skillfully; both avoid an English setting but convey reactions to English events of the time. These two dialogues did much to establish Socratic methods and Platonic thought in England.

Elyot exerted an outstanding influence through his *Dictionary.* He was the first man in England to analyze the need for a comprehensive work dealing with the classical Latin of the Renaissance and then to attempt a volume meeting that need. Most important of all for the future influence, he explained his Latin words in English idiom. Through his own three editions, the revisions of his work by Thomas Cooper, and the continued use of his material in Cooper's *Thesaurus,* Elyot's contribution to the English language extended through the Renaissance. As no English dictionaries existed, he influenced the language used by such writers as Spencer, Marlowe, and Shakespeare.

In the late sixteenth century and after, Elyot is often praised in a general way for his learning, enlargement of the language, and elegant style. In the *Governour* he deliberately added words of classical origin to enlarge the language. In later works he used words from his own knowledge of sheep, horses, and the general details of country life as well as words of native English origin. We need a complete, reliable study of his diction and his style before we can draw conclusions about his influence on the language. But the references to him by others suggest that he gave to many writers an awareness of words and style.

The *Governour* was an important influence because it mirrored the life of Elyot's own time in ways that have not been fully recognized. Elyot, his father, and other landed gentry carried government to all parts of England; and this practical experience must have stimulated Elyot's thinking about the qualities of good governors, though he found it expedient to use classical examples. For about seven years also, while he was clerk of the Council, Elyot had an unexcelled opportunity to watch good and bad qualities in governors, including the king himself. The court of Henry VIII and Catherine of Aragon lived in a world of music, dance, and song. Sir Thomas More, with theory and practice for both men and women, had been influencing the court to a classical education, making it desirable—almost fashionable. Colet, Grocyn, Linacre, and Lily, with their study in Italy and other Mediterranean countries, had contributed. So had Erasmus and Vives with their periods of residence in England. The Inns of Court, where most gentlemen spent at least a brief time, trained their students in song, dance, and the formalities of courtly behavior. The king had made physical pursuits, especially hunting and the use of the longbow, almost a way of life. Thus the *Governour* caught and reflected a many-sided life of England.

If Elyot did nothing but organize and report these characteristics of his time—and he probably did much more—he exerted an influence of magnitude. Though his effect on future writers is hard to measure because they drew from the classics and from other writers later than Elyot, many are indebted to him for incidents, ideas, and for idiom and diction. Some men who read the *Governour* may even have tried to shape their lives by it. Probably Elyot not only mirrored the best of his own time but did much to create Elizabethan life and the Elizabethan gentleman.

At least Elyot has a firm claim to recognition for the *Governour* because he was the first man writing in England and in English to recommend for the gentleman a combination of these things: first, a classical and literary education; second, physical development, including the use of the longbow, for peace and war; third, training for service in the government; fourth, religious and ethical development; fifth, artistic skill in painting, drawing, music, and the dance; sixth, a courtly, aristocratic behavior.

Perhaps as a literary man, in England only and in the sixteenth century only, Elyot reached and influenced a greater number of people than Sir Thomas More did. This statement is not meant to suggest that Elyot was a greater man, thinker, or writer; for he must in all ways be ranked below More. But Elyot's books were in English, and he wrote on many subjects. More's greatest single work was in Latin, his English works mainly dealt with religious controversy, and under Queen Elizabeth his life and writings were not favored for public discussion. In contrast, circumstances made it possible for Elyot to reach many people.

As a writer, Elyot lacked the creative imagination that prompted Erasmus' *Praise of Folly* and More's *Utopia*. He was not usually at home with irony or satire, though he used effective touches of it in *Pasquil the Plain*. He could not make a character live, as Erasmus was able to do, but his aims did not usually require characterization. He lacked the largeness of vision and the free play of mind that prompts men to "a speculative philosophy among friends," an intellectual mountain climbing to discover only where thought might lead. A writer who lacks these qualities may compensate by revealing himself, so that through him others discover themselves. But Elyot either lacked depths of self or he was incurably reticent—perhaps by nature and training, perhaps by the troubled times in which he lived. Hence he wrote nothing that would be chosen with no dissent as one of the great books of the world. He was for an age, not for all time. But in his age he exerted a sound, substantial influence, largely through his Platonic dialogues and Platonic thought, through his *Dictionary* and its two later editions, perhaps through his *Doctrinal of Princes* and his general concern with style and diction, and through *The Book Named the Governour*.

# APPENDIX I

## Sixteenth-Century Works with a Possible Relation to the Governour

1516. ERASMUS, *Institutio principis Christiani.*

*ca.* 1516. CASTIGLIONE, *Il Cortegiano* (published in 1528).

1517–1519. BUDÉ, *De l'institution du prince* (first published *ca.* 1547).

1518–1519. FRANCESCO PATRIZI, *De regno et regis institutione* (written before 1492).

1523. JUAN LUIS VIVES, *De institutione feminae Christiani.*

————. *De ratione studii puerilis.*

1530. JACOPO SADOLETO, *De libris recte instituendis.*

1531. JUAN LUIS VIVES, *De tradendis disciplinis.*

1542. JERONIMO OSORIO, *De nobilitate civili e nobilitate Christiani.*

1545. ROGER ASCHAM, *Toxophilus.*

*ca.* 1550–1560. THOMAS BECON, *The Catechism* (sections on education); *The Christian Knight.*

1555. ANON., *The Institucion of a Gentleman.*

1559. WM. CUNNINGHAM, *The Cosmographical Glasse.*

1563. LAURENCE HUMFREY, *The Nobles, or of Nobilitye.*

1570. ROGER ASCHAM, *The Scholemaster.*

1570. THOMAS BLUNDEVILLE. *Of Councils and Counselors* (an English reworking of *El consejo i consejeros del principe,* 1559).

1572. JOHN BOSSEWELL, *Workes of Armorie.*

1572. SIR HUMPHREY GILBERT, *Queene Elizabethes Achademy,* EETS, ex. ser., Vol. 8 (1898).

1574. JOHN HIGGINS, *The first part of the Mirour for Magistrates* (preface).

1576. WM. BLANDY, *The Five Bookes of Civill and Christian Nobilitie* (trans. of Osorio).

1576. RICHARD ROBINSON, *A Morale Methode of Civil Policie,* abridged out of Franciscus Patricius.

*ca.* 1576. THOMAS WHYTHORNE, *Autobiography,* ed. and publ. by Jas. M. Osborn, 1961, 1962.

1577 (?). JOHN NORTHBROOKE, *Spiritus est vicarius Christi . . . A Treatise wherein Dicing, Dauncing . . . Are Reproved.*

1580. THOMAS FORREST, *A Perfite Looking Glasse for All Estates* (a trans. of three orations by Isocrates).

1581. WM. BLANDY, *The Castle or Picture of Pollicy, showing . . . the parts of a commonwealth.*

1581. RICHARD MULCASTER, *Positions.*

1582. ⸺. *The First Part of the Elementarie.*

1582. STEFANO GUAZZO, *The Civile Conversation* (three books trans. by Geo. Pettie and the fourth by Bartholomew Young).

1586. JOHN CASE, *The Praise of Musicke.*

1586. WM. WEBBE, *A Discourse of English Poetry.*

1588. WM. KEMPE, *The Education of Children in Learning.*

1589. GEORGE PUTTENHAM, *The Arte of English Poesie.*

1595. WM. JONES, *A Discourse whether a Nobleman by Birth or a Gentleman by Desert Is Greater in Nobilitie* (trans. from G. Baptista Nenna).

1596. EDMUND COOTE, *The Englishe Scholemaister.*

1597. NICHOLAS LING, *Politeuphia.*

1600. THOMAS FLOYD, *The Picture of a Perfit Common Wealth.*

1606. LODOWICK BRYSKETT, *A Discourse of Civill Life.*

1607. JAS. CLELAND, *The Institution of a Young Noble Man.*

1611. GEORGE MORE, *Principles for Yong Princes.*

1612. JOHN BRINSLEY, *Ludus literarius.*

1622. ⸺, *A Consolation for Our Grammar Schooles.*

1622. HENRY PEACHAM, *The Compleat Gentleman.*

# APPENDIX II

## Alleged Influences of Elyot
## on Other Writers

BROOKS, HAROLD F. "Shakespeare and the *Governour*, Book II, Chap. 13. Parallels with *Richard II* and the *More* Addition," *Shakespeare Quarterly*, XIV, no. 3 (1963), 196–199. The author argues for some influences of Elyot, unnoticed before, on *Richard II*, *Two Gentlemen of Verona*, *Julius Caesar*, and Hands D's additions to the play of *Sir Thomas More*.

BUSH, DOUGLAS. "Julius Caesar and Elyot's *Governour*," *MLN*, LII (1937), 407–408. In the emphasis upon pride in Julius Caesar just before his death, Elyot and Shakespeare and more alike than Plutarch and Shakespeare.

CONKLIN, W. T. "Two Further Notes on Shakespeare's Use of Elyot's *Governour*," *University of Texas Studies in English*, X (1930), 66–69. Elyot probably did not influence Shakespeare's characterization of Coriolanus, because there is a close likeness between Shakespeare and Plutarch. But there is a likeness between Elyot's serious handling of Alexander's killing his dear friend Clitus in the *Governour* and Shakespeare's humorous slanting of the same episode in *Henry V*.

HARCOURT, L. W. VERNON. "The Two Sir John Fastolfs," *Transactions of the Royal Historical Society*, 3rd. ser., IV (1910), 47–62. A historical character Fastolf was once committed to prison by Justice Gascoigne; this incident was the basis for the story of a conflict between Prince Hal and the justice, but Elyot's story of a conflict between Hal and the justice is still unproved when it is examined by all the available legal details.

PHIALAS, PETER G. "Shakespeare's Henry V and the Second Tetralogy," *SP*, LXII (1965), 155–175. The most important idea dramatized in Shakespeare's political plays is that success in public life depends on the ability to reconcile its demands with the claims of the individual life. Richard II, Henry IV, York, Gaunt, Falstaff, and Hotspur are examples. The author then comments on Henry V's concern with both political and nonpolitical values. The same combination of values was stressed by the humanists; he cites as an example the passage from Elyot on a ruler (III, iii), asking him to know himself and to realize that every man owns his own soul and body, etc. Also Henry's insistence to his soldiers in the night before Agincourt that he is a man like them seems to echo Elyot.

SARGENT, RALPH M. "Sir Thomas Elyot and the Integrity of the *Two Gentlemen of Verona*," *PMLA*, LXV (1950), 1166–1180. The theme of friendship versus love is developed by many Elizabethans, including Lyly, Peele, and Sidney. In *The Two Gentlemen of Verona* Shakespeare "presents the two ideals . . . in what might be called the purest Renaissance form." All three characters show that they understand the code of friendship between men: Proteus violates it deliberately but repents; Sylvia reproaches him for violating it; Valentine observes the code when he offers to give up Sylvia, but since he knows what she will do, he is not guilty of treachery to her.

SLEDD, JAMES. "A Footnote on the Inkhorn Controversy," *University of Texas Studies in English*, XXVIII (1949), 49–56. The lexicographers "appear to be in the mainstream of Elizabethan English. . . . Refusing the opportunity to innovate too freely, Elyot and Cooper fitted sound English idiom to their Latin." They "collected the riches of the language; but they did not introduce many new words."

STARNES, D. T. "Notes on Elyot's *The Governour*," *RES*, III (1927), 37–46. Elyot had a considerable influence on Higgins, *The Mirror for Magistrates*, 1578; Northbrooke, *A Treatise against Dicing, Dancing* . . . 1586; Webbe, *A Discourse of English Poetry*, 1588; and Puttenham, *The Art of English Poesie*, 1588.

————. "Elyot's 'Governour' and Peacham's 'Compleat Gentleman,' " *MLR*, XXII (1927), 319–322. Peacham prescribes the same authors for the same reasons, often in similar order and wording; like Elyot he emphasizes the need for geography; he summarizes Elyot's material on dancing, and he borrows, almost literally, his ideas on riding, running, and wrestling.

————. "Shakespeare and Elyot's *Governour,*" *University of Texas Studies in English,* VII (1927), 112–132. Works probably inspired by the *Governour* were *De l'institution du prince* by Budé, 1547, and *De educandis principum liberis,* by Sturm, 1570. His "influence is obvious" in the anonymous *Institution of a Gentleman,* 1555; *Toxophilus,* 1545; *Schoolmaster,* 1570; Peacham, *The Complete Gentleman,* 1622, and many other works. Shakespeare probably took the incident about Prince Hal's imprisonment and the king's attitude to justice in *Henry IV,* Part II, direct from Elyot. Speeches on order and degree in *Henry V,* in *Troilus and Cressida,* and in *Coriolanus* may owe something to the *Governour.* Other plays with echoes of the *Governour* are these: *Richard II, The Merchant of Venice, All's Well that Ends Well, Measure for Measure, Timon of Athens,* and *The Winter's Tale.*

————. "The Picture of a Perfit Common Wealth," *University of Texas Studies in English,* XI (1931), 32–41. This work by Thomas Floyd, 1600, has "scarcely a page that does not reflect the thought or use the actual language of the *Governour.*" Floyd also used Nicholas Ling's *Politeuphia, Wit's Common Wealth,* 1597, 1598.

————. "Sir Thomas Elyot and the 'Sayings of the Philosophers,'" *University of Texas Studies in English,* XIII (1933), 5–35. The author traces through the sixteenth and the early seventeenth centuries the history of the lives and sayings as a type of writing and then shows the relationship of the authors and the compilers to Elyot's *Governour* and his other works.

————. "Thomas Cooper's Thesaurus," *University of Texas Studies in English,* XXVIII (1949), 15–48. For years "the place of the *Thesaurus* was unique, and . . . its influence on lexicography in England was far-reaching."

————. "Thomas Cooper and the *Bibliotheca Eliotae,*" *University of Texas Studies in English,* XXX (1951), 40–60. Cooper made real progress in the revision of Elyot's *Bibliotheca:* he chose his authorities carefully, improved the arrangement of entries, emphasized the gender and inflection of nouns, and stressed both classical Latin and idiomatic English.

————. "Sir Thomas Elyot and the Lanquet-Cooper Chronicle," *University of Texas Studies in English,* XXXIV (1955), 35–42. In Lanquet's *Epitome* and its later editions known as *Cooper's Chronicle,* thirty-nine or more passages were written by Elyot. Also his sketches, such as those on St. Augustine, Albion, and Britannia were "reprinted in full" by Grafton in his *Chronicle,* but he gave the credit for them to Cooper.

————. "Sir Thomas Elyot *Redivivus,*" *University of Texas Studies in English,* XXXVI (1957), 28–40. Elyot had considerable influence on John Bossewell, *Works of Armory,* 1572, 1579; on John Forrest, and his annotations for *A Perfect Looking Glass for All Estates,* 1580, in which Forrest paraphrases material from *The Doctrinal of Princes,* the *Governour,* and *The Image of Governance;* on James Cleland, *The Institution of a Young Noble Man,* 1607; and on George More, *Principles for Young Princes,* 1611.

STENBERG, THEODORE. "Sir Thomas Elyot's Defense of the Poets," *University of Texas Studies in English,* X (1926), 121–145. Elyot "anticipated Sidney, Webbe, and Puttenham (or whoever wrote *The Art of English Poesie*) by a half century"; hence he should be called the father of English criticism in the Renaissance. His influence on Webbe is more certain than it is on the others, since Webbe spoke of his own work as compiled, and the parallels with Elyot are numerous.

SPENSER. *The Works of Edmund Spenser.* Variorum edition. (Baltimore, 1932–1957). The editors point out many likenesses between Elyot and Spenser, though they do not usually insist on a direct influence. See Indexes under *Elyot,* in these various volumes:

Elyot's shamefastness and continence. Guyon's adventure in *F.Q.* Vol. 2.

*Castle of Health* for certain ideas. Vols. 1, and 7, Pt. 2.

*Defence of Good Women* and Vives in Herde's translation. Britomart's ability to rule and her stress on temperance. Vol. 3.

Great houses and castles as memorials to owners. Vol. 7, Pt. 2.

Friendship in *Governour* (II, xi, xii). Vol. 4.

Elyot's conservative ideas about the social order—courtesy, nobility, justice—and his efforts to restore English words. Vols. 5, 6, and 7, Pt. 1.

# APPENDIX III

## Authorities, Chiefly Medical, for The Castle of Health

ACTUARIUS. *See* Johannes Actuarius.

AËTIUS. Early 6th century A.D. A Greek and a court physician at Byzantium. He wrote a sixteen-book compilation. The first eight books were published at Venice, 1534; and a complete Latin translation appeared at Basel in 1542. He gave the best account in antiquity of diseases of the eye, ear, nose, throat, and teeth.

ALEXANDER OF TRALLES. 525–605? A Byzantine who settled in Rome and may have taught as well as practiced there. He had originality and was a first-class observer who gave accounts from experience of insanity, gout, dysentery, and cholera. His prescriptions often include Byzantine charms.

APOLLODORUS. Perhaps the Stoic philosopher, before the Christian era.

APOLLONIUS. *ca.* 4 B.C. A wandering philosopher and mystic who wrote a life of Pythagoras.

APPIANUS. A Greek historian of Alexandria who flourished under the Antonines.

ARISTOXENUS (Arestoxenus). A disciple of Aristotle, a musician, and the author of many treatises on history and philosophy. His books on music are the earliest ones extant.

ARNOLD OF VILLANOVA. 1235–1311. A man of strange contradictions. He was a pioneer in classifying diseases and opposed scholastic dogma. He was connected with the Montpellier school in France. He sometimes suggested prayers to saints as a method of relieving diseases.

AUGUSTINUS, AUGUSTINE DE. 16th century. Wolsey's personal physician, and a nephew of Ghinucci, Bishop of Worcester. Later he was a physician to Henry VIII.

AVENZOAR (ABENSOAR). 1113–1162. An empiricist who expressed ideas contrary to Galen and opposed dialectical speculation in medicine. He discovered the itch mite and was a careful observer of many things. But he did harm by refusing to consider surgery part of medicine.

AVERROES. 1126–1198. A Spanish Moslem, born in Cordova, better known as a philosopher and a freethinker than as a physician. He tried to base a system of medicine on the neo-Platonic modification of Aristotle's philosophy.

AVICENNA or IBN SINA (AUYCEN). 980–1037. A court physician to caliphs in the Mohammedan and Jewish periods. He died in the prime of life because of sensual excesses. Though he was popular as a practitioner, his *Canon* was a bad influence because he placed ratiocination above firsthand investigation. He also stopped progress in surgery by opposing it and using cautery instead.

CATO THE CENSOR. 234–149 B.C. A Greek-hater who believed that Greek physicians meant to kill Romans. He used gibberish for dislocations, cabbage as a household remedy, and folk charms for sick oxen.

CELSUS, AURELIUS CORNELIUS. ca. 25–35 A.D. The greatest of the Latin medical writers. Probably he was not a physician himself but believed that he could write on medicine with valuable results. He was ignored by physicians in his day. His work *De re medicina* was one of the earliest medical books to be printed, 1478, at Florence, and went through many editions. Its first four books deal with diseases treated by diet and regimen. His accounts of diseases and of surgical practices are amazing.

DAMASCENE. See Mesuë the Older.

DEMOCRITUS OF ABDERA. 460–360 B.C. The first man to state an atomic theory, that everything, including the soul and the body, is made up of atoms of various shapes and sizes.

DIOCLES OF CARYSTUS. 3rd century B.C. A son of the physician Archidamus and a student of anatomy, considered by antiquity as the greatest practitioner after Hippocrates. He was the author of a series of works dealing with the causes of symptoms.

DIOSCORIDES, PEDACIUS. In the service of Nero, 54–68 A.D. He was a Greek army surgeon who used his travel to study plants. His work is the authoritative source of the *materia medica* of the ancients. He wrote on medical botany as an applied science, and men followed his descriptions for some sixteen centuries.

GALEN. 131–201 A.D. The greatest Greek physician after Hippocrates and the founder of experimental physiology. He was a skillful practitioner; but as he had too ready an answer for every problem, he tended to establish a system of medical philosophy as a substitute for the Hippocratic observation of facts. He stopped progress because men considered him infallible.

FICINO, MARSILIUS. 1433–1499. One of several, including Pico della Mirandola, who looked for the rational explanations back of magic and astrology and opposed witchcraft. Thus the influence on medicine was indirect but real.

GUAINERIO, ANTONIO. 15th century. He belonged to the school of Montpellier and was one of the leading medical writers of his time.

HALY BEN ABBAS (HALYABBAS). Died in 994. He was a Persian magician of the Mohammedan and Jewish period. His *Royal Book* was the canon for 100 years and then was superseded by the *Canon* of Avicenna, but at Salerno it was the sole source for a knowledge of anatomy in the hundred years between 1070 and 1170.

HIPPOCRATES. 460–370 B.C. The greatest of Greek physicians and perhaps the greatest of all physicians. He lived in the great period of Athenian democracy. He developed the art of clinical examination, using senses and mind in his diagnosis with complete honesty and respect for the patient. He separated medicine from occult arts and from philosophy, organized it into a systematic science, and based it on the highest ethics, the "Hippocratic oath."

ISAAC BEN SOLOMON, or ISAAC JUDAEUS. (850–940 or 950). A medical writer of Jewish origin, in the Eastern Caliphate. He wrote a book on uroscopy, and one on dietetics (published in 1487) which deserved its later popularity. *Opera omnia Isaaci* (Lione, 1515) offers more proof of his importance in the Renaissance.

JESUS, son of SIRACH. 180 B.C. He is the author of a tribute to
physicians.

JOHANNES ACTUARIUS. His dates are uncertain but he was a
Greek physician, one of the last of the Byzantine writers.
Though he maintained the view that urine is a filtrate of
the blood and wrote an elaborate treatise which perpetu-
ated the theory, he was also the first to use a graduated
glass for examining urine. His writings were popular,
with many editions in the sixteenth century.

JOHANNITIUS (JOHANNICIUS), or HONAIN BEN ISAAC. 809-873.
He has been called "the Erasmus of the Arabic Renaissance." He translated Hippocrates, Galen, Oribasius, and
Paul of Aegina, and was the leading medical man of his
day in Baghdad. He wrote a commentary on Galen's
*Microtechne* and also the oldest treatise in Arabic on
diseases of the eye.

MACHAON and PODALIRIUS. In Homer's catalogue of ships the
two are mentioned as leaders commanding thirty vessels
and as the sons of Aesculapius. Both were good physicians,
skilled in extracting weapons, binding up wounds, and
using soothing drugs.

MESUË THE OLDER, or JOHANNES MËSUE, or JANUS DAMASCENUS.
777-837. He practiced medicine in Baghdad and (though
a Christian) became director of the hospital there. He
left works on dietetics and gynecology; his most important
work was *Aphorisms,* first published in Bologna in 1489.

MESUË THE YOUNGER. 10th or 11th century. A pharmacist,
perhaps a pseudo-pharmacist in the period of decadence
of Arabian medicine. He was the alleged compiler of a
compendium of drugs.

ORIBASIUS (325-403 A.D.). A courtier, friend, and physician to
Julian the Apostate. He recorded the knowledge of others
instead of originating it; but he named his sources and
quoted them with precision. He explained Galen with
special care and did much to establish him as an authority.
He wrote a seventy-volume encyclopedia of medicine, and
though it has been lost, his *Synopsis,* made for his son,
is extant. His *Euporista,* a popular treatise on medicine,
avoided all superstition and used the best information
known to his time.

PAULUS CELIUS. Not in the available histories of medicine.
Perhaps Elyot meant Caelius Aurelianus, a 5th-century

urologist who had sensible, humane treatments for insanity, used sunbaths for chronic ailments, and reproduced
a lost work of Soranus. Or perhaps he meant Aurelius
Cornelius Celsus, above.

PAUL OF AEGINA (Paulus of Egineta). 625–690. The last of
the Greek eclectics and compilers and the last great
Byzantine. He studied in Alexandria and then went to
Rome. He wrote an *Epitome* in seven books, the seventh
being on surgery. He gave original accounts of various
difficult operations.

PINDAR THE POET. *ca.* 522–443 B.C. The great lyric poet of
Greece. In his third Pythian ode he sings of Aesculapius
as a healer so proficient that Pluto accused him of dimin-
ishing the number of shades; so he was destroyed by a
thunderbolt and became an object of worship.

PLINY THE ELDER. 23–79 A.D. Author of a *Natural History,*
books XX-XXXII dealing entirely with medicine. He
gives many unusual facts about plants and drugs and some
glimpses of Roman medicine. His was "one book of
classical antiquity which was read steadily throughout the
Dark Ages. . . ."

PLINY THE YOUNGER. 61 or 62–*ca.* 113 A.D. Nephew and heir of
Pliny the Elder and a patron of learning. His preceptor
was Quintilian. He had no apparent connection with
medicine, though Elyot said that he had read both Plinys.

PODALIRIUS. *See* Machaon above.

PYTHAGORAS. 580–489 B.C. A good geometer who held a belief
about the mystical power of numbers. His numberlore
exerted influence on the Hippocratic doctrine of crises
and critical days, with a tendency to assign fixed periods
to the resolution of different diseases.

RHAZES (RASIS). 860–932. A great clinician who gave the first
accurate accounts of measles and smallpox. He left a great
compilation from many sources but added original material from studies of his patients. Though a Galenist in
theory, he followed Hippocrates in his practice.

RUFUS OF EPHESUS. 98–117 A.D. A great eclectic who lived in
the reign of Trajan. He described the structure of the
eye, noted first that pulse, heartbeat, and systole are
synchronous, and gave the first descriptions of the bubonic
plague and other diseases. His treatise on gout was trans-

lated into Latin in the sixth century. He added new compounds to *materia medica* and was a good surgeon.

SERENUS SAMONICUS or QUINTUS SERENUS. 5th century A.D. He wrote a didactic poem on popular medicine, the *Liber medicinalis*.

SORANUS EPHESUS (EPHESIUS). *ca.* 100 A.D. The leading authority in antiquity on gynecology, obstetrics, and pediatrics. He worked in Alexandria and then in Rome, during the time of Trajan and Hadrian. His comments on midwifery and diseases of women had no real additions for about 1,500 years. He made a diagnosis of rickets. He studied anatomy, observed cases and symptoms with exactness, and left precise details about diets and operations.

THEOGNIS. *ca.* 549 B.C. A Greek poet of Megara, who wrote much of the early elegiac poetry.

The sources for information about Elyot's authorities in *The Castle of Health* are chiefly these works: Arturo Castiglioni, *A History of Medicine*, trans. and ed. by E. B. Krumbhaar (New York, 1947); F. H. Garrison, *An Introduction to the History of Medicine* (Philadelphia, London, 1960); *Nouvelle Biographie Genérále; Enciclopedia Italiana;* Sir Paul Harvey, *The Oxford Companion to Classical Literature* (Oxford, 1940); and Lemprière's *Classical Dictionary*, rev. by F. A. Wright (London, 1948).

# NOTES

## CHAPTER I. *Return From an Embassy*

1. *Calendar of State Papers . . . Relating to English Affairs . . . Venice,* ed. by Rawdon Brown, IV (London, 1871), no. 701. The report is dated November 24, 1531, but the incident happened about seven weeks earlier. See also *Calendar of Letters and Papers, Foreign and Domestic, of the Reign of Henry VIII,* IV, V, Index; IV, Introduction, p. cclxxx, hereafter cited as *L. and P.* Items in these volumes will usually be cited by number only; in long items, sections of an item will be given in parentheses or pages will be given and identified as pages.
2. *L. and P.,* V, 941, 989, also 1312, 1358, and Index; Dom David Knowles, *The Religious Orders in England:* III, *The Tudor Age* (Cambridge, 1959), Chaps. XVII–XIX.
3. Nicholas Harris Nicolas, *The Privy Purse Expences of King Henry the Eighth,* 1529–1532 (London, 1827), pp. 217–223, for Anne's return to Durham House, gifts brought to the king, etc.; or see *L. and P.,* V, pp. 758–759.
4. Neville Williams, *The Royal Residences of Great Britain* (London, 1960), Chap. 6.
5. Edward Edwards, *Libraries and Founders of Libraries* (London, 1865), p. 157. He estimates that in 1530–1532 Henry spent £10,800 for jewels, not including plate, and a little over £100 for books and bindings.
6. *L. and P.,* V, 1377.
7. Ernest Law, *The Royal Gallery of Hampton Court* (London, 1898), no. 563 and pp. 203–204. The picture is used only because it comes nearest of available portraits to the descriptions of the king by foreigners about 1531–1532. Art historians dis-

agree about its date, some of them placing it as late as 1535 or 1536 because of the scroll. The youthful face and figure as well as the costume seem earlier. The beard does little to date it; Henry wore a beard at times in the 1520's, and, according to Falier, in 1531. Professor Heckscher has suggested that this portrait is atypical and though he has not seen the original, he is tempted to say that it may be "either a late copy of a genuine portrait or possibly the fusion of two types."

8. *Calendar of State Papers . . . Venice,* IV, no. 694.
9. K. T. Parker, *The Drawings of Hans Holbein . . . at Windsor Castle* (London, 1945), p. 40, also Plate 15. The drawing of Elyot is usually dated about 1532.
10. Garrett Mattingly, *Catherine of Aragon* (Boston, 1941), p. 216.
11. Nicholas Pocock, *Records of the Reformation,* II (Oxford, 1870), 329–331. See *L. and P.,* V, Appendix 15, for a brief summary. The questions as used here follow the substance and usually the exact wording of the original, with some liberties of omission or arrangement.
12. *L. and P.,* V, 1077; also *Calendar of Letters . . . between England and Spain,* ed. by Pascual de Gayangos, IV, Pt. II (London, 1882), no. 957.
13. *L. and P.,* V, 171, p. 85.
14. *L. and P.,* V, 707, 737.
15. Mattingly, pp. 347–349, places Anne's physical surrender after the death of Warham, August 23, 1532. His view seems convincing.
16. Wilhelm Schenk, *Reginald Pole . . .* (London, New York, Toronto, 1950), Chap. II. Or see other standard lives of Pole.

CHAPTER II. *Early Background and Family*

1. Support for Elyot's details on excavation was given by visitors at the Dissolution: "it is in very good state, with much new building of stone and brick." See Knowles, *The Religious Orders in England:* III, *The Tudor Age* (Cambridge, 1959), 315.
2. Wills used here and in future chapters are listed in *Index of Wills Proved in the Prerogative Court of Canterbury, 1383–1558,* ed. by J. C. C. Smith (London, 1893, 1895), British Record Society—hereafter cited as *Index of Wills . . . P.C.C.* The will of Erasmus Pime is listed in Vol. III of the same series. For Sir Richard Elyot, see H. H. S. Croft (ed.), *The Boke Named the Gouernour,* I (London, 1883), Appendix A; and for Sir Thomas Elyot, see Stanford E. Lehmberg, *Sir Thomas Elyot: Tudor Humanist* (Austin, Texas, 1960), Appendix II. Photostats of all of them, including the Elyots, have been secured from the Probate Registry, Somerset House. The chief wills are these:

1492. Dalamer, Sir Thomas, Knyght.
    Berks.; Syon, Middlesex. . . . . . .   22 Doggett.
1492. Dalamere, Lady Elizabeth.
    Burial at Syon, Middlesex. . . . . .   10 Vox.
1511. Fetiplace, Richard, squyer.
    Estshifford, Berks. . . . . . . . . .   1 Fetiplace.
1514. Kyngeston, John. Chelrey, Berks. . . .   34 Fetiplace.
1515. Besylis, Wm., esq. Besylslye, Berks.; Oxford.   6 Holder.
1517. Fyndern, Sir Wm., knt.
    Carleton, Camb.; Berks., etc. . . . . .   36 Holder.
1521. Barrowe, Sir Mores, knt. Ive churche, Wilts.   9 Maynwaryng.
1522. Elyot, Sir Richard, knt. Wilts,
    Oxford, London, Berks. . . . . . .   24 Maynwaryng.
1524. Fetyplace, John. Esthifford, Berks. . . .   F 28 Bodfelde.
1524. Fetyplace, Thomas, knt. Berks. . . . .   32 Bodfelde.
1526. Besellis, Dame Alice. Syon, Middlesex;
    Berks.; Oxford. . . . . . . . . .   8 Porch.
1529. Feteplace, Wm. Chilrey, Berks.; Wilts. . .   6 Jankyn.
1531. Codryngton, Dorathe. Syon, Middlesex. .   13 Thower.
1531. Barow, Dorathe. Hants; Wilts. . . . .   12 Thower.
1541. Kingeston, Dame Susan. Chelrey, Berks. .   28 Alenger.
1546. Elyot, Sir Thomas, knt. Camb., Dorset,
    Hants, Somerset, Wilts. . . . . . .   14 Alen.
1582. Pime, Erasmus, esq. Brymore,
    Cannington, Somerset. . . . . . . .   7 Rowe.

3. *Calendar of the Patent Rolls, Henry VII,* II (London, 1916), 188; *L. and P.,* I (London, 1920), 833 (12), 1365 (19); *Notes and Queries,* VIII (1853), 276.

4. See Note 2, for this and other references to wills. Where I have used the term *trustees,* Elyot uses *feoffees* and *recoverers,* the accurate legal terms.

5. E. Lipson, *The History of the Woollen and Worsted Industries* (London, 1921), p. 233.

6. E. Lipson, *The Economic History of England,* II (London, 1947), 11–12, 69.

7. See Note 6.

8. W. K. Jordan, *The Forming of the Charitable Institutions in The West of England* . . . 1480–1660 (Philadelphia, 1960), pp. 6–7. See also E. M. Carus-Wilson, *Medieval Merchant Venturers* (London, 1954), Chap. I, on Bristol; G. D. Ramsay, *The Wiltshire Woollen Industry* (London, 1943); *A History of Wiltshire,* IV (London, 1959), 43–45, etc. (This is the Victoria County History.) In the fourteenth century, if not earlier, Bristol men had set up looms in their houses, where they employed other men.

9. E. G. R. Taylor, *Tudor Geography, 1485–1583* (London, 1930), pp. 9–10.

10. *Wiltshire: The Topographical Collections of John Aubrey,* ed. by John E. Jackson (London, 1862), pp. 9–13.
11. *Aubrey's Brief Lives,* ed. by Oliver Lawson Dick (London, 1949), pp. 278–279. Abraham Fraunce, protected by the Countess of Pembroke after Sidney's death, emphasized her and Ivychurch in titles; see any biographical sketch of Fraunce.
12. *Wiltshire Archaeological and Natural History Magazine,* I (1854), 68–91; XIV (1874), 320–331, and other articles. The term *humanist,* whenever used in this work, means one who stressed the accurate translation of the classics of Greece and Rome and their application to the improvement of contemporary life.
13. *L. and P.,* XV, p. 547; *Victoria History of the County of Essex,* II (London, 1907), 120.
14. *Calendar of the Patent Rolls, Henry VII,* I (London, 1914), 476–479, 504, and Index; also Vol. II, Index. As there are several men named John Michell, identification remains uncertain.
15. P.R.O., C 1/199/63. The document was called to my attention and a photostat secured for me by Mrs. Olive D'Arcy Hart, 21 Addison Avenue, Holland Park, London W. 11.
16. John Hutchins, *The History and Antiquities of the County of Dorset,* III (Westminster, 1868), 30; for later lists without her name, see pp. 31–32; *L. and P.,* XIV, Pt. I, 586.
17. For the daughters of Richard Fettiplace, see *The Four Visitations of Berkshire,* Harleian Society Publications, 56 (London, 1907), Pt. I, 28; George Lipscomb, *The History and Antiquities of the County of Buckingham,* III (London, 1847), 71–75; George J. Aungier, *The History and Antiquities of Syon Monastery* (London, 1840), Index; and the will of Dame Susan Kingston, listed above, Note 2. The Codringtons remain uncertain because the name itself seems to appear in strangely different forms.
18. See *L. and P.,* Vols. for 1539, 1540, and following, under the individual names in the Index or under Court of Augmentations.
19. For further details see Chap. VI of this work, Notes 5 and 6.
20. Croft (ed.), *Gouernour,* I (London, 1883), xix–clxxxix; Lehmberg, see Note 2 above.

CHAPTER III. *West Country Landed Gentry: Their Ideas and Attitudes*

1. H. S. Bennett, *English Books and Readers, 1475–1557* (Cambridge, 1952), p. 29.
2. For a list of the wills, see Chap. II of this work, Note 2.
3. Lysons, *Magna Britannia,* I (London, 1806), 260–261; John Nichols, *Bibliotheca topographica Britannica* (London, 1790),

Pt. II, pp. 72–83, with paging beginning again in Part II and often inaccurate.

4. John Stow, *The Chronicles of England* . . . (London, 1580), pp. 890, 902–903. *STC* 23333.

5. P.R.O., C 1/199/63.

6. *L. and P.,* I, Pt. I (London, 1920), 885 (13), records the grant to him of the livery of his lands, with these properties named.

7. Charles Edward Mallet, *A History of the University of Oxford,* I (London, 1924), 348–349; *Victoria History of the County of Oxford,* III (London, 1954), 163; *DNB* under Fleming.

8. *L. and P.,* XV, pp. 548, 549; XVI, no. 745, f. 22; XVII, no. 258, f. 20.

9. G. M. Trevelyan, *Illustrated English Social History,* I (London, New York, Toronto, 1950), 68; Eileen Power, *Medieval English Nunneries* (Cambridge, 1922), Chap. I, also Chaps. III, VIII; *Victoria History of the County of Essex,* II (London, 1907), 115–120.

10. H. S. Bennett, *Life on the English Manor: A Study of Peasant Conditions* (Cambridge, 1938), p. 173; *The Pastons and their England* (Cambridge, 1951); also "The Reeve and the Manor in the Fourteenth Century," *EHR,* XLI (1926), 358–365; A. Abram, *English Life and Manners in the Later Middle Ages* (London, 1913); Edward L. Cutts, *Parish Priests and their People* (London, 1898); G. G. Coulton, *The Medieval Village* (Cambridge, 1925); Paul M. Kendall, *The Yorkist Age* (New York, 1962).

CHAPTER IV. *Unknown Years. 1503–1510.*

1. *Calendar of the Patent Rolls, Henry VII,* I, II (London, 1914, 1916), Index.

2. John Stow, *The Chronicles of England* . . . (London, 1580), pp. 876–877, though he erroneously names *Thomas* instead of *Richard* Elyot; Charles H. Hopwood, *A Calendar of the Middle Temple Records* (London, 1903), p. 2.

3. W. S. Holdsworth, *A History of English Law,* II (London, 1923), 486–492.

4. Sir John Fortescue, *De laudibus legum Anglie,* ed. by S. B. Chrimes (Cambridge, 1949), Chap. L.

5. Hopwood, pp. 2–4.

6. Fortescue, Chap. L.

7. *Calendar of the Patent Rolls, Henry VII,* II, 539.

8. Holdsworth, p. 487.

9. *L. and P.,* I (London, 1920), 11 (9); 82, p. 39; also 205 and 963.

10. *L. and P.,* I, 1836 (14).

11.  Charles E. Mallet, *A History of the University of Oxford*, I (London, 1924), 143–144, 410–414; Hastings Rashdall, *The Universities of Europe in the Middle Ages*, ed. by Powicke and Emden, III (London, 1951), 353–376.
12.  F. M. Nichols, *The Epistles of Erasmus*, II (London, New York, Bombay, 1904), no. 441, p. 331.
13.  Peal Hogrefe, *The Sir Thomas More Circle* (Urbana, 1959), Chap. V, where these ideas are documented.
14.  Roberto Weiss, "Cornelio Vitelli in France and England," *Journal of the Warburg Institute*, II (1938–39), 219–226; M. Burrows, *Collectanea*, sec. ser., OHS, XVI (Oxford, 1890), 332–379.
15.  Elizabeth F. Rogers, *St. Thomas More: Selected Letters* (New Haven and London, 1961), pp. 94–103, for the standard translation by T. S. K. Scott-Craig.
16.  See Note 13 above.
17.  P. S. Allen, *Opus epistolarum Des. Erasmi Roterodami*, XII (Oxford, 1958), Index; or Rogers, Index.
18.  Rogers, pp. 2, 6.
19.  Nichols, *The Epistles*, I (London, New York, Bombay, 1901), no. 112; also pp. 270, 283, 302, 313–314, 334, 372.
20.  Nichols, II, nos. 457, 459, 568.
21.  Rogers, p. 77.
22.  Sir Thomas Elyot, *Dictionary* (London, 1538), A 5. "*cogitetisque, apud vosipsos, id operis iam coeptum ab equite britanno, barbarissimo scilicet, utpote in paternis tantum aedibus educato, nec ab anno aetatis duodecimo ab altero quopiam preceptore literis instructo, sibi ipsi nimirum duce tam in scientiis liberalibus, quam in utraquè philosophia: quod procul abest, ut ostentando dicam vel arroganter: sed ut gratiis DEO OPT. MAX. cum a me tum ab his, quibus hic meus liber fuerit utilis, utrinque redditis: alii musarum uberiori benefitio freti, meo quidem exemplo, parem aut mariorem operam aggredi, pro sua Republica non dubitarent.*" STC 7659.
23.  *A History of Wiltshire*, V (London, 1957), 357. (This is the Victoria County History.)
24.  C. W. Boase, *Register of the University of Oxford*, OHS, I (Oxford, 1885), 104, 131.
25.  *Calendar of the Patent Rolls, Henry VII*, Index; *L. and P.*, Indexes for the years named; A. L. Rowse, *Tudor Cornwall* (London, 1947), Index; also Chap. II, Note 2 of this work.
26.  Beatrice White, *The Vulgaria . . .*, EETS, 187 (London, 1932), 142, for the list of Linacre's translations from Galen. For other facts about Linacre, see *L. and P.*, Indexes, from about 1509 to 1524. Elyot's high praise of Linacre (in the *Governour*, I, xvi, and in the 1541 edition of *The Castle of Health*, Book II, Chap.

32) for his eloquent and exact translation of Galen's *De sanitate tuenda* and for his worth as a physician to Henry VIII lends some support to the idea of a personal relationship.

27. Holdsworth, II, 498–499.
28. Holdsworth, II, 503–510; and IV (London, 1924), 264.
29. Fortescue, Chap. XLIX.
30. John Stow, *A Survey of London*, ed. by C. L. Kingsford, I (Oxford, 1908), 78.
31. Edward Waterhouse, *Fortescutus illustratus, or a Commentary on . . . De laudibus legum Angliae* (London, 1663), pp. 544, 546. Waterhouse inserts the material usually known as the Bacon report between Chaps. XLIX and L.
32. Charles T. Martin, *Minutes of Parliament of the Middle Temple,* I (London, 1904), 34, 5, 13–14, 37.
33. Holdsworth, II, 490–491. The rule, he adds, was sometimes relaxed; and they were by no means restricted to this practice.
34. Thomas Stapleton, *The Life and Illustrious Martyrdom of Sir Thomas More,* trans. by Philip E. Hallett (London, 1928), p. 44.
35. Edward Hall, *Henry VIII* (London, 1904), I, 1–26, for funeral, coronation, and jousts.
36. Martin, I, 35–36.
37. Nichols, *The Epistles,* I, no. 210, p. 457.

CHAPTER V. *Middle Temple. Clerk of Assize, Western Circuit. 1510–1522*

1. William Roper, *The Lyfe of Sir Thomas Moore, knighte,* ed. by Elsie V. Hitchcock, EETS, 197 (London, 1935), 5–6.
2. Charles Trice Martin, *Minutes of Parliament of the Middle Temple,* I (London, 1904), 34. An item on p. 68 about assigning a "Master Elyot" to the chamber of "Master Ynglefeld" is indexed under *Richard* but probably belongs to his son *Thomas,* since Richard had moved to one of the inns for serjeants-at-law.
3. Martin, pp. 16, 17, 22, and Index.
4. William Dugdale, *Origines juridiciales* (London, 1666), p. 193.
5. Sir John Fortescue, *De laudibus legum Anglie,* ed. and trans. by S. B. Chrimes (Cambridge, 1949), Chap. XLIX; for the Bacon report see Edward Waterhouse, *Fortescutus illustratus, or a Commentary on . . . De laudibus legum Angliae* (London, 1663), material between Chaps. XLIX–L, pp. 539–546.
6. Dugdale, pp. 204–205.
7. Martin, I, 42.
8. *The Paston Letters,* ed. by Jas. Gairdner, II (London, 1904), p. 206, for item on two men who accepted the office at Middle and Inner Temple, to have excuses for being away from their wives.

9. Martin, I, 33–34. For parallels at other inns, see Baildon, *Records of the Society of Lincoln's Inn: The Black Books,* I (London, 1897), Index of Subjects.
10. William Herbert, *Antiquities of the Inns of Court and Chancery* (London, 1804), pp. 248–259; Martin, *Minutes.*
11. Herbert, pp. 212–217; W. S. Holdsworth, *A History of English Law,* II (London, 1923), 506–508.
12. William C. Bolland, *A Manual of Year Book Studies* (Cambridge, 1925), pp. 62–64.
13. Dugdale, pp. 194–195.
14. *L. and P.,* I (London, 1920), II, III, IV, Indexes under Elyot, Circuits, or Western Circuit.
15. *L. and P.,* Indexes for the years named.
16. *L. and P.,* I (London, 1920), 1836 (14), for the appointment as Justice of the Common Pleas; also Index in this and other volumes under the years named.
17. *L. and P.,* II, Index under Circuits.
18. Wm. D. Cooper, "Expenses of the Judges of Assize . . . Western and Oxford Circuits, 1598–1601," *Camden Miscellany,* IV (1858), 15–43, also the Introduction, pp. 3–14. This is Vol. 73 in the whole series. The source is a MS in the hands of Lord Petre, a descendant of Justice Walmesley.
19. Holdsworth, I (London, 1922), 275–276; Kenneth Pickthorn, *Early Tudor Government: Henry VII* (Cambridge, 1934), pp. 56–57.
20. *Statutes of the Realm,* ed. by Luders, Tomlins, Raithby, *et al.* (London, 1810–1817), I, II, III. The details can be checked easily, either with or without use of the Index.
21. Holdsworth, I, 288–289.
22. Kenneth Pickthorn, *Early Tudor Government: Henry VIII* (Cambridge, 1934), p. 21. In Wiltshire, 56 men were named to serve from 1495 to 1509; 33 from 1509 to 1514; 21 in February, 1515; and 26 in November, 1515, when Thomas Elyot's name first appeared.
23. Holdsworth, I, 289; *Fyrst the booke for a Justyce of peace . . .* (London, 1550), fol. 3.
24. Holdsworth, IV (London, 1924), 138–142, 148–150; *Fyrst the booke . . .* fols. 4–8; Wm. Lambarde, *Eirenarcha* (London, 1581), First Book, Chaps. 20–25. The last two works are listed as *STC* 14880 and *STC* 15163.
25. *Warwick County Records,* ed. by S. C. Ratcliff and H. C. Johnson, IV (Warwick, 1938), ix–x. See Conyers Read, *William Lambarde and Local Government* (Ithaca, 1962), pp. 15–18, for Lambarde's account of himself and his father-in-law.
26. *Calendar of the Caernarvonshire Quarter Sessions Records,* ed. by W. Ogwen Williams, I (London, Bradford, 1956), xxxiii–xxxix, xlvi, lxxxiv–cviii; *Warwick County Records,* VI (Warwick,

1941), xx–xxvii; Holdsworth, IV, 142–151; *Rolls of the Gloucestershire Sessions of the Peace, 1361–1398,* ed. by Elizabeth G. Kimball (Kendal, 1942), p. 21, where it is noted that one peer was present at all sessions but one, and only one lawyer was on the commission. (The volume named last is Vol. 62 in the Bristol and Gloucestershire Archaeological Society series.)

27. Holdsworth, I, 297–298; IV, 77–79; Pickthorn, *Early Tudor Government: Henry VII,* pp. 61–63.
28. Pickthorn, p. 68.
29. Holdsworth, I, 291–292.
30. P. S. Allen, *Opus epistolarum Des. Erasmi Roterodami,* I, II (Oxford, 1906, 1910), for Table of Letters.
31. *L. and P.,* I, Pt. II (London, 1920), pp. 1537–1538; also Vol. II, Index, under Richard Elyot or under Hants.
32. *The Herts Genealogist and Antiquary,* I (Harpenden, Herts, 1895), 79.
33. William Berry, *County Genealogies, Pedigrees of the Families of Hants* (London, 1833), p. 70.

CHAPTER VI. *General Problems. Clerk of the Council. ca. 1522–1530.*

1. See list of wills, Chap. II, Note 2.
2. F. W. Weaver, *Somerset Medieval Wills, 1501–1530,* sec. ser., Somerset Record Society, XIX (London, 1903), 217–219; Charles T. Martin, *Minutes of Parliament of the Middle Temple,* I (London, 1904), 34; *Index of Wills . . . P.C.C.,* II (London, 1895).
3. F. A. Inderwick, *A Calendar of the Inner Temple Records,* I (London, 1896), Index under Port; *L. and P.,* I (London, 1920), 82, p. 43, and Index. For Little Carlton see *The Victoria History of the County of Cambridge,* II, 20.
4. Henry Ellis, *Original Letters,* first ser., II (London, 1824), 113–119. See this reprint for original spelling.
5. Stanford E. Lehmberg, *Sir Thomas Elyot: Tudor Humanist* (Austin, Texas, 1960), pp. 26, 189.
6. *Index of Wills . . . P.C.C.,* I (London, 1893), 1521. Sir John Cutte. F 12 Maynwaryng. See also *L. and P.,* Index for years named. He received many grants, was on many commissions, had attended the king at the Field of the Cloth of Gold, and was Under Treasurer of England from 1515 to his death.
7. W. H. Dunham, Jr., "The Ellesmere Extracts from the '*Acta Consilii*' of King Henry VIII," *EHR,* LVIII (1943), 301–318; "Henry VIII's Whole Council and its Parts," *HLQ,* VII (1943), 7–46; "Wolsey's Rule of the Whole Council," *AHR,* XLIX (1943–44), 644–662.
8. *L. and P.,* IV, 1939, p. 864; III, 417, 703, 873.

9. G. R. Elton, *The Tudor Revolution in Government* (Cambridge, 1953), pp. 63–64.
10. *Statutes of the Realm,* III (London, 1817), 21 Henry VIII, c. 16, p. 298.
11. W. S. Holdsworth, *A History of English Law,* I (London, 1922), 412–413; I. S. Leadam, *Select Cases in the Court of Requests* (London, 1898), Introduction. It is Vol. 12 in the publications of the Selden Society.
12. See Note 4 above.
13. *L. and P.,* I (London, 1920), 1462 (26); 1662 (55); IV, 1939 (9), p. 869. See also 4231, p. 1865, and 6490 (1). For other items about Eden see IV, V, Indexes.
14. A. F. Pollard, "Council, Star Chamber, and Privy Council under the Tudors," *EHR,* XXXVII (1922), 348; or see entire article, pp. 337–360.
15. William Roper, *The Lyfe of Sir Thomas Moore, knighte,* ed. by Elsie V. Hitchcock, EETS, (London, 1935), 197, 62–63 and 42–43.
16. *L. and P.,* IV, Appendix 133.
17. *L. and P.,* I, Addenda I, Pt. I (London, 1929), 530.
18. *L. and P.,* IV, 4313 (14), 5508 (1).
19. Joel Hurstfield, *The Queen's Wards* (London, New York, Toronto, 1958), Part I, "The Revival of Royal Wardship"; also Holdsworth, III (London, 1923), 62–68.
20. Holdsworth, III, 510–520. He says that Glanvill's theories were contrary to the practice in his own time.
21. *P.R.O.,* C/1/199/63, a chancery suit brought by Richard Elyot and his wife Alice, late the wife of Thomas Daubridgecourt, states that Daubridgecourt had as issue two sons and three daughters; Wm. Berry, *County Genealogies, Pedigrees of the Families of Hants* (London, 1833), pp. 70–71, names two sons, Thomas and John, a daughter Mary, who married Reginald Pym, and a daughter Jane.
22. *L. and P.,* XIV, Pt. I, 403 (38), dated February 11, 1539. For the difficulties in the process, see Hurstfield, pp. 168–176, or Chap. 9 entire.
23. Martin, *Minutes,* I, 149.
24. *Index of Wills . . . P.C.C.,* III, Erasmus Pime, 7 Rowe.
25. S. Reed Brett, *John Pym* (London, 1940), pp. 264–265.
26. Lehmberg, p. 34. He cites P.R.O., C/1/1016/62–64.
27. *L. and P.,* III, IV, Index under Elyot for the years named.
28. *L. and P.,* IV, 4321 and Appendix 176. See *Lists and Indexes: Proceedings in the Court of Star Chamber,* XIII, Vol. I (London, 1901), p. 140, no. 204, for a suit against Sir Thomas More, suggesting that such suits were efforts to shift the blame to officials. These papers are Bundle XXII, Henry VIII.
29. *L. and P.,* IV, 4914, 5373, 6141; V, 978 (6); IX, 457, 493; XI,

641; Dom David Knowles, *The Religious Orders in England: III, The Tudor Age* (Cambridge, 1959), p. 72.
30. *L. and P.*, IV, V, Index under dates given.
31. *Calendar of the Patent Rolls, Henry VII*, II (London, 1916), pp. 230, 357.
32. Garrett Mattingly, *Catherine of Aragon* (Boston, 1941), p. 368.
33. Stow, *Survey of London*, ed. by C. L. Kingsford, I (Oxford, 1908), 88; G. M. Trevelyan, *Illustrated English Social History*, I (London, New York, Toronto, 1950), 89.
34. Roper, *The Lyfe*, p. 21.

## CHAPTER VII. *Authorship. Doubtful Works. The Gouvernour, 1531*

1. Constance W. Bouck, "On the Identity of Papyrius Geminus Eleates," *Trans. of the Cambridge Bibliographical Society*, II, Pt. V (1958), 352–358. Some who noted the problem earlier assumed that Eleates is a place name.
2. E. P. Goldschmidt, *The First Cambridge Press in its European Setting* (Cambridge, 1955), pp. 1–20; S. C. Roberts, *A History of the Cambridge University Press, 1521–1921* (Cambridge, 1921), pp. 1–14.
3. Goldschmidt.
4. Bouck.
5. Sir Thomas Elyot, *Bibliotheca Eliotae* (London, 1542), under *Britania*.
6. H. H. S. Croft (ed.), *The Boke Named the Gouernour*, I (London, 1883), cxxv–cxxvii.
7. Mr. Thomas S. Wragg, Librarian and Keeper of Collections at Chatsworth, answered my inquiry, saying that the previous history of the copy that belonged to the Duke of Devonshire but was given to the British Museum in 1957 is unknown. Mr. H. M. Nixon, Deputy Keeper of Printed Books, British Museum, wrote that neither volume indicates the person for whom it was originally intended. I have since examined both copies at the British Museum. C. 8. c. 15. and C. 132. i. 9.
8. *Papyrii Gemini Eleatis Hermathena*, ed. by Henry Bradshaw (Cambridge, 1886); Henry Bullock, *Oratio*, ed. by Bradshaw and Jenkinson (Cambridge, 1886), p. 22, for list of six known copies and another fragment of *Hermathena*.
9. Roger Ascham, *Toxophilus* (London, 1545), Book A, fol. 36$^v$ (misnumbered for 39). Ascham also praised Elyot's learning and his bringing regard to the nobility.
10. Goldschmidt, Bouck, and *DNB*. Twyne's history is listed in *STC* as 24407. Perhaps it has not been thoroughly examined for its possible relationship to Elyot.

11. Goldschmidt, pp. 16–18; *DNB;* F. M. Nichols, *The Epistles of Erasmus,* II (London, 1904), nos. 436, 441, 557.
12. See Note 8 above.
13. Edward Powel, *Propugnaculum* (London, 1523), at Folger Shakespeare Library.
14. *A History of Wiltshire,* III (London, 1956), 389, 185–186. (This is the Victoria County History.)
15. *STC.*
16. Folger Shakespeare Library, MSS L. b. 550, Account Book, 1549–1600. For the *Governour,* fol. 194, no. 104; for others, fol. 63, nos. 32, 33, 34; and fol. 64, no. 53.
17. Sears Jayne and Francis R. Johnson, *The Lumley Library: The Catalogue of 1609* (London, 1956), Index. Lord Lumley's translation of Erasmus, *Institutio principis Christiani,* made about 1550, when he was sixteen years old, is catalogued.
18. Elisabeth Holmes, "The Significance of Elyot's Revision of the *Gouernour,*" *RES,* new ser., XII (1961), 352–363.
19. John M. Major, *Sir Thomas Elyot and Renaissance Humanism* (Lincoln, Neb., 1964). For Aristotle, see pp. 144–152 chiefly; Plutarch, 152–160; Cicero, 141–144; Quintilian, 160–163; Seneca, 163–166; Isocrates, 166–169; Plato, 7–9, 174–177, and in Chaps. 5–9 ideas that are not summarized here.
20. P. S. Allen, *Opus epistolarum Des. Erasmi Roterodami,* XII (Oxford, 1958), Index; J. E. Sandys, *A History of Classical Scholarship,* II (Cambridge, 1908), 171.
21. Major, pp. 40–43, 156–157.
22. Major, pp. 44–45.
23. W. H. Woodward, *Studies in Education during . . . the Renaissance* (Cambridge, 1906), Chap. IV.
24. Woodward, *Vittorino da Feltre and Other Humanist Educators* (Cambridge, 1905); see for P. P. Vergerius, Lionardo Bruni D'Arezzo, Aeneas Sylvius, and Battista Guarino.
25. Major, pp. 60–67.
26. Pearl Hogrefe, "Elyot and 'the Boke Called Cortigiano in Ytalion,'" *MP,* XXVII (1930), 303–309. The writer no longer holds the extreme views implied here about the influence of Castiglione.
27. Pearl Hogrefe, *The Sir Thomas More Circle* (Urbana, 1959), pp. 108–112 for earlier statements of these views.
28. Major, Part II, Chap. 3.
29. Major, Part II, Chap. 2.
30. Anon., *The Institucion of a Gentleman* (London, 1568), G 1. The 1555 edition is not available. See also Appendix II of this work for summary of article by Starnes alleging that influence is obvious.
31. Cunningham, *The Cosmographical Glasse* (London, 1559), Preface.

32. Bossewell, *Workes of Armorie* (London, 1572), fols. 8, 16–17, 41, 122–125, 129, 130.
33. D. T. Starnes, "Notes on Elyot's *The Governour,*" *RES,* III (1927), 37–46.
34. Aristotle, *The Politics,* trans. by H. Rackham (London, New York, 1932), Book VIII, iv–vii.
35. Other works examined are these: Richard Robinson, *A Morale Methode of Civile Policie,* 1576 (abridged from Patrizi); Mulcaster, *Positions,* 1581; Lodowick Bryskett, *A Discourse of Civill Life,* 1606; James Cleland, *The Institution of a Young Noble Man,* 1607.
36. Whythorne, *Autobiography,* ed. by Jas. M. Osborn (Oxford, 1961), p. 239, also pp. 65, 112. Or see the 1962 edition, p. 199 and Index under Elyot.
37. [Case], *The Praise of Musicke* (Oxford, 1586), Preface.
38. Sir John Davies, *Poems,* ed. by Clare Howard (New York, 1941), pp. 65–108. Two twentieth-century poets have made some use, though not in Elyot's spirit, of the chapters on dancing: see T. S. Eliot, *Four Quartets* (New York, 1943), "East Coker," I; and Peter Viereck, *Terror and Decorum* (New York, London, 1949), the "Ballad of the Jollie Gleeman," and "Graves Are Made to Waltz On." I am indebted to Norris Yates for the suggestion on Viereck.
39. The others and the works examined are these: Richard Mulcaster, *Positions,* 1581; Wm. Kempe, *The Education of Children in Learning,* 1588; Edmund Coote, *The Englishe Scholemaister,* 1596; John Conybeare, *The Letters and Exercises of the Elizabethan Schoolmaster,* written about 1580 to 1594 and published in 1905; John Brinsley, *Ludus literarius,* 1612, and also *A Consolation for our Grammar Schooles,* 1622; Chas. Hoole, *A New Discovery of the Old Art of Teaching Schoole,* written about 1660 but published in 1913.
40. Henry Peacham, *The Complete Gentleman,* ed. by Virgil B. Heltzel (Ithaca, 1962), p. 7.
41. Ernest Barker, *Traditions of Civility* (Cambridge, 1948), pp. 132–136, is among those supporting the idea, if support is needed.

CHAPTER VIII. *The* Governour. *Individual and English Ideas*

1. For the attitude of Erasmus and Continental humanists on rhetoric and wisdom see Hanna H. Gray, "Renaissance Humanism: The Pursuit of Eloquence," *JHI,* XXIV (1963), 497–514.
2. H. H. S. Croft (ed.), *The Boke Named the Gouernour,* II (London, 1883), 132–133.

3. Foster Watson, *The English Grammar Schools to 1600* (Cambridge, 1908), p. 50.

4. Elyot, *Of the Knowledge whiche maketh a wise man* (London, 1533), fol. 19. In fol. 17 also Elyot compares the man of eloquence and wisdom to a painter. If the painter does not "conceive in his mind the hole proporcion of the image" before he begins and also while he is painting, his work will be imperfect; and though he may please the ignorant, wise men will perceive an imperfection. So a speaker who joins knowledge, wisdom, and sound reasoning with eloquence will please and profit all hearers. Perhaps Elyot had learned from Holbein.

5. Pearl Hogrefe, *The Sir Thomas More Circle* (Urbana, 1959). See Index for documentation of sources.

6. Castiglione, *The Book of the Courtier,* trans. by Chas. S. Singleton (Garden City, 1959), p. 242, for references in this paragraph. This edition is cited for general ideas because it is available and is indexed.

7. Pearl Hogrefe, "Sir Thomas Elyot's Intention in the Opening Chapters of the Governour," *SP,* LX (1963), 133–140, for this writer's view. For the opposite view, see Stanford E. Lehmberg, "Sir Thomas Elyot and the English Reformation," *Archiv für Reformationsgeschichte,* XLVIII (1957), 91–111; or *Sir Thomas Elyot: Tudor Humanist* (Austin, Texas, 1960), Chap. 3. Leslie G. Warren, "Humanistic Doctrines of the Prince" (Univ. of Chicago, Diss., 1937) argued that the *Governour* was propaganda for the secular power, it is said, but I have not seen his work.

8. Peter G. Phialas, "Shakespeare's Henry V and the Second Tetralogy," *SP,* LXII (1965), 155–175, discusses influences from Elyot on kings in both private and public life and on the thoughts of Henry V the night before Agincourt.

9. Castiglione, pp. 77–82.

10. Edward Waterhouse, *Fortescutus illustratus* (London, 1663), pp. 539–546.

11. Castiglione, pp. 67–70, 74, 77–78, 102, 104–105, 135.

12. Garrett Mattingly, *Catherine of Aragon* (Boston, 1941), p. 38.

13. Mattingly, pp. 129, 132.

14. See Note 10, above.

15. Clement C. Parker, *The Art of Archery* (Norristown, Penn., 1948). His version is based on an English translation by H. Walrond, publ. in the *Archers' Register,* 1902–3. About 1515, a printed version based on a manuscript at Toulouse appeared in France.

16. *Statutes of the Realm,* III (London, 1817), 3 Henry VIII, c. 3, for 1511–12; 33 Henry VIII, c. 9, for 1541–42. See Index for statutes between these dates. For earlier laws, see Vols. I, II, Indexes.

17. *L. and P.,* II, 395.
18. George A. Hansard, *The Book of Archery* (London, 1841), pp. 37–38.
19. N. H. Nicolas, *The Privy Purse Expences of King Henry the Eighth,* 1529–1532 (London, 1827), Index under Arrows and Bows; or *L. and P.,* Index, under these and other years.
20. *L. and P.,* XII, Pt. II, 617 (10), dated August, 1537.
21. Hansard, p. 41; *Shakespeare's England,* II (Oxford, 1916), 385. Neither source gives documentation, but the details are both traditional and probable.
22. Sir John Smythe, *Certain Discourses Military,* ed. by J. R. Hale (Ithaca, 1964).

CHAPTER IX. *Ambassador to the Emperor. 1531–1532.*

1. *Calendar of Letters . . . England and Spain,* ed. by Pascual de Gayangos, IV, Pt. II (London, 1882), no. 788. He uses *Vullyot* for *Elyot,* but the intent seems clear.
2. *Calendar of Letters,* no. 641, p. 71; *L. and P.,* V, 112 (Feb. 21, 1531); William Roper, *The Lyfe of Sir Thomas Moore, knighte,* ed. by Elsie V. Hitchcock, EETS, 197 (London, 1935), 103–104, and 126, Note.
3. *L. and P.,* IV, Index; *State Papers,* VII (London, 1849), CCXXXVI, CCXLVI.
4. *L. and P.,* IV, Index; *State Papers,* VII, CCLXVI; *DNB.*
5. *L. and P.,* V, Index.
6. *L. and P.,* V, Index; *DNB* has no biography of him but see details under Stephen Vaughan.
7. *L. and P.,* V, Index; A. F. Pollard, *Thomas Cranmer and the English Reformation* (London, 1926), Index; J. G. Ridley, *Thomas Cranmer* (Oxford, 1962), Index.
8. *L. and P.,* V, VI, VII, Indexes; *State Papers,* VII, CCCXXXIV.
9. *L. and P.,* VI, VII, Indexes; *DNB.*
10. *L. and P.,* VI–IX, Indexes; for Wyatt's poem, Ruth Hughey, *The Arundel Harington Manuscript of Tudor Poetry,* I (Columbus, Ohio, 1960), 170–172 and Notes in Vol. II.
11. Garrett Mattingly, *Catherine of Aragon* (Boston, 1941), pp. 347–349.
12. H. H. S. Croft (ed.), *The Boke Named the Gouernour,* I (London, 1883), lxxvii–lxxxi.
13. *Calendar of Letters . . . England and Spain,* IV, Pt. I (London, 1882), 898, p. 382; or *L. and P.,* V, 773.
14. Croft, I, lxxxv–lxxxviii.
15. *L. and P.,* V, 574 for Vaughan, and 910 for Augustine. Augustine speaks also of his long-continued friendship for Elyot, from the time when Wolsey was in power.

16. See Note 12 above.
17. *L. and P.*, V, 1077; VI, 465, p. 207; and VII, 121. See *Governour*, I, xxiv, Elyot's praise of Henry VII as a strong king who brought order to his country, as evidence of his practical conservatism in government.
18. John M. Major, *Sir Thomas Elyot and Renaissance Humanism,* (Lincoln, Neb., 1964), p. 107, suggests a material reward from the emperor but offers no evidence.
19. *L. and P.*, VI, 1370–1371.
20. Mattingly, *Renaissance Diplomacy* (London, 1955), pp. 244–246, 249.
21. *Calendar of the Patent Rolls, Henry VII*, II (London, 1916), pp. 595, 604; *L. and P.*, I (London, 1920), 112; *Calendar of Letters* . . . *England and Spain*, II (London, 1866), 19.
22. *L. and P.*, I (London, 1920), 1948 (95).
23. Mattingly, *Catherine of Aragon*, pp. 273–274.
24. *L. and P.*, IV, 5322, 5323, 5501, 5620, 5938; *Calendar of Letters* . . . *Spain*, III, Pt. II (London, 1877), 632, 678, 679, 680.
25. Mattingly, *Catherine of Aragon*, pp. 398–405.
26. *Calendar of Letters* . . . *Spain*, V, Pt. I (London, 1886), no. 142, p. 430; Mattingly, *Catherine of Aragon*, p. 405; also pp. 246, 360–362.
27. *L. and P.*, VII, 962, 969, and Index.
28. *L. and P.*, VII, 1270 and Index.
29. *L. and P.*, VIII, 327, 345, 346, 892.
30. Facts about executions and about former conspirators who rallied to support the king after the death of Catherine can be verified in the *DNB* and other standard sources.

CHAPTER X. Pasquil the Plain. Of the Knowledge Which Maketh a Wise Man. *Events, 1532–1533.*

1. H. H. S. Croft (ed.), *The Boke Named the Gouernour,* I (London, 1883), lxxxv–lxxxviii. See for original spelling.
2. Henry Ellis, *Original Letters,* first series, II (London, 1824), 113–119. See for original spelling.
3. W. S. Holdsworth, *A History of English Law,* I (London, 1922), 65–69; IV (London, 1924), 122; Kenneth Pickthorn, *Early Tudor Government: Henry VII* (Cambridge, 1934), p. 61; Sir Anthony Fitzherbert, *The Newe Boke of Justices of the Peas* (London, 1538), fols. 24–37.
4. Croft, *Gouernour,* I, xcvi–xcvii for original spelling.
5. C. H. Cooper, *Annals of Cambridge,* I (Cambridge, 1842), 361.
6. Croft, I cii–ciii for original spelling.
7. Croft, I, xciv–xcv for original spelling.
8. *L. and P.*, VI, 562, pp. 249, 247.
9. *L. and P.*, VI, 465; or *Calendar of Letters* . . . *England and Spain*, IV, Pt. II, Cont. (London, 1882), 1072.

10. The edition of *Pasquil,* listed by E. Gordon Duff, *Bibliotheca Pepysiana,* Pt. II: *A Descriptive Catalogue of the Library of Samuel Pepys* (London, 1914), p. 21, as 1532 proves, on examination at Magdalene College, to be one of 1533. Probably this error contributed to the listing in the *STC,* 1926, of a 1532 copy at Jesus College.

11. *L. and P.,* V, 1658. The *NED* gives nothing earlier than the two uses by Elyot. The word does not appear in Elyot's *Dictionary,* 1538, or in the 1548 revision by Cooper.

12. *NED* under Pasquil.

13. *Pasquil the Playne* (London, 1533), photostat of the H.E.H. Library copy, used at the F.S. Library. The brevity and the repetition make it unnecessary and almost impossible to give exact references to ideas.

14. *L. and P.,* V, 171, p. 85.

15. Elyot, *Of the Knowledeg [sic] whiche maketh a wise man* (London, 1533). *STC* 7668. The second edition is not dated, but the Berthelet design with 1534 in the border indicates the earliest possible date. It is *STC* 7669. A letter from Elyot to Cromwell (Harley MS 6989, fol. 33, British Museum) is probably related to this work, as Lehmberg suggested in *Sir Thomas Elyot: Tudor Humanist,* pp. 123–24. Elyot is sending Cromwell a little treatise, he says, made to comfort himself and others of equal "debilitie." The material is important and requires careful reading, although he is only recalling to his readers what natural reason has taught them. He asks Cromwell to defend him against those with minds so fevered that all good council seems bitter, and also, when he shall find opportunity, to recommend one of these books [here he changes to the plural] to the king. This is the last English book he plans to make unless the desire of his friends compels him. But if permitted to live in quiet, he hopes to act so that none may accuse him of wasting his time. Perhaps his "bringer" carried to Cromwell copies of both *Pasquil* and *Of the Knowledge Which Maketh a Wise Man.* The letter adds to the evidence that Elyot was making every effort to influence Henry VIII.

16. Kurt Schroeder, *Platonismus in der Englischen Renaissance vor und bei Thomas Elyot* (Berlin, 1920) includes a reprint; it was reprinted also by Edwin J. Howard (Oxford, Ohio, 1946).

17. *Of the Knowledeg . . .* (1533), fols. A2–A7.

18. *Of the Knowledeg . . . ,* fols. 16–17, 102. For the passage on good and evil see fol. 61.

19. Edwin J. Howard, "Some Words in Sir Thomas Elyot's *Of the Knowledge Which Maketh a Wise Man,*" *MLN,* LVIII (1943), 396–397. He emphasizes simplicity of diction.

20. See Dialogue IV, entire, for the kinds of adversities and for the discussion of great honor.

21. Fol. 64. See Chap. IX of this work, Note 2, on the time when Elyot and the emperor spoke of Henry's losing More as a counselor; also H. W. Donner, "The Emperor and Sir Thomas Elyot," *RES,* II (1951), 55–59.
22. Edwin J. Howard, in the Introduction to his edition, pp. xxx–xxxi, mentioned the likeness in Plato and More, as others have also done.
23. Thomas Stapleton, *The Life and Illustrious Martyrdom of Sir Thomas More,* trans. by Philip E. Hallett (London, 1928), pp. 158–159.

CHAPTER XI. A Sermon of Holy Saint Cyprian *and Pico's* Rules of a Christian Life. *Events 1534.*

1. *L. and P.,* VII, 121; or *Calendar of Letters . . . Spain,* ed. by Pascual de Gayangos, V, Pt. I (London, 1886), no. 8.
2. *Statutes of the Realm,* III (London, 1817), 25 Henry VIII, c. 12.
3. *Statutes,* c. 14.
4. *Statutes,* c. 19, 20, 21, 22.
5. *L. and P.,* VII, 362.
6. *L. and P.,* VII, 1090; *DNB;* David Knowles, *The Religious Orders in England:* III, *The Tudor Age* (Cambridge, 1959), Index.
7. Knowles, XVII, XVIII, XIX; Maurice Chauncy, *The Passion and Martyrdom of the Holy English Carthusian Fathers,* trans. by Radcliffe (London, 1935) pp. 59–61; other standard sources.
8. *L. and P.,* VIII, 1001; Garrett Mattingly, *Catherine of Aragon* (Boston, 1941), pp. 276–277.
9. *DNB; L. and P.,* VII, 129–134, 1607, for Forrest; VI, VII, Indexes, for Powell.
10. Sir Thomas Elyot, *A Swete and Devoute Sermon of Holy saynt Cyprian . . .* and *The Rules of a Christian Lyfe* (London, 1534). *STC* 6157. The 1539 edition is also dated on the title page. It is *STC* 6158. Both editions are at the F.S. Library. The dedication to Dame Susan is retained in 1539.
11. Elyot, *Cyprian* (1534), fols. A2–A4.
12. J. H. Blunt, *The Myroure of oure Lady,* EETS, ex. ser., 19 (London, 1873), xxix–xxx. The picture of the effigy of a nun in the robes of Syon House is reproduced opposite p. xxiii.
13. George Lipscomb, *The History and Antiquities of the County of Buckingham,* III (London, 1847), 75. The picture of Dame Susan's effigy shows her in nun's robes. See p. 71 for an account of her sister, Anne Purefoy.
14. C. F. R. Palmer, "Notes on the Priory of Dartford in Kent," *Archaeological Journal,* XXXIX (1882), 177–179, gives an instance, about 1518–1527, of a prioress granted the right to re-

ceive "any well-born . . . widows of good repute, to dwell perpetually in the monastery, with or without the habit, according to the custom of the monastery. . . ."

15. *L. and P.,* XV–XX, Indexes under individual names, under Syon House, or Court of Augmentations; *The Four Visitations of Berkshire,* Vol. 56 (London, 1907), p. 28, Harleian Society Publications.

16. Geo. J. Aungier, *The History and Antiquities of Syon Monastery* (London, 1840).

17. Mattingly, *Catherine of Aragon* (Boston, 1941), pp. 231–232.

18. Knowles, pp. 215–216.

19. E. W. Benson, *Cyprian* (London, New York, 1897); F. W. Farrar, *Lives of the Fathers* (London, 1907).

20. John M. Major, *Sir Thomas Elyot and Renaissance Humanism* (Lincoln, Neb., 1964), pp. 104–106.

21. William Roper, *The Lyfe of Sir Thomas Moore, knighte* (London, 1935), ed. by Elsie V. Hitchcock, EETS, Vol. 197, p. 102. Authorities differ about the number of gold pieces Cyprian gave his executioner. More also used St. Cyprian (as well as Ambrose, Bernard, Cassian, and dominantly St. Augustine) in his *Dialogue of Comfort,* written during his imprisonment, April 17, 1534, to July, 1535. See Leland Miles, "Patristic Comforters in More's *Dialogue of Comfort,*" *Moreana* (November, 1965), 9–20. While Miles is possibly right in conjecturing that More's attention may have been "drawn or re-drawn to Cyprian" through Elyot's work, brought to him in prison, it seems more reasonable to assume that both Elyot and More had been familiar with Cyprian since the edition of Erasmus, 1519–20, and that More had been reading the works of all these patristic fathers *before* he went to prison, as a preparation for his certain ordeal. See also Note 23, below.

22. Sir Thomas More, *The workes* (London, 1557), pp. 1–20; R. W. Chambers, *Thomas More* (London, 1948), p. 92.

23. P. S. Allen, *Opus epistolarum Des. Erasmi Roterodami,* IV (Oxford, 1922), 1000; XII (Oxford, 1958), p. 30.

24. *Statutes,* III, 26 Henry VIII, c. 1, 2, 3, 13, 22, 23.

25. Paul L. Hughes and Jas. F. Larkin, *Tudor Royal Proclamations,* I (New Haven, London, 1964), nos. 158, 161.

26. *Archaeologia,* XXXIII (London, 1849), 352–353, for transcript of the letter, in original spelling, by Sir Henry Ellis. See *L. and P.,* VII, 1559, for summary under date of 1534.

27. Elizabeth F. Rogers, *St. Thomas More: Selected Letters* (New Haven, London, 1961), pp. 212–214, for More's views on a general council of the church as authority. A view of papal infallibility came later in history.

CHAPTER XII. *Other Translations. ca. 1530–1535*

1. Pearl Hogrefe, *The Sir Thomas More Circle* (Urbana, 1959), pp. 188–191, where the ideas are documented.
2. Erasmus, *Opera omnia*, IV (Lugduni Batavorum, 1703), Table of Contents; F. M. Nichols, *The Epistles of Erasmus*, II (London, New York, and Bombay, 1904), pp. 77, 80–81, 110–112, 249.
3. Sir Thomas More, *Utopia*, ed. by J. H. Lupton (Oxford, 1895), p. 216.
4. Vives, *De tradendis disciplinis*, trans. and ed. by Foster Watson as *Vives: On Education* (Cambridge, 1913), pp. 253, 193, 158 and Index.
5. H. H. S. Croft (ed.), *The Boke Named the Gouernour*, I, II (London, 1883), Indexes.
6. Plutarch, *Moralia*, trans. by F. C. Babbitt, I (London, Cambridge, Mass., 1949), x, xv.
7. C. R. Thompson, *The Translations of Lucian by Erasmus and St. Thomas More* (Ithaca, 1940), pp. 23–28, 13–17, 20, 22; P. S. Allen, *Opus epistolarum Des. Erasmi Roterodami*, I (Oxford, 1906), 187.
8. Nichols, *The Epistles*, I (1901), nos. 154, 156.
9. Erasmus, *Opera omnia*, IV, 611–616; *Institutio principis Christiani*, trans. by Lester K. Born as *The Education of a Christian Prince* (New York, 1936), p. 135.
10. *Howe One Maye take profite of his enemyes* (London, 1533?). Photostat of H.E.H. Library copy. STC 20052.
11. *L. and P.*, IV, 6248 (22); H. R. Plomer, *Wynkyn de Worde and his Contemporaries* (London, 1925); C. G. H. Davenport, *Thomas Berthelet* (Chicago, 1901).
12. Croft, I, clxv–clxvi.
13. H. B. Lathrop, *Translations from the Classics into English, from Caxton to Chapman, 1477–1620* (Madison, 1933), p. 41.
14. Stanford E. Lehmberg, *Sir Thomas Elyot: Tudor Humanist* (Austin, Texas, 1960), p. 128, Note.
15. *Howe One Maye take profite*, fols. 5ᵛ, 6, 13.
16. *The maner to chose and cherysshe a frende* (London, 1533?), fols. 14, 15ᵛ–16.
17. *The maner*, fol. 14ᵛ.
18. Sir Thomas Elyot, *The Education or bringinge up of Children* (London, 1535?). Photostat of H.E.H. Library copy. *STC* 20057.
19. See Note 11 above.
20. Plutarch, *Moralia*, I, xxiii–xxviii.
21. Croft, I, 322–327; Wm. Berry, *County Genealogies, Pedigrees of the Families of Hants* (London, 1833), p. 288, for the list of four sons and three daughters.

22. *A Dialogue betwene Lucian and Diogenes* (London, n.d.). Photostat of H.E.H. Library copy. *STC* 16894.
23. Lathrop, p. 320 and Index.
24. James Wortham, "Sir Thomas Elyot and the Translation of Prose," *HLQ*, XI (1947–48), 219–240.
25. Lehmberg, p. 18.
26. Wortham. The phrase-by-phrase method, he says, was well used by Poyntz and badly used by Wyatt, who followed phrase for phrase, almost word for word, with little regard for English syntax.
27. Sir Thomas Elyot, *The Doctrinall of princis* (London, 1534?). F.S. Library. *STC* 14278. The preface and the "Addicion" have been supplied by reproductions from the Newberry Library, *STC* 14277.
28. For Hervet, see *Nouvelle Biographie Générale* (Paris, 1958); Lathrop, pp. 32, 48–50. He had worked with Lupset in Paris, supervising one of Linacre's translations of Galen, had tutored a son of Geoffrey Pole in England, and had translated Xenophon at Pole's request.
29. Elyot, *The Doctrinall*, Aii, preface to edition of *STC* 14277.
30. J. M. Major, *Sir Thomas Elyot and Renaissance Humanism* (Lincoln, Neb., 1964), pp. 166–169.
31. Roger Ascham, *Toxophilus* (Westminster, 1902), p. 86.
32. Lathrop, pp. 42–43; *Isocrates*, with English trans. by Geo. Norlin, I (London, Cambridge, Mass., 1954), pp. xv–xxx.
33. Lathrop, p. 43.
34. Wortham, pp. 237–240.

CHAPTER XIII. The Castle of Health, *1536–1539 (1539, 1541). Events ca. 1535–1536.*

1. *L. and P.*, VIII, 149 (52).
2. Garrett Mattingly, *Catherine of Aragon* (Boston, 1941), pp. 416–419; H. A. L. Fisher, *The History of England, 1485–1547*, V (London, New York, Bombay, 1934), 348–357; *L. and P.*, VIII, 661, 666, 726, 786.
3. Fisher, pp. 384–388, or other standard sources.
4. *L. and P.*, X, 601; *Calendar of Letters . . . England and Spain*, V, Pt. II (London, 1888), no. 43, pp. 84–85.
5. Garrett Mattingly, *Renaissance Diplomacy* (London, 1955), p. 249.
6. *Statutes of the Realm*, III (London, 1817), 25 Henry VIII, c. 21, p. 469; *L. and P.*, VIII, 73–76.
7. Fisher, pp. 374–375.
8. Fisher, p. 380, with estimates based partly on Stow.
9. *L. and P.*, X, 975; *DNB*.

10. *Statutes of the Realm,* III, 28 Henry VIII, c. 10.
11. Fisher, pp. 391-392.
12. H. H. S. Croft (ed.), *The Boke Named the Gouernour,* I (London, 1883), cxvi-cxvii; *L. and P.,* X, 1233, for the date, 1536.
13. *L. and P.,* XI, 1217 (20); XII, Pt. II, 157, 1150 (15).
14. The first edition, in the Yale Medical Library, will probably be listed in the new *STC* as 7642.5. Two editions of 1539, quarto and octavo, a quarto edition of 1541, and another probably 1544 will be listed. When this information came to me, several known copies had not yet been checked. The 1541 edition has been issued in the Scholars' Facsimiles and Reprints.
15. Arturo Castiglioni, *A History of Medicine,* trans. and ed. by E. B. Krumbhaar (New York, 1947), Chapter XV.
16. For Linacre see *L. and P.,* I-IV, Indexes; other standard sources.
17. F. M. Nichols, *The Epistles of Erasmus,* III (London, New York, and Bombay, 1918), 764, for the dedication to Aufinius.
18. Louis B. Wright, *Middle-Class Culture in Elizabethan England* (Chapel Hill, 1935), pp. 581-587; items in *STC.* Typical items are these: *Here begynneth a Newe Boke of Medecynes . . . the Treasure of Pore Men,* 1526 (?); *Here beginneth a Good Booke of Medicines,* 1539, with about nine printings by 1600; Thomas Paynell, *A moche profitable Treatise against the Pestilence,* 1534; Thomas Moulton, *This is the Myrrour or Glasse of Helth,* 1539 (?), reprinted about 15 times before 1600; R. Jonas, *The byrth of Mankynde,* 1540, a translation of a German book that was again trans. by Thomas Raynald in 1545 and reprinted many times; Thomas Vicary, *A profitable Treatise of the Anatomie of Mans Body,* 1548, and revived in 1577. (For the first two see *STC* 24199 and 24200.)
19. Thomas Whythorne, *The Autobiography,* ed. by Jas. H. Osborn (Oxford, 1961), pp. lix, 19, 112; or the edition with modern spelling, pp. 11, 98.
20. Whythorne, p. 239, Footnote; in the 1962 ed., p. 199.
21. Thomas Cogan, *The haven of health* (London, 1584), 4ᵛ.
22. Account Books of the Wm. More Family, 1549-1600, MSS L. b. 500, at the F.S. Library. Andrew Maunsell, *The Second Parte of the Catalogue* (London, 1595), p. 5, also listed *The Castle. STC* 17669.
23. Sir Thomas Elyot, *The Castell of Helthe* (London, n.d.). Estimates are 1536-39. I am indebted to the Librarian of Historical Collections, Yale Medical Library, for reproductions of the title page and the preface.
24. Elyot, *The Castel* (London, 1539), A2-A3. Photostat of the H.E.H. Library copy. *STC* 7643.
25. Elyot, *The Castel* (London, 1541), A2-A4. *STC* 7644. (Scholars' Facsimiles and Reprints.) See Thomas Morley, *A Plain . . . Introduction to Practical Music,* 1597, for his protest that he is not

taking a living away from honest teachers of music. This work has been ed. by R. Alec Harmon and published in 1952.

26. Beatrice White, *The Vulgaria*, EETS, 187 (London, 1932), xxxviii; Paul L. Hughes and Jas. F. Larkin, *Tudor Royal Proclamations*, I (New Haven, London, 1964), no. 216.

27. Sir Thomas More, *The workes* (London, 1557), pp. 243–244, or Third Book, Chapter 16, in any edition.

28. Sir Thomas Elyot, *Governour*, III, xi, xxii, xxvi, xxx.

29. Fielding H. Garrison, *An Introduction to the History of Medicine* (Philadelphia, London, 1960), pp. 129–131.

30. Garrison, pp. 130–131.

31. Elyot, *The Castel* (1541), I$_v$, X 3, O 2. For Elyot's praise of Linacre in the *Governour* see I, xvi.

32. Garrison, p. 163; Castiglioni, p. 385.

33. Elyot, *The Castel*, X 3, G 2$^r$, I$^r$, U$^r$, X 3$^r$, Y.

CHAPTER XIV. *The* Dictionary, *1538 (1542, 1545). Events, 1537–1538.*

1. H. A. L. Fisher, *The History of England, 1485–1547*, V (London, New York, Bombay, 1934), 407–419; *DNB*.

2. For the execution of Forrest, see *DNB*, or Henry B. Wheatley, *London, Past and Present*, III (London, 1891), 255–256; for letters between Forrest and the queen, *L. and P.*, VII, 129–135.

3. *DNB*, under *Becket*, for facts; for effects outside England, Fisher, pp. 426–427.

4. Craig R. Thompson, *The Colloquies of Erasmus* (Chicago, London, 1965), pp. 285–286.

5. Fisher, pp. 433–434.

6. *DNB* under the individual names of Poles, or other standard sources. As Geoffrey Pole broke under torture and gave some evidence, his life was spared.

7. *L. and P.*, XII, Pt. I, 182 for details about Elyot; see also 79 (2), 127, 211, 261–270; F. A. Inderwick, *A Calendar of the Inner Temple Records*, I (London, 1896), 44, 46, 97.

8. *L. and P.*, XII, Index under Parkyns; G. R. Elton, *Star Chamber Stories* (London, 1958), pp. 19–51, "The Fool of Oxford."

9. *L. and P.*, XII, Pt. I, 539 (21).

10. *L. and P.*, XII, Pt. II, 157; 1150 (15).

11. *L. and P.*, XII, Pt. II, 911.

12. *L. and P.*, XIII, Pt. I, 1519 (12).

13. *L. and P.*, XIII, Pt. I, 291, 292.

14. Stanford E. Lehmberg, *Sir Thomas Elyot: Tudor Humanist* (Austin, Texas, 1960), pp. 158–161. For a similar suit against Elyot's father, see I. S. Leadam, *Select Cases in the Court of Requests*, Selden Society, 12 (London, 1898), 11–12.

15. Sir Henry Ellis, Transcript of two letters by Elyot, *Archaeologia,*
    XXXIII (1849), 351–354. This version has the original spelling.
    Croft and Strype placed the letter in 1536; the editors of *L. and
    P.,* XIII, Pt. II, 854, in November, 1538. I have added para-
    graphing for clarity.
16. Lehmberg p. 153.
17. H. H. S. Croft (ed.), *The Boke Named the Gouernour,* I (Lon-
    don, 1883), cxxxii.
18. Fisher, pp. 407–408, 415–416.
19. The 1542 edition is not listed in the *STC,* but a number of
    copies are now known—at the British Museum, National Library
    of Scotland, University of Illinois.
20. Cooper's revisions are listed under Elyot, *STC* 7661, 7662, 7663.
    A 1587 edition of Cooper's *Thesaurus* has been listed, but Dr.
    D. M. Rogers of the Bodleian Library has proved that the title
    leaf is a "later fake," prefixed to an imperfect copy of the 1578
    edition. Mr. Leo Hansen, Keeper of Printed Books, Bodleian,
    gives me this information.
21. Sir Thomas Elyot, *Dictionary* (London, 1538), A2ᵛ–4, for the
    preface. *STC* 7659.
22. Vives, *De tradendis disciplinis,* trans. by Foster Watson as *Vives:
    On Education* (Cambridge, 1913), pp. 131, 133, 139.
23. For a Latin version of the letter, see Croft, I, cxl–cxli.
24. For Columella, see J. Lemprière, *Classical Dictionary,* ed. by F.
    A. Wright (London, 1948).
25. DeWitt T. Starnes, *Renaissance Dictionaries* (Austin, Texas,
    1954), Chap. VI.
26. He cited Perottus and Valla 7 or 8 times each; Budé, Donatus,
    and Gellius 9 or 10 to 13 each. Pompey Festus, a Roman gram-
    marian, 2nd century B.C., gave the meaning and etymology of
    every word he listed and added valuable information about
    early Roman life.
27. Chas. E. Raven, *English Naturalists from Neckham to Ray* (Cam-
    bridge, 1947), pp. 42–44.
28. Sir Thomas Elyot, *Bibliotheca Eliotae: Eliotis Librarie* (London,
    1542), British Museum.
29. Elyot, *Bibliotheca* (1542), A2–A3.
30. Starnes, pp. 55–56.
31. Starnes, Chapter VI. New sources include a Latin-French
    *Dictionarium,* 1538, by Robert Stephanus; a tenth-century lexi-
    con by Suidas, with much biographical and geographical infor-
    mation, reprinted by Aldus, 1514; the *Commentariorum linguae
    Latinae,* 1538, by Stephen Doletus, French humanist; and Petrus
    Crinitus, *Vitae poetarum Latinarum,* for details on ten Latin

poets; and additional details from Pliny and the medieval bestiaries.

32. Examples from A to E include also the Albanenses, whose eleven heresies he analyzes, Arrius, Basilides, Berengarius, the Caiani, Carpocrates, the Cataphriges, and Cherinthus.

33. I am indebted to Mr. John Crow, University College, London, for the suggestion on the dating.

34. Elyot, *Bibliotheca Eliotae* (London, 1545). British Museum copy. *STC* 7660. Lloyd E. Berry, University of Illinois, is preparing a complete edition of Elyot's works. He plans to examine every available copy in England and the United States of every edition published in Elyot's lifetime, including the editions of the dictionary.

35. Elyot, *Bibliotheca* (London, 1548), A3$^v$–4.

36. Starnes, p. 109.

37. Starnes, Chapters I–V. See for other works and editions.

38. Vives, pp. 133–134.

39. John Palsgrave, *Lesclarcissement de la langue francoyse* (London, 1530). *STC* 19166. See *L. and P.,* III, 3680, for indentures with Pynson as early as 1523.

40. John Baret, *An Alvearie or Triple Dictionary in Englishe, Latin, and French* (London, 1573), "To the Reader," pages not numbered. *STC* 1410. An edition of 1580 added a fourth language, Greek.

41. D. T. Starnes and E. W. Talbert, *Classical Myth and Legend in Renaissance Dictionaries* (Chapel Hill, 1955), p. 29. See Chaps. III, IV for further borrowings from the *Thesaurus.*

42. Starnes and Talbert, p. 17; T. W. Baldwin, *William Shakespeare's Small Latine & Lesse Greek,* I (Urbana, 1944), p. 710.

43. Richard Sherry, *A Treatise of Schemes and Tropes* (London, 1550), dedicatory epistle, A3. Photostat of the H.E.H. copy.

44. John Leland, *Collectanea,* V (London, 1744), p. 144. It is ironic that Leland's attack on Polydore Virgil for questioning the authenticity of the King Arthur stories appears in this same volume.

45. Starnes, *Renaissance Dictionaries.* p. 141.

46. A photostat of Cooper's tribute has been furnished me by the Newberry Library. See Note 20 above.

47. Starnes, pp. 128, 288–289.

48. Professor Lucyle Hook, Barnard College, found the letters of Peter Bold to Theophilus, 7th. Earl of Huntingdon, among the Hastings papers at the H.E.H. Library. She plans to publish them.

49. Starnes, Chaps. VI–VIII.

CHAPTER XV. The Banquet of Sapience. The Defense of Good Women. *Events, 1539–1540*

1. H. A. L. Fisher, *The History of England,* 1485–1547, V (London, New York, Bombay, 1934), 434–437; J. D. Mackie, *The Earlier Tudors, 1485–1558* (Oxford, 1952), pp. 425–427.
2. *Statutes of the Realm,* III (London, 1817), 31 Henry VIII, c. 14; 32 Henry VIII, c. 10.
3. *L. and P.,* XIV, Pt. II, 572 (3 viii); XV, 14.
4. John Stow, *A Survey of London,* ed. by Chas. L. Kingsford, I (Oxford, 1908), 88–89, 179, also 91; Fisher, 348, 386, and Index.
5. Roger B. Merriman, *Life and Letters of Thomas Cromwell,* I (Oxford, 1902), 61, 303–304.
6. Garrett Mattingly, *Catherine of Aragon* (Boston, 1941), pp. 368–369.
7. A. G. Dickens, *Thomas Cromwell and the English Reformation* (London, 1959), pp. 38–39.
8. *DNB* under Powell and Abell; Mattingly, pp. 276–277.
9. *L. and P.,* XIV, Pt. II, 619 (37); XV, 282 (6).
10. *L. and P.,* XVI, 107 (7).
11. *L. and P.,* XIV, Pt. II, 236 (m. 11. d, p. 72); 780 (4).
12. Stanford E. Lehmberg, *Sir Thomas Elyot: Tudor Humanist* (Austin, Texas, 1960), p. 158.
13. *L. and P.,* XV, 436 (41).
14. *L. and P.,* XV, 1027 (16).
15. Sir Thomas Elyot, *The Bankette of Sapience* (London, 1539). *STC* 7630. I have examined a photostat of the H.E.H. Library copy of this edition, and I have used also the 1545 edition. No sound conclusion can be drawn about the differences in editions until they have been carefully edited.
16. Hoyt E. Hudson, *The Epigram in the English Renaissance* (Princeton, 1947), Chap. I.
17. D. T. Starnes, "Sir Thomas Elyot and the 'Sayings of the Philosophers,'" *Studies in English: The University of Texas Bulletin,* no. 13 (1933), pp. 5–35.
18. Leicester Bradner and Chas. A. Lynch, *The Latin Epigrams of Thomas More* (Chicago, 1953), Introduction, pp. xi–xiv.
19. D. T. Starnes, *Proverbs or Adages by Des. Erasmus,* Englished by Richard Taverner, a facsimile (Gainesville, Ga., 1956), Introduction, pp. v–xii; F. M. Nichols, *The Epistles of Erasmus,* I (London, New York, Bombay, 1901), p. 442. I have not been able to examine *The 'Adages' of Erasmus* (Cambridge, 1964), by Margaret M. Phillips.
20. J. L. Vives, *An Introduction to wysedome,* trans. by Rycharde Morysine (London, 1540). *STC* 24847.
21. *The Bankette of Sapience* (London, 1539), introduction and dedication to the king.

22. H. B. Lathrop, *Translations from the Classics into English, from Caxton to Chapman, 1447–1620* (Madison, Wis., 1933), pp. 71–72; Lehmberg, p. 131. Seneca, 64 citations; Cicero, 56; Solomon, 50; St. Augustine, 41; Ecclesiastes, 34; St. Jerome, 26; St. Paul, 23; Plutarch, 14.

23. Thomas Whythorne, *The Autobiography*, ed. by Jas. M. Osborn (Oxford, 1962), p. 53; or p. 65, in the 1961 edition. For the music, see Whythorne, *Songs for five voices* (London, 1571), Song 11. F. S. Library. *STC* 25584.

24. Wm. Baldwin, *A treatise of morall phylosophy* (London, 1550), Chap. XXVIII, fol. H5ᵛ.

25. Elyot, *The Defence of Good Women* (London, 1540), not listed in *STC*. I have used the "line-for-line and letter-for-letter reprint" of this first edition (Oxford, Ohio, 1940) and have also examined the unique copy at the H.E.H. Library. I have used the 1545 edition, *STC*, 7658.

26. For *Surry*, see D7 in the 1540 edition, and C8 in the 1545 edition, or p. 51 in the modern reprint.

27. Mattingly, Index, for the places where Catherine lived in her later years.

28. *L. and P.*, XV, 872, 925.

29. Preserved Smith, *Erasmus* (New York, London, 1923), Chap. XI.

30. Craig R. Thompson, *The Colloquies of Erasmus* (Chicago, 1965), pp. 217, 267, 86. See also "Marriage," p. 114; "The Epithalamium of Peter Gilles," p. 223; "The Lower House, or The Council of Women," p. 441.

31. Among those who assumed that Elyot had Catherine of Aragon in mind, see Foster Watson, *Vives and the Renascence Education of Women* (London, 1912), pp. 211–213; Lehmberg, pp. 174–177.

CHAPTER XVI. The Image of Governance. A Preservative against Death. *Last Years, 1541–1546*

1. *L. and P.*, XVI, 580 (18).

2. *L. and P.*, XVI, 678 (31).

3. *L. and P.*, XVI, 1489, p. 700, f. 167 b.

4. *L. and P.*, XVII, 443 (24); 714 (4); 1012 (52); 1154 (96); Browne Willis, *Notitia Parliamentaria*, I (London, 1730), 190.

5. *L. and P.*, XVIII, Pt. I, 226 (8); 832, p. 468; 982, p. 546, 115 b.

6. *L. and P.*, XVIII, Pt. II, 449 (79); XXI, Pt. II, 472.

7. *L. and P.*, XIX, Pt. I, 273, p. 152; 274, p. 159. Some property transactions in Vol. XIX seem to concern another Thomas Elyot.

8. *L. and P.*, XX, Pt. I, 622, 623.

9. *L. and P.*, XXI, Pt. I, 91.

10. Sir Thomas Elyot, *The Image of Governance* (London, 1541). *STC* 7664. As the colophon is dated 1540 and the title page 1541, probably the printer finished setting up the book proper late in 1540; then Elyot gave him the preface and the Table later. These and the title page he set up in 1541.
11. Elyot, *Image* (1541), a2–b2.
12. H.H.S. Croft (ed.), *The Boke Named the Governour*, I (London, 1883), cxlix.
13. Pierre Bayle, *The Dictionary, Historical and Critical*, II (London, 1735), 770, under *Encolpius*, for Bayle's view, also that of Selden and Wotton.
14. Erasmus, *Institutio principis Christiani*, ed. and trans. by Lester K. Born as *The Education of a Christian Prince* (New York, 1936), pp. 194, 198.
15. Elyot, *Governour*, I, xii; II, x; III, iii, x, xxi.
16. George Ticknor, *History of Spanish Literature*, I (New York, 1849), 540–545, 553–554.
17. See *STC* or standard histories of literature for editions.
18. Mary Lascelles, "Sir Thomas Elyot and the Legend of Alexander Severus," *RES*, II (1951), 305–318.
19. Lascelles, pp. 314–317. She says also that Whetstone used episodes from Elyot in his *Mirror for Magistrates of Cities* and that Ben Jonson burlesqued episodes from it in *Bartholomew Fair*.
20. Lascelles, pp. 317–318.
21. F. M. Nichols, *The Epistles of Erasmus*, I (London, New York, Bombay, 1901), pp. 364–369.
22. Elyot, *The Image*, entire. It seems impossible to give page references for this summary.
23. Sir Thomas Elyot, *A Preservative agaynste deth* (London, 1545), preface A2–A4ᵛ. *STC* 7674.
24. See *Ars moriendi* in *STC*, nos. 786–793, between 1490–1506; Sister Mary Catherine O'Connor, *The Art of Dying Well* (New York, 1942).
25. For the anonymous work see *STC* 24221.
26. *DNB* or other standard sources.
27. John Archer Gee, *The Life and Works of Thomas Lupset* (New Haven, London, 1928), pp. 265–290.
28. P. S. Allen, *Opus epistolarum Des. Erasmi Roterodami*, X (Oxford, 1941), 2824, 2884; Erasmus, *Preparation to deathe* (London, 1538), translator not named. *STC* 10505, copy at F. S. Library.
29. John Fisher, *The English Works*, ed. by Mayor (London, 1876, 1935), EETS, ex. ser. XXVII, 351–363.
30. Sir Thomas More, *The workes* (London, 1557), Table.
31. *DNB* and *STC*, under these names. Frith or Tracy, *The Preparation to the Cross with the Preparation to Death*, ca. 1530;

John Bradford, *A Fruitful Treatise against the Fear of Death,* before 1555; Thomas Becon, *The Sick Man's Salve,* 1561.

32. Elyot, *A Preservative agaynste deth,* first part of the book and C5$^v$ for conventional ideas and the use of authority.

33. Elyot, C4.

34. Elyot, A8.

35. Elyot, B$^v$.

36. Elyot, D4.

37. Elyot, D$^v$–D3. For free will see also the *Governour,* III, iii, and *Pasquil the Playne* (1533), fol. 27$^v$ for the sardonic comment about the need to warn the master, "onles thou thinkest that every man shall be called of god, as saint Paule was, who was elected."

38. *L. and P.,* V–XX, Indexes; W. P. Baildon, *The Records of . . . Lincoln's Inn: The Black Books,* I (London, 1897), 203, 213 and Index; *Victoria History of the County of Cambridge,* II (London, 1948), 33–34.

39. See *DNB* or standard histories of literature.

40. For Elyot's will see Chapter II, Note 2. The will of Alington's father is listed in *Index of Wills . . . P.C.C.* as 1526, 14 Porch. See *Victoria History of Cambridge,* II, Map II, opposite p. 3, for Alington residences.

41. For William Raynsford, see *L. and P.,* VIII, XI, XII, Indexes. The will of a Sir Wm. Raynsford in *Index of Wills . . . P.C.C.* as 1557, Oxford, F 11 Wrastley, may be that of Elyot's friend.

42. Charles T. Martin, *Minutes of Parliament of the Middle Temple,* I (London, 1904), 81, 86, 90, and Index; *The Victoria History of the County of Huntingdon,* II (London, 1932), 359, 367. One of the two bays of the detailed monument as pictured has the figures of Sir Jas. Dyer and his wife, Margaret Barrow, kneeling and facing each other. This bay, it is said, was erected by a grandnephew of Sir James. See also *DNB.*

# SELECTED

# BIBLIOGRAPHY

ALLEN, P. S. *Opus epistolarum Des. Erasmi Roterodami* . . .
12 vols. Oxford, 1906–1958.

AUNGIER, GEORGE J. *The History and Antiquities of Syon Monastery.* London, 1840.

BERRY, WILLIAM. *County Genealogies, Pedigrees of the Families of Hants.* London, 1833.

BOUCK, CONSTANCE W. "On the Identity of Papyrius Geminus Eleates," *Transactions of the Cambridge Bibliographical Society,* II, Pt. V (1958), 353–358.

CASTIGLIONE. *The Courtier,* trans. by Charles S. Singleton. This edition is available and is indexed. Garden City, New York, 1959.

CASTIGLIONI, ARTURO. *A History of Medicine,* trans. by E. B. Krumbhaar. New York, 1947.

COOPER, WILLIAM D. "Expenses of Judges of Assize . . . Western and Oxford Circuits," *Camden Miscellany,* IV (1858), 15–43.

CROFT, H. H. S. (ed.) *The Boke Named the Gouernour.* London, 1883. 2 vols.

DUGDALE, WILLIAM. *Origines juridiciales.* London, 1883. 2 vols.

DUNHAM, W. H., JR. "The Ellesmere Extracts from the '*Acti Consilii*' of King Henry VIII," *EHR,* LVIII (1943), 301–318; "Henry VIII's Whole Council and its Parts,"

*Huntington Library Quarterly,* VII (1943–44), 7–46;
"Wolsey's Rule of the Whole Council," *AHR,* XLIX
(1943–44), 644–662.

ELTON, G. R. *Star Chamber Stories.* See "The Fool of Oxford,"
pp. 19–51. London, 1958.

ERASMUS. *Colloquies,* trans. and ed. by Craig R. Thompson.
Chicago, 1965.

————. *Institutio principis Christiani,* ed. and trans. by Lester
K. Born as *The Education of a Christian Prince.* New
York, 1936.

FISHER, H. A. L. *The History of England,* 1485–1547. Vol. V
in *The Political History of England.* London, New York,
and Bombay, 1906.

FORTESCUE, SIR JOHN. *De laudibus legum Anglie,* ed. and
trans. by S. B. Chrimes. Cambridge, 1949.

GARRISON, FIELDING H. *An Introduction to the History of
Medicine.* Philadelphia, London, 1960.

GOLDSCHMIDT, E. P. *The First Cambridge Press in its European
Setting.* Cambridge, 1955.

GREAT BRITAIN. GOVERNMENT DOCUMENTS.
*Calendar of Letters . . . between England and Spain.*
London, 1862–1954. Vols. II-VIII deal with the reign
of Henry VIII. 13 vols. and 2 supplements.
*Calendar of Patent Rolls, Henry VII.* London, 1914, 1916.
2 vols.
*Calendar of State Papers . . . Venice.* London, 1864–
1898. 9 vols.
*Calendar of Letters and Papers, Foreign and Domestic,
of the Reign of Henry VIII.* London, 1862–1910. 21
vols. in 33 parts. Also I (1920), 3 parts; and *Addenda,*
I (1929–32), 2 parts.
*State Papers.* VII. London, 1830–1852. 11 vols.
*Statutes of the Realm.* Ed. by Luders, Tomlins, Raithby,
*et al.* I, II, III. London, 1810–1828. 11 vols.

HERBERT, W. *Antiquities of the Inns of Court and Chancery.*
London, 1804.

HOLDSWORTH, W. S. *A History of English Law.* London, 1922–
1952. 13 vols.

HOLMES, ELISABETH, "The Significance of Elyot's Revision of the *Gouernour*," *RES*, new series, XII (1961), 352–363.

HOGREFE, PEARL. *The Sir Thomas More Circle*. Urbana, 1959.

HURSTFIELD, JOEL. *The Queen's Wards*. London, 1958.

HUTCHINS, JOHN. *The History and Antiquities of the County of Dorset*. 3rd edition. Westminster, 1868–1873. 4 vols.

JAYNE, SEARS AND FRANCIS R. JOHNSON. *The Lumley Library: The Catalogue of 1609*. London, 1956.

KELSO, RUTH. *The Doctrine of the English Gentleman in the Sixteenth Century*. Urbana, 1929.

KNOWLES, DAVID. *The Religious Orders in England: III, The Tudor Age*. Cambridge, 1959. 3 vols.

KNOWLES, DAVID AND R. N. HADCOCK. *Medieval Religious Houses: England and Wales*. London, 1953.

LAMBARDE, WILLIAM. *Eirenarcha*. London, 1581.

LASCELLES, MARY, "Sir Thomas Elyot and the Legend of Alexander Severus," *RES*, II (1951), 305–318.

LEADAM, I. S. *Select Cases in the Court of Requests*. London, 1898.

LEHMBERG, STANFORD E. *Sir Thomas Elyot: Tudor Humanist*. Austin, Texas, 1960.

LIPSCOMB, GEORGE. *The History and Antiquities of the County of Buckingham*. London, 1847–1851. 4 vols.

MAJOR, JOHN M. *Sir Thomas Elyot and Renaissance Humanism*. Lincoln, Neb., 1964.

MARTIN, CHARLES T. *Minutes of Parliament of the Middle Temple*. London, 1904–1905. 4 vols.

MATTINGLY, GARRETT. *Catherine of Aragon*. Boston, 1941.

——. *Renaissance Diplomacy*. London, 1955.

MORE, SIR THOMAS. *Utopia,* trans. and ed. by J. H. Lupton. Oxford, 1895.

——. *The Workes . . . in the Englysh tonge*. London, 1557.

MORE, WILLIAM. Account Books. MSS L. b. 550. Folger Shakespeare Library.

NICHOLS, F. M. *The Epistles of Erasmus*. London, New York, Bombay. 1901–1918. 3 vols.

NICOLAS, NICHOLAS HARRIS. *The Privy Purse Expences of King Henry the Eighth*. London, 1827.

PARKER, CLEMENT C. *The Art of Archery* (a modern version of *Lart Darcherie*). Norristown, Penn., 1948.

———. *Compendium of Works on Archery*. Philadelphia, 1950.

PEACHAM, HENRY. *The Complete Gentleman*, ed. by Virgil B. Heltzel. Ithaca, 1962.

PICKTHORN, KENNETH. *Early Tudor Government: Henry VII*. Cambridge, 1934.

POLLARD, A. F., "The Council under the Tudors," *EHR*, XXVII (1922), 337–360.

———. *Thomas Cranmer and the English Reformation*. London, 1926.

———. *Henry VIII*. London, New York, and Toronto, 1951.

———. *Wolsey*. London, New York, and Toronto, 1929.

POWER, EILEEN. *Medieval English Nunneries*. Cambridge, 1922.

QUARTER SESSIONS.

> *Calendar of the Caernarvonshire Quarter Sessions Records*, ed. by W. Ogwen. London and Bradford, 1956.

> *Gloucestershire Sessions of the Peace*, 1361–1398, ed. by Elizabeth G. Kimball. Kendal, 1942 (Vol. 62, Bristol and Gloucestershire Archaeological Society series).

> *Warwick County Records*, IV, VI, ed. by Ratcliff and Johnson. Warwick, 1935–1964. 9 vols.

READ, CONYERS. *Bibliography of British History. Tudor Period, 1485–1603*. 2nd ed. Oxford, 1959.

RIDLEY, J. G. *Thomas Cranmer*. Oxford, 1962.

ROGERS, ELIZABETH F. *The Correspondence of Sir Thomas More*. Princeton, 1947.

———. *St. Thomas More: Selected Letters*. New Haven, London, 1961.

ROPER, WILLIAM. *The Lyfe of Sir Thomas Moore* . . . ed. by Elsie V. Hitchcock. EETS, Vol. 197, (London, 1935).

STAPLETON, THOMAS. *The Life and Illustrious Martyrdom of Sir Thomas More*, trans. by Philip E. Hallett. London, 1928.

STARNES, DEWITT T. *Renaissance Dictionaries*. Austin, Texas, 1954.

————. *Proverbs or Adages by Des. Erasmus . . . Englished by Richard Taverner*, a facsimile. Gainesville, Ga., 1956.

————. Articles listed in Appendix II.

STOW, JOHN. *A Survey of London*, ed. by C. L. Kingsford. Oxford, 1908. 2 vols.

VICTORIA COUNTY HISTORIES: Cambridge, Essex, Oxford, Huntingdon, Wiltshire, etc.

VIVES, J. L. *De tradendis disciplinis*, trans. and ed. by Foster Watson as *Vives: on Education*. Cambridge, 1913.

WATERHOUSE, EDWARD. *Fortescutus illustratus, or a Commentary on . . . . De laudibus legum Angliae*. London, 1663. See pp. 539–546 for the material on the Inns of Court, usually referred to as the Bacon report.

WILLS. *The Index of Wills Proved in the Prerogative Court of Canterbury*. 1383–1558. Ed. by J. C. C. Smith for the British Record Society. London, 1893, 1895.

WOODWARD, W. H. *Studies in Education during the Age of the Renaissance*. Cambridge, 1906.

————. *Vittorino da Feltre and Other Humanist Educators*. Cambridge, 1905.

WORTHAM, JAMES, "Sir Thomas Elyot and the Translation of Prose," *Huntington Library Quarterly*, XI (1948), 219–240.

# INDEX